Pro Business Activity Monitoring in BizTalk 2009

Jeff Sanders and Geoff Snowman

Apress®

Pro Business Activity Monitoring in BizTalk 2009

Copyright © 2009 by Jeff Sanders and Geoff Snowman

ISBN-13 (pbk): 978-1-4302-1914-9

ISBN-13 (electronic): 978-1-4302-1915-6

9 8 7 6 5 4 3 2 1

Lead Editors: Mark Beckner and Jon Hassell

Technical Reviewer: Dave Rodriguez

Editorial Board: Clay Andres, Steve Anglin, Mark Beckner, Ewan Buckingham, Tony Campbell, Gary Cornell, Jonathan Gennick, Michelle Lowman, Matthew Moodie, Jeffrey Pepper, Frank Pohlmann, Ben Renow-Clarke, Dominic Shakeshaft, Matt Wade, Tom Welsh

Project Manager: Sofia Marchant

Copy Editor: Ami Knox

Associate Production Director: Kari Brooks-Copony

Production Editor: Candace English

Compositor: Diana Van Winkle

Proofreader: Nancy Bell

Indexer: Brenda Miller

Cover Designer: Kurt Krames

Manufacturing Director: Tom Debolski

Distributed to the book trade worldwide by Springer-Verlag New York, Inc., 233 Spring Street, 6th Floor, New York, NY 10013. Phone 1-800-SPRINGER, fax 201-348-4505, e-mail orders-ny@springer-sbm.com, or visit http://www.springeronline.com.

For information on translations, please contact Apress directly at 2855 Telegraph Avenue, Suite 600, Berkeley, CA 94705. Phone 510-549-5930, fax 510-549-5939, e-mail info@apress.com, or visit http://www.apress.com.

Apress and friends of ED books may be purchased in bulk for academic, corporate, or promotional use. eBook versions and licenses are also available for most titles. For more information, reference our Special Bulk Sales–eBook Licensing web page at http://www.apress.com/info/bulksales.

The source code for this book is available to readers at http://www.apress.com. You will need to answer questions pertaining to this book in order to successfully download the code.

To Lisa and our joint project currently under a 9 ½ month development phase—I can't wait for "go-live."
—Jeff Sanders

This book is dedicated to my mother, Doris Snowman, who passed away shortly before publication.
—Geoff Snowman

Mediocrity can talk; but it is for genius to observe.

—Benjamin Disraeli, British Prime Minister and Novelist

Contents at a Glance

PART 1 ■ ■ ■ Introducing BAM

PART 2 ■ ■ ■ Working with BAM Tools

PART 3 ■ ■ ■ Capturing Application Data for BAM

PART 4 ■ ■ ■ Advanced Topics in BAM

Contents

PART 1 ■■■ Introducing BAM

PART 2 ■■■ Working with BAM Tools

PART 3 ▪▪▪ Capturing Application Data for BAM

PART 4 ■ ■ ■ Advanced Topics in BAM

Foreword

Jeff first approached me for a little advice on this book at the Microsoft Professional Developer Conference in October 2008. After he described his plan for the book, the first words out of my mouth were, "It's about time." Jeff, being the great guy that he is, didn't take any offense at all and understood what I meant right off the bat.

What I meant is that BAM has been the secret weapon of the advanced BizTalk and .NET developer for far too long. It's not unusual for people to walk up to me and strike up a conversation around BizTalk projects that they've worked on. Being a bit of a snarky guy, I always ask for their thoughts on BAM early in the conversation. Depending on the answer, I can just about always tell how good a BizTalk developer they are from that single question. It's only the deeply insightful developer who ever seems to get to BAM.

I've always thought this odd. Mastering BAM isn't as easy as falling off a turnip truck, but neither is it the hardest technology that I've ever learned (not by a long shot!). Sure there are many, many features in BizTalk Server to occupy any earnest enterprise application developer for hours and hours. I firmly believe that BAM should be the first thing a BizTalk developer learns right after Orchestration.

We develop enterprise class applications for customers. Whether those customers are from the same organization as we are or we're doing spec work for an outside company, pleasing customers is usually high on the list of requirements. Pleasing customers includes leaving them with a feeling of confidence in the work and in us personally as developers and service providers. Confidence stems from trust: trust in our insight into their specific problem solution and trust of our code to provide insight into the internal workings of that system. This is the core value of BAM. Opening up an insightful view into an opaque system for the operations staff and end users builds trust and confidence (and more often than not, repeat business).

The investment it takes to learn BAM and to put it in every major application we build is miniscule—especially when compared to the comfort our customers feel from the trust gained via insight into the system. This book is your first step into becoming a more insightful enterprise developer, not to mention a developer who can easily impress at cocktail parties with your advanced knowledge of BizTalk Server and .NET development. (But be quick! Once this book makes the rounds, the secret will be out of the bag, and everyone will be doing BAM.)

Michael Woods
Group Product Manager
Developer Platform Technical Product Management
Microsoft Corporation

About the Authors

JEFF SANDERS is a group manager/solution architect with Avanade in the US East region, where he focuses on BizTalk, SharePoint Server, WCF, WF, and .NET, and reducing complexity. Avanade is a global IT consultancy specializing in applied solutions based on the Microsoft enterprise platform and is co-owned by Accenture and Microsoft.

Jeff speaks at local and regional user groups and code camps. He was a cowriter of the BizTalk 2006 R2 Microsoft certification exam, as well as other Microsoft PRO-level exams, and has served on Alpha reviews. He is one of few to have achieved a perfect score on the BizTalk 2006 exam. He was a technical reviewer of *Pro Mapping in BizTalk Server 2009* (Apress, 2009) and *WCF Multitier Services Development with LINQ* (Packt Publishing, 2008). Jeff holds a degree in journalism and mass communications from Elon University.

GEOFF SNOWMAN is a lead programmer analyst in the Internet Business Unit of GEICO, where he works with BizTalk Server, Windows Communication Foundation, and service-oriented architecture. Prior to joining GEICO, Geoff was a senior consultant with Microsoft Consulting Services. At Microsoft, Geoff helped customers to implement SOA on Microsoft technology, working with the complete Microsoft application platform.

Geoff is a frequent and popular speaker at user groups, conferences, and code camps. Geoff has been in computing since 1983. He has an M.A. degree in computer science from Cambridge University and is a Microsoft Certified Professional Developer, Microsoft Certified Database Administrator, and Microsoft Certified Technology Specialist. Geoff has been working with BizTalk Server since the tech preview version of BizTalk 2000.

About the Technical Reviewer

DAVID RODRIGUEZ is the founder of CoBiz Solutions Group, LLC, based in Seattle, Washington. He delivers to his clients an in-depth focus on connecting companies to their employees, partners, and systems through the use of process reengineering and software development that leverages the Microsoft technology stack, white-box solutions, and other leading technologies.

Over the years, David has delivered projects for clients of all sizes throughout the United States. His projects have ranged in nature from line-of-business application development to enterprise integration solutions. David's technical credentials include Microsoft Technology Specialist (MCTS): BizTalk Server 2004/2006, Microsoft Certified Solutions Developer for .NET (MCSD), and Microsoft Certified Application Developer for .NET (MCAD). In addition, David is certified in project management by the University of Washington.

David resides in his native Seattle where he spends his free time exploring the city and the backwoods of the Pacific Northwest. David can be reached at `david.rodriguez@cobizgroup.com` for advice on BizTalk Server development and implementations, integration initiatives, or any other consulting opportunities.

Acknowledgments

I would like to thank Mark Beckner for asking me to write a book on BAM, and for his and Jon Hassell's incredible amounts of patience during the writing process. Thank you both for sticking by us and for ensuring that the first book focused purely on BAM wouldn't be a mediocre one. I want to thank the team at Apress, especially Sofia, Ami, and Candace. The publishing industry, as with many industries, is going through some very tough times. While many companies are just throwing content out there to see what sticks, I'm proud to be associated with one that takes the opposite approach of releasing only the highest quality material at the right time. What you, dear reader, see before you is the result of over ten months of brainstorming, collaboration, constant refinement, fact-checking, and updating to ensure that your money is well spent and that the high standards of writing, editing, and production are maintained.

Thanks to our official technical reviewer, David Rodriguez, for his technical validation and for keeping the writing focused. Thanks, too, to our unofficial technical reviewer, Bryan Corazza, for bringing his BAM experience and suggestions to the project.

Thanks to Geoff Snowman, without whom this book would have never happened. Geoff and I worked together previously in consulting roles and knew one another from our involvement in local users groups. While I had done some BizTalk work before, it was Geoff's demos of a "$30,000 file copy tool" that piqued my interest in BizTalk and BAM. I knew that fighting to bring Geoff onboard this project would bring it not only increased credibility, but also a deep experience base with BAM. During the course of this book, collectively we've both experienced major occupation transitions, two unfortunate losses, a new life on the way, and numerous personal and professional obstacles that stole many hours of writing time. Through it all, having someone to rely on whom I could trust to keep the original intent of the book intact made overcoming those obstacles all the easier. I eagerly look forward to our next project together.

I would be remiss not to mention the many people who have helped to shape this book, either directly or indirectly. To Kevin O'Riordan, Rudi Rihani, Ken Serauskis, and Douglas Johnston of Avanade, thanks for the encouragement, support, and words of wisdom on work/life balance. To Gary Gentry and Rajeev Ramesh of Avanade, thank you for pushing me further beyond what I thought possible. To Stephen Thomas of BizTalkGurus.com and Larry Beck of Avanade, thanks for the open doors, IM conversations, and fervent interest in SOA. I wouldn't have considered writing were it not for Dan Kahler, who has always encouraged me to go further. Words cannot express the gratitude to the many who have given me sage-like mentorship through the years, especially Ron Baldwin, Steve Samuelson, Steve Bridges, Brian Birsa, Shawn Ward, Scott Bolden, Bill Price, and Randy Wilson. Thanks to bloggers like Jesus Rodriguez, Dion Hinchcliffe, Keith Lim, and Andy Shen, who helped turn five-minute breaks into fifteen-minute ones. Thank you to Microsoft, especially the Connected Systems Division, for continuing to put out solid products and investing in improving them through the years.

Personally, I would like to thank Dick Gawlik (miss you, man) and Rick Lobo for keeping a watchful eye, and my family and friends for understanding. Most of all, however, I have to thank my wife, Lisa Sanders, for her support and love, and for being able to patiently read many a book while I wrote mine. Lisa, you've always inspired me.

Jeff Sanders

I would like to start by thanking the entire team at Apress for their support during the writing of this book. Without Sofia Marchant, our project manager, this book would not have happened. She has been the glue that held the project together. Our editors, Jon Hassell and Mark Beckner, provided constant support and encouragement. If you can understand the book, it's thanks to Ami Knox, our copy editor, who turned our scribbling into English. Candace English led the production effort and turned our Word docs into the book you hold in your hand. In addition, I thank all the other team members at Apress whose names I don't know but without whom the book would not exist. Thanks also to Dave Rodriguez for his diligent review of the entire book.

Thanks to Jeff Sanders, who brought me in to the project and has constantly pushed to make this the best book we could write. I've enjoyed working with you. What are we going to write about next?

I owe thanks to several people at Microsoft. I'll start with the Connected Systems Division, who created a great product and are a source of genuine innovation. Bashar Badawi, Dave Ateek, Scott Zimmerman, and Alex Starykh were wonderful colleagues who taught me many things. Thanks also to Cesar Larrea, D. P. Brightful, and the entire Mid Atlantic States application platform team. Thanks to all my friends with Developer and Platform Evangelism, too numerous to mention by name. Gary Hughes, a legend within Microsoft Consulting Services, is a wonderful manager and great friend who encouraged me to get started on the project. Thanks to all the Microsoft customers who forced me to go deep by giving me challenging problems to work on. I would also like to thank John Callaway of QuickLearn, whose BizTalk Server Deep Dive is the best technical training I have ever attended.

On a personal note, I would like to thank Dr. Bob Hehir for his friendship and advice. Thanks to Mark Frederiksen, my MICSUG co-conspirator. Thanks to Vishwas Lele and Scott McHugh of Applied Information Sciences. Finally, I would like to thank my wife, Susan Snowman, for her constant support and encouragement. Without her I would be nothing.

Geoff Snowman

Introduction

Business Activity Monitoring (BAM) is one of the more powerful tools within the Microsoft application platform, but until now, it hasn't been used as widely as it should be. There are two reasons for this. One reason is that BAM isn't widely understood. Not a lot of material is available that teaches BAM concepts to developers, and even many BizTalk developers don't know much about BAM. We hope this book will start to spread knowledge of BAM more widely.

The second reason many people overlook BAM is because it ships as part of BizTalk Server. This gives many people the impression that BAM is only relevant to developers building BizTalk applications. In fact, nothing could be further from the truth. BAM can be used to monitor any application that uses Windows Communication Foundation (WCF) or Windows Workflow Foundation (WF) without writing any code. For other .NET applications, a few simple calls to the BAM API give you access to the power of the BAM infrastructure. Although BAM works well with BizTalk Server and should be used with just about every BizTalk application, every .NET developer should also be aware of the benefits of BAM. If Microsoft sold BAM as an SOA monitoring solution at the same price as the BizTalk license that includes BAM, it would be a bargain.

This overlooking of BAM is unfortunate, because BAM bridges the gap between business processes and business intelligence to provide rich capabilities for real-time business intelligence. If you have business processes or web services implemented on the Microsoft application platform, BAM provides a high-performance infrastructure for monitoring the behavior of your systems and brings a powerful real-time component to any business intelligence strategy.

How This Book Is Organized

In this book, you'll learn how to apply BAM to your projects. Part 1 teaches you the basics of BAM. Chapter 1 provides an introduction to BizTalk and BAM and describes some of the industry trends that make BAM important. Chapter 2 describes BAM installation and configuration. In Chapter 3, you'll implement your first simple BAM project, which monitors a web service written in WCF. This project will give you an overview of all the steps required for a BAM implementation. Chapter 4 describes how BAM fits into some application architectures.

Part 2 shows you how to apply BAM to BizTalk projects. Chapter 5 teaches you how to build an observation model. The observation model defines the data that will be captured by BAM. Chapter 6 describes how to wire up a BizTalk application for BAM. In Chapter 7, you'll learn how to present BAM data to end users.

Part 3 goes deeper into capturing data from .NET applications. Chapter 8 fleshes out the information you'll need to work with BAM and WCF. In Chapter 9, you'll see an example of using BAM with WF. Chapter 10 covers the BAM API.

Part 4 is about advanced topics in BAM. Chapter 11 covers integrating BAM with BI tools. Chapter 12 covers relationships, which allow you to link multiple BAM activities together. Chapter 13 covers administering a BAM system in production. In Chapter 14, you'll learn a powerful design pattern for monitoring a BizTalk system using BAM. Finally, Chapter 15 wraps up by talking about some possible future directions for BAM.

This book will give you a strong understanding of BAM that you can apply to your applications, whether you're a WCF, WF, BizTalk, or .NET developer.

Book Requirements

To learn BAM, you will need to implement BAM solutions, and that requires a development machine. We provide many practical exercises throughout the book, and it's essential to have a development machine with the following prerequisites:

- BizTalk Server 2009 or BizTalk Server 2006 R2, including all optional components

- SQL Server (SQL Server 2008 or SQL Server 2005 if you have BizTalk Server 2009, SQL Server 2005 or SQL Server 2000 if you have BizTalk Server 2006 R2)

- Visual Studio (Visual Studio 2008 if you have BizTalk Server 2009, Visual Studio 2005 if you have BizTalk Server 2006 R2)

If you're running all these products on a single machine, 1GB of memory is a bare minimum, and 2GB is strongly preferred.

Who This Book Is For

We wrote this book for anyone who wants to know what's happening in their organization, right now!

Developers building WCF, WF, or BizTalk applications will learn how to monitor those applications without writing extra code. Architects will discover how to bridge service-oriented architecture, business process management, and BI. Decision makers will see what's happening inside business processes. BI specialists will comprehend how BAM provides real-time capabilities that supplement any BI strategy. Business users and analysts will learn how BAM allows them to understand what's happening in the business every minute of every day.

PART 1

■ ■ ■

Introducing BAM

In Part 1, you'll learn the basics of Business Activity Monitoring (BAM). Chapter 1 provides an overview of BAM and compares BAM with BI. Chapter 2 will teach you how to select the server configuration for BAM. Chapter 3 will lead you through a very simple, but complete, BAM project, where you will capture data from a WCF service. Chapter 4 will describe how BAM can be used in a variety of different software architectures.

■ ■ ■

Welcome to Business Activity Monitoring!

Business Activity Monitoring (BAM) provides real-time business intelligence by capturing data as it flows through a business system. By using BAM, you can monitor a business process in real time and generate alerts when the business process needs human intervention. Although many vendors, including IBM and Oracle, sell BAM solutions, this book focuses on the Microsoft BAM tools. Microsoft's BAM is a feature of Microsoft BizTalk Server that was first introduced in BizTalk Server 2004. The current version of BAM is a flexible infrastructure that captures data from Microsoft's full line of service-oriented architecture (SOA) offerings: Windows Communication Foundation (WCF), Windows Workflow Foundation (WF), .NET applications, and BizTalk Server.

In this book, you'll gain an in-depth understanding of the BAM tools in BizTalk Server 2009 and learn how to apply the tools to your project, whether you're building on BizTalk Server, WCF, WF, or some other set of tools. If you're a BizTalk developer, you'll learn how to provide your end users with information about how your BizTalk application behaves. However, BAM provides value to any application built on the Microsoft platform, whether or not you're using BizTalk Server. If you're using WCF or WF, you can use BAM to instrument your application, often without modifying your code. If you're writing .NET code, you can call the BAM API to make use of the low-latency data capture provided by BAM. BAM allows information workers to monitor a business process in real time, regardless of which tools are being used to implement the process.

This chapter provides an introduction to BAM. The chapter first outlines some of the technology trends that provide the context for the development of BAM. We'll briefly review service-oriented architecture, business process management (BPM), and business intelligence (BI). Next, we describe the benefits of BAM, followed by an overview of the architecture and functions of BizTalk Server 2009. Finally, the chapter ends on an overview of BAM, describing the data sources that can be used with BAM, the observation models that define the data to capture, and the ways to present BAM data.

Technology Trends

In this section, we'll review some recent trends in enterprise architecture. BAM builds on service-oriented architecture, business process management, and business intelligence, and a short review of these trends will be helpful in your understanding of BAM.

Service-Oriented Architecture and BAM

BAM is often used to capture data from applications built using service-oriented architecture principles. SOA is a style of architecture based upon message passing between systems, where the goal is to expose data and services in a loosely coupled fashion that makes it easy to create composite services. SOA projects typically follow four principles:

- *Boundaries are explicit*: Calling a service may require crossing a network, crossing a security boundary, or marshalling data between different representations. Service-oriented designs pay attention to the costs of boundary crossing; messages are passed explicitly instead of being implicitly created by method calls.

- *Services are autonomous*: Services are versioned and managed independently of their clients. Changes in implementation details are irrelevant to the clients.

- *Services share schema and contract, not class*: In SOA, there's a bright line between the external interfaces to the service and the internal implementation of the service. The interfaces to the service are typically defined using Web Services Description Language (WSDL). Implementation details, such as classes, are hidden from the client. All interaction with the service is through endpoints defined by contracts.

- *Service compatibility is based upon policy*: Information such as service-level agreements and security policy isn't captured by a service's WSDL. Instead, tools such as WS-Policy are used to capture information on service policies.

Typical goals of SOA projects include opening up data in legacy systems to new uses, reusing functionality, composing services into new capabilities, promoting business agility, and lowering the cost of developing new systems. Often, systems within the enterprise are exposed as web services. These services can be composed into new capabilities, which are consumed by new applications. BAM is commonly used to capture messages flowing between services, and Microsoft's implementation of BAM does an excellent job of monitoring a system built on Microsoft's SOA tools: WCF, WF, and BizTalk Server. Several examples in the book will teach you how to use BAM in an SOA.

Business Process Management and BAM

Many BAM projects are used to monitor the behavior and performance of business processes in a business process management system. As the name implies, BPM systems manage business processes. There are two major flavors of BPM: Integration-Centric Business Process Management Systems (IC-BPMS) and Human-Centric Business Process Management Systems (HC-BPMS).

IC-BPMS are concerned with moving data between systems. The IC-BPMS marketplace evolved out of the Enterprise Application Integration (EAI) space, and IC-BPMS are focused on moving messages between software systems. As an example, consider an insurance company. When a new policy is written, the underwriting system must notify the accounting system, so it can start collecting premiums. When a claim comes in, the claims system should verify coverage using the underwriting system, and then notify the accounting system that the claim should be paid. Each of these business processes could be managed by IC-BPMS. Microsoft's IC-BPMS offering is BizTalk Server.

HC-BPMS are concerned with workflows that connect people. As an example, consider how a distributor of medical devices manages its product catalog. A salesperson visits a hospital and receives a request for a device that is not in the catalog. The salesperson may request that the device be added to the catalog, but several departments must review the request before the item can be sold. The catalog desk will review the request and determine whether an equivalent device from another manufacturer is already carried. Perhaps the distributor carries a similar product in its own brand that it would prefer to sell. If the product is approved by the catalog desk, vendor management will need to approve the vendor, and a purchasing agent will need to agree to a price with the manufacturer. Each of these steps will require human intervention. HC-BPMS have capabilities for delegating tasks when a person is on vacation and escalating tasks if they don't get done within the expected time. Microsoft's HC-BPMS offering is Microsoft Office SharePoint Server with workflows created using Share-Point Designer.

In many cases, HC-BPMS and IC-BPMS are used together to implement a business process. Let's return to the insurance claim example we described previously. In most cases, the claim will be paid immediately, and IC-BPMS (in this case, BizTalk Server) will verify coverage with the underwriting system and then notify the accounting system to pay the claim. However, the claims system runs a fraud detection algorithm that identifies suspicious claims. For those claims, IC-BPMS will initiate a human-centric workflow in HC-BPMS (in this case, Microsoft Office SharePoint Server) that will ensure the claim is reviewed before payment. This would be implemented by using BizTalk's SharePoint adapter to write a message from the claims system into a SharePoint document library, and then initiating a SharePoint workflow based on the document arriving in the library.

One of the most common uses for BAM is to track the progress of a business process. BAM can be used to report on the status of an individual process, to summarize the state of a collection of business processes by providing aggregate data, or to send alerts to a person or system when issues arise with a process. In our example, BAM provides end-to-end visibility within both systems.

Business Intelligence and BAM

BAM adds real-time capabilities to business intelligence systems. Forrester defines BI as "A set of methodologies, processes, architectures, and technologies that transform raw data into meaningful and useful information used to enable more effective strategic, tactical, and operational insights and decision-making." Typical BI systems transfer data from operational systems to a data warehouse using some kind of extract-transform-load (ETL) tool. Data in the warehouse is aggregated to allow for ad hoc analysis using reporting tools. Information workers work with data in the data warehouse to understand the state of the enterprise, analyze trends, and perform "what-if" analyses. One way to think about a BI system is to view it as a way to make data in the underlying operational systems visible to the business.

BI initiatives are a powerful tool for aligning execution with strategy. Corporate Performance Management (CPM) tools can provide direct feedback on how well the tactics adopted by the organization are supporting the strategic goals established at the executive level. Well-chosen key performance indicators (KPIs) can measure the performance of the organization and allow analysis of causes of success or failure.

Traditional BI systems have limitations, however. Many BI systems don't work in real time. Usually, the data load happens on a periodic basis: hourly, daily, or weekly. Because of this, data in a typical BI system is primarily historical and cannot be used to generate an alert when business conditions change or action is needed by management. Many BI systems expect to load their data from a traditional database and don't support grabbing data from an in-flight process in the BPM. Adding BAM capabilities increases the value of a BI system by providing real-time data.

Don't think of BAM as a competitor to BI, and don't assume that your organization needs to make a choice between deploying traditional BI systems and deploying BAM. In many cases, the BAM infrastructure will be used to feed data into a traditional data warehouse. A comprehensive performance management strategy will use both BI and BAM to view both the current status of processes and the trends that drive performance.

The Benefits of BAM

BAM captures data from your business systems, providing real-time monitoring of a business process. In the same way that a BI system makes data in your transactional database visible to information workers, BAM captures data from your BPM system or SOA solution and makes it available to nontechnical users. The main benefits of BAM are

- BAM automates data capture and aggregation.
- BAM provides real-time visibility into business processes.
- BAM can alert users.
- BAM can capture data asynchronously.

Let's review each of the advantages of BAM before drilling into the implementation details.

BAM Automates Data Capture and Aggregation

There's an important difference between the typical data sources used by BAM and BI. BI systems typically either load data from an operational database via ETL or use hybrid online analytical processing (HOLAP) to build data aggregations over relational data. BAM loads data from events as they are processed by an application or BPM system. Events can be Biz-Talk messages, WCF service calls, WF activities, or API calls. BAM makes life very easy for the developer who wants to monitor processes built on BizTalk applications, WCF services, or WF workflows by automatically capturing data without requiring any application changes.

Once data has been captured, it can be automatically aggregated into summary views, either in real time or during a scheduled cube build.

BAM Provides Real-Time Visibility into Business Processes

The difference in data sources leads to a different emphasis between the way BAM and BI data is used. BI data is often used for historical and "what-if" analysis, or in an attempt to understand performance trends. BAM data is typically used for a short-term picture of what's happening in an organization right now or to analyze the behavior of a business process.

BAM Can Alert Users

Because BAM provides a real-time, event-driven infrastructure, it can alert your users when something requires their attention. Alerts can be based either on a specific instance of a process, such as an order that hasn't shipped 48 hours after being received, or on the aggregate behavior of a process, such as more than 500 orders being received in a week, a business situation that calls for extra staffing to be brought in. BAM alerts can be sent to one or more people, for example by e-mail, or can be used to initiate an automated process such as a BizTalk orchestration.

BAM Can Capture Data Asynchronously

Obviously, it would be easy for a developer to write .NET code that logged to a database each time a BizTalk message was transmitted. This would have performance implications, however, because each service call would be delayed by a network round-trip to the database server. Because BAM provides a technology known as a *buffered event stream* within the BAM API, with background services that capture events and write them to the BAM Primary Import (BAM PI) database, BAM can capture event data with minimal impact on the performance of the system that's being monitored.

BizTalk Server Overview

Because BAM ships as a feature of BizTalk Server, and many BAM projects use BizTalk Server as one of the sources of data, this section will provide a brief overview of BizTalk Server. Readers with BizTalk experience will probably want to skip to the next section.

Microsoft BizTalk Server 2000 was marketed as a ".NET Enterprise server that unites, in a single product, enterprise application integration (EAI) and business-to-business (B2B) integration." It included such features as messaging between applications, document tracking, process orchestration, and XML tools. While BizTalk's goals have remained more or less consistent since that time, it's grown to encompass numerous industry, business, and architectural trends. The current version integrates several technologies that make transformational change possible. BizTalk Server 2004 was a major change in the BizTalk architecture, as BizTalk moved from the component object model (COM) to .NET. Since that time, BizTalk Server 2006, BizTalk Server 2006 R2, and BizTalk Server 2009 have built on the architecture, adding support for radio frequency identification (RFID), electronic data interchange (EDI), and rich integration with the Visual Studio Team System project model.

Many Microsoft server products provide a rich set of tools focused on a common theme. As an example, SQL Server provides several tools focused on data: the core database engine, SQL Server Analysis Services, SQL Server Reporting Services, and SQL Server Integration Services. Another example is Microsoft Office SharePoint Server, which provides several tools focused on collaboration: document libraries, enterprise search, content management, forms-driven business process, team sites, and the business data catalog. The BizTalk Server tools are focused on systems integration. The tools include a messaging engine, adapters for external systems, orchestration and long-running business processes, a business rules engine, EDI tools, an RFID infrastructure, endpoint and trading partner management, and BAM. Very few BizTalk projects use every tool in the toolbox, but together these tools make up a powerful kit for building integration solutions.

Today, BizTalk is a hugely successful integration product, with over 8,000 customers worldwide. In late 2008, BizTalk's customer base included

- 90% of the Fortune Global 100

- 12 of the 15 largest retailers in the world

- 5 of the 10 largest hotel chains in the world

- 6 of the 8 largest U.S. pharmaceutical companies

- 4 of the 5 largest U.S. electronics parts manufacturers

- 9 of the 10 largest U.S. telecommunications companies

- 5 of the 8 largest U.S. chemical companies

- 4 of the 5 largest railroads in the U.S.

- 9 of the 10 largest insurance companies in the world

- 23 of 27 EU member governments

BizTalk Messaging

The core of BizTalk Server is the messaging engine, illustrated in Figure 1-1. BizTalk Messaging provides a publish-subscribe engine built on a SQL Server database called the *message box*. The BizTalk administrator configures a receive port that tells an adapter to listen at a specific location. As an example, a receive port might listen for XML files dropped into a specific folder. Once the adapter picks up an inbound interchange, the adapter hands it to a receive pipeline. The receive pipeline is a collection of .NET components that can validate message structure, disassemble messages from text or binary formats into XML, break batches of messages into individual messages, or do any other custom processing that the developer chooses. The receive pipeline may call a map, which transforms the inbound message into another format, and then the message is published into the message box, a SQL Server database.

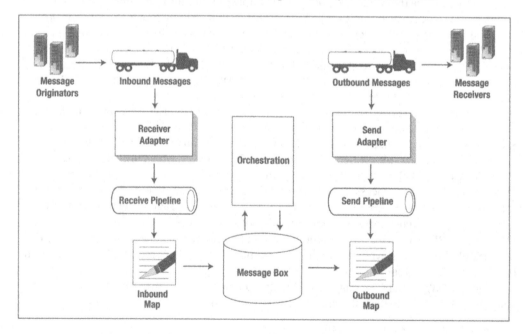

Figure 1-1. *Publish-subscribe messaging in BizTalk Server*

The message box is the heart of BizTalk; it contains information on in-flight messages and subscriptions. Two types of service can subscribe to an inbound message: send ports and orchestrations. A send port is in some ways the mirror image of a receive port. When a send port picks up an outbound message, the message can be mapped to another format, and is then passed to a send pipeline. The send pipeline can assemble the message into a non-XML format, validate the message, encrypt the message, or perform other custom processing. Next the message is passed to an adapter that transmits the message. As an example, a send port might use the FTP adapter to transmit the file to a server on the Internet via File Transfer Protocol (FTP).

BizTalk Adapters

Adapters are the secret sauce that allows BizTalk to talk to other systems. An adapter is a piece of software that can connect to an external data source, technology, or application. Adapters have been part of BizTalk since the first version. In BizTalk Server 2004, a new adapter framework based on .NET was included in the new BizTalk architecture. In BizTalk Server 2006 R2, an additional adapter framework built on WCF was added. With most adapters, connecting to an external system is as simple as a few mouse clicks.

Most adapters can be configured as either send or receive ports, although there are a few exceptions. The SMTP adapter is an example of a send-only adapter, and the POP3 adapter is a receive-only adapter. Adapters are loosely categorized into adapters that work with specific applications, such as the SAP adapter, adapters that work with data, such as the IBM DB2 adapter, and adapters that work with technologies or protocols, such as the HTTP and MSMQ adapters. Table 1-1 lists the adapters available in BizTalk Server 2009.

Table 1-1. *Adapters in BizTalk Server 2009*

Adapter	Category
SAP (WCF Adapter Framework)	Application
Siebel (WCF Adapter Framework)	Application
Oracle e-Business Suite (WCF Adapter Framework)	Application
Oracle Database (WCF Adapter Framework)	Data
Microsoft SQL Server (WCF Adapter Framework)	Data
SAP	Application
PeopleSoft Enterprise	Application
JD Edwards OneWorld XE	Application
JD Edwards EnterpriseOne	Application
Siebel	Application
ODBC Adapter for Oracle Database	Data
IBM DB2	Data
Microsoft SQL Server	Data
Host Files (Mainframe: VSAM; AS/400: Physical Files)	Technology
TIBCO Rendezvous	Technology

Continued

Table 1-1. *Continued*

Adapter	Category
TIBCO Enterprise Message Service	Technology
Host Applications (Mainframe: CICS and IMS; AS/400 VSR)	Technology
WebSphere MQ (Client-based)	Technology
WebSphere MQ (Direct)	Technology
MSMQ/MSMQT	Technology
EDI (X.12, HIPAA, and EDIFACT)	Technology
File	Technology
FTP	Technology
HTTP	Technology
SOAP	Technology
WSE 2.0	Technology
WCF WS-HTTP	Technology
WCF Basic-HTTP	Technology
WCF Net-TCP	Technology
WCF Net-MSMQ	Technology
WCF NetNamedPipe	Technology
WCF Custom	Technology
WCF Custom Isolated	Technology
SMTP	Technology
POP3	Technology
Windows SharePoint Services (WSS 2.0 and 3.0)	Technology

BizTalk Orchestration

The orchestration engine builds on messaging to provide support for business logic and long-running business processes. The screenshot in Figure 1-2 is an example of a BizTalk orchestration that implements a design pattern called *parallel convoy*. This orchestration is part of a purchase order process. In this system, a purchase order can only be processed when two messages have arrived: an order detail message from the web site and a credit card approval message from a third-party credit card processor. The orchestration waits for both messages to arrive, and then uses a map to create a message that contains both order details and credit card payment information. This message is then sent to the ERP system for processing.

Orchestration is part of the publish-subscribe messaging model. Orchestrations receive incoming messages by creating subscriptions in the message box. When an orchestration sends a message, it is published to the message box, where it can be picked up by a send port or another orchestration.

Two facilities provided by BizTalk Orchestration for dealing with long-running business processes are *correlation* and *compensation*. As an example of correlation, imagine an orchestration that sends a purchase order to a supplier and needs to receive the corresponding purchase order acknowledgment. Using correlation, the orchestration would initialize a correlation set that contains the order number when the outgoing message is sent. BizTalk will use the correlation set to create a special subscription in the message box that receives acknowledgments with the correct purchase order and routes them to the correct instance of the orchestration.

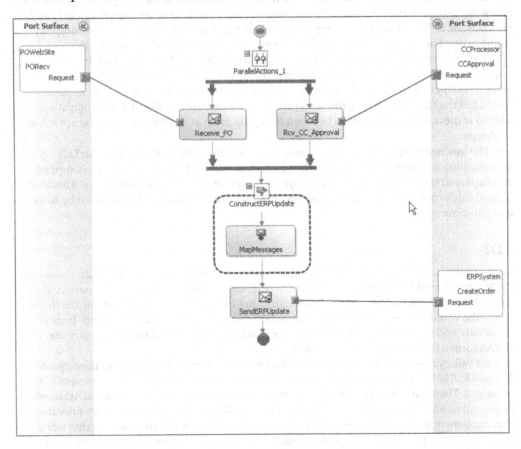

Figure 1-2. *A BizTalk orchestration*

Compensation is a technique to deal with long-running transactions and can be thought of as the "undo" to the execution of an orchestration. Traditional database transactions are atomic, which means that they succeed or fail as a unit. Integration processes often need transactions that last too long to be implemented as atomic transactions. To continue the example, sending the purchase order to the supplier, and receiving a response, should be implemented as a transaction. However, it may take several hours to receive the response from the supplier, so this can't be implemented as an atomic database transaction. Also, sending the message to the supplier has an effect outside BizTalk, so it can't be simply rolled back. Compensation is the set of actions that need to be taken if a transaction needs to be cancelled after it has started. Unlike rolling back an atomic transaction, compensation may take additional steps to recover from the failed transaction, such as updating other systems or e-mailing users to let them know about the failed transaction.

Business Rules Engine

The business rules engine allows business logic to be separated from the application. As an example, consider a car dealer who has branches in several states. The taxes on a car depend on the state where the car is sold, the state where the new owner lives, the type of car, and the status of the owner. In some states, Native Americans or veterans receive special treatment for car taxes. As well, tax rules can change with each jurisdiction's financial year. The company wants to open additional branches in new states, so it will need to add new tax logic.

It would certainly be possible to implement the tax rules as .NET code, but that would require a developer to get involved every time the rules were modified. Instead, a business analyst could create and modify tax policies in the business rules engine, and the application would call the tax policy during the sales process. By using the business rules engine, it's possible to achieve a clean separation between the application and business rules that are subject to change.

The business rules engine, or BRE, may be called from within an executing BizTalk orchestration or directly using C# code from an interfacing application. Rules are compiled and deployed to the engine, and may be dynamically altered as conditions change. This level of flexibility provides the robust conditional logic processing functionality required by BPM and real-time systems.

EDI

In addition to traditional EAI within an organization, BizTalk is widely used for B2B connectivity. The traditional EDI formats, X12 and EDIFACT, are the most widely used formats in B2B; X12 is the dominant format in the United States, and EDIFACT is the dominant format in the rest of the world. In the United States, transaction formats mandated by the Health Insurance Portability and Accountability Act (HIPAA) are widely used in the healthcare industry; the HIPAA formats are based on the X12 standards.

BizTalk provides pipeline components that can assemble and disassemble messages in X12 and EDIFACT. The pipeline components can deal with batching and debatching of EDI messages. They can also generate acknowledgments, such as X12's 997 Functional Acknowledgement or AS2's Message Disposition Notification (MDN). Special pipelines are provided that implement the AS2 protocol, which transmits EDI files securely over the Internet using HTTP and SMIME. BizTalk ships with schemas for all the popular versions of X12 and EDIFACT. The BizTalk Administration Console provides features for administering EDI trading partners and setting the EDI options for each partner.

RFID

Radio frequency identification is used to track the movement of physical goods. One example of RFID that's familiar to commuters in the Northeast region of the United States is the E-ZPass system. An E-ZPass is a tag that's mounted on a car windshield. As the car passes through a highway tollbooth, the tag is automatically detected by an antenna in the tollbooth, and the toll is charged to the driver's credit card. RFID tags are widely used in manufacturing, distribution, and retailing to track the movement of inventory. BizTalk provides a software infrastructure for RFID that uses a driver model to interface with a wide variety of RFID hardware.

BizTalk Server 2009 adds support for RFID devices that run the Windows Mobile and Windows CE operating systems.

Management and Operations

BizTalk provides a variety of tools for developing BizTalk solutions and managing BizTalk servers. A set of add-ins for Visual Studio 2008 allows message schemas, maps, orchestrations, and pipelines to be developed. The BizTalk Administration Console allows administrators to create receive and send ports, manage services, set up EDI trading partners, view subscriptions, and handle suspended messages.

System Monitor (PerfMon) can be used to check the performance of BizTalk applications, and System Center Operations Manager (SCOM) can be used to monitor the health of your BizTalk group. Send ports, receive ports, and orchestrations can be configured to track messages. Tracked messages are copied to a special database after processing so that it's possible to examine all the messages that have passed through the system. In earlier versions of BizTalk Server, a separate tool called Health and Activity Tracking (HAT) was used to examine tracked data, but in BizTalk Server 2009, tracked data was added to the Administration Console, shown in Figure 1-3.

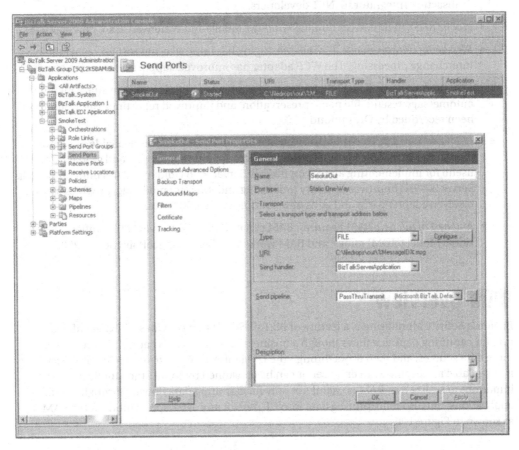

Figure 1-3. *The BizTalk Administration Console*

What's New in BizTalk Server 2009

There are a number of new features in BizTalk Server 2009:

- *Platform alignment*: BizTalk Server now supports Windows Server 2008, SQL Server 2008, Visual Studio 2008, and virtualization using Windows Server 2008's hypervisor technology (Hyper-V). BizTalk artifacts are now fully integrated into Visual Studio Team System's application life-cycle management, supporting TFS source code control, automated builds via MSBuild, and unit testing via Visual Studio Test. Visual Studio now supports debugging BizTalk maps, pipeline components, and orchestrations.

- *Administration*: The Administration Console now supports access to Health and Activity Tracking (HAT) data.

- *SOA registry*: BizTalk Server now provides a new registry based on UDDI 3.0.

- *New adapters*: New adapters based on the WCF Adapter Framework have been provided for Oracle e-Business Suite and Microsoft SQL Server.

- *New legacy integration features*: BizTalk Server now includes a WCF channel for communicating with WebSphere MQ. The WCF Service for Host Applications exposes the Transaction Integrator to .NET developers.

- *Mobile RFID*: RFID devices running Windows Mobile and Windows CE are now supported.

- *Messaging improvements*: BizTalk Messaging has improved support for recoverable interchange processing. The WCF adapter has improved support for transactions.

- *EDI improvements*: The EDI pipelines now support multiple message attachments, automessage resend, file name preservation, and improved reporting. The system has been recertified by Drummond.

- *ESB Guidance 2.0*: The Enterprise Service Bus (ESB) Guidance is available as a download from Microsoft's Patterns & Practices group. It provides code and guidance that is useful for implementing an ESB on BizTalk Server. ESB Guidance 2.0 is built on BizTalk Server 2009. It improves itinerary processing and itinerary modeling, provides a new resolver-adapter pack, and adds new features to the ESB Portal.

- *And best of all, new BAM Features*: BAM can now use SQL Server 2008 Unified Dimensional Model (UDM) cubes, and BAM works with PerformancePoint Server 2007.

BAM Overview

Business Activity Monitoring is a feature of BizTalk Server that provides a flexible infrastructure for capturing data as it flows though a business process. Data is captured from one or more data sources, and then flows through the BAM infrastructure to a set of databases, where it is available for display to an end user or can be consumed by some other application. It's important to realize that BAM is useful not only for capturing data flowing through BizTalk applications, but also for capturing data in WCF, WF, or any .NET application via the BAM API, as shown in Figure 1-4.

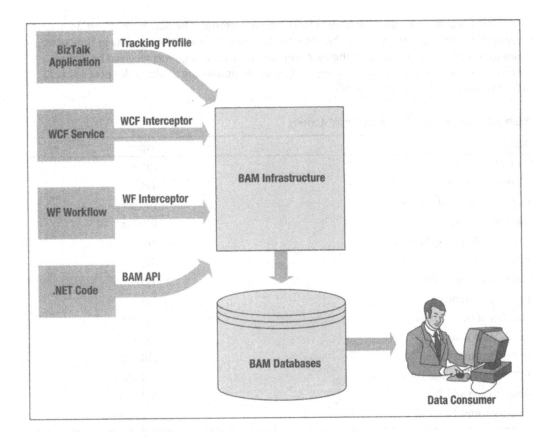

Figure 1-4. *Data flow in BAM*

When you implement a BAM project, you have to answer three key questions:

- What data should be captured?
- Where does the data come from?
- How will the data be presented to the user?

The following sections will look at each of these three areas in turn.

Observation Model: What Data Should Be Captured?

All BAM projects start by creating an observation model. The observation model defines the data that is captured from the business system and the way the data is displayed. On most projects, the observation model is defined by a business analyst working in Excel, using the BAM Add-In for Excel. Observation models contain two types of artifacts: activities and views. It's important to understand that the observation model doesn't define how the data is captured; it only defines the data of interest and the way that data will be presented to data consumers.

A BAM activity is a collection of data fields and milestones. The data may be text data, or it may be numeric data captured as either floats or integers. Milestones are points in time when something occurred, for example, the date and time that a message was received by BizTalk or a WCF service was called. As an example, if we were monitoring a sales order process, we might capture the data listed in Table 1-2.

Table 1-2. *The Example Purchase Order Activity*

Name	Type
Order Number	Integer
Customer Name	Text
Customer Account Number	Integer
Discount Percentage	Integer
Customer Industry (NAICS)	Text
Salesperson	Text
Customer State or Province	Text
Customer Country	Text
Number of Order Lines	Integer
Total Order Value	Float
Order Date and Time	Milestone
ERP System Message Date and Time	Milestone
Invoice Date and Time	Milestone
Ship Date and Time	Milestone

■**Note** The North American Industry Classification System (NAICS) is a system for classifying economic data, where each industry is given a standard code. As an example, the code 33994 is used for the manufacturing of office supplies other than paper.

If you examine the data, you'll see that not all the data in the purchase order is captured by BAM. The order also includes the customer street address, but this isn't captured because none of the users who use BAM data are interested in this level of detail.

A BAM view provides information on how the data in the activity will be presented to the user. Often, there will be several views onto the same activity, supporting different roles within the organization. In addition to simple data and milestones, a view can include aggregations and dimensions.

■**Note** You'll find much more detail on activities and views in Chapter 5.

In our purchase order example, we might have three audiences for BAM data: the sales manager, the shipping manager, and the IT help desk.

The sales manager is primarily interested in tracking the performance of the sales team by industry and state. The sales manager's view might be a four-dimensional Excel pivot table, with the dimensions being order date, salesperson, customer industry, and geography (see Table 1-3). At each cell in the cube, the measures would be total orders, average order value, and number of orders.

Table 1-3. *The Sales Manager View*

Name	Type
Order Date	Time Dimension
Customer Industry (NAICS)	Data Dimension
Salesperson	Data Dimension
Customer State and Country	Data Dimension
Number of Orders	Sum of Integers
Total Order Value	Sum of Floats
Average Order Value	Average of Floats

The shipping manager is concerned with getting orders out in a timely manner, but is too busy to look at a report on a regular basis. Instead, BAM should notify the shipping manager when an order takes more than 48 hours to ship. Occasionally, the shipping manager needs to report on average time to ship and would like a report that shows the average number of hours to ship an order by week.

The shipping manager will use the BAM Portal to display his view on the data and will also have an alert configured to e-mail the order number when an order has not shipped within 48 hours (see Table 1-4).

Table 1-4. *The Shipping Manager View*

Name	Type
Order Date	Time Dimension
Number of Orders	Sum of Integers
Average Invoice Time	Average Duration
Average Ship Time	Average Duration

The IT Help Desk is called when the status of an order needs investigation. The help desk wants to be able to determine the date and time an order was received, sent to the ERP system, and invoiced. However, the order values are considered confidential information that should not be visible to the help desk. The help desk will also use the BAM Portal to view data, and the help desk view is just a subset of the original activity without any aggregation, as shown in Table 1-5.

Table 1-5. *The IT Help Desk View*

Name	Type
Order Number	Integer
Customer Name	Text
Customer Account Number	Integer
Order Date and Time	Milestone
ERP System Message Date and Time	Milestone
Invoice Date and Time	Milestone
Ship Date and Time	Milestone

Data Sources: Where Does the Data Come From?

The four data sources most commonly used with BAM are BizTalk applications, WCF services, WF workflows, and .NET applications that work with the BAM API.

- *BizTalk applications*: BAM can capture data from fields in BizTalk messages or BizTalk context properties. BAM can also capture milestones from the date and time a BizTalk message is received or sent. Data capture from BizTalk is configured using the Tracking Profile Editor (TPE), shown in Figure 1-5. The TPE provides a simple click-and-drag user interface that makes it easy for the developer to specify the data that is captured.

■**Note** Chapter 6 is focused purely on the Tracking Profile Editor, including its major concepts, hands-on exercises, and deployment.

- *WCF services*: BAM can capture data from the SOAP envelope in a WCF request, response, or fault message. The captured data is specified using an interceptor configuration (IC) file, an XML file that is created by a developer. The service's app.config is modified to load the BAM components at run time.

■**Note** Chapter 3 covers a basic walkthrough of a BAM project that uses the WCF interceptor. The WCF interceptor is covered in greater detail in Chapter 8.

- *WF workflows*: BAM can capture milestones from WF activities. Like WCF services, an IC file is used to specify the data that must be captured, and BAM components must also be loaded at run time.

■**Note**   Chapter 9 contains more information about the WF interceptor.

- *BAM API*: .NET code can write data directly into BAM using an API. Code that isn't executing in BizTalk will use either the `BufferedEventStream` or `DirectEventStream` classes. These two classes have different performance and reliability characteristics, but the bottom line is that it's easy to write .NET code that interfaces with the BAM API. If you need to instrument code on another platform, such as J2EE, all the standard Java/.NET interop techniques can be used, including creating a web service in .NET that calls the BAM API.

■**Note**   The BAM API is described in Chapter 10.

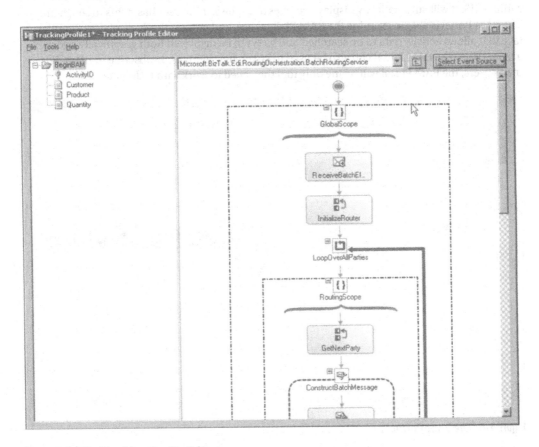

Figure 1-5. *The Tracking Profile Editor*

Databases and Consuming Data: How Will the Data Be Presented to the User?

After events pass through the BAM infrastructure, they are initially stored in a database called BAM Primary Import. This database contains a set of tables for each BAM activity.

There are two types of views: real-time aggregation and scheduled. Real-time aggregation views will be created as SQL Server views in BAM PI. Scheduled views are implemented by building OLAP cubes on a periodic basis. Older data may be migrated out of BAM Primary Import to the BAM Archive database.

The tables and views that bm.exe builds are quite straightforward; standard reporting tools, such as SQL Server Reporting Services or Microsoft Office PerformancePoint Server, can easily consume the data. Developers familiar with ADO.NET or LINQ will have no difficulty programming against the databases. You can assume that the database structures will be maintained in future product versions.

In many cases, you won't need to build your own client. BizTalk provides two prebuilt clients for BAM data: the BAM Portal and BAM Excel spreadsheets. The BAM Portal, shown in Figure 1-6, is an ASP.NET application that can be installed with BizTalk Server, if your system is running IIS. It will automatically display activities and views, if the user has rights to see them. The BAM Portal is able to examine the BAM PI database, and automatically display a user interface that allows activity data to be searched and views to be displayed both graphically and as a pivot table. The BAM Portal can also be used to create new alerts and subscribe to them. For many users, the BAM Portal will be the only tool they need to work with BAM data.

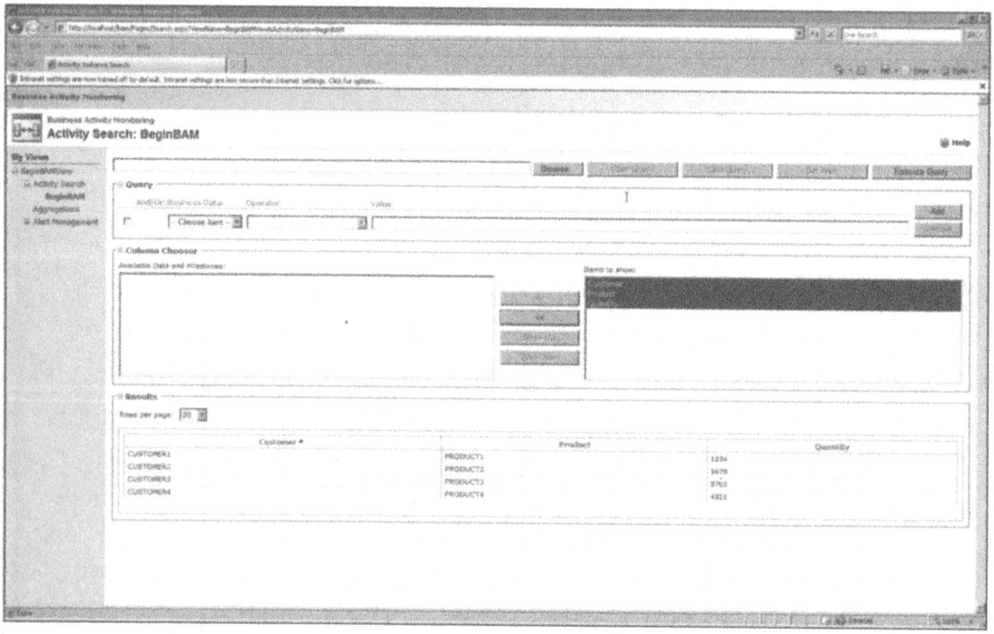

Figure 1-6. *The BAM Portal*

However, some users will prefer to work with the Excel client. Each time you build a new view with the BAM Add-In for Excel, a live pivot table is built in the spreadsheet that is linked to the BAM data. If you have users who love Excel, they will be delighted to learn that they can use their favorite tool to analyze BAM data. You can enable them to connect to the BAM databases by just e-mailing them the spreadsheet that is built by the add-in.

BAM alerts are built on SQL Server Notification Services. When SQL Server Notification Services are available, alerts can be created that will either send an e-mail or create a file when a particular condition occurs. BAM Alerts are often used to notify a person, typically by e-mailing a human-readable message. However, a BAM alert can also write an XML file, and this can be read by a receive port that initiates a BizTalk orchestration, allowing BizTalk to act on the alerted condition.

■**Note** Chapter 7 describes working with the BAM Portal and the Excel client. Chapter 11 has detailed examples of using Microsoft BI tools such as SQL Server Reporting Services to display BAM data.

Summary

This chapter introduced BAM in the context of several important technology trends. The first section introduced SOA, BPM, and BI. The next three sections described the benefits of BAM, and then provided an overview of BizTalk Server and the new features of BizTalk Server 2009. The final section introduced BAM as a tool for capturing data that flows through business systems, especially systems built on BizTalk Server, WCF, WF, and .NET. That section also mentioned three important questions: What data does BAM need to capture? Where does the data come from? How is the data presented to the user?

In the remainder of Part 1, you'll learn more of the basics of BAM, starting with configuration options and how to install BAM in Chapter 2.

CHAPTER 2

■■■

Installing and Configuring BAM

Installing and configuring BizTalk is not a straightforward process. Although it's become easier in each version, installation is made more complex by the large number of subsystems and technologies that are required in a BizTalk installation. That is still true in BizTalk Server 2009.

The installation and configuration process for BAM is no different. It involves planning and design of your BAM server architecture and roles, installing several prerequisites, the installation processes, and configuration.

Because of the technical complexity of BizTalk Server and BAM, Microsoft offers official installation and configuration guides for BizTalk, which may be downloaded from http:// www.microsoft.com/downloads/details.aspx?displaylang=en&FamilyID=9c697e02-d1bc-4684- 8748-28b3a292d5bf. Available as of the time of the publication of this book are guides on how to install

- BizTalk Server 2009 in a multicomputer environment

- BizTalk Server 2009 on Windows Vista

- BizTalk Server 2009 on Windows Server 2003

- BizTalk Server 2009 on Windows Server 2008

- BizTalk Server 2009 on Windows XP

- BizTalk Server 2009 via upgrade from BizTalk Server 2006

- BizTalk RFID Mobile

- BizTalk RFID on Windows Server 2003 or 2008

- BizTalk Server RFID on Windows XP or Vista

Additionally, Microsoft has published a troubleshooting document for BizTalk Server 2009 setup.

With BizTalk Server 2006 R2, Microsoft had also published a separate, stand-alone document on considerations when installing BAM, found at http://go.microsoft.com/ fwlink/?LinkId=81041. As of the publication of this book, that document had yet to be updated for BizTalk Server 2009.

We have found these documents to be somewhat reliable, with some noted issues surrounding sequence of events and hotfix installation (hopefully these issues will be addressed and corrected). By and large, the guides target the broadest audience possible, and as such, don't provide context surrounding questions you should ask specifically as they relate to BAM.

This chapter will attempt to bridge that gap by providing specific context surrounding

- How BAM software is structured
- Designing your BAM architecture
- Optimizing your BAM architecture
- Creating a BAM Virtual PC for the exercises in this book

This chapter will not cover the installation of BizTalk Server 2009.

How BAM Software Is Structured

As part of a marketing effort, the BizTalk team created a series of posters illustrating the concepts of BizTalk and BAM. While the BAM poster (available for download at http://www.microsoft.com/downloads/details.aspx?FamilyID=193CD7A4-E271-46BB-B4EE-8434DFA779A0&displaylang=en) is visually arresting and provides a great high-level visualization of the many BAM software components, without diving into several sets of documentation, it's unclear as to where the various components reside or where they are conceptually installed.

Software for BAM falls into three major categories: presentation and tools, service façade and processing, and a database and platform services. Chapter 3 will cover more about the different roles within a BAM deployment, and who uses which tools.

Presentation and Tools

Software within this category is used for the visual presentation of data or tools with which a user will interface.

The BAM Portal

The BAM Portal is an ASP.NET-based application used for the consumption of BAM data. It may be used by all roles within a BAM project. It is installed as part of the BizTalk Server 2009 installation process and configured under the BAM Portal tab. It may be installed on any Windows server that runs IIS, as long as that server is joined to the same BizTalk Server group. It is then accessed by any data consumer with access to a web browser. While the BAM Portal may be installed on the same server as BizTalk, it is generally recommended you install it on a separate server dedicated to BAM and BAM tools.

The BAM Client: bm.exe and the BAM Add-In for Excel

The BAM Client tools are the core tools for building BAM solutions. The BAM Management utility, or bm.exe, provides for end-to-end management and deployment of BAM. The BAM Add-In for Excel provides for the creation of observation models to be deployed to the BAM infrastructure, and the capabilities to consume BAM data within Excel via a data connection (known as *Live Workbooks*). The tools of the BAM Client are used by business analysts, developers, system administrators, and data consumers. The BAM Client is installed as part of the BizTalk Server installation process, and configured under the BAM Tools tab. As per the installation instructions, ensure that you have already installed Microsoft Office

Excel before installing the BAM Client. The BAM Client may be installed on the same server or another computer than BizTalk Server. It is generally recommended that a copy of the BAM Client be installed on each BizTalk server and each client desktop.

Information Worker Tools: Microsoft Office Excel, Microsoft Office InfoPath, Microsoft Office Visio

Microsoft Office Excel, along with the BAM Add-In for Excel, is used to create observation models and consume data from Live Workbooks. Microsoft Office InfoPath is used to create XML-based forms for submission to a WCF service (optional). Microsoft Office Visio is used to create business process diagrams. Business analysts, developers, and data consumers use these tools, which are installed as part of the Microsoft Office 2007 installation software. It is generally recommended that a licensed instance of these tools be installed on the desktops of business analysts and developers, while data consumers require only Excel for data consumption.

The Orchestration Designer for Business Analysts

The Orchestration Designer for Business Analysts (ODBA) may also be used to define BAM activities and business processes. As its name suggests, business analysts use this tool. It is installed as part of a stand-alone web download and requires Microsoft Visio to function. It is generally recommended that ODBA be installed on business analysts' desktops.

The Tracking Profile Editor

The Tracking Profile Editor (TPE) is used to map activities within a BizTalk orchestration or orchestrations to an observation model. This tool, which is for BAM developers, is installed as part of the BizTalk Server installation software and configured as part of the BAM Tools tab. It is generally recommended that an instance of the TPE be installed on developers' desktops.

Visual Studio 2008

Visual Studio 2008 serves as the basis for the BizTalk Server development environment and as a means to create interceptor configuration (IC) files. BAM developers rely on this tool. It is installed as part of a stand-alone installation from the Visual Studio 2008 installation media. It is generally recommended that a licensed instance of Visual Studio 2008 be installed on the desktops of BAM developers.

Microsoft Office SharePoint Server

Microsoft SharePoint Server may be integrated with BAM and the BAM data stores by serving as a portal mechanism to display BAM data or by using the MOSS dashboard and portal to display KPIs from the BAM API (views); and/or may integrate the MOSS BDC with BAM using custom code. This tool, used by business analysts, developers, and data consumers, is installed as part of its stand-alone installation media and involves a great deal of planning. Integration between a SharePoint farm and a BizTalk group must be a carefully designed effort. It is generally recommended that a licensed version of SharePoint be installed on its own server farm. If the integration is performed via a data-enabled SharePoint web part, the web part must be deployed to each server in the farm using SharePoint Central Administration. The account utilized by the web part should have the necessary permissions to the BAM SQL Server databases. SharePoint Server is accessed by data consumers via web browser or mobile device.

Microsoft SQL Server Reporting Services

Microsoft SQL Server Reporting Services (SSRS) may be integrated with BAM and the BAM Primary Import database to build reports against the data stored within BAM. Using this tool, business analysts and developers design reports and data consumers view those reports. It is important to have Visual Studio 2008 installed before attempting installation of SSRS. SSRS is installed as part of the installation media included with SQL Server 2008. Depending upon the amount of network traffic and usage, it is generally recommended you install SSRS on its own server. Reports are then consumed by data consumers' desktops via web browser or e-mail.

Microsoft PerformancePoint Server

Microsoft PerformancePoint Server is Microsoft's Enterprise Performance Management application used to host dashboards and scorecards. It may be integrated with BAM by utilizing BAM data as the measurable objectives for scorecards and dashboards. Used by business analysts, developers, and data consumers, PerformancePoint Server is generally installed to its own server and accessed via web browser from the desktops of its users.

Custom .NET Applications: Web, Windows, and Console

If you have built any custom .NET applications, whether they be web-based using ASP.NET or Silverlight, desktop-based using Windows Forms or WPF, or console-based, they may access BAM data and serve as a presentation medium via the BAM API. These applications are consumed by data consumers. Custom .NET applications differ in their deployment strategy, but if they access the BAM API, the only requirement is that they be able to interface with SQL Server views (the only officially supported mechanism).

Service Façade and Processing

Software within this category is used to provide an application programming interface with which to interact with BAM, to process and track BAM data, or to monitor the processing and tracking of BAM data.

BAM Eventing: The BAM API, WCF, and WF Interceptors

BAM Eventing is the name for the collection of DLLs, executables, and config files that encompass the BAM API, WCF interceptor, and WF interceptor. BAM Eventing software is used to write data to the BAM data stores from a custom .NET application, a WCF service, or a WF workflow and is installed by the system administrator or BAM developer. BAM Eventing is required on any server or client that wishes to report data to BAM via one of these technologies. For instance, if you wish to instrument your WCF service, BAM Eventing must be installed on the machine hosting the WCF service as well. BAM Eventing is installed using the BizTalk Server 2009 installation media under the Additional Software selection.

BAM Web Services: Management and Query

The BAM Web Services, included as part of BizTalk Server 2006, largely serve to support the BAM Portal and its functionality. As a result, they are not a supported means for querying data for BAM or for managing BAM (however, the SQL Server views and bm.exe, respectively, are). They are not used by any role in a supported fashion; however, BAM developers have been known to use them to create custom BAM portals. When the BAM Portal is installed via the BizTalk Server 2009 installation media, these web services are created in the same web site within their own virtual directories. They require special permissions by default. It is generally recommended that you don't use these web services unless you wish to build your own BAM portal, as they are unsupported.

BAM Interceptor Performance Counters

The BAM interceptor performance counters provide real-time data on the BAM interceptors via Performance Monitor. Typically used by systems administrators, these counters are installed as part of the BizTalk Server 2009 installation media. In order for the counters to function, BAM Eventing software must first be installed on the server.

BAM Tracking Host

Because BizTalk Server 2009 is optimized for performance, the primary orchestration execution and messaging engines are not geared toward moving messages to the BizTalk Tracking (DTA) or BAM databases. It is therefore recommended that a dedicated background process, the tracking host, be created with this intent. The tracking host exists to move DTA and BAM data from the BizTalk Message Box database to the BizTalk Tracking and BAM Primary Import databases. The tracking host is usually configured by developers and system administrators. It is part of BizTalk and therefore is installed as part of the BizTalk Server 2009 installation process from the BizTalk Server 2009 installation media.

WCF Services and WF Workflows

WCF services and WF workflows are technologies that serve as components of larger applications or solutions. BAM may be used to intercept data from these two technologies. Business Analysts create an observation model of the data to be monitored, while developers and system administrators develop and configure this integration, and data consumers actually use the data. Because they are components of larger applications, WCF services and WF workflows are installed as part of those larger applications. In order for data to be intercepted from them, the BAM Eventing software must be installed on the same server(s) on which the WCF and/or WF host reside.

Database and Platform Services

Software within this category is used for the storage and analysis of BAM data, including data created as a result of that storage (e.g., BAM alerts).

SQL Server Notification Services and the BAM Alert Provider for SQL Notification Services

Noticeably absent from SQL Server 2008 is SQL Server Notification Services. BAM utilizes Notifications Services, a technology from SQL Server 2005, as its implementation medium for BAM alerts. This is done by creating a BAM alert provider. Although it is architecturally messy and involves downloading hotfixes and the SQL Server 2005 Notification Services stand-alone components, the BAM alert provider may still be used within BizTalk Server 2009. BAM alerts are designed by the business analyst role, developed by the BAM developer role, deployed by the systems administrator role, and consumed by the data consumer role. They are installed using a series of stand-alone downloads from the Internet, as well as the BizTalk Server 2009 installation media. Notification Services include three separate roles as well: provider, generator, and distributor. Depending upon the number of BAM alerts you expect to generate, you may distribute these roles across multiple servers to provide for greater scalability (by modifying the application definition file). However, in general, it is recommended that Notification Services be installed on a single BAM-specific server.

SQL Server Analysis Services

SQL Server Analysis Services provides advanced analytical capabilities to BAM. Specifically, the BAM Analysis database is stored in SQL Server Analysis Services. It is installed as part of the SQL Server installation process using the SQL Server media. Analysis Services for BAM Aggregations is then installed atop SQL Server Analysis Services.

SQL Server

SQL Server is the persistence and storage mechanism for BAM data. BAM installs several SQL Server databases, and utilizes the SQL Server technologies quite comprehensively. SQL Server, used by system administrators, is installed in the BizTalk Server and BAM installation process with its own stand-alone media. It is generally recommended that SQL Server be installed on its own server(s). Depending upon your needs, the BAM databases (Primary Import, Archive, Star Schema, Analysis, and Notification Services) may be installed on different SQL Servers entirely. The installation documentation provides the necessary requirements for doing so. The BAM databases may also be shared across multiple BizTalk Server groups.

Designing Your BAM Architecture

The BAM software components were designed with flexibility in mind, providing the ability to install all components on a single server or distribute the components across multiple servers. With an understanding of the purpose of each component and a general recommendation of its conceptual installation, designing a logical and physical BAM architecture becomes a great deal easier.

The three categories of BAM software don't necessarily map to physical installation location on a one-to-one basis. Instead, the design of a BAM architecture is usually based upon role and function. Where traditional deployment topologies include production, staging/UAT, test/QA, and development environments, BAM adds the dimension of roles.

Server Role Topology

If you're a systems administrator, an applications developer, or a business analyst, you'll inter-face with BAM and BizTalk in different ways. Typically, a BAM server role topology involves three structured environments: run-time, design-time, and usage-time. Each of these envi-ronments may or may not include a production, staging/UAT, test/QA, and development environment depending upon need. Members within a role will utilize different environments based upon function.

Generally, the server role topology maps to the deployment topology as shown in Table 2-1.

Table 2-1. *A Recommended Server Role Topology to Deployment Topology Mapping*

	Development	Test/QA	Staging/UAT	Production
Run-time		✓	✓	✓
Design-Time	✓			
Usage-Time		✓	✓	✓

The Run-Time Environment

The BAM run-time environment (RTE) is where BizTalk and BAM processing occurs. It includes software components from all three categories. A basic BizTalk and BAM run-time environment can include the following (see Figure 2-1):

- BAM API
- BAM WCF interceptor
- BAM WF interceptor
- BAM tracking host
- Analysis Services for BAM Aggregations
- BAM alert provider
- SQL Server Notification Services
- BAM databases
- BizTalk run time
- BizTalk send and receive hosts
- BizTalk databases

While all of these components may be installed on the same server, availability and scal-ability will be greatly compromised in doing so.

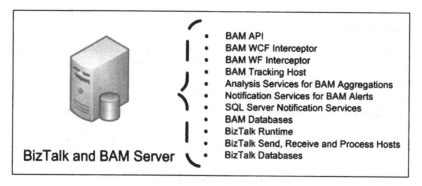

Figure 2-1. *An example of a single-server BAM software installation*

As the number of WCF services and WF workflows being intercepted and the number of applications utilizing the BAM API grows, so too will the load on the server. Fortunately, the BAM Eventing software may be installed on multiple servers, making these technologies easy to scale out.

As the number of orchestrations executing and messages being received, transformed, and sent grows, so too will the load on the BizTalk in-process or isolated hosts allocated on the BizTalk server to handle the load. Because BizTalk servers may be added to the group, the hosts may be scaled across multiple machines. Additional BizTalk Message Box databases may be added as well to handle load. However, cross-cutting every BizTalk host instance is the ability to track. The BizTalk host instances are optimized for message exchange, not tracking. It is generally recommended that a separate host be allocated for tracking purposes. The tracking host should be run on two servers running BizTalk Server for redundancy purposes. Optimal performance conditions dictate that at least one tracking host service exist per BizTalk Message Box database, and that for redundancy purposes, an extra tracking host service be on the ready (that is, the total number of tracking hosts should be $n+1$ where n represents the number of BizTalk Message Box databases).

Analysis Services, as you may imagine, has the potential to introduce additional performance bottlenecks as load grows. Real-time aggregation is a memory-intensive operation. The SQL Server architecture and BizTalk configuration wizard provides the ability to scale Analysis Services out into its own server or series of servers if need be.

In general, BAM alerts are not memory intensive. We've seen BAM projects where numerous BAM alerts have been created, and then later refined and reduced in number to include only those of the most interest. Conversely, we've seen BAM projects where only a few BAM alerts were created initially, but the number later expanded as the scope of data flowing into BAM increased. Over time, you may wish to segregate BAM alerts and the Notification Services component onto its own server.

The BAM databases may also be installed on different servers than the BizTalk databases as load grows. The individual BAM databases themselves may also be installed on different servers to distribute load.

It's very important to note that BizTalk is an optional component with BAM. BAM may be installed for the sole purpose of monitoring WCF services or WF workflows, with no monitoring of BizTalk orchestrations whatsoever. Because it is part of the BizTalk server installation, however, most BAM implementations include BizTalk's execution engine.

Initially, a basic and common BAM run-time environment begins with four servers, configured as shown in Figure 2-2.

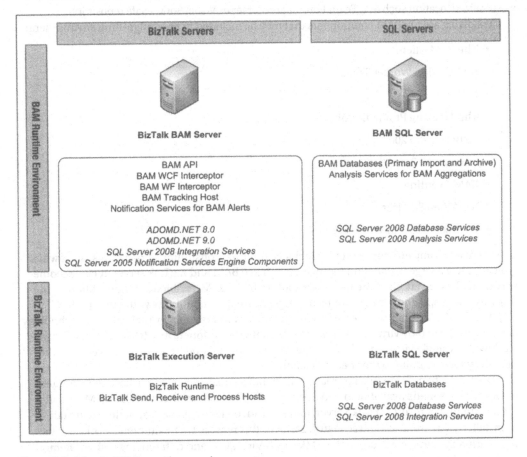

Figure 2-2. *A basic BAM run-time environment*

To provide even greater availability, and due to cost and space concerns, multiple, clustered SQL servers and a BizTalk Server group should be included in your topology. You may also consider test/QA, staging/UAT, and production instances for each of these four server roles.

The Design-Time Environment

The Design-Time Environment (DTE) is where the design and creation of BAM solutions occurs. This design occurs on workstations allocated for business analysts and BAM/BizTalk developers.

BAM solutions tend to be quite resource and artifact intensive. A standard set of tools should be made available for both roles, while the artifacts generated by those tools should be stored in a centralized location such as a Team Foundation Server or Visual SourceSafe repository.

Following are the BAM components that may be included in the design-time environment:

- The BAM Client

- Information Worker Tools

- ODBA

- The Tracking Profile Editor

- Visual Studio 2008

- Custom .NET applications

- BAM Eventing

- BAM Web Services

- WCF services and WF workflows

In a usage-time environment that includes multiple consuming applications, all of which typically have a large installation footprint much like BAM and BizTalk server, it can become very difficult to install all of the necessary tools to build BAM-enabled solutions. Many of the tools also have specific configurations that may cause incompatibility with other tools.

An effective technique to remedy this challenge is workstation virtualization, a technology used to rapidly deploy virtual machine images to BAM developers and BAM business analysts worldwide. A single virtual machine image may be created, updated, and deployed with the necessary tools to build to the specific scenario.

One of the benefits to this approach is also that a consistent, standardized development environment is made available to end users. BAM tools, such as Microsoft Excel, Microsoft Visual Studio, Microsoft BizTalk Server, and so forth, do take a great deal of time to install, uninstall, repair, and update (see Figure 2-3). For this reason, we recommend workstations use a virtualization technique, such as Microsoft Virtual PC and differencing disks or Remote Desktop, to help to overcome this hurdle.

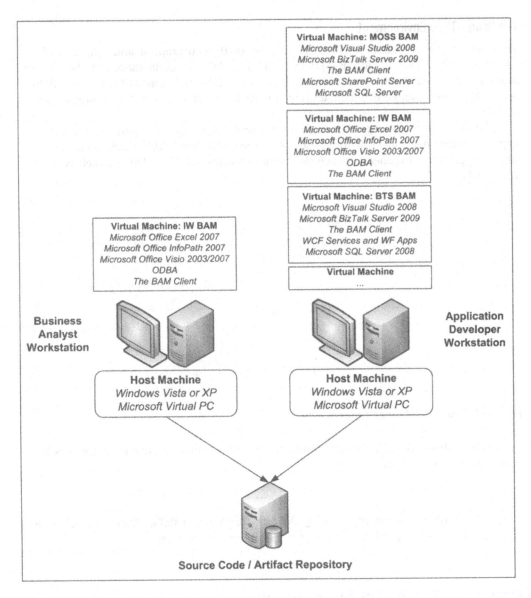

Figure 2-3. *A basic BAM design-time environment*

The Usage-Time Environment

The usage-time environment (UTE) of BAM focuses on the consumption and utilization of data produced by BAM. Because BAM data is stored in a SQL Server database and a SQL Server Analysis Services database, applications such as the BAM Portal, Microsoft PerformancePoint Server, Microsoft SharePoint Server, and custom .NET applications may all take advantage of BAM.

The structure of the usage-time environment server topology (see Figure 2-4) will vary depending upon need. By its definition, a usage-time environment will include some consuming application. In general, most BAM solutions use the BAM Portal or an Excel Live Workbook.

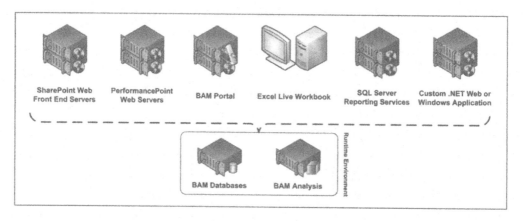

Figure 2-4. *A basic BAM usage-time environment*

For peak demand times, the servers that host the BAM Portal should include network load balancing to better distribute the load.

■**Note** For specific suggestions on consuming BAM data through custom .NET applications as well as integration points with PerformancePoint and SharePoint, please see Chapters 7 and 11.

Operating Systems per Environment

BizTalk Server 2009 is supported on Windows Server 2008, Windows Server 2003, Windows XP with Service Pack 3, and Windows Vista with Service Pack 2. Deciding upon which is a matter of the purpose of the BAM installation itself.

Servers existing within the run-time environment and the usage-time environment, including separate production, staging/UAT, and test/QA environment instances, should run Windows Server 2008 or Windows Server 2003.

Workstations within the design-time environment should run Windows Vista or Windows XP for development purposes including the rapid prototyping of BAM and BizTalk scenarios.

Currently, BizTalk Server 2009 is not supported on beta versions of Windows 7 or Windows Server 2008 R2.

Licensing

Because it is not a server component of BizTalk, but falls under the category of additional software, the licensing model for BAM differs from that of BizTalk. An additional license is not required when installing BAM on more than one server.

The BizTalk Server 2009 licensing FAQ includes the following:

You are required to have a valid processor license for each processor on which you install any component of the "server software." However, you may install "additional software" on any number of internal devices for use solely in conjunction with the server software or other additional software. Additional software includes (but is not limited to):

- *BizTalk administration and monitoring tools*

- *BizTalk-related schemas and templates*

- *Development tools*

- *Master Secret Server or Enterprise Single Sign-On*

- *Software development kits (SDKs)*

- *Business Activity Monitoring Event Application Programming Interface (API) and Administration Tools*

- *BAM Interceptors for Windows Workflow Foundation and Windows Communication Foundation*

- *Business Activity Services*

Any components not specified "additional software" in your licensing materials are considered server software and require a valid processor license when utilized.

Optimizing Your BAM Architecture

With physical space becoming increasingly expensive in data centers and heat dissipation and energy consumption continuing to be major issues in on-premise hosting, one of the more common practices utilized is virtualization technology.

Virtualization technologies are typically utilized in production and staging/UAT environments using Microsoft's Hyper-V technology, and on the design-time environment workstation in Windows Vista using Microsoft's Virtual Server or Microsoft Virtual PC.

Microsoft offers a full guide to virtualization of BizTalk on the Hyper-V platform, currently written for BizTalk 2006 R2. Because the underlying architecture of BizTalk Server 2009 is nearly identical to that of BizTalk 2006 R2, the guide may also be used for the virtualization of BizTalk Server 2009. The guide may be found online at http://msdn.microsoft.com/en-us/library/cc768518.aspx and may be downloaded from http://go.microsoft.com/fwlink/?LinkId=123100.

The guide is divided into four major sections: "Getting Started," "Deploying BizTalk Server on Hyper-V," "Evaluating BizTalk Server Performance on Hyper-V," and "Testing BizTalk Server Performance on Hyper-V."

Virtualizing BizTalk, much like the virtualization of any technology, may incur some degree of performance degradation. Fortunately, Microsoft also provides two very strong guides to optimizing BizTalk performance:

- The Microsoft BizTalk Server Optimization Guide, which may be downloaded at `http://technet.microsoft.com/en-us/library/cc296643.aspx`

- The Microsoft BizTalk Server Performance Optimization Guide, which may be downloaded at `http://msdn.microsoft.com/en-us/library/cc558617.aspx`

Additionally, there are numerous professional services organizations with expertise in BizTalk that are able to help with your installation.

Creating a BAM Virtual PC for the Exercises in This Book

In order to perform the many exercises throughout this book, you'll need to create your own Virtual PC image. While we won't go through the process in painstaking detail (that's what the installation and configuration guides are for), the general process for building a BAM development ready Virtual PC is as follows:

1. Download and install Microsoft Virtual PC.

2. Create and configure a new virtual machine with at least a 16GB dynamically expanding master drive and a 16GB dynamically expanding data disk.

3. Install Windows Server 2008 on the virtual machine image.

4. Install critical Windows updates.

5. Enable Internet Information Services.

6. Install Microsoft Office Excel.

7. Install Visual Studio 2008 with SP1.

8. Install SQL Server 2008.

9. Install SQLXML 3.0 with SP3.

10. Install Microsoft Management Console 3.0.

11. Install prerequisites for MQSeries Agent (optional).

12. Install SQL Notification Services.

13. Install SQL Server 2005 with SP2.

14. Install Windows SharePoint Services.

15. Disable the Shared Memory Protocol.

16. Join the local administrators group.

17. Configure the Application Event Log.

18. Install BizTalk Server.

19. Verify your installation.

20. Configure BizTalk Server.

21. Enable TCP/IP and named pipes.

22. Enable DTC on the local host server.

Summary

This chapter detailed the many software components of BAM and provided insight into the three server role topologies typically found in a BAM solution: run-time environment, design-time environment, and usage-time environment. The chapter also included recommendations as to which of these server role topologies should be duplicated in production, staging/UAT, test/QA, and development deployment environments. The chapter also examined the typical BAM components that are installed on each server in the server role topology.

The chapter included the considerations that must be undertaken when planning and deploying a BAM environment, including operating systems, virtualization, and licensing. The chapter concluded with instructions on how to set up a virtual machine using Microsoft Virtual PC to perform the exercises found in this book.

Now that your BAM development computer is ready, the next chapter will get your hands dirty in a real-world BAM scenario and walk you through creating your first BAM project.

CHAPTER 3

■■■

Your First BAM Project

One of the most underutilized capabilities of BAM is to capture data from Windows Communication Foundation (WCF). Your first BAM project, in this chapter, will focus on using BAM and WCF. In this chapter, you will also learn about the four roles in a BAM project: business analyst, developer, system administrator, and data consumer.

The chapter starts by describing the responsibilities of these roles, and then walks through a simple BAM project step by step. This sequence of exercises, which captures data from a simple WCF service, shows how BAM provides value even if your organization doesn't use BizTalk Messaging or BizTalk Orchestration.

Who Participates in a BAM Project? Roles and Responsibilities

People who participate in a BAM project are usually assigned to the following roles: business analyst, developer, system administrator, and data consumer. This section provides an overview of the responsibilities of each of these roles. On real BAM projects, it's not unusual for a single person to play all of these roles. When you're learning, however, it will be much easier to understand the process and tools if you think about the tasks handled by separate roles.

When you are working on a BAM project, we recommend identifying the owners for each of these roles, outlined in Figure 3-1, to help ensure the process is handled as smoothly as possible.

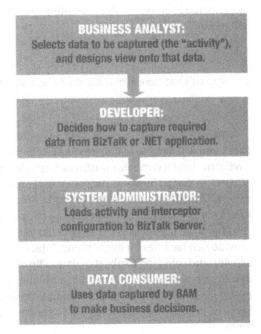

Figure 3-1. *Roles and responsibilities in a BAM project*

Business Analyst

As we discussed in Chapter 1, BAM provides visibility into business transactions as they pass through a business system. BAM can capture data in a message or message header, and BAM can also capture the time that a message passed through the system. The business analyst will perform two steps in a BAM project:

- *Define one or more activities*: As an example, an activity might contain data captured from a purchase order process that runs as a BizTalk orchestration.

- *Define one or more views of the activities*: As an example, the purchasing manager and the manufacturing scheduler might want to see different views of the data in the purchase order activity.

In BAM, the word *activity* is used to mean a set of data that is captured from a business process. Each field in an activity will be text data, integer data, float data, or a milestone. Text, integer, and float data is typically captured from a BizTalk message, a BizTalk message context, or a WCF service parameter. Milestones capture the date and time that something happened, such as the time a message was received by a BizTalk orchestration.

Activities are implemented as a collection of tables in SQL Server. Each activity is a single row of data, but for performance reasons BizTalk breaks the activity into different tables representing completed activities and in-process activities. You won't need to script the tables by hand; the BAM tools will automatically build the correct tables from an activity description laid out by the business analyst.

■**Note** You'll find more information on the BizTalk databases in Chapter 13.

Two tools can be used to create an activity: Microsoft Excel or Microsoft Visio. To use Excel, you will need to install the BAM Add-In for Excel. For Visio, you will need to use the Orchestration Designer for Business Analysts (ODBA), a Visio add-in that allows business analysts to design business processes and create BAM activities. Unless business analysts are using ODBA for process design, it's usually easier for them to work in Excel, as views, other than a simple default view, can only be created using Excel.

Views are used to show the captured data in a format that's helpful to the end user. Views provide rich facilities for aggregating data, using dimensions to analyze progress through an activity, and selecting a subset of data. The concept of a view will be very familiar to SQL Server developers, and BAM views can be implemented as SQL Server views over the tables that represent the BAM activity. For performance reasons, however, you may prefer to use Analysis Services to create aggregations. Views are created using Microsoft Excel with the BAM Add-In for Excel.

■**Note** Chapter 5 covers activities and views in much more detail.

Once the business analyst has completed work, the data captured by BAM and the data displayed by BAM have been defined. The definitions are exported from Excel as an XML file and handed to the system administrator.

Developer

Once the business analyst has designed the abstract data requirements in the activity, the developer maps the data requirements to concrete implementation. The developer does this by wiring up the activity to the business process or technology, specifying which field in a BizTalk message or WCF parameter will be stored in the activity tables. As described in Chapter 1, the most common sources for captured data are as follows:

- *BizTalk messages and orchestrations*: In a BizTalk project, the developer will use a tool called the Tracking Profile Editor (TPE) to specify how data is captured from the business process. Fields in a message payload or message context can be captured as data, and message timestamps can be captured as milestones.

■**Note** The TPE is described in Chapter 6.

- *WCF services*: With WCF services, the BAM developer creates an interceptor configuration (IC) file that specifies which items in a SOAP packet should be captured in the activity.

■**Note** Chapter 8 covers the WCF interceptor.

- *Windows Workflow Foundation (WF) workflows*: With WF workflows, the BAM developer creates an IC file that specifies which WF activities should be tracked using BAM.

■**Note** Chapter 9 covers the WF interceptor.

- *.NET-based applications*: Any .NET application can use the BAM API to write data to a BAM activity, either directly using the `DirectEventStream` class or through a buffer using the `BufferedEventStream` class.

■**Note** Chapter 10 goes into more detail on the BAM API.

System Administrator

Activities and views are implemented as SQL Server tables and views. The business analyst will export an activity definition file from Excel and hand it off to the developer and the system administrator. Once the developer has completed mapping the conceptual to the physical using an IC file, the developer will turn that IC file over to the system administrator.

Using these two inputs, the system administrator will use the BAM Management utility, bm.exe, to load the activity definition into SQL Server. (Yes, it really is named BM, which, in our opinion, is a poor naming choice. With a little experience, however, the output won't be nearly as fragrant.) In addition, when using the WCF and WF interceptors, BM is used to load the interceptor configuration file. Finally, the system administrator is usually responsible for setting appropriate permissions to allow the application to write to BAM. As an example, a WCF service that uses the interceptor must run as an account that is a member of the BizTalk Application Users group. You'll see examples of all three administration steps in Exercise 3-5.

System administration is a straightforward process, and these deployment tasks will typically take a few minutes each. This is a critical role, however, because BAM deployment to production will require someone with permissions to create tables and views in SQL Server. In the United States, organizations that need to comply with Sarbanes-Oxley (SarbOx) requirements will usually have strict separation between the development team and the administration team.

Data Consumer

Every BAM implementation exists to provide data to a consumer. In most organizations, the data consumers are either business users or IT personnel, but they could include customers, suppliers, or other business partners.

- *Business users*: In the majority of BAM implementations, the consumer of the data is an information worker within the business. As an example, a purchasing manager might track performance of the purchasing process by using a BAM implementation that monitors the flow of purchase requests, purchase orders, and invoices. A manufacturing scheduler might use another view onto the same data to understand how inventory is flowing to a just-in-time manufacturing facility.

- *IT users*: In some cases, IT chooses to use BAM data internally and not expose it to business users. Uses for BAM within IT include providing forensic data to resolve support incidents and providing message counts to support capacity planning.

BAM data is stored in SQL Server tables and views, so any tool that can consume data from SQL Server can be used. Custom applications that use ADO.NET, ADOMD.NET, XMLA, SQL Server Reporting Services, or Microsoft Office PerformancePoint Server can all be used with BAM data.

BizTalk Server also provides the BAM Portal, an ASP.NET application that can display and search data from any BAM activity or view. For many BAM projects, the best choice is to provide the BAM Portal to data consumers, and then consider building a custom solution to view the data later when the users ask for additional functionality that the portal can't provide. In Exercise 3-8, you'll see data in the portal, and in Exercise 3-9 you'll look at the underlying SQL Server databases.

The Project: Monitoring a WCF Service

In this series of exercises, you'll create a simple WCF service and then use BAM to monitor it. You'll perform the following steps:

1. In Exercise 3-1, you will implement a simple WCF service using Visual Studio 2008. For simplicity's sake, you'll implement the service as a console application, although real services are more likely to be hosted in Internet Information Server (IIS) or Windows Activation Service (WAS). In a real project, developing the service would be done by a developer.

2. In Exercise 3-2, you will develop a simple client for the WCF service. This is another developer task.

3. In Exercise 3-3, you will design a BAM activity that defines the data to capture. You'll create the activity using Microsoft Excel with the BAM add-in. In a real project, this would be a business analyst task.

4. In Exercise 3-4, you will write an interceptor configuration file that defines how to capture data from the WCF service. You'll create the file by editing the XML. Because the developer understands the details of the service implementation, this task would typically be done by the developer.

5. In Exercise 3-5, you will deploy the activity and interceptor configuration using BM, a command-line tool. This is a system administrator task.

6. In Exercise 3-6, you will modify the service's app.config file to load the BAM Tracking Service. This is another developer task.

7. In Exercise 3-7, you will execute the service using the client. Exercises 3-7 through 3-9 simulate the application running in production; the business users or data consumers would typically be using the application to get their work done.

8. In Exercise 3-8, you will look at the activity data using the BAM Portal. Analyzing data would be another data consumer function.

9. In Exercise 3-9, you will look at the activity data using SQL Server Management Studio. Although business users and data consumers probably wouldn't use Management Studio to look at data in the real world, they might use a tool like SQL Server Reporting Services to view reports based on BAM data.

EXERCISE 3-1. CREATING A WCF SERVICE (DEVELOPER TASK)

In the first exercise, you'll create a simple WCF service that will be monitored in later exercises. If you haven't seen WCF before, you can think of this program as similar in nature to an ASP.NET web service.

1. Open Visual Studio 2008. From the File menu, select New ➤ Project to create a new project. Select a C# Console Application, and name it BeginBAMHost.

2. From the File menu, select Add ➤ New Project. Add a Visual C# class library project called BeginBAMSvc. When developing WCF applications, we recommended building the service implementation in a separate project from the service host.

3. In the Solution Explorer window, right-click the References folder of BeginBAMSvc and select Add Reference. Select the System.ServiceModel library (see Figure 3-2), and then click OK. System.ServiceModel is the main library for WCF.

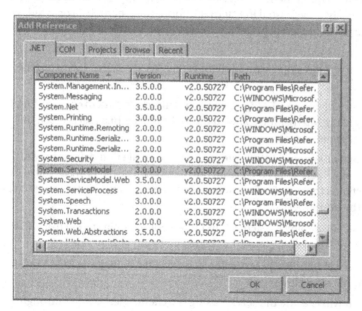

Figure 3-2. *Adding a reference to System.ServiceModel*

4. In the Solution Explorer window, double-click Class1.cs to open the file in the editor. Replace the entire contents of the file with the code shown in Listing 3-1.

Listing 3-1. *The Interface and Implementation for the WCF Service*

```
using System;
using System.ServiceModel;

namespace BeginBAMSvc
{
    [ServiceContract]
    interface ISalesOrder
```

```
    {
        [OperationContract]
        int Create(string customerID, string productID, int productCount);
    }

    public class SalesOrder : ISalesOrder
    {
        int ISalesOrder.Create(string customerID,
            string productID, int productCount)
        {
            Console.WriteLine("Create Order. " +
                "Customer: {0} Item: {1} Quantity: {2}",
                customerID, productID, productCount);
            return 0;
        }
    }
}
```

This code defines a simple interface called BeginBAMSvc.ISalesOrder. The interface contains one method: Create. The [ServiceContract] attribute on the interface indicates that the interface defines the contract for a WCF web service. The [OperationContract] method indicates that the Create method will be exposed by the web service. The class SalesOrder implements the interface. For simplicity, the implementation simply logs the method call to the console.

5. In the Solution Explorer window, right-click BeginBAMSvc and select Rebuild to confirm that the project builds.

6. In the Solution Explorer window, right-click the References folder of BeginBAMHost and select Add Reference. Select the System.ServiceModel library, and then click OK.

7. In the Solution Explorer window, right-click the References folder of BeginBAMHost and select Add Reference. Click the Projects tab, select BeginBAMSvc, and then click OK.

8. In the Solution Explorer window, double-click the program.cs file in the BeginBAMHost project to open the file in the editor. Replace the entire contents of the file with the code shown in Listing 3-2.

Listing 3-2. *The Service Host Console Application*

```
using System;
using System.ServiceModel;

namespace BeginBAMHost
{
    class BamHost
    {
        static void Main(string[] args)
        {
            ServiceHost serviceHost =
                new ServiceHost(
                typeof(BeginBAMSvc.SalesOrder));
```

```
            serviceHost.Open();
            Console.WriteLine("Press <ENTER> to terminate.");
            Console.ReadLine();
            serviceHost.Close();
        }
    }
}
```

This code creates a new ServiceHost that will expose an instance of the SalesOrder class as a WCF service. The Open method tells WCF to start listening to any endpoints associated with the service. This code doesn't define the address of the endpoint, which will be defined in a config file.

9. In the Solution Explorer window, right-click the BeginBAMHost project and select Add ➤ New Item. Create an application configuration file called app.config.

10. Replace the entire contents of the app.config file with the code in Listing 3-3.

Listing 3-3. *The app.config File for the WCF Service*

```xml
<?xml version="1.0" encoding="utf-8" ?>
<configuration>
  <system.serviceModel>
    <services>
      <service name = "BeginBAMSvc.SalesOrder"
          behaviorConfiguration="mexBehavior">
        <host>
          <baseAddresses>
            <add baseAddress="http://localhost:8200/BeginBAM"/>
          </baseAddresses>
        </host>
        <endpoint address="" binding="basicHttpBinding"
            contract="BeginBAMSvc.ISalesOrder" />
        <endpoint address="mex" binding="mexHttpBinding"
            contract="IMetadataExchange" />
      </service>
    </services>
    <behaviors>
      <serviceBehaviors>
        <behavior name ="mexBehavior">
          <serviceMetadata httpGetEnabled="True"/>
        </behavior>
      </serviceBehaviors>
    </behaviors>
  </system.serviceModel>
</configuration>
```

This configuration file specifies that there will be a service that is implemented by an instance of the BeginBAMSvc.SalesOrder. There will be two endpoints for the service. One endpoint will be at address http://localhost:8200/BeginBAM and will accept SOAP messages over HTTP. The other endpoint will be at http://localhost:8200/BeginBAM/mex and will accept requests for the service's Web Services Description Language (WSDL) over HTTP. The serviceBehaviors element indicates that the WCF service should be able to provide WSDL on request.

Caution This WCF service doesn't perform any administrative functions, so it should be run using an account that is NOT a member of the administrators group. Why make life easy for intruders?

---

11. If the account that will run the WCF service is not a member of the Administrators group, add the account to the BizTalk Application Users group.

12. If the account that will run the WCF service is not a member of the Administrators group and you are running Windows Server 2003, download the Windows Support Tools for Windows Server, install them on your machine, and then run the following command:

```
"C:\Program Files\Support Tools\httpcfg.exe"
    set urlacl /u http://+:8200/BeginBAM/ /a "D:(A;;GA;;;BU)"
```

Note To locate the download for the Windows Support Tools, search the web for "Windows Support Tools."

---

13. Alternatively, if the account that will run the WCF service is not a member of the Administrators group and you are running Windows Server 2008 or Windows Vista, run the following command:

```
"C:\Windows\System32\Netsh.exe" http add urlacl
    url=http://+:8200/BeginBAM/ sddl="D:(A;;GA;;;BU)"
```

In the same way that files have an access control list (ACL) and can only be read by accounts that have permissions on those files, each URL has an ACL associated with it. The ACL controls which accounts can listen on the URL. If a WCF service wants to listen on a specific URL, the account running the service must have permissions on that URL.

By default, all URLs have local administrators in their ACL. This means to create a service that listens on a specific URL, the account needs to either be a member of the local administrators group or be added to the ACL for the group. It's not recommended to run services as members of the administrators group, so you need to give your account permissions to create the URL http://localhost/BeginBAM/.

In Windows Server 2003, the tool that administers permissions on URLs is HTTPCFG. The syntax is

```
httpcfg set urlacl /u <Your URL> /a <Access Control List>
```

In Windows Server 2008, the tool that administers permissions on URLs is NETSH. The syntax is

```
netsh http add urlacl url=<Your URL> sddl=<Access Control List>
```

The plus sign in the URL specifies the local server name, and the rest of the URL is the virtual directory name that the service listens on.

The URL is straightforward enough, but how do you specify an access control list? The answer is that you manipulate these permissions using Security Descriptor Definition Language (SDDL). Security descriptors can be very long and complex, with hundreds of characters where each character is a specific permission. The string `"D:(A;;GA;;;BU)"` is the simplest possible descriptor that will get your service running.

`D:` means that this is a discretionary access control list; it defines who has access to some resource, in this case the URL. A means grant access. GA is the `SDDL_GENERIC_ALL` flag. It means that the SIDs listed in the ACL have all permissions over the resource. Finally, BU is the `SDDL_BUILTIN_USERS` flag, which tells you that all users in the domain have this permission. The bottom line is that the commands allow any user, including nonadministrators, to create a listener on your URL.

Note For much more information on this topic, search the web for "Security Descriptor Definition Language."

---

14. In the Solution Explorer window, right-click the Begin BAM Host project and select Set as StartUp Project.

15. Press the F5 key to confirm that the service builds and executes. If the service doesn't execute, check all the code to ensure that you entered it correctly. Leave the service running, as you'll call it in the next exercise.

EXERCISE 3-2. CREATING A CLIENT FOR THE WCF SERVICE (DEVELOPER TASK)

In this exercise, you'll create a test client for the simple WCF service. This will be used to call the service when you test your BAM implementation.

1. Leave Visual Studio 2008 from the previous exercise open, and open a second copy of Visual Studio 2008. You want to have two copies of Visual Studio open at the same time: one for the client and another for the service.

2. In the new copy of Visual Studio, from the File menu select New ➤ Project to create a new project. Select Visual C# Windows Forms Application, and name the application BeginBAMClient.

3. In the Solution Explorer window, right-click the References folder and select Add Service Reference. Enter the address `http://localhost:8200/BeginBAM`, and then click the Go button. If you see an error message, check that the service is running and that the address matches the address you entered in the service's `app.config` file. Enter **SalesOrder** in the Namespace text box, and then click OK.

4. Open the Toolbox, and drag three labels to the form. Select the first label, press F4, and then enter **Customer :** in the Text property. Select the second label, press F4, and then enter **Product :** in the Text property. Select the third label, press F4, and then enter **Quantity :** in the Text property.

5. Using the Toolbox, drag three text boxes to the form. Select the first text box, press F4, and then enter **CUSTOMER1** in the Text property and **Customer** in the name property. Select the second text box, press F4, and then enter **PRODUCT1** in the Text property and **Product** in the name property. Select the third text box, press F4, and then enter **1234** in the Text property and **ProductQuantity** in the Name property.

6. Using the Toolbox, drag a button to the form. Select the button, press F4, and enter **Create Order** in the Text property.

7. Arrange the controls so they look as shown in Figure 3-3.

Figure 3-3. *Control layout in the WCF client*

8. Double-click the Create Order button, and enter the following code:

```
SalesOrder.SalesOrderClient proxy = new
    SalesOrder.SalesOrderClient();
proxy.Create(Customer.Text, Product.Text,
    int.Parse(ProductQuantity.Text));
```

The code calls the WCF service when the button is clicked. The entire file should look like what you see in Listing 3-4.

Listing 3-4. *The Client for the WCF Service*

```
using System;
using System.Collections.Generic;
using System.ComponentModel;
using System.Data;
using System.Drawing;
using System.Linq;
using System.Text;
using System.Windows.Forms;

namespace BeginBAMClient
{
```

```
public partial class Form1 : Form
{
    public Form1()
    {
        InitializeComponent();
    }

    private void button1_Click(object sender, EventArgs e)
    {
        SalesOrder.SalesOrderClient proxy =
            new SalesOrder.SalesOrderClient();
        proxy.Create(Customer.Text, Product.Text,
            int.Parse(ProductQuantity.Text));
    }
}
}
```

9. Check that the service is still running, click the copy of Visual Studio that contains the client, and press F5. The client should start, and the form should appear. Click the button, and then look at the window where the service is running. You should see the data from the client being displayed by the service, as shown in Figure 3-4.

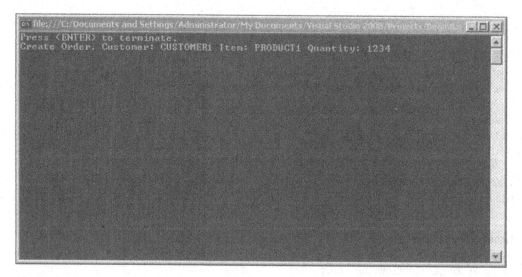

Figure 3-4. *The WCF Service displaying data entered at the client*

10. Shut down both the client and the service while you set up the BAM activity, but leave Visual Studio running.

EXERCISE 3-3. BUILDING A BAM ACTIVITY AND VIEW (BUSINESS ANALYST TASK)

You have created a simple WCF service and a simple test client. Now that the preliminaries are complete, you can build a BAM solution to track calls to the service. The first step is to create a BAM activity and a BAM view that will be used to capture and display the BAM data.

1. Open Excel and create a new workbook.

2. Open the Excel Add-Ins Management dialog box. In Excel 2007, click the Office button, and then click the Excel Options button (see Figure 3-5). Click Add-Ins, select Excel Add-Ins from the Manage drop-down box, and then click Go (see Figure 3-6). In Excel 2003, select Add-Ins from the Tools menu.

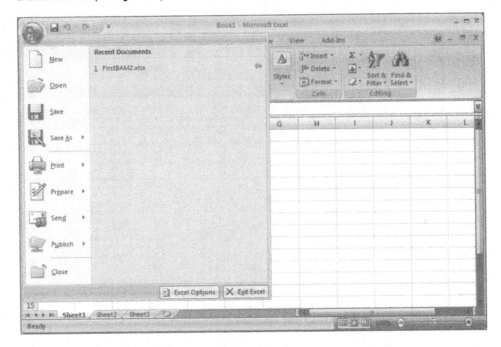

Figure 3-5. *Setting Excel options in Excel 2007*

3. The Business Activity Monitoring Add-In should be enabled. If it's not enabled, check the check box beside it, as shown in Figure 3-7, and click OK. If it is enabled, just click OK to close the dialog box.

4. In Excel 2007, click the Add-Ins tab in the Office Ribbon, and then select BAM Activity from the BAM menu. In Excel 2003, select BAM Activity from the BAM menu on the menu bar.

5. Click the New Activity button.

6. Enter **BeginBAM** in the Activity Name text box.

7. The BAM activity specifies the list of data that BAM will capture. The WCF service created in Exercise 3-1 has three parameters. The activity will capture each of the parameters. Click New Item to bring up the New Activity Item dialog box (see Figure 3-8). Enter **Customer** as the item name, **Business Data – Text** as the item type, and **50** as the maximum length of the data. Click OK to return to the New Activity dialog box.

8. Create another item with Product as the item name, Business Data – Text as the item type, and 50 as the maximum length of the data. Click OK to return to the New Activity dialog box.

9. Create a third item with Quantity as the item name and Business Data – Integer as the item type. Click OK to return to the New Activity dialog box (see Figure 3-9).

10. Click OK to close out the new activity.

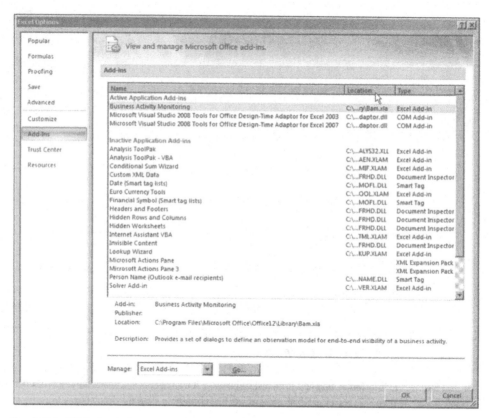

Figure 3-6. *Click the Go button to manage Excel add-ins in Excel 2007.*

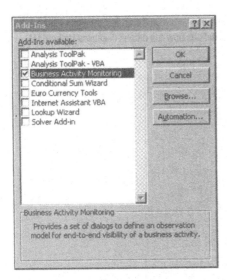

Figure 3-7. *The Add-In Management dialog box*

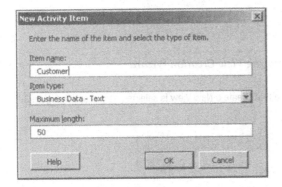

Figure 3-8. *The New Activity Item dialog box*

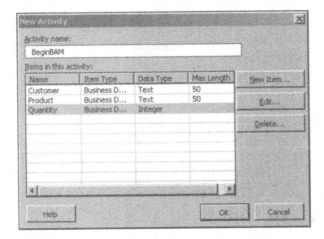

Figure 3-9. *The New Activity dialog box, showing the activity*

11. Click OK again, and the Business Activity Monitoring View Creation Wizard will start, as shown in Figure 3-10. While the activity defines the data that is captured, the view defines how the data is displayed in the BAM Portal.

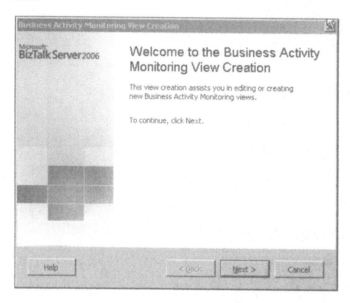

Figure 3-10. *The Business Activity Monitoring View Creation Wizard*

12. Click Next to continue to the next page, ensure that Create a New View is selected as you see in Figure 3-11, and then click Next again.

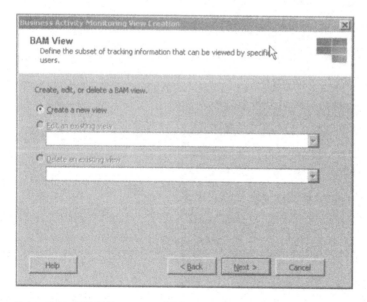

Figure 3-11. *BAM View page of the wizard*

13. As shown in Figure 3-12, enter **BeginBAMView** as the view name, check the check box for the BeginBAM activity, and click Next.

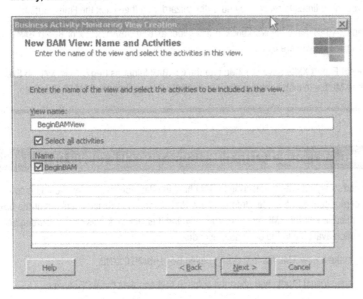

Figure 3-12. *New BAM View: Name and Activities page of the wizard*

14. Check the Select All Items check box (see Figure 3-13), and then click Next.

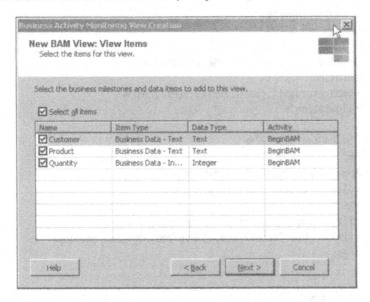

Figure 3-13. *New BAM View: View Items page of the wizard*

15. The rest of the wizard supports adding additional features to the view, such as groups of milestones, aliases for data items, aggregations, and dimensions. In this exercise, the simplest possible view is ideal, so just click the Next button three more times to reach the end of the wizard, and then click the Finish button.

16. Make a new folder called `C:\BAM`. Save the workbook in this folder as `BeginBAM.xlsx` or `BeginBAM.xls`, depending on the version of Excel you are using.

17. From the BAM menu, select Export XML. Save the XML into the `C:\BAM` folder as `BeginBAM.XML`. In Exercise 3-5, you will use the XML file to install the activity into the BAM Primary Import (BAM PI) database.

EXERCISE 3-4. CREATING AN INTERCEPTOR CONFIGURATION FILE (DEVELOPER TASK)

Now that you have an activity and view, it's time to describe to BAM how the data for the activity should be collected. This is done in an interceptor configuration file. Unfortunately, BizTalk doesn't provide a tool out of the box for building IC files, so you will need to edit the XML by hand. You may find it easier to do this step by cutting and pasting from the completed solution available in the book source code.

1. Using Windows Explorer, make a new XML file in `C:\BAM` called `BeginBAMIC.XML`.

2. If Visual Studio is closed, open Visual Studio and open the solution that contains the WCF service.

3. In the Solution Explorer window, right-click the solution and select Add ➤ Existing Item. Select the `BeginBAMIC.XML` file from `C:\BAM` and enter the code shown in Listing 3-5.

Listing 3-5. *The Interceptor Configuration File*

```
<?xml version="1.0" encoding="utf-8" ?>
<ic:InterceptorConfiguration
 xmlns:ic="http://schemas.microsoft.com/BizTalkServer/2004/➥
10/BAM/InterceptorConfiguration"
   xmlns:wcf="http://schemas.microsoft.com/BizTalkServer/2004/➥
10/BAM/WcfInterceptorConfiguration">

 <ic:EventSource Name="SalesOrderSource"➥
     Technology ="WCF"➥
     Manifest ="BeginBAMSvc.ISalesOrder, BeginBAMSvc,➥
     Version=1.0.0.0, Culture=neutral, PublicKeyToken=null">
   <wcf:NamespaceMappings>
     <wcf:Namespace Prefix ="order" Uri="http://tempuri.org/"/>
     <wcf:Namespace Prefix="s" Uri="http://www.w3.org/2003/05/soap-envelope" />
   </wcf:NamespaceMappings>
 </ic:EventSource>

 <ic:BamActivity Name="BeginBAM">
   <ic:OnEvent IsBegin="true" IsEnd ="true"➥
      Name ="Create" Source="SalesOrderSource">
    <ic:Filter>
     <ic:Expression>
```

```
        <wcf:Operation Name="GetServiceContractCallPoint" />
        <ic:Operation Name="Constant">
          <ic:Argument>ServiceRequest</ic:Argument>
        </ic:Operation>
        <ic:Operation Name="Equals" />
      </ic:Expression>
    </ic:Filter>

    <ic:CorrelationID>
      <ic:Expression>
        <wcf:Operation Name="AutoGenerateCorrelationToken"/>
      </ic:Expression>
    </ic:CorrelationID>

    <ic:Update DataItemName="Customer" Type="NVARCHAR">
      <ic:Expression>
        <wcf:Operation Name ="XPath">
          <wcf:Argument>//order:customerID</wcf:Argument>
        </wcf:Operation>
      </ic:Expression>
    </ic:Update>
    <ic:Update DataItemName="Product" Type="NVARCHAR">
      <ic:Expression>
        <wcf:Operation Name ="XPath">
          <wcf:Argument>//order:productID</wcf:Argument>
        </wcf:Operation>
      </ic:Expression>
    </ic:Update>
    <ic:Update DataItemName="Quantity" Type="INT">
      <ic:Expression>
        <wcf:Operation Name ="XPath">
          <wcf:Argument>//order:productCount</wcf:Argument>
        </wcf:Operation>
      </ic:Expression>
    </ic:Update>
  </ic:OnEvent>
 </ic:BamActivity>

</ic:InterceptorConfiguration>
```

The IC specifies that the arguments for the WCF service should be captured in the BAM activity.

```
<?xml version="1.0" encoding="utf-8" ?>
    <ic:InterceptorConfiguration
      xmlns:ic="http://schemas.microsoft.com/BizTalkServer/2004/➡
          10/BAM/InterceptorConfiguration"
      xmlns:wcf="http://schemas.microsoft.com/BizTalkServer/2004/➡
        10/BAM/WcfInterceptorConfiguration">
```

The header specifies that this file is an IC and defines a couple of namespaces that will be used in the XML file.

```
<ic:EventSource Name="SalesOrderSource"➥
    Technology ="WCF"➥
    Manifest ="BeginBAMSvc.ISalesOrder, BeginBAMSvc,➥
    Version=1.0.0.0, Culture=neutral, PublicKeyToken=null">
    <wcf:NamespaceMappings>
      <wcf:Namespace Prefix ="order"➥
        Uri="http://tempuri.org/"/>
      <wcf:Namespace Prefix="s"➥
        Uri="http://www.w3.org/2003/05/soap-envelope" />
    </wcf:NamespaceMappings>
  </ic:EventSource>
```

The EventSource element specifies the source of the events that BAM will capture. The name is used later in the IC to refer to this source of events. A more complex IC might have multiple event sources. The Technology element specifies whether this capture is WCF or WF. The Manifest element is the decorated type name of the interface that defines the service contract. BeginBAMSvc.ISalesOrder is the interface name, and BeginBAMSvc is the name of the assembly that contains the implementation.

```
<ic:BamActivity Name="BeginBAM">
```

The BamActivity element specifies the activity name that you used in the Excel file. In a more complex example, data could be stored in several activities. The namespace definitions will be used later in the file in an XPath expression that defines the data to capture.

```
<ic:OnEvent IsBegin="true" IsEnd ="true"➥
  Name ="Create" Source="SalesOrderSource">
  <ic:Filter>
    <ic:Expression>
      <wcf:Operation Name="GetServiceContractCallPoint" />
      <ic:Operation Name="Constant">
        <ic:Argument>ServiceRequest</ic:Argument>
      </ic:Operation>
      <ic:Operation Name="Equals" />
    </ic:Expression>
  </ic:Filter>
```

The OnEvent element indicates that you should capture the BAM data when the Create method is called on the assembly defined in SalesOrderSource EventSource. IsBegin="true" specifies that this will create a new row in the database. IsEnd="true" specifies that you aren't going to write additional data to the row later.

The filter expression tells BAM to capture data when a request is received by the WCF service. You must have a filter expression, but in a simple request-response service, this filter will always capture data on every call.

```
<ic:CorrelationID>
  <ic:Expression>
    <wcf:Operation Name="AutoGenerateCorrelationToken"/>
  </ic:Expression>
</ic:CorrelationID>
```

Usually, BAM will need to capture data at multiple points in the business process. When that happens, you'll store some unique identifier in the correlation ID that you can use to identify the business process. As an example, if every step in the process is aware of the order number, you could use order number as a correlation ID to ensure that BAM always writes to the same row in the database. In this simple exercise, you will only write to the BAM activity once, and you can use a random number as the correlation ID.

```
<ic:Update DataItemName="Customer" Type="NVARCHAR">
  <ic:Expression>
    <wcf:Operation Name ="XPath">
      <wcf:Argument>//order:customerID</wcf:Argument>
    </wcf:Operation>
  </ic:Expression>
</ic:Update>
```

The Update element uses an XPath expression to define the data BAM will capture from the SOAP packet passed to the WCF service. DataItemName indicates the column in the BAM activity that this item should be stored in. The XPath operation specifies the data to capture. The order prefix was defined in the EventSource element to refer to the http://tempuri.org/ namespace. This XPath expression captures a customerID element that has the correct namespace anywhere in the body of the SOAP packet.

```
<ic:Update DataItemName="Product" Type="NVARCHAR">
  <ic:Expression>
    <wcf:Operation Name ="XPath">
      <wcf:Argument>//order:productID</wcf:Argument>
    </wcf:Operation>
  </ic:Expression>
</ic:Update>
<ic:Update DataItemName="Quantity" Type="INT">
  <ic:Expression>
    <wcf:Operation Name ="XPath">
      <wcf:Argument>//order:productCount</wcf:Argument>
    </wcf:Operation>
  </ic:Expression>
</ic:Update>
```

Two additional Update elements specify the other two items of interest.

```
    </ic:OnEvent>
  </ic:BamActivity>


</ic:InterceptorConfiguration>
```

The final lines of the file just close out the previous elements.

EXERCISE 3-5. DEPLOYING THE ACTIVITY AND IC FILE (SYSTEM ADMINISTRATOR TASK)

Now that you have the BAM activity and view file, and the IC file, you can load the files into BAM. Loading the activity will automatically create database tables to store the data that the business analyst selected.

■Note The `bm.exe` file requires administrator permissions, so you will need to run the next step as a local administrator.

---

1. Open a new command line from the Start menu.

2. Enter the following commands:

```
cd c:\BAM
path %path%;C:\Program Files\Microsoft BizTalk Server 2009\Tracking
bm deploy-all -DefinitionFile:beginBAM.xml
bm deploy-interceptor -Filename:beginBAMIC.xml
bm add-account -AccountName:<your account name> -View:BeginBAMView
```

As an example, if your account name is MACHINE1\Janet, you would enter the last command as follows:

```
bm add-account -AccountName:MACHINE1\Janet -View:BeginBAMView
```

The first line sets the current folder to `c:\bam`. The second line sets the command-line path to include the folder where `bm.exe` is installed. The command-line path is a list of folders that are searched when a command name is entered. If you can't run the `bm.exe` command after setting the path, use Windows Explorer to check where BizTalk was installed and then reenter the path command so that the path points to `bm.exe`.

The third line (`bm deploy-all`) deploys the activity and view that were exported by Excel (see Figure 3-14). After this command, the correct data structures will have been set up in SQL Server to capture BAM data.

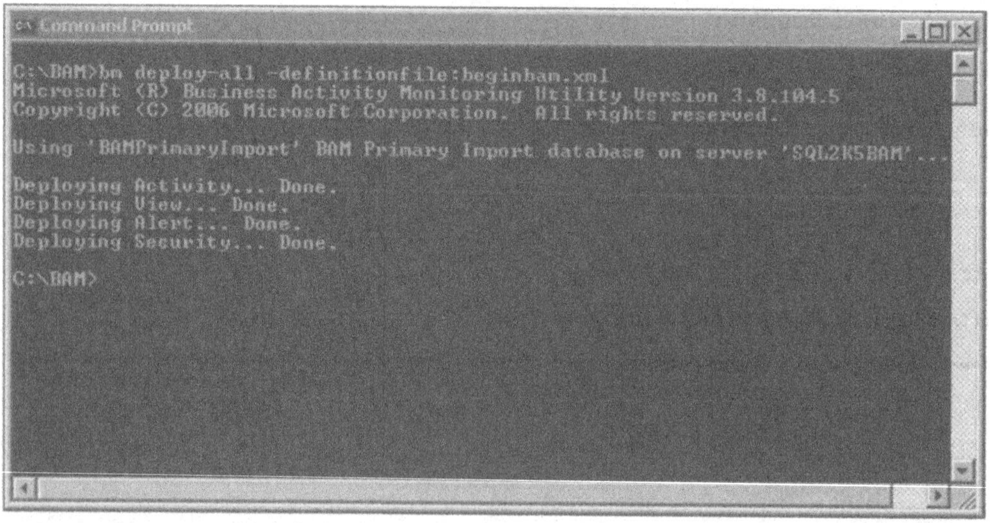

Figure 3-14. *Deploying the activity and the view*

The fourth line (bm deploy-interceptor) deploys the interceptor configuration file (see Figure 3-15). This tells BAM which parameters of the WCF service should be captured, and where they should be stored.

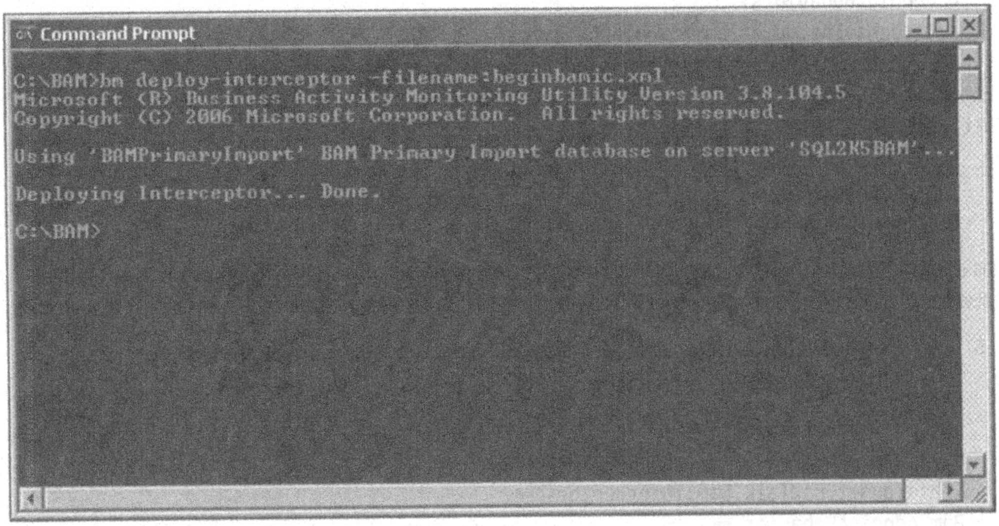

Figure 3-15. *Deploying the interceptor configuration*

The final line (bm add-account) gives your account permissions to view the data associated with the BAM view. If you don't run this command, you will be able to see the portal, but you won't see any data. If you are a local administrator, you can skip this step, but the recommended practice is that you work with the portal using a non-administrator account.

EXERCISE 3-6. MODIFYING APP.CONFIG (DEVELOPER TASK)

At this point, the WCF service has been created, the data that BAM should capture has been selected, and where the data should be captured from has been specified. Before you can test the service, you will modify the WCF service configuration to load the BAM components. Note that no changes are needed in the code, and the service does not need to be recompiled. The only changes are in the app.config file.

1. If Visual Studio is not open, open it now, and load the solution that contains the WCF Service.

2. In Solution Explorer, double-click the app.config file to open it in the editor.

3. Find the endpoint element that specifies the basicHttpBinding endpoint. Modify it by adding a reference to bamEndpointBehavior, so it reads as follows:

```
<endpoint address="" binding="basicHttpBinding"➥
  contract="FirstBAMService.ISalesOrder"➥
behaviorConfiguration="bamEndpointBehavior"/>
```

This change tells WCF that when this endpoint is called, WCF should inject the behavior specified later in the file with the name bamEndpointBehavior.

4. Find the behaviors element. After the end of the serviceBehaviors element, add this endpointBehaviors element:

```
<endpointBehaviors>
    <behavior name="bamEndpointBehavior">
      <bamServiceBehaviorExtension ConnectionString=➥
"Integrated Security=SSPI;Data Source=localhost;➥
Initial Catalog=BAMPrimaryImport;"
             PollingIntervalSec="1500" />
    </behavior>
</endpointBehaviors>
```

This element tells WCF to load the BAM service behavior extension when bamEndpointBehavior is invoked, and it also provides the BAM components with the connection string to the BAM PI database.

5. After the /behaviors tag that closes out the list of behaviors, add the following element:

```
<extensions>
  <behaviorExtensions>
    <add name="bamServiceBehaviorExtension"➥
type="Microsoft.BizTalk.Bam.Interceptors.➥
Wcf.BamEndpointBehavior,➥
Microsoft.BizTalk.Bam.Interceptors, Version=3.0.1.0,➥
Culture=neutral, PublicKeyToken=31bf3856ad364e35" />
  </behaviorExtensions>
</extensions>
```

This section tells WCF the type that it should load from the Global Assembly Cache (GAC) when the BAM components are loaded.

After the changes, the entire app.config file should look like this:

```
<?xml version="1.0" encoding="utf-8" ?>
<configuration>
  <system.serviceModel>
    <services>
      <service name = "BeginBAMSvc.SalesOrder"➥
behaviorConfiguration="mexBehavior">
        <host>
          <baseAddresses>
            <add baseAddress="http://localhost:8200/BeginBAM"/>
          </baseAddresses>
        </host>       <endpoint address="" binding="basicHttpBinding"➥
            contract="FirstBAMService.ISalesOrder"➥
            behaviorConfiguration="bamEndpointBehavior"/>
        <endpoint address="mex" binding="mexHttpBinding"➥
          contract="IMetadataExchange" />
      </service>
```

```
    </services>
    <behaviors>
      <serviceBehaviors>
        <behavior name ="mexBehavior">
          <serviceMetadata httpGetEnabled="True"/>
        </behavior>
      </serviceBehaviors>
      <endpointBehaviors>
        <behavior name="bamEndpointBehavior">
          <bamServiceBehaviorExtension ConnectionString=➥
"Integrated Security=SSPI;Data Source=localhost;➥
Initial Catalog=BAMPrimaryImport;"
              PollingIntervalSec="1500" />
        </behavior>
      </endpointBehaviors>
    </behaviors>
    <extensions>
      <behaviorExtensions>
        <add name="bamServiceBehaviorExtension"➥
type="Microsoft.BizTalk.Bam.Interceptors.➥
Wcf.BamEndpointBehavior,➥
Microsoft.BizTalk.Bam.Interceptors, Version=3.0.1.0,➥
Culture=neutral, PublicKeyToken=31bf3856ad364e35" />
      </behaviorExtensions>
    </extensions>
  </system.serviceModel>
</configuration>
```

EXERCISE 3-7. EXECUTING THE SERVICE (DATA CONSUMER TASK)

It's time to test the BAM implementation.

1. Start the WCF service.

2. Start the client.

3. Enter some data, and then click the Create Order button. Check that the console application displays the data you entered.

4. Change the data in the client and call the web service again. If you call the service several times with different data, you will have more to look at it in the next exercises.

EXERCISE 3-8. LOOKING AT THE DATA USING THE BAM PORTAL (DATA CONSUMER TASK)

The BAM Portal is an application supplied with BizTalk Server that can display data in a BAM view. The BAM portal can read the data model associated with a BAM view and will automatically display the data in a user-friendly format.

1. Open a copy of Internet Explorer. Enter `http://localhost/bam` in the address bar, and then press Enter. You should see the BAM Portal, as shown in Figure 3-16.

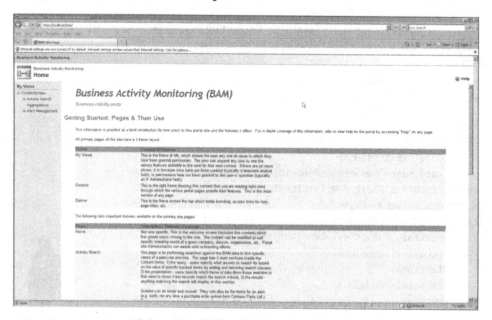

Figure 3-16. *The BAM Portal*

2. At the left-hand side of the portal is a navigation bar. Click the Activity Search link, and then click the name of the view: BeginBAMView. This will bring up the Activity Search screen (see Figure 3-17).

3. The left-hand column in the column chooser should contain a list of all the data items in the view. Select all of the items, and click the >> button near the center of the screen. This will move the items to the Items to Show column. Click the Execute Query button, and you should see your data displayed in the Results pane near the bottom of the screen. If you see data, stand up and give yourself a round of applause. If not, we include some debugging suggestions later in the chapter in the "Debugging the Exercise" section.

4. You can use the Activity Search screen to select the data you want to see. Near the top of the screen is the Query pane. Using the first drop-down in the Query pane, select the customer item. In the second drop-down, select Is Exactly. In the Value text box, enter the name of one of the customers in your data. As an example, if the customer column contains the name CUSTOMER1, you can enter **CUSTOMER1**. Click the Add button near the right of the screen, and then click the Execute Query button again. You will see orders for only that customer in the Results pane.

5. The client should still be running. Call the WCF service again, and then click Execute Query in the BAM Portal. The new data should be visible in the portal as soon as the query is executed again.

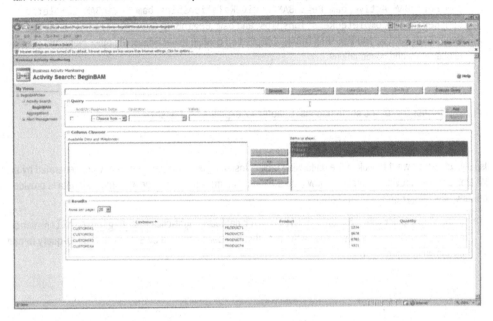

Figure 3-17. *The Activity Search screen*

■**Note** Chapter 7 includes information on other features of the BAM Portal, including working with aggregations and alerts.

EXERCISE 3-9. LOOKING AT THE DATA USING SQL SERVER MANAGEMENT STUDIO

The BAM Portal is really just an ASP.NET application on top of the BAM Primary Import database. Sometimes, it will be beneficial to look at data directly.

1. Open SQL Server Management Studio, and connect to the database engine on your SQL Server. You will see several BAM-related databases: BAMAlertsApplication, BAMAlertsNSMain, BAMArchive, BAMPrimaryImport, and BAMStarSchema. BAMPrimaryImport is the database that is used initially by the BAM infrastructure to store data. BAMAlertsApplication and BAMAlertsNSMain are used by SQL Server Notification Services to support BAM alerts. BAMArchive is used to archive older BAM data that has been removed from BAMPrimaryImport to improve performance. BAMStarSchema is used by jobs that construct views in SQL Server Analysis Services.

2. In SQL Server Management Studio, examine the BAMPrimaryImport database. You will see several tables and SQL Server views that support your BAM activity and BAM view. You will see table names like bam_BeginBAM_Active, bam_BeginBAM_ActiveRelationships, bam_BeginBAM_Completed, bam_BeginBAM_CompletedRelationships, and bam_BeginBAM_Continuations. The tables bam_BeginBAM_Active and bam_BeginBAM_Completed contain the activities; the other tables are used by relationships and continuations.

■Note Chapter 6 explains continuations. Chapter 12 explains relationships.

Usually, you won't want to look at the underlying tables. Instead, you'll use the views that were generated by the BM tool, as these provide a simplified view onto the data. The most useful perspective into your data is provided by the view bam_BeginBAM_AllInstances.

3. In the Views folder within the BAMPrimaryImport database, right-click bam_BeginBAM_AllInstances and select Open View. You will see all the data that has been captured by BAM in an easy-to-query format, as shown in Figure 3-18.

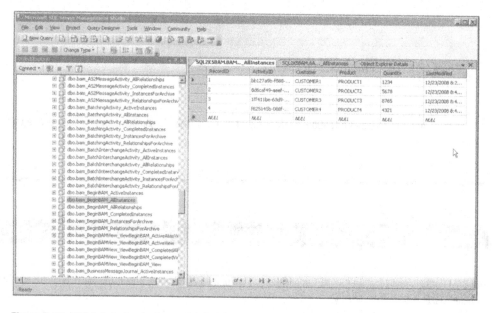

Figure 3-18. *BAM data in the bam_BeginBAM_AllInstances view, displayed in SQL Server Management Studio*

■Note Chapter 11 provides more information on working with the BAMPrimaryImport database using tools like SQL Server Reporting Services and Microsoft Office PerformancePoint Server.

Debugging the Project

If you saw the BAM data, congratulations! If not, here are a few tips and tricks for debugging the project.

Setup

The following tips will help you troubleshoot problems with BAM setup and configuration:

- *Do you see the BAM Add-In in Excel?* If the BAM Add-In for Excel is missing, check to see whether you can find a file called `C:\Program Files\Microsoft Office\Office12\Library\BAM.xla`. If you have this file, you should be able to enable the BAM Add-In for Excel using the Add-In Management dialog box. If you don't have it, the BAM tools are not installed. Use Add/Remove Programs to check the BizTalk Server installation and ensure the BAM client, which is found under Additional Software, is installed.

- *When you attempt to deploy the activity, you see the error message* "ERROR: The BAM deployment failed. Unable to determine the BizTalk SKU. Retrieving the COM class factory for component with CLSID {C6432-2C34810BE8CD} failed due to the following error: 80040154." If you get this error message, BAM is not installed on your machine. Use Add/Remove Programs to check the BizTalk Server installation and ensure that BAM is installed. Ensure you have the following components: Portal Components, including Business Activity Monitoring; Developer Tools and SDK; Server Runtime; Administration Tools and Monitoring, including the Windows Communication Foundation Administration Tools; Additional Software, including BAM Alert Provider, BAM Client, and BAM Eventing. Run the BizTalk Configuration tool and ensure all BAM components are configured.

- *When you start the WCF service, it fails.* Debugging the service shows the exception "The type 'Microsoft.BizTalk.Bam.Interceptors.Wcf.BamEndpointBehavior, Microsoft.BizTalk.Bam.Interceptors, Version=3.0.1.0, Culture=neutral, PublicKeyToken=31bf3856ad364e35' registered for extension 'bamServiceBehaviorExtension' could not be loaded." If you get this error message, the BAM components for WCF are not installed correctly. Use Add/Remove Programs to check the BizTalk Server installation and ensure that the Developer Tools and SDK option is installed. Run the BizTalk Configuration tool and ensure all BAM components are configured.

- *When you browse to the BAM Portal, you get the message* "The page cannot be found. The page you are looking for might have been removed, had its name changed, or is temporarily unavailable." If you get this message, either the BAM Portal is not installed or BAM is not configured. Use Add/Remove Programs to check the BizTalk Server installation. Check that the Portal Components feature, including Business Activity Monitoring, is installed. Run the BizTalk Configuration tool and ensure all BAM components are configured.

- *When you browse to the BAM Portal, you get the message "Service Unavailable."* This message can occur when the application pool running the BAM Portal has an identity that is not a member of the IIS_WPG group. Use IIS Administrator to check the account that is running the BAM Portal, and then check the account is a member of the IIS_WPG group.

- *In a 64-bit system, you are unable to see the BAM Portal.* The BAM Portal requires that IIS be set up in 32-bit mode. You can do this using the following command:

```
cscript %SYSTEMDRIVE%\inetpub\adminscripts\adsutil.vbs ➥
SET W3SVC/AppPools/Enable32bitAppOnWin64 1
```

Note More information on setting up your machine for the exercises can be found in Chapter 2.

Activity and View

The following tips will help you troubleshoot problems with the BAM observation model:

- *When you browse the web portal, you get the message "No View to Display."* You can check which activities and views are installed by using these commands:

```
bm get-activities
bm get-views
```

- *When you browse the web portal, you get the message "No View to Display."* However, BM indicates the activity and view were installed correctly. This probably means that your account doesn't have permission to see the view. Try rerunning this command:

```
bm add-account -AccountName:<your account name> -View:BeginBAMView
```

- *When you browse the web portal, you get the message "No View to Display."* BM indicates the activity and view were not installed. Take a look at the XML file that you believe contains the activity and view. The XML format is fairly simple, and reading the file should confirm that the activity and view were defined correctly. If they don't exist, try rerunning this command:

```
bm deploy-all –definitionFile:beginBAM.xml
```

- *You receive error messages when you attempt to deploy the activity.* You can check which activities and views are installed by using these commands:

```
bm get-activities
bm get-views
```

Remove all activities and views by using the following commands, and then try the deployment again:

```
bm remove-activity –Name:<activity name>
bm remove-view –Name:<view name>
```

Interceptor Configuration

The following tips will help you troubleshoot problems with the IC file:

- *You receive error messages when you attempt to deploy the interceptor configuration.* You can check which interceptor configurations are installed by using this command:

```
bm get-interceptorlist
```

  Remove all interceptor configurations by using the following command, and then try the deployment again:

```
bm remove-interceptor –Activity:<activity name>
```

- *When you start the WCF service, it fails.* Debugging the service shows an exception of type `Microsoft.BizTalk.Bam.Interceptors.BamInterceptorException`. Exceptions of this type usually indicate syntax errors in the interceptor configuration file. The message associated with the exception may provide some help in debugging the syntax error.

- *You see the view in the BAM Portal, but data has been captured for only some of the fields.* If only some of the fields are collecting data, an error exists in the `<ic:Update>` elements in the interceptor configuration file. Check this area of the file carefully for typos, and remember that uppercase is not the same thing as lowercase.

- *You see the view in the BAM Portal, but no data has been captured.* If BAM data isn't captured, one of three errors occurred: the BAM components aren't loaded, the interceptor configuration file wasn't installed, or the interceptor configuration file was incorrect. Check that `app.config` has been modified to set up the endpoint behavior, check the interceptor configuration carefully against the sample in the exercise, and rerun BM to confirm that the interceptor configuration file was deployed correctly. You can check which interceptor configurations are installed by using this command:

```
bm get-interceptorlist
```

  If the interceptor configuration is deployed, either it isn't being loaded or it contains an error. You can test to see whether the interceptor configuration is being loaded by deliberately putting a syntax error into the file. Undeploy the interceptor configuration. Make a copy of the correct interceptor configuration, and then remove this line:

```
<ic:Operation Name="Equals" />
```

  Redeploy the interceptor configuration, and then restart the WCF application. If the application generates an exception, the interceptor configuration is being loaded. If no exception is seen, the interceptor configuration is not being loaded.

  If the interceptor configuration is being loaded, the error is somewhere in the `<ic:Update>` elements at the end of the file. Make sure that `DataItemName` matches the name in the activity definition file. Check that `<wcf:Argument>` matches the parameter name in the interface definition.

  If the interceptor configuration isn't being loaded, the error is either in the `app.config` file or the `<ic:EventSource>` element. Review these carefully, comparing them with the sample code.

Summary

In this chapter, you learned about the different participants in a BAM project. You also went through an extended set of exercises that implemented a simple BAM view into a WCF service. The exercises took you through the following tasks:

1. Create a simple WCF service.

2. Create a client for the service.

3. Create an activity and view that define the data to be captured and how it will be displayed.

4. Create an interceptor configuration file that defines where the data will be captured from.

5. Deploy the activity, view, and IC using the bm.exe tool.

6. Modify app.config to specify that the BAM components are loaded.

7. Test the service.

8. Display the captured data.

9. Examine the captured data in the database.

Some of the characteristics of BAM that were described in Chapter 1 have been illustrated by the exercises:

- *Automated data capture and aggregation*: The WCF service was already coded and compiled before you started the BAM implementation. Although the configuration process has several steps, no code changes are needed in the WCF service, and no additional code for data capture is written. It's also worth noting that the sample application is a straightforward .NET application, and was not implemented using BizTalk Messaging or BizTalk Orchestration.

- *Real-time visibility into business processes*: Captured data is immediately visible in the BAM Portal. There's no need to wait for an ETL cycle to run. Instead, as soon as the method is called, data is collected and visible to a nontechnical user.

- *High-performance infrastructure*: Although this test case didn't put much load on your service, it's good to know that the infrastructure is designed to scale for heavy load.

In Chapter 4, you'll learn about some different application architectures and see how they can be used with BAM.

■ ■ ■

Where BAM Fits in Your Business

Many BizTalk architects elect not to implement BAM because they believe that BAM doesn't fit some specific architectural model. This idea is a misconception; BAM may be implemented in any number of scenarios, including many that don't even use BizTalk Server's core engine. This chapter covers BAM in various business and architectural models.

Most people think of BizTalk as an integration server. While BizTalk provides second-to-none integration capabilities, a BizTalk server may also serve as the foundation for a number of different connected systems architectures. This chapter includes a discussion of BAM in multiple business and architectural models, focusing on how BAM may be used to enhance and instrument the model. After reading this chapter, you should know the advantages of BAM in the enterprise and where BAM fits in the business or architectural model you currently support.

When BizTalk Server 2000 was released, it was marketed as a ".NET Enterprise server that unites, in a single product, enterprise application integration (EAI) and business-to-business (B2B) integration." It included such features as administration, document tracking, orchestration, messaging, and XML tools. While BizTalk's core functionality has remained more or less consistent since that time, it's grown to encompass additional technologies that support a wide range of capabilities.

You may be evaluating BizTalk, currently have BizTalk in place to solve a business need, have implemented multiple BizTalk servers, or simply be examining a means to get more from your existing BizTalk implementation. Fortunately, BizTalk Server is not a tool geared toward solving a single problem. BAM can be used with a wide variety of applications and architectures, including business to business (B2B), service-oriented architecture (SOA), enterprise service bus (ESB), business process management (BPM), composite applications, and others.

BAM in a B2B Business Model

BAM is widely used in business-to-business, business-to-consumer (B2C), and consumer-to-consumer (C2C) applications. In these solutions, BizTalk serves as a brokering mechanism between two parties.

One example of a B2B scenario is in the healthcare industry. A healthcare provider may send patient claims submitted when an individual visits a doctor to a folder exposed by an insurance company that is accessed by BizTalk's File adapter. The file is retrieved, decrypted, validated, transformed, and acted upon; for instance, the message is sent to a third-party billing company to determine the amount, after meeting a deductible, for which the patient is responsible (see Figure 4-1).

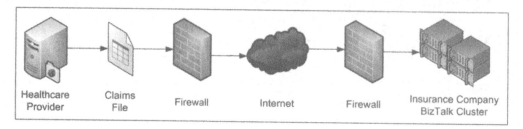

Healthcare Provider   Claims File   Firewall   Internet   Firewall   Insurance Company BizTalk Cluster

Figure 4-1. *Sample B2B scenario*

In this scenario, BAM provides touchpoints into the overall claims processing process. A BAM activity called Monthly Claims Processed may be defined, with data items including

- Processing Begins
- Processing Error Occurs
- Processing Completes
- Claim Value
- Patient ID
- Provider

The activity could be used to create a view that includes

- Number of Claims
- Total Claim Amount
- Most Claims per Patient
- Fewest Claims per Patient
- Largest Claim Amount
- Smallest Claim Amount

As the claims are processed, BAM may provide real-time notification that claims processing has completed, or that a claim amount over a specific threshold has been filed, and perform some action in real time. Business decisions may be made as claims are processed, providing a true benefit to the business as the claims processor doesn't have to wait two to three months before analyzing tens of millions of records and acting on the results.

BAM in a B2C Business Model

The B2C model is much like the B2B one, except that a consumer instead of a business is the originator or recipient of a message. An example of a B2C scenario is the retail industry. A personal care product company may create a Silverlight-based web application to use as a product storefront. Internet users add items to their basket and submit an order. The Silverlight-based application calls into a Windows Communication Foundation (WCF) end-point exposed by BizTalk server, which activates a BizTalk orchestration and passes an XML copy of the order to BizTalk.

BizTalk then disassembles the XML message into messages representing each line item and publishes separate messages to the BizTalk message box. An orchestration subscribes to those published messages and generates messages to send to an order fulfillment system, a logistics and packaging application, and a CRM system to send an e-mail to the consumer (see Figure 4-2).

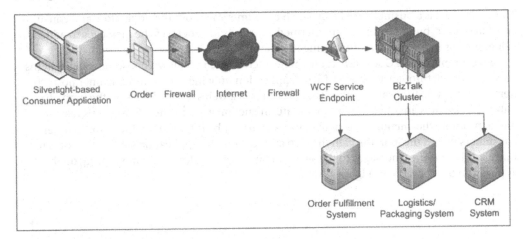

Figure 4-2. *Sample B2C scenario*

BAM provides real value in a B2C model because of its real-time nature. A BAM activity called Product Activity could be created, including milestones such as

- Date Order Placed
- Estimated Shipping Date

Data items could also be defined, such as

- Quantity Ordered
- Product
- Price

A real-time view could provide aggregate data such as

- Total Quantity (Measure)
- Total Price (Measure)
- Product (Data Dimension)
- Order Date (Time Dimension)

As orders are processed by BizTalk, BAM may notify the marketing department that a popular product has been identified and is outselling other products, signal suppliers to expedite shipping of raw materials, and perhaps even increase the price of the product. In real time, the business may realize a greater profit margin or modify its supply chain to adjust to changing market conditions, as opposed to a traditional BI solution that requires more time for data to be gathered and analyzed.

BAM in a C2C Business Model

The C2C model is a business model in which consumers are both the originators and consumers of messages, but many times, an intermediary relays or processes the messages to add value, such as in brokering or interchange scenarios.

An example of a C2C scenario is an online auction site that allows consumers to list items they wish to sell through an ASP.NET web application utilizing AJAX. The consumer posts the item, and the web application submits to BizTalk, via a web service, details on the item. BizTalk then executes an orchestration to initiate an auction area, to check the seller's history, and to promote the auction via e-mail to users who may be interested in the item. As other consumers bid on the item through the web application, the application sends those bids to BizTalk, which routes messages to the seller and performs performance monitoring on the application using BAM (see Figure 4-3).

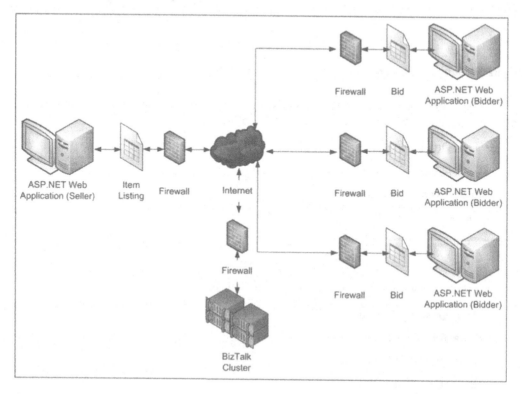

Figure 4-3. *Sample C2C scenario*

BAM is once again a valuable tool in a C2C model because of its real-time nature. BAM activities may be defined and implemented to identify performance degradation on the web site, signaling BizTalk to send a message to virtualization software to allocate more processing power for the application. A BAM activity could be defined to identify a flood of bids from the same IP, potentially indicating either a script that is automated to bid for the user or even a denial of service attack from a user trying to exclude other users from bidding on the item by flooding the server with ping requests or garbage REST-based posts.

In the B2B, B2C, and C2C scenarios, BizTalk is key to the architecture of the scenario, providing endpoint surfacing, transformation, business process execution, and routing, and BAM provides crucial real-time business intelligence (BI).

BAM and SOA

Chapter 1 introduced the concept of service-oriented architecture. Microsoft's main offering for developing services is WCF. WCF provides a "best of breed" solution for service development, combining the advantages of previous Microsoft connected systems technologies including .NET Remoting, COM+, MSMQ, ASP.NET Web Services, and the Web Services Enhancements (WSE). WCF services surface functionality via endpoints described using Web Services Description Language (WSDL) based upon a client-server model (see Figure 4-4).

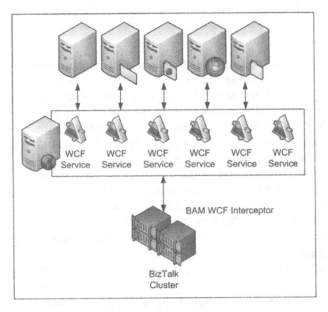

Figure 4-4. *BizTalk and BAM in an SOA*

BAM's WCF interceptor is used to directly provide monitoring capabilities to WCF services and entire business processes that traverse WCF service boundaries. BAM's ability to intercept requests made to WCF services and to monitor Windows Workflow Foundation (WF) workflows is one of the most powerful service-oriented capabilities of BAM.

> **Note** Much more information on the WCF and WF interceptors appears in Chapters 8 and 9.

BAM activities may be defined for individual WCF services to monitor and instrument their execution throughout the process life cycle. As an example, a telecommunications company that owns fiber optic and telephone networks could implement an SOA using WCF services to expose its product information, billing interfaces, and customer information. The telecom company allows its partners to bundle its products with their own service offerings on the telecom company's network and submit order request messages through the WCF endpoints.

A BAM activity could be created with a milestone of product availability date and data items such as product monthly service fee, customer geographic location, and product minutes included. As WCF service calls occur, BAM monitors the services. Using continuations, service flow can be monitored across service execution boundaries to create one BAM activity entity. If the telecom company had metric thresholds in place to realize that the one product plan was outselling all other plans for customers in a specific region, the telecom company could then shift its telecom networking resources, including network availability and support staff, to better service those customers on that plan, ensuring fewer busy signals.

BAM and ESB

ESB is an architectural model of application-to-application (A2A) connectivity that provides rich flexibility and loose coupling. An ESB uses a transport layer such as BizTalk's message box or message-oriented middleware to provide services with a set of event-driven technologies, and supports distributed processing for greater scalability. SOA and ESB are based on the same principles and technologies: XML, SOAP, abstraction of endpoints, and so forth. ESBs, however, provide additional capabilities not inherent to SOA such as service orchestration, process choreography, routing, and richer management (see Figure 4-5).

ESB terminology refers to on-ramps, off-ramps, and itineraries. An on-ramp is a service that allows a message to be submitted to the ESB, an off-ramp allows a message that has travelled across the ESB to be transmitted to an external system, and an itinerary is the data in the message header that specifies how the message should be routed by the ESB.

In fact, Microsoft provides a download that gives guidance on how to build an ESB on the BizTalk Server infrastructure; version 2.0 of the ESB Guidance shipped with BizTalk Server 2009. The APIs, framework, and tools lessen the total time to market to deploy an ESB on the Microsoft stack of technologies.

Let's consider an example in the field of medical research. A clinical study coordinator interfaces with enterprise servers such as active directory for authentication, a web server to host study documentation, a mobile server for remote access to data, and others. The corporate network also includes databases to host participant data information, e-mail and portal servers to provide collaboration and content management, and BizTalk servers to provide for line-of-business integration. There are also pre-existing legacy servers, Java and other messaging systems on the network and on the extranet to which the coordinator has access.

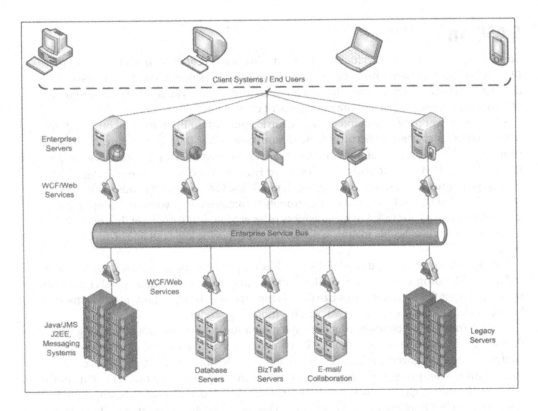

Figure 4-5. *BizTalk and BAM in an ESB*

At the beginning of a study, the coordinator uses a web application hosted on the web server. After entering some basic study information, the web application creates a message that is submitted to a WCF service. The WCF service is an on-ramp to the ESB; on-ramps translate the message into a standard message schema that all systems interfacing with the ESB support. Within the message content header is a predefined path by which the message is expected to follow, referred to as an *itinerary*. The message is routed to a number of systems that interface with the bus, including a directory server to allocate study administrators, the e-mail system to send study information to participants, database servers to record that the study was initiated, and legacy payroll systems to open escrow accounts for study participants to receive payments for their participation. In each interface, the message from the bus is transferred to the host system off-ramp for processing; reply messages are returned on the bus. Each time new clinical data is acquired, it is submitted to an on-ramp, and the itinerary routes it to the correct systems.

As clinical data flows through the ESB, BAM can capture that data and summarize it in real time. As an example, BAM could capture data on changes in patient cholesterol level and blood pressure, and provide summary data to the physicians managing the study. This allows safety and efficacy of the medication under study to be reviewed in real time during the trial. BAM activities and views could be created to monitor all calls made to WCF services from both the ESB and each of the systems that interface with the bus.

BAM and BPM

The concept of BPM was introduced in Chapter 1. Business process management systems (BPMS) seek to automate a business process. An example business process would be a purchasing workflow, where the creation of a purchase order causes an approval request to be sent to each approver in turn in the management chain.

BizTalk Server provides an integration-centric approach to BPM, focused on workflow between different systems. Microsoft Office SharePoint Server (MOSS) workflows and blackpearl from K2 are examples of human-centric BPMS, focused on workflow between people. BizTalk Server 2004 shipped with a feature called Human Workflow Services (HWS), which attempted to provide human-centric BPMS capabilities. HWS was never widely adopted and was quickly abandoned by Microsoft; we strongly recommend that you don't adopt HWS on any of your projects. BizTalk Server's business rules engine (BRE), however, has been widely adopted, providing a flexible means to define domain-specific logic outside of application code.

In the future, we expect that a WF host technology, codename Dublin, will become a central part of Microsoft's BPM strategy. Microsoft's business process modeling tools have been weak until recently; we expect tools like the M language and the Quadrant modeling tool will be used to significantly strengthen Microsoft's modeling products.

As an example of a business process implementation, let's consider a purchasing workflow used at a large defense contractor. The company works on a variety of government contracts, and each government contract has specific rules for authorizing purchases. On some contracts, employees of the company can approve any necessary purchase. On another contract, the rule might be that any purchase greater than $10,000 needs to be approved by the government. On a third contract, the rule might be that total purchases from a single vendor greater than $1,000,000 in a single calendar year require government approval. The defense contractor has an ERP system, but the purchasing capability in the ERP system is incapable of implementing the complex rules for approving purchases. The company would, however, like to use the ERP system's screens for creating and tracking purchase requests.

One way to meet this need would be to use BizTalk to capture new purchase requests created by the ERP system, and hand them off to a workflow in either MOSS or K2 (see Figure 4-6). The workflow tool would implement the purchase approval workflows and hand the approved or rejected order request back to BizTalk, which would update the ERP system. When goods are received, the workflow system would be used to track the goods and update the ERP system with the arrival date.

In this environment, BAM would be used to monitor the purchasing process. Each order in the ERP system could include a date when order approval is needed and also a date when the goods themselves are needed. When a purchase request is transmitted to the workflow system by BizTalk, BAM would capture data about the request. In addition, it would capture data when the approved request is returned and when the goods are received.

BAM data would be used by the business in two ways: to monitor the purchase process and to generate alerts when deadlines are missed.

Monitoring the purchase process would require an aggregated view to provide summary information on how the process is performing. The view would probably contain measures like average time to approve a purchase order and average time for goods to be delivered after an order is approved. The data could be broken down by department, item categories, or supplier so that the efficiency of different departments or suppliers could be compared.

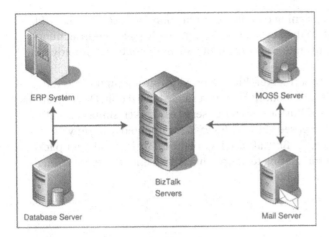

Figure 4-6. *BizTalk in BPM*

■**Note** Chapter 5 contains information on creating aggregated views of BAM data.

Because each purchase request contains deadlines, BAM can be used to monitor whether the process is completed within the deadlines. BAM can raise alerts when specific conditions arise in the data, either at an aggregate level or for individual items. BAM could raise an alert when a purchase request is not approved before the approval deadline, or when goods are not received before the delivery deadline. Alerts can also be raised, however, for issues that affect all items. As an example, an alert can be raised when the average time to approve a purchase request is more than seven days or when multiple orders from a vendor miss their delivery deadline.

■**Note** Chapter 7 contains information on creating alerts.

BAM and Composite Applications

Composite applications are the very definition of "Do More with Less." Composite applications compose multiple existing services into a new application. In the Web 2.0 world, composite applications are often referred as *mashups*. In the enterprise space, composite applications rely heavily on exposing line-of-business systems such as ERP or manufacturing control systems via APIs, services, or adapters. These endpoints are referred to as the *service façade* and provide access to existing functionality. Services become the building blocks for various applications; their function remains the same, but their usage differs depending upon the caller.

Great care must be taken when designing composite applications, as legacy system APIs may have undesirable side effects when the black box hides too much, when a transactional model has not been fully developed, or state and caching of data have not been properly implemented and considered.

Because of its origins as an integration server, BizTalk provides strong support for the composition of multiple distinct units of functionality into a single logical unit. Orchestrations may be used to compose calls to line-of-business systems, services, or even simply execute in-line C#. The orchestration may be exposed via a WCF service or initiated using any of BizTalk's receive adapters (see Figure 4-7). BizTalk also has a Line of Business adapter pack, which provides prebuilt adapters for integrating to various line-of-business systems through WCF, and a toolkit for building custom adapters.

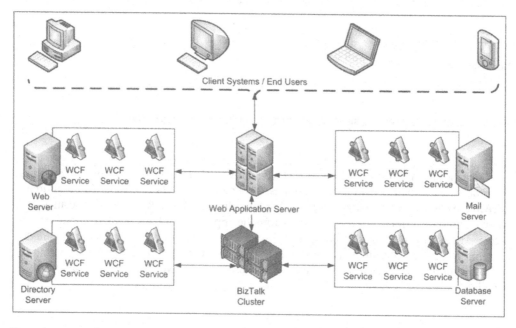

Figure 4-7. *BizTalk as a composite application host*

Because composite applications are composed from multiple service endpoints, either WCF or web services, BAM may be used to instrument and monitor them. As an example, consider an e-learning company that develops several services to expose the functionality of its core domain-specific objects: student, parent, teacher, content, scheduling, billing, and so forth. Each service provides a WSDL contract describing the messages it can accept. Some of the services, such as the billing service, interface with BizTalk by calling another WCF service that BizTalk exposes to execute an orchestration. The benefit of this architecture is that multiple applications can take advantage of each service.

One application allows for counselors to examine a student's curriculum and suggest a plan tailored to meet the needs of the student, while fitting within an acceptable tuition cost. Another application, implemented as a Windows service, queries the student service to determine a student's preferences for learning sessions, and then uses the scheduling service to allocate a time period to hold the instructional session. Once the session is complete, the application contacts the billing service, instantiates a BizTalk orchestration, and generates an invoice.

BAM activities and views could be created to identify the most popular scheduling times, to remediate billing problems due to students not showing up, to adjust lesson plans to better contour them to the needs of the student and the ability of the parent to pay, and so on. Composite applications seek to present multiple application interfaces; BAM unifies those interfaces into one holistic view. As messages flow through the services, BAM provides a single source that crosses boundaries and breaks open silos of information.

Summary

Regardless of the architectural model, both BizTalk and BAM may be utilized in that model to provide instrumentation of business processes, as well as alter the behavior and ultimate outcome of those processes in real time.

BAM and BI solutions utilize many of the same foundational concepts, including metrics for decision making that are based on date, time, or data values. BAM and BI differ in how the metrics are implemented, however. The most important difference is BAM's focus on real-time information, where some BI implementations are focused on historical information. Where both BAM and BI expose similar front-end technologies to the user, the middle tier and data stores for both differ widely.

This concludes Part 1, which introduced the basic concepts of BAM, including installation, configuration, and a simple walkthrough of your first BAM project, and provided context of where BAM fits into your business.

Part 2, beginning with the next chapter, builds upon the introduction, providing instructions on using the BAM toolset with BizTalk Server. Chapter 5 describes the tools that business analysts use on a BAM project to specify the data that will be captured and how it will be displayed.

PART 2

■■■

Working with BAM Tools

In Part 2, you will learn how to work with the BAM tools. Each of the chapters in this part builds on concepts and ideas that you learned in Part 1.

There are three major parts to any BAM solution: event definition, event processing, and event consumption.

Chapter 5, focused on defining events, describes more advanced concepts in activities and views, and centers on the business analyst tools: the BAM Add-In for Excel and the Orchestration Designer for Business Analysts (ODBA). You've already seen one simple example of an activity and a view in Chapter 3. BAM allows much richer views to be created that include aggregations and time-based measurements. As you go through Chapter 5, you'll see several examples of creating BAM views to support specific roles in the organization.

Chapter 6, focused on event processing, describes the Tracking Profile Editor (TPE). This tool is used to select the data that is captured from BizTalk Messaging and BizTalk Orchestration. In Chapter 3, you also saw an example of capturing data from WCF. Unlike WCF, where building the interceptor configuration file requires editing XML by hand, the TPE allows data to be selected by a simple click-and-drag process, building the tracking profile for you.

Chapter 7, focused on event consumption, covers using the BAM Portal and Excel spreadsheets, and using data directly from the SQL Server databases. You've already taken a look at the BAM Portal in Chapter 3. In Chapter 7, you'll see some more advanced options for consuming data.

By the end of Part 2, you will understand how to use the BAM tools to define, process, and consume events for your solution.

■ ■ ■

CHAPTER 5

The BAM Observation Model

In this chapter, we'll focus on the data BAM will collect and how it will be displayed. The end result is referred to as a *BAM observation model*, the conceptual definition of the activities you wish to observe using BAM.

Before diving into the observation model, we'll present a method to keep your BAM artifacts organized. Without a predefined BAM project type within Visual Studio, it can become tedious to track and manage your many BAM files. In this section, you'll learn how to use source code control with BAM. The next section describes activities, the basic building blocks of any BAM solution. Activities specify the data that will be captured from the business process; they simply specify field names and types. The following section introduces a sample application that will be used in Chapters 5, 6, and 7, and includes an exercise to build the sample activity. After that, we'll describe the Orchestration Designer for Business Analysts (ODBA), an alternative tool for building activities. We'll then cover views, which are used to specify how data is displayed. Views allow data to be aggregated and analyzed based on the BI concept of measures and dimensions. The final section describes the BAM Management (BM) tool that is used to deploy activities and views into production.

Setting Up a BAM Solution

One of the reasons developers often struggle with BAM solutions is that BAM solutions aren't contained within a single logical container. While Visual Studio does have a BizTalk solution project type, it doesn't have a BAM counterpart. Over time, having to search for BAM artifacts without a structured means of storage adds a great deal of time to the development and deployment of a BAM solution—time that could better be spent refining the business process. While your solution may be observing the data flowing throughout your business, sometimes there's no one observing the way you organize your code.

The following exercise creates a simple project container to hold your BAM artifacts. This is a project that doesn't compile, but it will provide you the ability to get at your BAM artifacts from within a centralized location using a tool that should be familiar to you, Visual Studio 2008. You don't have to set up this project to make BAM work, but if you do, it will make working with source code control much easier, allowing you to keep all artifacts associated with your project in your source code control system.

EXERCISE 5-1. SETTING UP A BAM SOLUTION

This exercise will demonstrate how to create and organize a BAM solution to reduce the amount of time needed to manage BAM artifacts.

Note This exercise assumes that BizTalk and BAM have been installed according to the recommendations in Chapter 2. It also assumes that your BizTalk server topology has already been configured, and that the necessary prerequisites, such as Visual Studio 2008, have been installed.

---

1. Start Visual Studio 2008.

   If you have a BizTalk solution, open it, and then from the File menu select Add ➤ New Project.

2. If you don't have an existing BizTalk solution, select New Project from the File menu.

3. In the left-pane, click the BizTalk Projects node in the tree view. If you don't have a BizTalk Projects node, it's likely that Visual Studio 2008 was not installed when BizTalk Server 2009 was installed. If this is the case, you'll need to repair the BizTalk server installation from the Control Panel.

4. Select Empty BizTalk Server Project. In the Name text box, select a name that uniquely identifies your BAM solution (see Figure 5-1). In general, it's best to name the project file according to the business function or business process you are attempting to instrument. A standard naming convention we like to follow is [CompanyName].[Business Project].[Business Process].BAM—for example, Apress.ProBAM2009. Publishing.BAM.

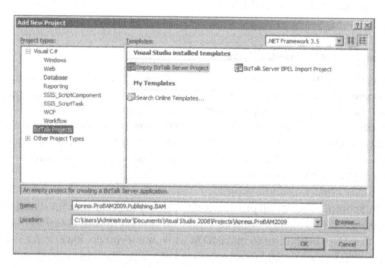

Figure 5-1. *Naming the BAM project*

5. Ensure that the location listed for your project is in the same location as the other projects in your solution. For a Windows Vista or Windows Server 2008 solution, the location would be C:\Users\[User Name]\ Documents\Visual Studio 2008\Projects\Apress.ProBAM2009.Publishing.BAM.

6. Click the OK button.

7. Right-click the solution name in Solution Explorer, and select Properties.

8. Select Configuration Properties ➤ Configuration. Uncheck the Build and Deploy check boxes for the BAM project.

9. Once the new project has been created, identify the artifacts your BAM solution will store: Excel workbooks, BAM definition files, WCF interceptor configuration files, WF interceptor configuration files, tracking profiles, ODBA process designs, BM scripts, and so forth.

10. Create a folder within your BizTalk solution for each artifact type, as shown in Figure 5-2. To do this, right-click your project, and select Add ➤ New Folder for each artifact type. When the folder appears in Solution Explorer, enter the name of the folder. If you mistype an artifact type, simply click it, and press the F2 key to rename it.

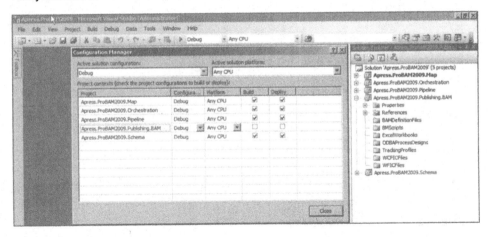

Figure 5-2. *Adding project folders*

11. Click the solution at the top of the hierarchy, and then from the File menu select Save All.

12. Open Windows Explorer, which should have been installed during the installation and configuration of BizTalk 2009.

13. Navigate to the Documents folder for the currently logged on user.

14. In the right pane, right-click and in the context menu that opens select New ➤ Shortcut.

15. When the Create Shortcut Wizard begins, click the Browse button, and navigate to the folder in which your BAM project resides. In our case, the project folder is C:\Users\<User Name>\Documents\Visual Studio 2008\Projects\Apress.ProBAM2009\Apress.ProBAM2009.Publishing.BAM.

16. Click Next.

17. Accept the default project name value for the BAM shortcut and click the Finish button.

18. This shortcut serves to centralize all BAM artifacts created by BAM tools, including the Tracking Profile Editor, Microsoft Excel, and Visual Studio 2008. When utilizing any of these tools, provided an artifact has not been stored in any other directory, the tool will default to the Documents folder of the currently logged on user. To save the artifact in the proper place, double-click the shortcut you have just created, navigate to the folder based upon the artifact type, and click Save (see Figure 5-3).

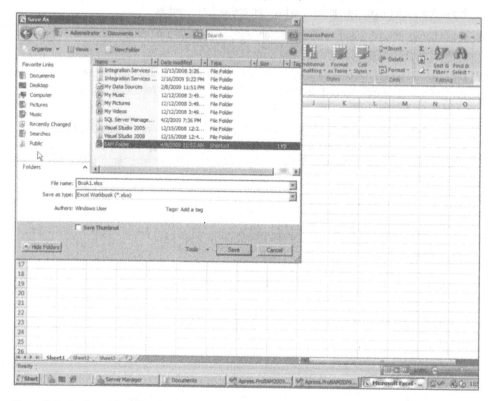

Figure 5-3. *Saving using the shortcut*

As the needs of your BAM solution grow, you may consider changing the BAM project name to be more specific. For instance, if you add code for custom event-stream processing, you will want to add a separate project with a different naming convention, such as Apress.ProBAM2009.Publishing.BAMCode. This makes deploying BAM much easier as the BAMCode project is compiled into a DLL and deployed to the BizTalk application.

■**Note** BizTalk and BAM solutions are not unlike other Visual Studio projects in that there is a need to keep project names short (less than 32 characters). Issues arise when project names, especially nested ones, expand beyond 32 characters. When choosing a naming convention, it's best to be as descriptive as possible, but also to bear this limit in mind. Remember, it's okay to abbreviate—just make sure you and your colleagues will know what the abbreviation stands for. Just like the saying goes, it's not as important to be right as it is to be consistent.

Capturing Data Using Activities

Activities are the heart of a BAM application. An activity is the set of fields that will be captured from a business process. Four types can be captured in an activity:

- *Business Data – Text*: This is stored as a SQL Server nvarchar, so it can store any Unicode character. When you create a text field, you must specify the maximum length of the text. The default is 50 characters.

- *Business Data – Integer*: This is stored as a SQL Server int.

- *Business Data – Decimal*: This is stored as a SQL Server float.

- *Business Milestone*: A business milestone is a date and time, usually captured from the date and time that a message was processed. It is stored as a SQL Server datetime.

As you create an activity, don't worry too much about how the data will be displayed to the user. Focus on the data items that need to be captured from your business process.

Two tools can be used to create an activity: Excel (via the BAM Add-In for Excel) and the Orchestration Designer for Business Analysts. Most of the time, Excel is preferred, because Excel can create the full range of activities and views, whereas ODBA can create only activities and simplistic default views. Activities and views could also be defined by editing the XML file by hand, but this is not recommended because it is inefficient and error prone.

At times a BAM implementation will hit a roadblock during analysis, due to a number of reasons:

- There are differences in perception as to how the business process actually operates.

- There are differences in terminology used throughout a process or between different participants in a business process.

- There are differences in how a milestone or a point of importance is defined, and even disagreement about whether it is relevant.

- There are differences in understanding as to the data available during a business process, where and when it is stored, how BizTalk is involved, and which aspects of that data are of importance.

- There are just "differences."

Before embarking on defining an observation model, we find that it's important to address these differences. It's crucial to the success of the project to ensure that

- Business processes are documented and well understood by both your team and the process participants.

- A data dictionary, glossary, or master data management tool exists that contains a clear definition of the data items to be captured.

- A roles definition document exists that contains a clear definition of the roles each participant plays.

- A business case and a functional case have been made for the activities and views that are to be defined, including relevance, timelines, audience, scope, and likelihood to change.

- An application architect, team lead, or information architect has collaborated with the business team to provide transparency into data currently available, as well as the data that could become available in working with partners or other data sources.

- Expectations are set properly, especially in fostering a collaborative environment. Each team member brings unique skills to the project, and the resultant output and effectiveness of the BAM solution is largely a reflection of that.

The Sample Scenario

In this section, we'll present the case study used in the exercises throughout Part 2. You may wish to note this page to refer back to it throughout Part 2.

The Arnold, Wilbur, and Olivia Corporation (AWO) is an international leader in specialty building material construction. AWO is known for innovation in building materials, especially in the area of environmentally sensitive building materials. One of AWO's business units manufactures custom building materials formed from recycled agricultural materials. Straw bale construction is eco-friendly because it is low cost, provides excellent thermal insulation, and is constructed from recycled rice straw that would otherwise be a waste product.

The majority of AWO's sales orders are generated by independent sales agents, who use a Windows application that estimates the cost of custom shapes and sizes of bales. Once the order is complete, the application sends it to a secure FTP site maintained by AWO. AWO also receives a few orders from a web site that allows contractors to order standard bale sizes.

A BizTalk application manages the sales order process. Receive locations monitor the FTP site and the MSMQ queue that transmits web orders. Each order starts an orchestration (see Figure 5-4) that includes the following steps:

1. Send the order to the Engineering department.

2. Receive a response from Engineering. Engineering will accept or reject the order depending on whether or not it meets state building codes.

3. Send the order to the Purchasing department for straw and fastener acquisition.

4. Receive a response from Purchasing that includes a promised date for the materials.

5. Send the order to the Accounting department.

6. Receive a response from Accounting that includes an order number.

Each agent has an agent number and sends a unique order number with each order. The combination of the agent number and the order number is able to uniquely identify any order. Engineering, Purchasing, and Accounting can return the agent number and order number with their responses, and the two numbers will be used to correlate their responses back into the correct orchestration.

In addition to the order number, Engineering's response includes an engineering control number that is used by Engineering's software systems to track the approval process. Engineering control numbers are unique.

If Engineering approves the order, it sends a message to the Manufacturing department using a separate BizTalk application that is based on BizTalk Messaging, with a send port subscribed directly to the receive port. This message doesn't include the order number, but it does include the engineering control number.

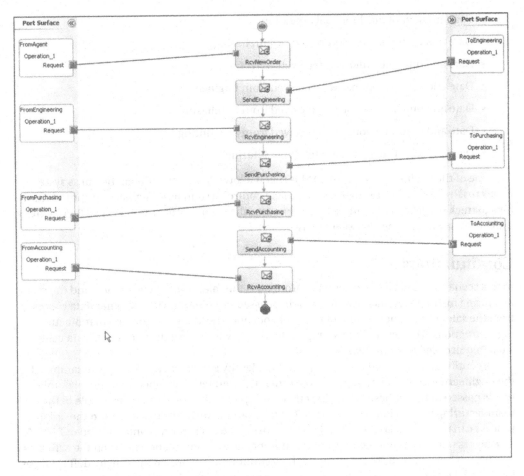

Figure 5-4. *The AWO sales order orchestration*

For each order, we will gather several pieces of data:

- Agent number
- Order number
- Engineering control number
- Engineering response, either accept or reject
- Volume of materials in the order
- Total number of bales
- Price of the order
- Customer name
- Customer postal code
- Customer state or province
- Customer country

- Total number of machine tool operations
- Date that materials were promised by Purchasing
- Date and time the order was received
- Date and time a response was received from Engineering
- Date and time a response was received from Purchasing
- Date and time a response was received from Accounting
- Date and time order was sent to Manufacturing

One of the business benefits of BAM is that it allows data from different business systems to be cross-referenced. The engineering project control system uses engineering control numbers to track orders, whereas the sales system uses the agent's order number. The BAM activity provides a cross-reference between the two.

Continuations

In this scenario, we need to capture data from both the sales order orchestration and the manufacturing instructions that pass through the messaging solution. The customer data comes from the sales order. The number of machine tool operations comes from the manufacturing instructions. To view these in a single activity, we will connect the two sets of data using a technique called *continuations*.

A continuation is a field that can be used to identify a business process. In the sample, if the Engineering department approves the order, it generates an engineering control number that is passed to the orchestration. The engineering control number is also available in the manufacturing instructions. This means that the manufacturing instructions and the order process can be connected into a single activity using the engineering control number. BizTalk developers refer to the engineering control number as the continuation between the activities.

It's not necessary to specify details of how continuation works in the activity definition, as long as all data items needed for continuation are present. In a BizTalk application, continuation details are set using the Tracking Profile Editor (TPE).

■**Note** Chapter 6 covers the TPE in detail and includes an exercise that implements a continuation.

EXERCISE 5-2. DEFINING AN ACTIVITY USING EXCEL

In this exercise, you will create an activity that defines the data captured from the AWO order process. The activity contains both milestones and business data. In Exercises 5-5, 5-6, and 5-7, you will use the activity as the basis for several BAM views.

1. Open Excel and create a new workbook.

2. Select BAM Activity from the BAM menu. (If the BAM menu is not loaded, see the instructions in Chapter 3, Exercise 3-3.)

3. Click the New Activity button. This brings up the New Activity dialog box.

4. Enter **Orders** as the activity name.

5. Click the New Item button.

6. Enter **AgentNumber** in the Item Name text box, and select the type Business Data – Text. Leave the default length of 50 characters. Your dialog box should look like the one in Figure 5-5. Click OK to return to the New Activity dialog box.

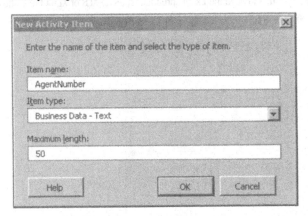

Figure 5-5. *The New Activity Item dialog box*

7. Add each of the data items shown in Table 5-1 by clicking the New Item button.

Table 5-1. *Data Captured in the Sample Activity for the AWO Order Process*

Name	Item Type/Data Type	Length
OrderNumber	Business Data – Text	50
EngControlNumber	Business Data – Text	50
EngineeringApproved	Business Data – Text	1
MaterialVolume	Business Data – Integer	N/A
BaleCount	Business Data – Integer	N/A
Price	Business Data – Decimal	N/A
CustomerName	Business Data – Text	50
CustomerPostalCode	Business Data – Text	20
CustomerState	Business Data –Text	2
CustomerCountry	Business Data – Text	50
ToolOperations	Business Data – Integer	N/A
MaterialsPromised	Business Data – Text	20
OrderReceived	Business Milestone	N/A
EngineeringResponse	Business Milestone	N/A
PurchasingResponse	Business Milestone	N/A
AccountingResponse	Business Milestone	N/A
ManufacturingReceived	Business Milestone	N/A

■**Note** As you enter the data fields, Excel will automatically sort them into alphabetical order.

8. Once you have entered all the fields in the activity, as shown in Figure 5-6, click OK twice, and the View Creation Wizard appears. Cancel the wizard, and save the Excel spreadsheet as an XLS or XLSX file in the ExcelWorkbooks folder in your BAM solution.

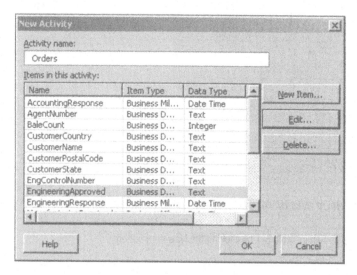

Figure 5-6. *The New Activity dialog box showing the completed Orders activity*

Orchestration Designer for Business Analysts

Orchestration Designer for Business Analysts is an add-in for Microsoft Visio that allows non-technical users to define a business process. ODBA also allows a BAM activity to be created. It's less useful than the BAM Add-In for Excel, because its options for creating views are much less flexible. When an activity is created, a simple default view is built, but no other views can be created.

If you don't have ODBA installed, you will need to install it to do this exercise. Officially, ODBA works only with Visio 2003, and you can't use Visio 2007. However, there is an unsupported hack that will install ODBA on a machine running Visio 2007. The hack has worked for us in the past, but as with all hacks, there are no guarantees. You may find that the representation of the business data of interest on the drawing surface is ugly, but you should be able to right-click the business data and edit it correctly.

■**Note** ODBA is unsupported on Visio 2007. Back up your machine before attempting to install ODBA on Visio 2007, and be aware that Microsoft Support won't help you if this hack damages your system.

When ODBA is installed, it is looking for a specific registry entry. On a 32-bit machine, the registry entry is HKEY_LOCAL_MACHINE\SOFTWARE\Microsoft\Office\11.0\Visio. On a 64-bit machine, the registry entry is HKEY_LOCAL_MACHINE\SOFTWARE\Wow6432Node\ Microsoft\Office\11.0\Visio. If you want to do the hack, the procedure is as follows:

1. Start RegEdit.exe.

2. On a 32-bit machine, find the registry entry HKEY_LOCAL_MACHINE\SOFTWARE\ Microsoft\Office\12.0\Visio.

3. On a 64-bit machine, find the registry entry HKEY_LOCAL_MACHINE\SOFTWARE\ Wow6432Node\Microsoft\Office\12.0\Visio.

4. Right-click the registry entry you found, and export it to a file.

5. Use Visual Studio to edit the file and replace all instances of 12.0\Visio with 11.0\Visio.

6. In RegEdit, import the modified file.

If you have both Visio 2003 and Visio 2007 installed, you should configure ODBA to use Visio 2003. Again there's a hack for this, but this one is documented and supported by Microsoft. If you have both Visio 2003 and Visio 2007 installed on your system, you can ensure that ODBA runs in Visio 2003 using the following procedure:

1. Display the Start menu, and browse to BizTalk Server 2006.

2. Right-click Orchestration Designer for Business Analysts and select Properties.

3. Ensure that the target of the shortcut and the Start In folder both refer to the c:\Program Files\Microsoft Office\Visio 11\1033\ folder.

EXERCISE 5-3. DEFINING A BUSINESS PROCESS USING ODBA

This exercise will provide a simple example of defining a business process in ODBA for readers unfamiliar with the tool.

1. Confirm that you have either installed Visio 2003 or a hacked copy of Visio 2007.

2. Once you have Visio 2003 installed, visit http://go.microsoft.com/fwlink/?LinkId=47543 to download ODBA. Alternatively, browse to http://www.microsoft.com/downloads, search for ODBA, and then select BizTalk Server 2006 Orchestration Designer for Business Analysts.

3. Download the install executable, and then run it to unzip the installation files into a convenient directory. Browse to that directory, and run Microsoft BizTalk Server 2006 Orchestration Designer for Business Analysts.MSI. Check that ODBA installs correctly.

4. From the Start menu, select All Programs ➤ BizTalk Server 2006 ➤ Orchestration Designer for Business Analysts. You will see the Visio design surface with the ODBA template loaded.

5. Create a simple business process so you can add some milestones. Drag two Action shapes and an End shape to the design surface.

6. Double-click the first Action shape, and name it Rcv Message.

7. Double-click the second Action shape, and name it Send Message.

8. Click the Begin shape, and drag an arrow from the bottom of the shape to the Rcv Message shape.

9. Click the Rcv Message shape, and drag an arrow to the Send Message shape.

10. Click the Send Message shape, and drag an arrow to the End shape. Your design surface should resemble what you see in Figure 5-7.

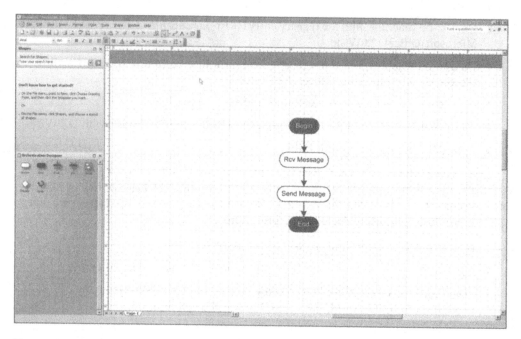

Figure 5-7. *A simple business process in ODBA*

<hr />

EXERCISE 5-4. DEFINING AN ACTIVITY USING ODBA

In this exercise, you will create a BAM activity using ODBA. This exercise assumes that you designed the business process described in Exercise 5-3.

1. If the Data of Interest shape is not visible (see Figure 5-8), from Visio's ODBA menu, select Show/Hide Business Data of Interest.

2. Right-click the Data of Interest shape, and select Edit Business Data Items. This will bring up the Business Data of Interest dialog box, as shown in Figure 5-9.

3. Click the Add button to bring up the Business Data Item Properties dialog box.

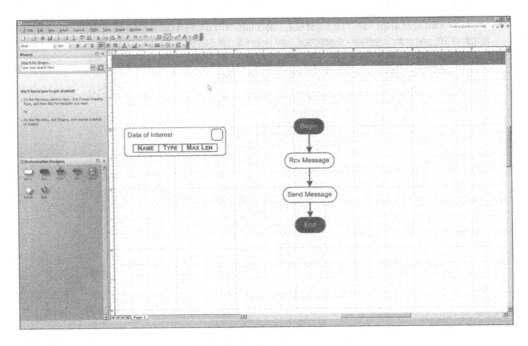

Figure 5-8. *ODBA showing the Data of Interest shape*

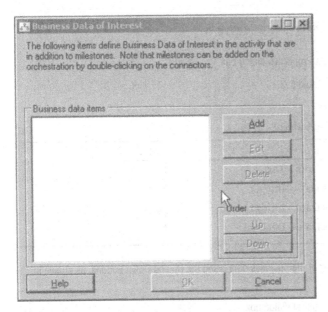

Figure 5-9. *The Business Data of Interest dialog box*

4. Enter **OrderNumber** in the Item Name text box, select Business Data – Text as the type, enter a maximum length of **20**, and enter a suitable description (see Figure 5-10).

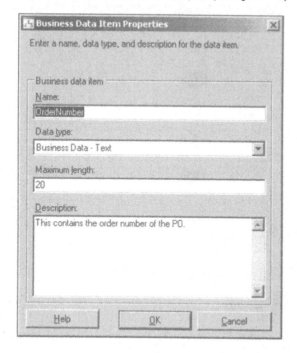

Figure 5-10. *The Business Data Item Properties dialog box*

5. Click OK to close the Business Data Item Properties dialog box.

6. Enter four more data items as listed in Table 5-2.

Table 5-2. *Data of Interest for the ODBA Activity*

Name	Type	Length
CustomerNumber	Business Data – Text	50
ItemCount	Business Data – Integer	N/A
BaleCount	Business Data – Integer	N/A
Price	Business Data – Decimal	N/A

7. If you wish, you can rearrange the order of the business data using the Up and Down buttons, as shown in Figure 5-11.

8. Click OK to close the Business Data of Interest dialog box.

9. Right-click the arrow between the Begin shape and the Rcv Message shape. Select Add Milestone to bring up the Milestone Properties dialog box. Enter **StartProcess** as the name of the milestone (see Figure 5-12).

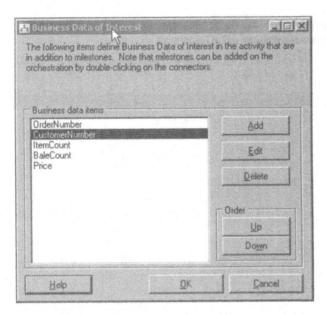

Figure 5-11. *The business data of interest for the ODBA activity*

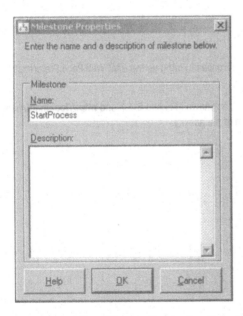

Figure 5-12. *The Milestone Properties dialog box*

10. Right-click the arrow from the Rcv Message shape to the Send Message shape, and create a milestone called SendMessage.

11. Right-click the arrow from the Send Message shape to the End shape, and create a milestone called EndProcess. Your activity should now resemble the one in Figure 5-13.

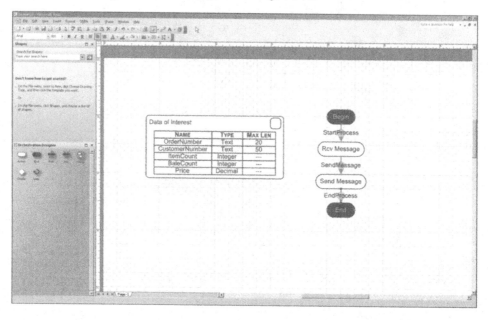

Figure 5-13. *The completed activity in ODBA*

12. From the ODBA menu, select Set BAM Web Page Preferences to bring up the BAM Web Page Preferences dialog box.

13. Enter the name **BaleOrders** in the Activity name field, as shown in Figure 5-14, and **http://localhost/bam** in the Web page URI field. Click OK. This sets the name of the activity.

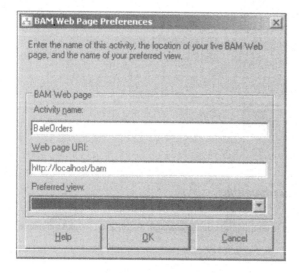

Figure 5-14. *The BAM Web Page Preferences dialog box*

14. From the ODBA menu, select Export BAM Definition File. Click the Browse button, use your shortcut within My Documents to navigate to the Visual Studio directory where your BAM solution is stored, and select the BAMDefinitionFiles folder. Save the file.

15. From the File menu, select Save, and then save the Visio diagram in your ODBAProcessDesigns folder.

Analyzing Data Using Views

If activities are the heart of BAM, views are the brains. A view does a lot more than just select the items to be displayed to a user; it can create value by adding aggregations and dimensions to the data gathered by an activity, or by combining data from multiple activities.

The following items can be included in a view:

- *Activity fields*: Of course, any field captured as part of the activity can be included in the view. Fields may be renamed by aliasing, and fields from multiple different activities may be displayed.

- *Durations*: A duration is the elapsed time between two business milestones. Durations can be used to measure elapsed time during a business process.

- *Milestone groups*: A milestone group is used to group milestones together. As an example, consider a business process in which an order is sent for engineering review. Any of three different messages could indicate that engineering review is complete. If each message was associated with a milestone, the three milestones could be grouped together into a milestone group called Engineering Review Complete.

- *Measures*: A measure is calculated from either fields in the activity or durations in the view, using one of these functions: sum, count, average, minimum, maximum. In the example scenario, marketing specialists are not really interested in the details of any specific order. Instead, they want to see an aggregate view that contains the average price of each order, the total price of all orders, the number of orders, and the total number of bales ordered. This is achieved by using measures.

- *Dimensions*: In addition to seeing the totals, the marketing specialists would like to analyze the performance of different sales agents in each state. This analysis is made possible by using dimensions to analyze the data. Think of the data as a cube, with dimensions as the edges of the cube. (This concept will be very familiar to anyone who has worked with SQL Server Analysis Services.) As an example, the marketing view has three dimensions, sales agent, customer state, and order date, as shown in Figure 5-15. Order date is a time dimension, and the other two dimensions are data dimensions. If you think about a cube, with customer state and country as the X dimension, sales agent as the Y dimension, and order date as the Z dimension, there will be a point in the cube for each combination of sales agent, customer state, and order date. At that point in the cube, the measures for that combination are stored: average price, total price, order count, and bale count. An analysis tool, such as Microsoft Excel, that is able to work with cubes can easily display either the measures at a specific point in the cube, such as orders for agent 57 in Maryland, USA on June 12, or the total value of all the measures along a dimension, such as average order value for each state and country for all sales agents on June 12.

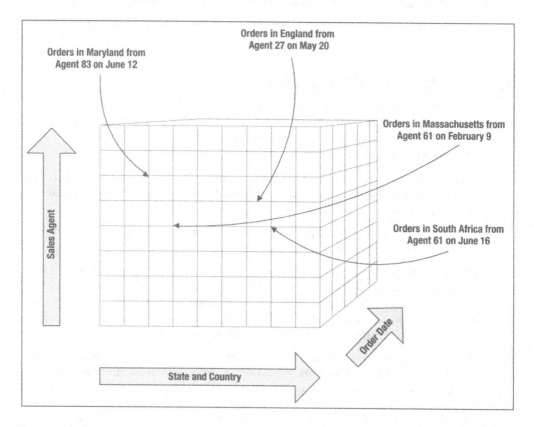

Figure 5-15. *The AWO marketing specialist view*

There are four types of dimensions:

- *Data dimension*: A data dimension classifies the data based on the value of a field. In the marketing specialist view, agent number and state/country are used as data dimensions.

- *Numeric range dimension*: A numeric range dimension is used to classify data items into ranges. At AWO, marketing specialists consider any order over $10,000 a large order, and provide special incentives to agents to bring in large orders. In the marketing specialist view, orders are divided into three ranges: Small ($0.00–$999.99), Medium ($1,000.00–$9,999.99), and Large ($10,000.00 and up). This classification is implemented using a numeric range dimension.

- *Time dimension*: Time dimensions are used to identify the date and time a milestone occurred. In the marketing specialist view, a time dimension is used so the marketers can compare performance of a specific agent over time.

- *Progress dimensions*: Progress dimensions track progress in a business process. A progress dimension divides a business process into stages. Each stage is defined as the time between two milestones. The chief operating officer (COO) of AWO is interested in the overall performance of the sales process, so the COO's view is based on a progress dimension (see Table 5-3).

Table 5-3. *The COO's Progress Dimension*

Stage	Start	End
OrderApproval	Order Received	Approved
Purchasing	Approved	Purchasing Complete
Design	Purchasing Complete	Manufacturing Instructions Sent

Although both progress dimensions and time dimensions are time-based, they have different purposes. Use a time dimension when you are interested in the actual date when something occurred. Use a progress dimension when you are interested in the duration or performance of a business process. The COO is interested in viewing performance trends over time, so the COO's view contains both a progress dimension and a time dimension. This allows the COO to understand whether performance is improving or getting worse from quarter to quarter.

When you design a view, consider whether the user is more interested in specific item details or aggregate data. Typically, an executive won't need to see the details of each individual order and will be much more interested in seeing aggregate data broken out along appropriate dimensions. However, a sales manager may be very interested in specific orders, and the sales manager's view may need to include item-level detail.

■**Tip** Before designing a view, ask yourself whether the view should include individual items or aggregate data. Generally, you'll want to pick one or the other. If you need both item-level data and aggregate data, you probably need two views. In the exercises, the COO and marketing views are aggregated views, and the manufacturing view is an item-level view.

Real-Time Aggregation

Another decision needs to be made when creating a view: should aggregations be calculated in real time? When a view that contains aggregations is created, it can be marked as a real-time aggregation view by selecting a button in the Excel spreadsheet. In a real-time aggregation view, each time a new item is added, a trigger calculates the new value of each aggregation. Obviously, this can affect performance, especially if a large volume of BAM data is being captured. If the view is not marked as real-time, aggregations will be calculated by building a SQL Server Analysis Services cube. The cube can be built on whatever schedule the DBA selects; we've seen projects that rebuild the cube as often as once per hour, and other projects that rebuild the cube as rarely as once per week.

The scheduled, cube-based view will have better performance during data capture, but the latest data won't be available until the cube is rebuilt. Use real-time aggregation when you have a small amount of data being captured or the benefits of real-time data outweigh the performance cost of the trigger.

EXERCISE 5-5. CREATING THE MANUFACTURING SCHEDULER VIEW

In this exercise, you will create the view that is used by AWO's manufacturing scheduler. This is a simple view that just displays an overview of individual orders.

1. Reopen the Excel spreadsheet created in Exercise 5-2.

2. From the BAM menu, select BAM View, and the BAM View Creation Wizard appears. Click Next to get to the next page.

3. Ensure Create a New View is selected, and then click Next.

4. Name the view Manufacturing. Select the Orders check box to ensure that data from the Orders activity is included in the view (see Figure 5-16). Click Next.

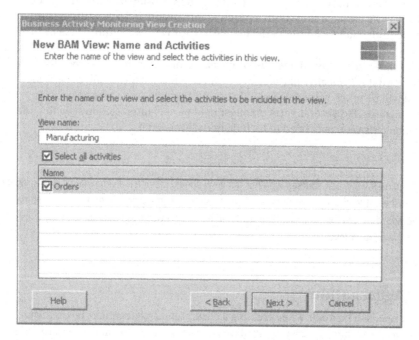

Figure 5-16. *The New BAM View: Name and Activities page of the BAM View Creation Wizard*

5. The next page of the wizard allows you to select the items that you would like to see in this view. The manufacturing scheduler isn't interested in the customer data, but just wants to see the level of effort required to produce each order. Select the following items:

- BaleCount
- EngControlNumber
- EngineeringApproved
- ManufacturingReceived
- MaterialsPromised
- MaterialVolume
- OrderNumber
- OrderReceived
- ToolOperations

6. Click Next to display the View Items page.

7. Click New Alias and select EngControlNumber from the drop-down box. Enter **ControlNumber** as an alias (see Figure 5-17).

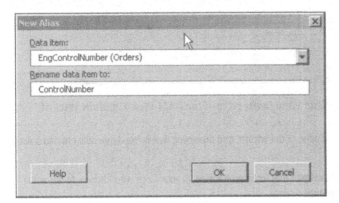

Figure 5-17. *Creating an alias*

8. Click New Alias and select EngineeringApproved from the drop-down box. Specify an alias of Approved for the field.

9. Click New Alias and select OrderReceived from the drop-down box. Specify an alias of OrderDate for the field.

10. Click EngControlNumber, and then click the Delete button. Click Yes to indicate you are sure you want to delete this alias.

11. Click EngineeringApproved, and then click the Delete button. Click Yes to indicate you are sure you want to delete this alias.

12. Click OrderReceived, and then click the Delete button. Click Yes to indicate you are sure you want to delete this alias.

These last few steps have renamed EngControlNumber, EngineeringApproved, and OrderReceived to new, friendlier names, as you can see in Figure 5-18.

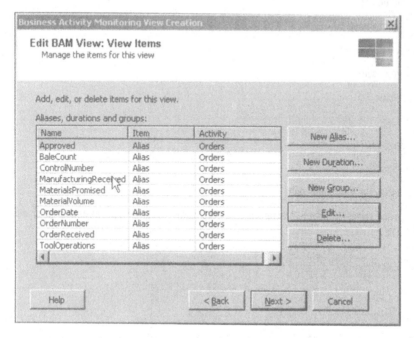

Figure 5-18. *The Edit BAM View: View Items page of the BAM View Creation Wizard*

13. Click Next until you reach the last page of the wizard, and then click Finish. You have now created a simple view.

14. Save the new version of the spreadsheet that includes the view in your `ExcelWorkbooks` folder with a unique name signifying its contents.

EXERCISE 5-6. CREATING THE MARKETING SPECIALIST VIEW

The Manufacturing view is fairly simple. It displays a subset of the fields from individual items and renames a couple of items. The Marketing team doesn't want to see individual items; they are much more interested in seeing aggregate data so they can tell how agents are performing in each state. In this exercise, you will build an aggregated view to support these queries.

1. Just as you did in the previous exercise, reopen the Excel spreadsheet if it's closed.

2. From the BAM menu, select BAM View, and the BAM View Creation Wizard appears. Click Next to get to the next page.

3. Ensure Create a New View is selected, and then click Next.

4. Name the view Marketing. Select the Orders check box to ensure that data from the Orders activity is included in the view. Click Next.

5. Select the following items:

   - AgentNumber

   - BaleCount

   - CustomerCountry

   - CustomerState

   - OrderReceived

   - Price

6. Click Next twice, until you reach the Aggregation Dimensions and Measures page.

7. Click New Dimension.

8. Enter **Customer** as the dimension name, select the dimension type of Data Dimension, and add Customer-Country and CustomerState to the dimension (see Figure 5-19).

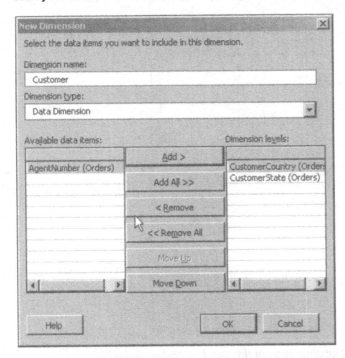

Figure 5-19. *Creating a data dimension in the New Dimension dialog box*

Note The order that items are added to a dimension is important. You should add CustomerCountry first, because CustomerCountry is the top-level item.

9. Click OK to return to the Aggregation Dimensions and Measures page.

10. Click New Dimension again, and enter **OrderSize** as the dimension name, select Numeric Range Dimension as the dimension type, and specify Price as the base data item. This dimension will be used to divide orders into small, medium, and large.

11. Click New Range to create a new range. Enter a range name of **Small**, and specify the From value as 0 and the To value as 1,000. This specifies that orders from $0 to $1,000 are small orders.

12. Click New Range to create a new range. Enter a range name of **Medium**, and specify the From value as 1,000 and the To value as 10,000. This specifies that orders from $1,000 to $10,000 are medium orders.

13. Click New Range to create a new range. Enter a range name of **Large**, and specify the From value as 10,000, and the To value as 1,000,000. This specifies that orders from $10,000 to $1,000,000 are large orders. Your New Dimension dialog should appear as shown in Figure 5-20.

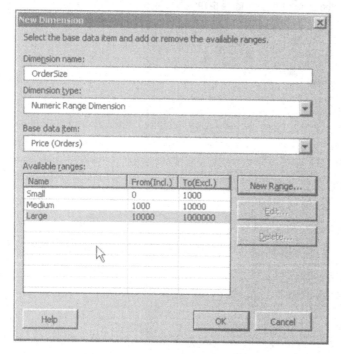

Figure 5-20. *Creating a range dimension in the New Dimension dialog box*

14. Click OK to return to the Aggregation Dimensions and Measures page.

15. Click New Dimension again, and enter **Agent** as the dimension name, select the dimension type of Data Dimension, and add AgentNumber to the dimension.

16. Click OK to return to the Aggregation Dimensions and Measures page.

17. Click New Dimension again, and enter **OrderDate** as the dimension name, select the dimension type of Time Dimension, use OrderReceived as the base business milestone, and select Year, Quarter, Month, Day, Hour, Minute as the display option. (In a real system, this would probably be too much detail, but in an exercise there's a good chance that all our data will be gathered on the same day, so we need to see the minutes.)

18. Click OK to return to the Aggregation Dimensions and Measures page.

19. Click New Measure, and enter **NumberOfBales** as the measure name, and select BaleCount as the base data item and Sum as the aggregation type (see Figure 5-21). This measure will be used to display the total number of bales that have been ordered.

Figure 5-21. *Creating a measure in the New Measure dialog box*

20. Click New Measure, enter **TotalPrice** as the measure name, and select Price as the base data item and Sum as the aggregation type. This measure will be used to display the total price of the orders.

21. Click New Measure, and enter **OrderCount** as the measure name. Select Count as the aggregation type, and the base activity will automatically default to Orders. This measure will be used to display the order count, based on the number of activity items in the activity.

22. Click Next until the last page of the wizard, and then click Finish.

23. Because you have created an aggregated view, the View Creation Wizard allows you to create a pivot table that will be the default display for the view. In the Pivot Table field list near the right of the screen, you can select the fields you would like to display. Choose TotalPrice, Agent, and Customer, to create a pivot table that shows total value of orders by geography and agent. You will see a pivot where the data area contains the total number of orders, sorted by agent and customer country.

24. Drag the customer country heading to the top of the pivot, and create a matrix, where each country is a column and each agent is a row. You will see numbers in the data area—these numbers aren't real data, they only exist to show that numbers will be displayed in that area when the pivot is live.

25. Save the new version of the spreadsheet that includes the view within your ExcelWorkbooks folder with a unique name signifying its contents. When you deploy the view to BAM, the new pivot table will be displayed on the BAM portal page, as shown in Figure 5-22.

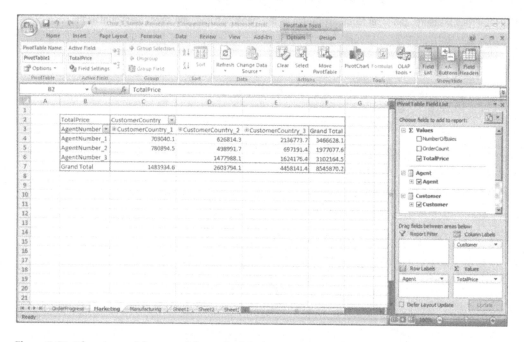

Figure 5-22. *The pivot table created from the Marketing view*

EXERCISE 5-7. CREATING THE COO VIEW

The COO is especially interested in understanding the overall performance of the order process, so the COO's view will include a progress dimension. Progress dimensions divide a business process into stages separated by milestones. In addition, durations will be used to measure the average time that an order spends at each stage in the process.

1. Just as you did in the previous exercise, reopen the Excel spreadsheet if it's closed.

2. From the BAM menu, select BAM View, and the BAM View Creation Wizard appears. Click Next to get to the next page.

3. Ensure Create a New View is selected, and then click Next.

4. Name the view OrderStatus. Select the Orders check box to ensure that data from the Orders activity is included in the view. Click Next.

5. Select the following items:

- AccountingResponse

- EngineeringResponse

- ManufacturingReceived

- OrderReceived

- Price

- PurchasingResponse

6. Click Next to bring up the View Items page.

7. Click New Duration. Create a duration called EngineeringReview that starts with the OrderReceived milestone and ends with the EngineeringResponse milestone. Set the time resolution to minute.

8. Create two more durations as shown in Table 5-4.

Table 5-4. *Durations in the Order Status View*

Duration Name	Start	End	Time Resolution
Purchasing	Engineering Response	Purchasing Response	Minute
EngineeringDesign	PurchasingResponse	ManufacturingReceived	Minute

9. Click Next to display the Aggregation Dimensions and Measures page.

10. Click New Dimension.

11. Name the dimension OrderProgress. Select the dimension type of Progress Dimension.

12. Click the New Milestone button. Name the progress milestone NewOrder, and select OrderReceived as the business milestone (see Figure 5-23).

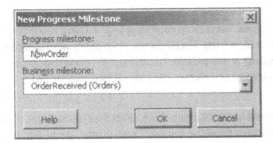

Figure 5-23. *Creating a progress milestone in the New Progress Milestone dialog box*

13. Click the New Stage button. Name the stage OrderApproval.

14. Click the New Milestone button. Name the progress milestone Approved, and select EngineeringResponse as the business milestone.

15. Click the New Stage button. Name the stage Purchasing.

16. Click the New Milestone button. Name the progress milestone PurchasingComplete, and select PurchasingResponse as the business milestone.

17. Click the New Stage button. Name the stage Design.

18. Click the New Milestone button. Name the progress milestone ManufacturingStart, and select ManufacturingReceived as the business milestone. Your New Dimension dialog box should now appear as it does in Figure 5-24.

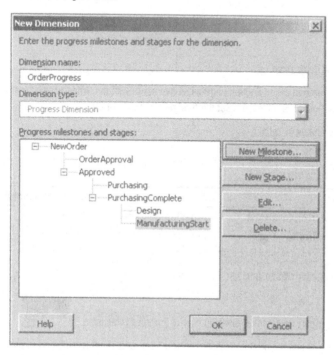

Figure 5-24. *The progress dimension*

This dimension divides order processing into three stages. The OrderApproval stage begins when a new order is received, and ends when a response is received from Engineering. The Purchasing stage begins when a response is received from Engineering, and ends when a response is received from Purchasing. The Design stage begins when a response is received from Purchasing, and ends when manufacturing instructions are transmitted to Manufacturing.

19. Click New Dimension again, and enter **OrderDate** as the dimension name, select the dimension type of Time Dimension, use OrderReceived as the base business milestone, and select Year, Quarter, Month, Day, Hour, Minute as the display option.

20. Click New Measure, and enter **TotalPrice** as the measure name, and select Price as the base data item and Sum as the aggregation type. This measure will be used to display the total price of the orders.

21. Click New Measure, and enter **OrderCount** as the measure name. Select Count as the aggregation type, and the base activity will automatically default to Orders. This measure will be used to display the order count, based on the number of activity items in the activity.

22. Click New Measure, and enter **AvgReviewTime** as the measure name, select Average as the aggregation type, and then select EngineeringReview as the base data item. This measure provides an average time for the engineering review process.

23. Click New Measure, and enter **AvgPurchasingTime** as the measure name, select Average as the aggregation type, and then select Purchasing as the base data item.

24. Click New Measure, and enter **AvgDesignTime** as the measure name, select Average as the aggregation type, and then select EngineeringDesign as the base data item.

The last three steps have created average durations for each of the process steps on the critical path. This allows performance of each department over time to be tracked. The Edit BAM View: Aggregate Dimensions and Measures page should now appear as it does in Figure 5-25.

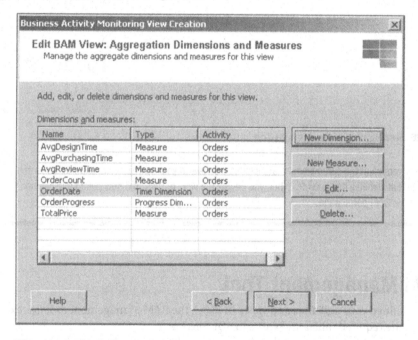

Figure 5-25. *The OrderProgress view*

25. Click Next until the last page of the wizard, and then click Finish.

26. In the pivot table, select OrderCount, TotalPrice, and Progress.

27. Click the Real-Time Aggregation button (see Figure 5-26). In Excel 2003, this button is on the BAM menu. In Excel 2007, it is in the Toolbar Commands area on the Add-Ins tab. Clicking this button ensures that status is updated on this view in real time.

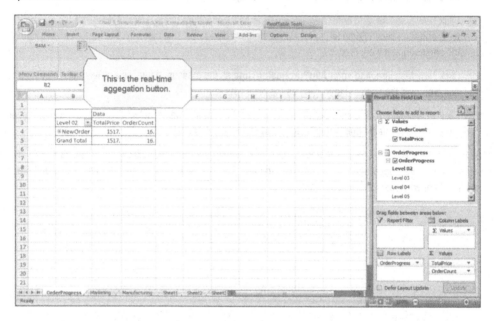

Figure 5-26. *Setting real-time aggregation*

28. Save the new version of the spreadsheet that includes the view to your `ExcelWorkbooks` folder with a unique name that signifies its contents. When you deploy the view to BAM, the new pivot table will be displayed on the BAM portal page.

The BAM Management Tool

Once you have defined your activities and views in Excel, the BAM Management tool (`bm.exe`) is used to create the required tables and views in SQL Server.

The most commonly used command with activities is `deploy-all`. The `deploy-all` command deploys the activities and views in an XML file or an Excel workbook to the BAM Primary Import (BAM PI) database. This command will automatically build the database tables and views needed to support your activities.

■**Note** You can only deploy an activity from an Excel workbook if you have Excel installed on the BizTalk server. If your production servers don't have Excel installed on them, you will need to export your BAM activity definition files to XML to deploy them in production.

If you wish to remove the activities, you can use the `remove-all` command. This will completely remove activities and views, deleting all data associated with them, so you may want to back up your BAM Primary Import database before using this command.

It's not unusual to find that after a BAM solution has been in production for a while, you want to add one or two additional fields to be captured. You can do this by modifying the activity definition file, and then using the `update-all` command. You can't remove a field from an activity, unless you're willing to completely delete the activity and then reload it.

The `get-activities` command will get a list of deployed activities, and the `remove-activity` command will remove an activity. `get-views` will get either a list of the views associated with a specific activity or a list of all views. The `remove-view` command will delete a specific view.

Each view has a specific list of accounts that are able to view the data. In the AWO example, only C-level executives should be permitted to see the data in the COO view. By default, administrators can see all views. You can use the `add-account`, `remove-account`, and `get-accounts` commands to manage the users who can see a view.

For real-time aggregation views, `get-RTAwindow` and `set-RTAwindow` manage the duration for the real-time aggregation.

Note `bm.exe` also has many other functions. Chapter 14 contains a complete list of all the commands provided by the `bm.exe` tool.

EXERCISE 5-8. DEPLOYING THE ACTIVITY USING BM

In this exercise, you will learn to use the `bm.exe` tool to administer BAM activities.

1. Open the last version of your spreadsheet. Using the BAM Add-In for Excel, from the BAM menu command, export the contents to XML. Save the file in your `BAMDefinitions` folder with a unique name. Our example assumes you have saved the file as the name `awo.xml`.

2. From the Start menu, right-click Command Prompt, and then select Run As Administrator. This will start a command shell with administrator privilege.

3. Change the directory to your `BAMDefinitions` folder.

Note You must be a local administrator to run the `bm.exe` command. These instructions assume that you have a single server installation and you used the default database names. If that is not the way your system is set up, you may need to add the `–Server` and `–Database` parameters to each of the following commands.

---

4. Enter the following commands:

```
path %path%;C:\Program Files\Microsoft BizTalk Server 2009\Tracking
bm deploy-all -definitionFile:awo.xml
bm add-account -AccountName:<your account name> -View:Manufacturing
bm add-account -AccountName:<your account name> -View:Marketing
bm add-account -AccountName:<your account name> -View:OrderProgress
```

Replace <your account name> with the name of your Windows user account in DOMAIN\USERNAME format. As an example, if you are logged on to a domain called AWOMANUF as user FREDDY, you would enter the following as the first add-account command:

```
bm add-account -AccountName:AWOMANUF\FREDDY -View:Manufacturing
```

These commands will deploy the activities and views, and then will give your account permission to see the views.

5. Enter the following commands:

```
bm get-activities
bm get-views
```

These commands will list the activities and views that were deployed.

6. Enter the following command:

```
bm get-accounts -View:Marketing
```

This command will list the users who can query the Marketing view.

Summary

In this chapter, you learned how to set up your BAM solution's artifacts, and how to create activities and views. Activities are the heart of BAM; they define the fields captured from your business process. Activities contain only four types: milestones, text, integers, and decimals. Views are used to define how data is presented to the user. Views add aggregations and dimensions into BAM, allowing for rich presentation of information. Usually, activities and views are designed by a business analyst, working in Microsoft Excel.

Chapter 6 covers the Tracking Profile Editor, which is used to connect your activities to a BizTalk application. The TPE is used by a developer who understands the schemas and orchestrations associated with the BizTalk application. In the exercises in Chapter 6, you wire up the activity you created in these exercises to the sample business process. In Chapter 7, you'll display live data from the sample using the BAM Portal.

CHAPTER 6

■■■

The Tracking Profile Editor

In Chapter 3, you learned about the four roles on a BizTalk project: business analyst, developer, system administrator, and data consumer. Chapter 5 covered the business analyst role, and showed you how to create an observation model that describes the data to be collected from a BizTalk application. This chapter describes a developer tool: the Tracking Profile Editor (TPE). The TPE is a graphical tool used to specify the messages, ports, and orchestration shapes that are the source of the data captured by BAM. In this chapter, you will learn to use the TPE to connect the observation model to a BizTalk application.

You can think of this process as specifying the implementation detail behind the abstract data model created by the business analyst. The output from this process is a tracking profile that specifies how data is captured from the BizTalk application.

Typically, the TPE will be used on a development server to build the tracking profile. Once the tracking profile has been applied and tested on the development server, it will usually be saved as a file with a `.btt` extension. The tracking profile file will then be transferred to the staging and production servers where it will be applied with a command-line tool called `bttdeploy`.

Note The TPE is only used when capturing data from BizTalk applications. It's not used when capturing other types of data such as WCF or WF, where interceptor configuration files are used instead.

Using the TPE is a fairly simple process based on click and drag. Normally, the TPE is used by a developer who is familiar with the details of the BizTalk application. In this chapter, you'll learn how to use TPE by working through several exercises. The exercises will involve

- Reviewing the sample BizTalk application

- Using the TPE to capture data from a BizTalk orchestration

- Using the TPE to capture data from BizTalk Messaging

- Using the TPE to set up a continuation

- Using `bttdeploy` to apply a tracking profile

TPE Overview

The TPE window has two panes, a BAM activity pane and a data source pane (see Figure 6-1). The BAM activity pane on the left-hand side of the screen contains a list of all the items in an activity. The data source pane contains data items, such as orchestrations or message schemas. To specify that a particular activity field contains a specific item, you drag that item from the data source to the activity item. In Figure 6-1, each of the fields in the activity has been associated with a data item.

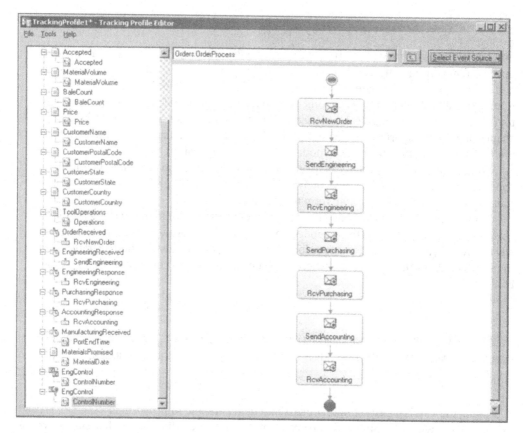

Figure 6-1. *The Tracking Profile Editor*

The following data source types can be displayed in the TPE:

- *Orchestrations*: Displays the flowchart associated with an orchestration.

- *Message payload schemas*: Displays a message schema.

- *Context property schemas*: Displays either a custom property schema that you create in Visual Studio or a standard set of context properties such as the SMTP context properties associated with the SMTP adapter.

- *Message property schema*: Displays a standard set of message properties: Service ID, Instance ID, Message ID, Service Class ID, Interchange ID, Session ID, Port Start Time, Port End Time, Size, and Part Count. These properties may not be available for every shape in an orchestration. As an example, if an orchestration doesn't contain any receive or send shapes, Message ID will never be populated. Message ID is guaranteed to exist for any receive or send shapes. If there is an error in a pipeline, Port Start Time and Port End Time will not be tracked for that interchange.

When an orchestration is displayed in the TPE, you can drag a shape from the orchestration to a milestone in the activity. This indicates that the date and time when the orchestration shape is executed should be stored in the milestone.

When a schema, context property list, or message property list is displayed in the TPE, you can drag a field from the schema or list to a business data item in the activity. As an example, if you have an integer in your message schema, you can drag it to a field in the activity of type integer.

When you capture milestone data from an orchestration, it's easy for BizTalk to decide when to capture the milestone. Each instance of the orchestration creates a new instance of the activity. However, when you capture message payload information from a schema, you may need to provide additional guidance about when to capture the data.

You can open a schema in the TPE in two ways: selecting the payload from an orchestration shape or opening a schema directly. If you open a schema by right-clicking a shape in the orchestration and selecting Message Payload Schema, Context Property Schema, or Message Property Schema, the TPE remembers the shape associated with the schema, and captures data when the shape is executed. However, you can also open a schema directly. In that case, after you set the message element or property associated with an activity field, you need to right-click the data item, select Set Port Mappings, and then specify the BizTalk port where the data will be captured. This allows the TPE to be used in messaging applications that don't have orchestrations, by picking the data item to capture from a message schema and then setting the receive or send port where that data item will be captured.

Several node types can be displayed in the left-hand pane of the TPE:

- *Activity and activity ID nodes*: The activity ID node contains the activity ID, which is a unique identifier associated with an instance of the activity. Most of the time, you will want to leave this node empty, and BAM will automatically generate a globally unique identifier (GUID). If your data contains a unique ID such as an order number or Social Security number, you can associate this with the activity ID instead.

- *Data item nodes*: In a typical tracking profile, the majority of the nodes are data item nodes. These represent the business data items in the activity, which will be captured from message payload schemas, context property schemas, or the message property schema. As an example, you will use this node type in Exercise 6-2 to capture the agent number and order number fields. These nodes are created by the business analyst in Excel or ODBA. If you connect several data items to an activity field, and more than one is processed, the last data item captured will be stored in the activity.

- *Business event nodes*: The second most common node type, these nodes represent the business milestones that will be captured from the date and time an orchestration shape is executed. As an example, you will use this node type in Exercise 6-2 to capture the date and time a new order was received. These nodes are created by the business analyst in Excel or ODBA. The time recorded for a shape is the time that the shape completes execution. If an expression shape calls a method that takes time to run, the event won't be recorded in BAM until the expression completes.

- *Continuation and continuation ID nodes*: Continuations are use to capture data from two different business processes or interchanges in a single activity. As an example, imagine that your process sends out a purchase order in an orchestration, but then receives a purchase order acknowledgement from your vendor in a different orchestration. If you want to see data from both the order and acknowledgment in a single activity, you will use a BAM continuation to correlate the two. Continuations aren't created in Excel or ODBA, they are implemented by the developer in the TPE.

Note Exercise 6-2 contains an example of a continuation.

- *Relationship nodes*: Relationships are used when an activity definition file contains more than one activity. As an example, imagine an organization that takes orders for custom manufactured parts. The business process for manufacturing each part is managed by an orchestration, and a BAM activity tracks information about each part. However, there's also an activity that contains information about the activity as a whole. The relationship between the order header activity and the order line item activity resembles a foreign key relationship in a database. In BAM, this is implemented using relationship folders.

Note Chapter 12 describes relationships in BAM.

- *Document reference URL nodes*: The WSS, File, and FTP adapters provide a property called MessageRefURL that contains the URL of the file. Document reference URL nodes can be used to capture that property. In this case, the BAM portal will display a link to the document.

EXERCISE 6-1. REVIEWING THE SAMPLE APPLICATION

Chapter 5 described a fictitious company called Arnold, Wilbur, and Olivia Corporation (AWO), and presented a sales order process built on BizTalk Server. In this exercise, you'll install the sample application and review the business process. The application includes both an orchestration that handles the majority of the sales order process and messaging that sends the manufacturing instructions from the engineering team to the factory. The BAM solution needs to capture data from both the orchestration and the manufacturing instructions.

■Note This exercise assumes that you have downloaded the sample code for the book from the Apress web site (http://www.apress.com). For information on the business process implemented by the sample, see Chapter 5.

1. Run the installation batch file for the sample code at C:\pro bam samples\chapter six\prepare.bat.

2. If you didn't complete the exercises in Chapter 5, run the batch file C:\pro bam samples\chapter five\ finished.bat. This will create the activity and views you need for the exercise.

3. Using Visual Studio 2008, open the solution Orders.sln in C:\pro bam samples\chapter six\code.

4. The solution contains two projects. The Orders project is the AWO sales order business process. The TestHarness project contains several maps that are used to simulate the actions of other software systems outside the business process.

5. Examine the OrderProcess orchestration, shown in Figure 6-2. You'll see that it's a fairly simple series of sends and receives. This business process is deliberately simplified so that you can focus on learning BAM techniques.

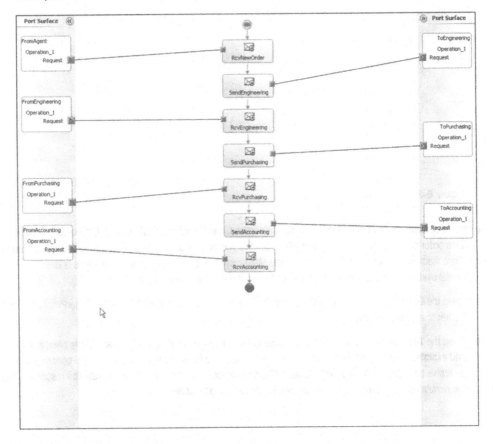

Figure 6-2. *AWO's sales order process*

6. In Solution Explorer, double-click each XSD file to examine the schemas in the Orders project. Each schema represents a message that is either sent or received by the sales order process.

7. From the Start menu, select BizTalk Server 2009 ➤ BizTalk Server Administration to open the BizTalk Administration Console.

8. Open the BizTalk Server group, and then open the Applications folder, shown in Figure 6-3.

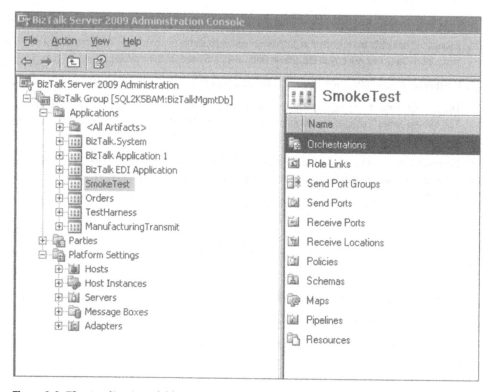

Figure 6-3. *The Applications folder*

The sample contains three applications: Orders, TestHarness, and ManufacturingTransmit. Orders contains the AWO sales order orchestration, ManufacturingTransmit is a messaging-only solution that transmits manufacturing instructions from the Engineering department to the Manufacturing department, and TestHarness is used to simulate external systems in the Engineering, Purchasing, and Accounting departments.

9. Open the Orders application, open the Orchestrations folder, and then double-click the OrderProcess orchestration to examine its bindings.

10. Open the TestHarness application, open the Send Ports folder, then double-click each of the send ports and examine their properties. For each send port, look at the Filter tab to examine how it is connected to a receive port. Also, examine the Outbound Maps tab to examine the maps that generate the responses from the simulated Engineering, Accounting, and Purchasing departments.

11. Open an instance of Windows Explorer, and browse to the `C:\pro bam samples\chapter six\filedrops` folder. You will see that this folder contains a batch file called `FileMove.bat`, shown in Listing 6-1.

Listing 6-1. *The `FileMove.bat` File*

```
set /a loopcount=0
:start
sleep 60
rem Advance orders one step in processmove "c:\pro bam samples\chapter six\➥
filedrops\toengineering\*.*"  "c:\pro bam samples\➥
chapter six\filedrops\tempengineering"
move "c:\pro bam samples\chapter six\filedrops\➥
topurchasing\*.*"  "c:\pro bam samples\chapter six\filedrops\temppurchasing"
move "c:\pro bam samples\chapter six\filedrops\➥
toaccounting\*.*"  "c:\pro bam samples\chapter six\filedrops\tempaccounting"
rem Advance the loop count variable
set /a loopcount=%loopcount%+1
rem Check for the fifth iteration
if %loopcount%==5 (goto :skip) else (goto :start)
:skip
rem Copy manufacturing instructions
move "c:\pro bam samples\chapter six\filedrops\manuftemp1\*.*"➥
    "c:\pro bam samples\chapter six\filedrops\manuftemp2"
rem Jump back to start of file
set /a loopcount=0
goto :start
```

This file is another part of the test harness that simulates the work of the Engineering, Purchasing, and Accounting departments. As an example of how the batch file works, consider the simulated behavior of the Engineering department. When the OrderProcess orchestration receives a new order, it immediately writes the order through a port called ToEngineering that stores the outbound file in a folder called `C:\pro bam samples\chapter six\filedrops\toengineering`. Once per minute, the `FileMove` batch file will move any files in the `toengineering` folder into the `tempengineering` folder. The TestHarness BizTalk application has a receive location pointed to `tempengineering` that will pick up the file, map it to the engineering response format, and write the file to the `fromengineering` folder. This simulates the behavior of the systems used by the engineering department and provides the message received in the RcvEngineering shape shown in Figure 6-1.

You may be wondering why the sample uses a batch file in addition to the TestHarness application. The batch file sleeps for 60 seconds between copies, slowing down the sales order process. One of the goals of the BAM implementation is to track the duration of the sales order process. If the process completed immediately, the BAM data showing progress would be less interesting to look at.

EXERCISE 6-2. USING THE TPE TO CAPTURE DATA FROM THE SAMPLE

In this exercise, you'll use the TPE to capture data from AWO's sales order orchestration.

Note You need to have administrative-level privileges to run the TPE.

---

1. From the Start menu, select BizTalk Server 2009, and then click Tracking Profile Editor. The TPE will open in a new window (see Figure 6-4).

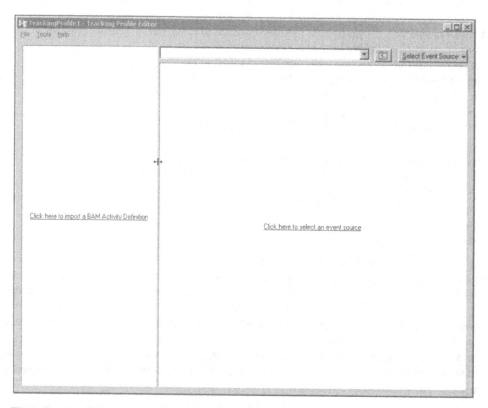

Figure 6-4. *The TPE just after it is loaded from the Start menu*

As mentioned previously, the TPE is divided into two panes: the activity pane on the left of the screen, and the event source pane on the right of the screen. The activity pane will contain a list of the items in the observation model that need to be captured. The event source pane will contain an orchestration or schema that is used the source of data being captured.

2. Click the link in the activity pane that is labeled "Click here to import a BAM Activity Definition."

A list of all activities deployed on the system will be displayed, as shown in Figure 6-5. In addition to activities you have deployed, you may see several activities that are defined by the EDI components, if you have the EDI/AS2 feature of BizTalk installed.

■**Note** BizTalk's EDI feature is primarily used to implement the X.12 and EDIFACT message formats that are often employed in B2B applications. If you're not familiar with EDI, don't worry, you don't need to use the EDI tools to implement BAM.

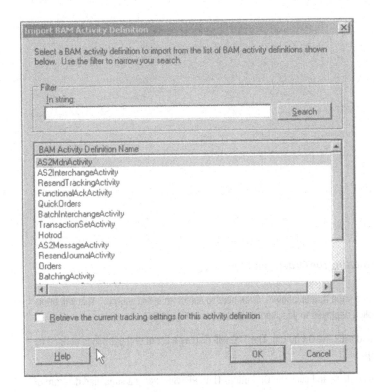

Figure 6-5. *The Import BAM Activity Definition dialog box*

3. Select the Orders activity. Leave the Retrieve the Current Tracking Settings for This Activity Definition check box unselected, and click the OK button to continue. Figure 6-6 shows how the TPE should appear after you've imported the Orders activity.

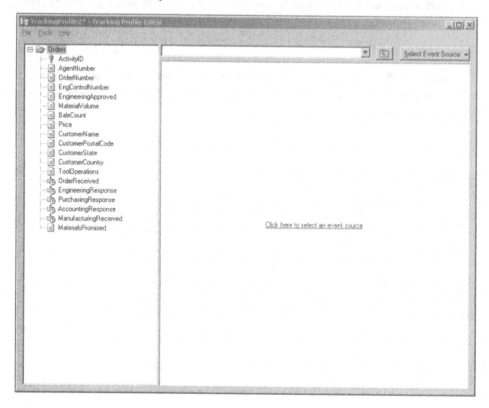

Figure 6-6. *The TPE after loading the Orders activity*

4. Click the link in the event source pane that is labeled "Click here to select an event source." This will bring up a list of all BizTalk assemblies deployed to your server, as shown in Figure 6-7.

5. Select the Orders assembly, and click the OK button. The TPE will display a list of orchestrations defined by the assembly (see Figure 6-8).

6. Select the OrderProcess orchestration, and click the OK button. The TPE will display a simplified diagram of the orchestration.

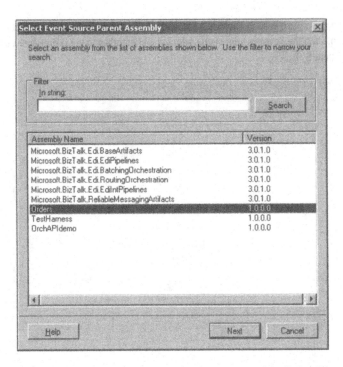

Figure 6-7. *The Select Event Source Parent Assembly dialog box*

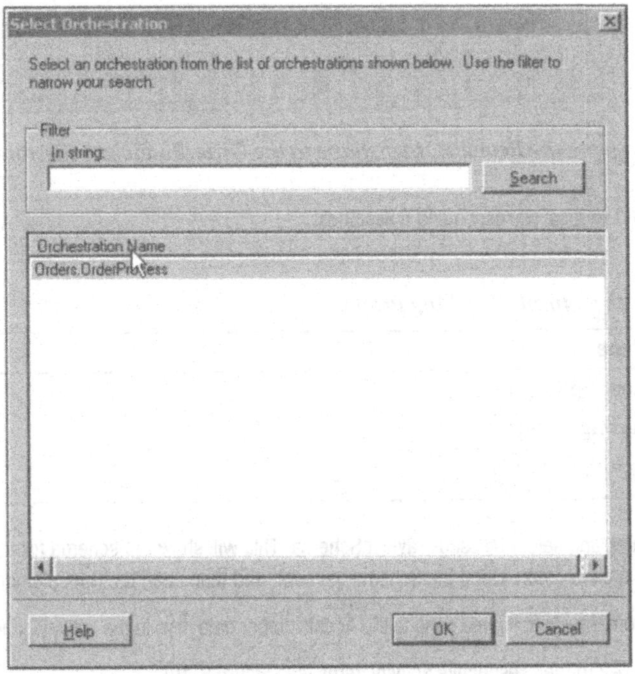

Figure 6-8. *The Select Orchestration dialog box*

7. Several of the milestones in the activity are used to capture the time when a particular message was sent or received by the orchestration. Drag the RcvNewOrder shape from the orchestration to the OrderReceived milestone in the activity (see Figure 6-9).

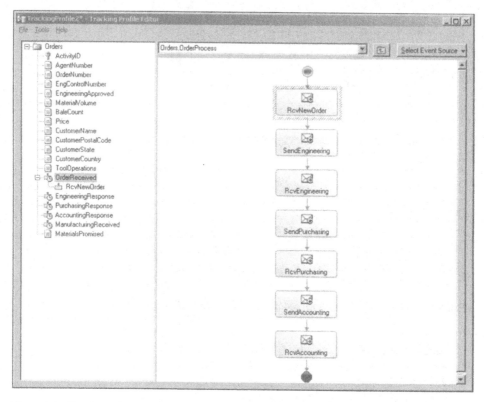

Figure 6-9. *The TPE after dragging the RcvnewOrder shape to the OrderReceived milestone*

8. Drag the shapes listed in Table 6-1 to their corresponding milestones.

Table 6-1. *Milestones Captured in the Sample Tracking Profile*

Orchestration Shape	Milestone
RcvEngineering	EngineeringResponse
RcvPurchasing	PurchasingResponse
RcvAccounting	AccountingResponse

9. Right-click the RcvNewOrder shape, and select MessagePayloadSchema. This will show the schema for the order message that activates the orchestration. Open the Schema element, and then open the Root element.

10. Drag the AgentNumber element from the event source pane to the AgentNumber data item in the activity pane.

11. Drag the elements listed in Table 6-2 to their respective activity items (see Figure 6-10).

Table 6-2. *Data Items Captured from the New Order Message in the Sample Tracking Profile*

Element	Activity Item
OrderNumber	OrderNumber
MaterialVolume	MaterialVolume
BaleCount	BaleCount
Price	Price
CustomerName	CustomerName
CustomerPostalCode	CustomerPostalCode
CustomerState	CustomerState
CustomerCountry	CustomerCountry

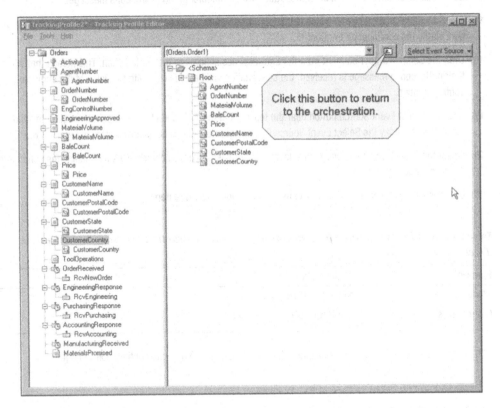

Figure 6-10. *The TPE after dragging the payload elements to the activity fields. The balloon points to the Return to Parent button.*

12. Click the Return to Parent button to return to the orchestration diagram.

13. Right-click the RcvEngineering shape and select Message Payload Schema.

14. Drag the elements shown in Table 6-3 to the activity indicated.

Table 6-3. *Data Items Captured from the Engineering Response Message in the Sample Tracking Profile*

Element	Activity Item
ControlNumber	EngControlNumber
Accepted	EngineeringApproved

You also need to capture the engineering control number in a continuation, as you will use this to match the orchestration with the manufacturing instructions message. Each row in the activity should include data from both an orchestration and a set of manufacturing instructions. That's the job of BAM continuations. Continuations are based on using a unique identifier to match data items that relate to the same instance of a business process. If you're familiar with correlation in BizTalk orchestrations, the concept of continuations will seem familiar to you. In this case, the continuation will match an orchestration with a manufacturing instructions message.

15. Right-click the Orders activity, which is the topmost element in the activity pane, and select New Continuation. Name the continuation EngControl.

16. Drag the ControlNumber element from the EngResponse schema to the continuation. This means that when the EngResponse message is received, the continuation will be initialized with the value of the engineering control number.

17. Click the Select Event Source button near the top-right of the TPE, and choose Select Messaging Payload. The TPE will display the Select Event Source Parent Assembly dialog box shown earlier in Figure 6-6.

18. Select the Orders assembly, and then select the ManufInstructions1 schema. This will display the schema for the manufacturing instructions.

19. Drag the elements listed in Table 6-4 to their corresponding activity items.

Table 6-4. *Data Items Captured from the Manufacturing Instructions Message in the Sample Tracking Profile*

Element	Activity Item
Material Date	MaterialsPromised
Operations	ToolOperations

20. Right-click the Orders activity, and select New Continuation ID. Name the continuation ID EngControl.

░**Note** The continuation ID must have the same name as the continuation created in step 26. The names are used to match up the continuation with the continuation ID.

21. Drag the ControlNumber element to the continuation ID.

22. Click the Select Event Source button, and then choose Select Messaging Property. Drag PortEndTime to the ManufacturingReceived activity item.

You have just set up several items that will be captured from the manufacturing instructions, which are transmitted through BizTalk Messaging. For each of these items, you need to specify the messaging port where the data will be captured.

23. Right-click the Operations element under the ToolOperations activity item, and then select Set Port Mappings.

24. In the port list, select ManufOut, as shown in Figure 6-11, and then click the > button to select this port.

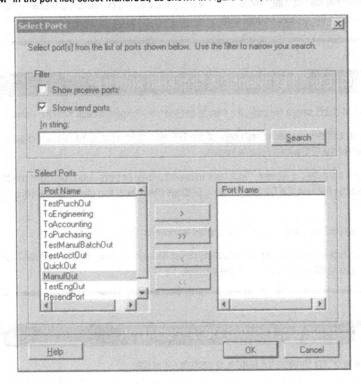

Figure 6-11. *The Select Ports dialog box*

25. You will also need to associate the ManufOut port with each of the items listed in Table 6-5.

Table 6-5. *Data Items Associated with the ManufOut Port in the Sample Tracking Profile*

Activity Item	Element	Port
ManufacturingReceived	PortEndTime	ManufOut
MaterialsPromised	MaterialDate	ManufOut
EngControl (Continuation ID)	ControlNumber	ManufOut

Now that the tracking profile has been built, you will save it as a file and also apply it to the server.

26. From the Tools menu, select Set Management Database. Confirm that the correct server and database names are set. The defaults are the local machine and the `BizTalkMgmtDB` database. In a typical single-machine development environment, these are the correct choice. If no changes are needed, click the Cancel button.

27. From the File menu, select Save As. Save the tracking profile in the `TrackingProfiles` folder that you created in Exercise 5-1. Use the file name `orderprofile.btt`. This will save a copy of the tracking profile in case you need to modify it later. (If you didn't do Exercise 5-1, save the file in any convenient folder.)

28. From the Tools menu, select Apply Tracking Profile. This will apply the tracking profile to the BizTalk management database and initiate the capture of BAM data.

EXERCISE 6-3. RECOVERING A TRACKING PROFILE

If you applied a tracking profile but didn't save a file copy, it's easy to get the tracking profile back from the database.

1. If the TPE is open, close it, and then reopen a fresh copy. If the TPE isn't open, start it. You'll want to perform this exercise using a copy of the TPE with no profile loaded.

2. Click the link in the activity pane that is labeled "Click here to import a BAM Activity Definition," and select the Orders activity. Select the Retrieve the Current Tracking Settings check box, and then click the OK button to continue.

3. When the activity loads, you will also see the currently-applied tracking profile.

4. If you want to remove the tracking profile from the database, select Remove Tracking Profile from the Tools menu, or use the `bttdeploy` utility covered later in this chapter.

EXERCISE 6-4. TESTING THE APPLICATION

In this exercise, you will run some orders through the sample to capture some data.

1. Open a copy of Windows Explorer, and navigate to `C:\pro bam samples\chapter six\filedrops`. Double-click `FileMove.bat` to start the batch file. It will loop until you close it.

■**Note** The batch file continually attempts to move files that are generated by the orchestration. If there are no files to move, the batch file will display an error message but continue operating. Don't worry about these error messages; this is how the batch file is supposed to work.

2. From the Start menu, select BizTalk Server 2009 ➤ BizTalk Server Administration to open the BizTalk Administrator. Open the BizTalk Server group, and then open the Applications folder. Right-click the Orders application, and then select Start. Start the TestHarness and ManufacturingTransmit applications in the same manner.

3. Copy several files from the Order Samples folder and drop them into the New Orders folder. About five minutes later, you should see the manufacturing instructions show up in the ToManuf folder. If you see files in this folder, the sample is working.

4. Open SQL Server Management Studio, and then connect to the database engine on the machine that has your BAMPrimaryImport database.

5. Open the Databases icon. Open the BAMPrimaryImport database, and then open Views. Right-click the dbo.bam_Orders_AllInstances view, and select Open View. If you see any data, BAM is capturing data from the sample.

■**Note** Chapter 7 is devoted to working with data captured by BAM. For more explanation of this view, see Chapter 7.

Applying a Tracking Profile in Production

Once you have tested a tracking profile on your development server, you will need to apply it in production. The bttdeploy utility is used to apply a tracking profile on a production server. The syntax for this command-line utility is quite simple:

```
bttdeploy.exe [options] <profile name>
```

Table 6-6 lists a couple options for bttdeploy.

Table 6-6. *bttdeploy Options*

Option	Description
/mgdb	Used to specify the BizTalk management database in the following format: <server name>[,port]\<database name>
/remove	Specifies that the profile is to be removed from the database

Here are some examples of valid calls to bttdeploy:

```
bttdeploy myprofile.btt
bttdeploy /remove myprofile.btt
bttdeploy /mgdb MYSERVER,1433\BIZTALKMGMTDB myprofile.btt
```

EXERCISE 6-5. APPLYING A TRACKING PROFILE IN PRODUCTION

In this exercise, you'll learn to use the `bttdeploy` tool to deploy a tracking profile.

1. From the Start menu, right-click Command Prompt, and select Run As Administrator. This will start a command shell with administrator privilege.

■**Note** You must be a local administrator to run the `bttdeploy` command. These instructions assume that you have a single-server installation and you used the default database names. If that is not the way your system is set up, you may need to add the `/mgdb` option to each of the following commands.

---

2. Change the directory to your Tracking Profiles folder.

3. Enter the following commands:

   ```
   path %path%;C:\Program Files\Microsoft BizTalk Server 2009\Tracking
   bttdeploy /remove orderprofile.btt
   ```

This command removes the tracking profile you created previously.

4. Enter the following command:

   ```
   bttdeploy orderprofile.btt
   ```

This command reapplies the tracking profile.

Cleaning Up with TP

This section contains a few tips and tricks for working with tracking profiles.

Limitations of TPE

The most important limitation of TPE is that it can only be used to capture data from BizTalk artifacts. If you want to use BAM to capture data from custom code, you'll need to use the BAM API.

■**Note** Chapter 10 covers the BAM API.

Some messages and elements can't be tracked with TPE. You can only track messages that have a schema that is known at design time, so you can't track messages of type string or System.XML.XMLDocument. Also, you can't capture data from repeated fields. As an example, if you have a purchase order message that contains multiple line items, you can capture data from the purchase order header, because each of those fields are unique, but you can't capture data from the line items, as they are repeated fields and there is no way to tell the TPE which instance to choose.

Some limitations exist on the length of data item names. The combined length of a folder name and data item instance value cannot be longer than 128 characters.

You also can't track any of the following orchestration shapes:

- Group (Task)

- Loop (While)

- Message Assignment

- Suspend

- Terminate

- Throw Exception

- Transform

You can work around this for some shapes by wrapping them in a nontransactional scope shape and tracking the scope, but this doesn't work for the Suspend and Terminate shapes, as they never fire the Shape End event.

Tracking Profile Storage

The TPE uses the databases listed in Table 6-7.

Table 6-7. *Databases Used by TPE*

Database	How Used
Management	Stores tracking profiles
BAM Primary Import	Stores interceptor configurations
DTA (Tracking)	XML data for orchestration status

BM can't show a list of currently applied tracking profiles. If you need to know the profiles that are applied on your server, query the bam_TrackingProfiles table in BizTalkMgmtDB.

When you apply a new version of a tracking profile, the previous version is also kept because existing instances of orchestrations may be using an older version of the tracking profile. New instances of the orchestration will always use the latest version. To remove older versions of the tracking profile, remove and then reapply the profile using either bttdeploy or TPE.

Summary

The Tracking Profile Editor is used to capture data from BizTalk messages or orchestrations. In this chapter, you learned about the different data sources and node types supported by the TPE. You did several exercises. In the first exercise, you examined the AWO sample application. In the second exercise, you built a tracking profile for the sample application. The tracking profile used a continuation to correlate messages flowing through two different BizTalk applications. In other exercises, you tested the AWO sample application, learned to recover a tracking profile using the TPE, and learned to deploy tracking profiles in production using bttdeploy.

The final chapter in Part 2 is Chapter 7, where you'll learn to display the data using the BAM Portal, Microsoft Excel, and data-access technologies.

CHAPTER 7

■ ■ ■

Consuming BAM Data and the BAM Portal

In Chapter 3, you learned how to capture data from a WCF service. In Chapter 6, you learned how to capture data from a BizTalk application. In this chapter, you'll learn how to use captured data. In most cases, the data will be displayed to a user, often a business manager who is interested the performance of a business process. BAM provides two out-of-the-box ways to display the data to a user: a web application called the BAM Portal and Excel pivot tables. Because these tools are provided with BizTalk Server and no development work is needed to use them, we have found that most of our clients prefer to use one of these two techniques to minimize development costs.

The data captured by BAM is stored in SQL Server. If you need more flexibility than the built-in tools provide, you can use any data access technique that works with SQL Server to read BAM data. BizTalk Server 2009 has some changes in the structure of the BAM Analysis database that allow Microsoft Office PerformancePoint Server 2007 to display BAM metrics; this is beneficial because earlier versions of BizTalk Server did not work well with PerformancePoint.

Note More about consuming BAM data from BI tools, such as PerformancePoint Server and SQL Server Reporting Services, may be found in Chapter 11.

This chapter will cover

- The BAM Portal
- Using Excel to view BAM aggregations in a pivot table
- The BAM databases
- Looking at data in SQL Server
- Enhancing BAM data with lookups

The BAM Portal

The BAM Portal is an ASP.NET application that is accessed through a web browser; it provides a simple interface for querying data in the BAM Primary Import database.

When you look at the BAM Portal, you will see each of the views that you can access in the left-hand navigation column. Each view will have three subpages associated with it: Activity Search, Aggregation, and Alert Management. If you don't see a view you expect, you should examine the security permissions on the view, which are managed using bm.exe. Each subpage provides a different way to work with the view.

Activity Searches

The Activity Search page (see Figure 7-1) is used to search for an instance of a BAM activity. As you'll recall from Chapter 5, each instance of a BAM activity contains information captured from a business process or message flow. Values captured in the observation model may be used to search in the BAM Portal.

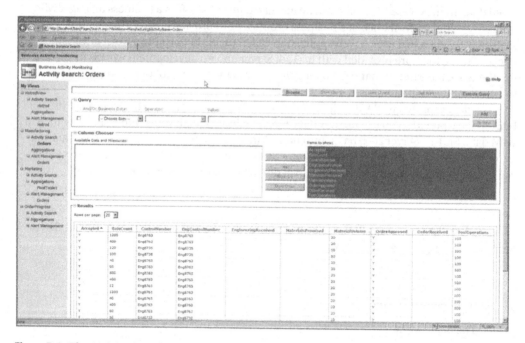

Figure 7-1. *The Activity Search page*

Queries are built using the Query Builder, which is found by selecting the view that interests you in the left-pane navigation, and then clicking Activity Search. You can create queries using dynamically built drop-down lists to provide search criteria. Adding and removing criteria alters the T-SQL query that is being built behind the scenes. Once the query is created, it may be stored and later reused, or used to define a BAM alert.

■**Note** Alerts are covered later in the chapter in the section "Alert Management" and in Exercises 7-2 and 7-4.

Aggregations

The Aggregation page (see Figure 7-2) provides a means to visually represent aggregated BAM data as a graph and pivot table. It is available for views that include aggregated data.

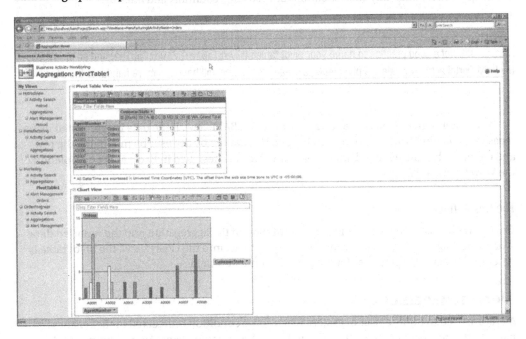

Figure 7-2. *The Aggregation page*

As described in Chapter 5, BAM views can provide measures and dimensions that support analytical processing. As BAM data is collected, data is aggregated in efficient, easy-to-query tables. Aggregations in BAM views have two flavors: scheduled and real-time.

A scheduled aggregation is represented within the BAM Analysis database as an OLAP cube and is a snapshot of your business data at a specific instance in time. A scheduled aggregation is best used when you want to examine where your business is at a date/time milestone. For instance, one client needs to have data at the conclusion of each month and each quarter. Scheduled aggregations worked best in this scenario and are more like traditional business intelligence solutions.

Real-time aggregation data is stored in the BAM Primary Import database and is updated using database triggers. Real-time aggregation is a powerful feature of the BAM infrastructure that is not available in more traditional BI stacks. As an example, you could watch the behavior of a business process and always have up-to-date values for how long the process is taking on average or the maximum length of time the process has taken for each hour in the last week.

Within the Aggregation page, two main areas display aggregation data: the Pivot Table View and the Chart View.

The Pivot Table View

If you've gone beyond the basics of Microsoft Excel, you'll be familiar with pivot tables. A pivot table is a data summarization tool that may display data organized in rows and columns, where the definitions of the rows and columns can be chosen by the user. Pivot tables also provide out-of-the-box functionality such as summation, sorting, counting, and filtering.

Note It's *not* a good practice to name your pivot tables PivotTable1, PivotTable2, and so on. When the BAM Portal actually renders a pivot table, a meaningful name will be much more helpful to the user.

Pivot tables make it easy to analyze the data in a BAM view, if the data is aggregated using measures and dimensions. The pivot table can be adapted by the user by modifying the rows and columns, but the default display is the one that was designed in Excel at the completion of the View Creation Wizard.

The Chart View

The Chart View is simply a graphical representation of the aggregation and the reported data. When you drag and drop items from the Chart Field list into the Chart View, the pivot table is synchronized and the graph is changed to reflect the new fields.

Alert Management

Alerts are used to notify a user or system when some condition is detected in the business data. Alerts are created in the Activity Search and Aggregation pages. As an example, in the Manufacturing view's Activity Search page, you could create an alert that would notify you when an order had a bale count of more than 400. In the Marketing Aggregations view, you could create an alert that would fire when an agent generates more than 20 orders in one state.

Alerts can be used to detect problems in the behavior of business processes. As an example, imagine a web site that sells electronic equipment. If more than 1,000 printers are sold from the site in less than one hour, users may be taking advantage of an errant coupon code or a problem with the web site. An alert could be raised to notify site managers that the situation should be investigated.

Alerts aren't useful, however, until they have a subscriber. When an alert is created, the portal will display the Alert Management page (see Figure 7-3). This page allows you to create a subscription to an alert. Two types of subscriptions are available: file and e-mail. A file subscription writes a file when the alert triggers, and an e-mail subscription sends an e-mail. You can have as many subscriptions as you want to a single alert, so you can have both file and e-mail subscriptions for the same alert.

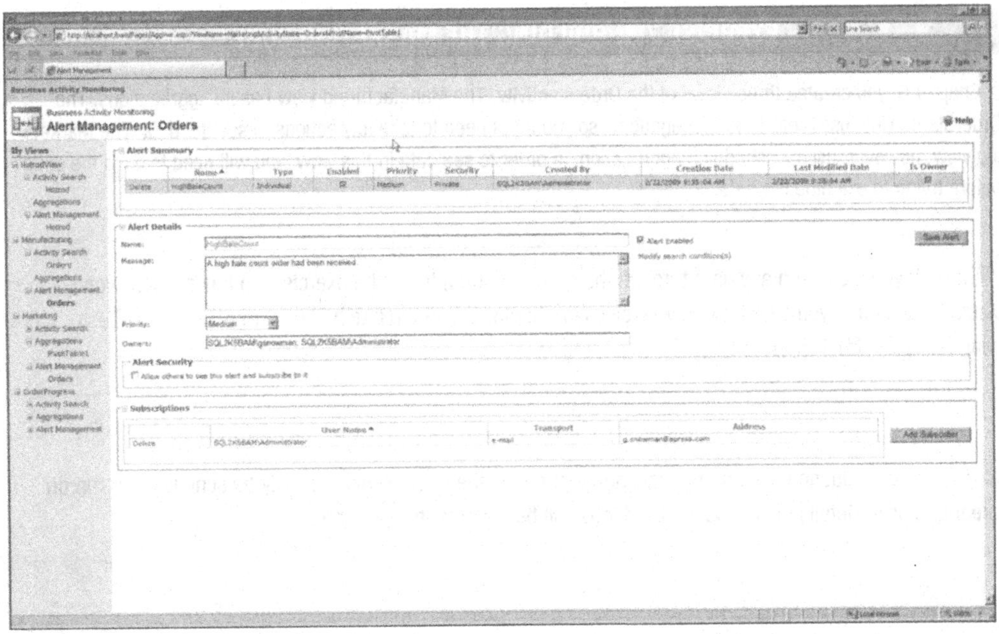

Figure 7-3. *The Alert Management page*

The obvious way to use alerts is to notify a person about a business situation, but there's another way to use them that automates the response. An alert subscription can write the alert to a file folder. There's no reason that file folder can't be a BizTalk Server receive location. That would allow a BizTalk orchestration to be automatically activated in response to a BAM alert. In turn, the BizTalk orchestration can call .NET code or a web service that automatically handles the alert situation.

At AWO, when a large order is received, temporary staff must be added at the factory to cope with the order. A BAM alert identifies the large order and writes a file using a file subscription. That file is picked up by a BizTalk receive port and written into a Microsoft Office SharePoint Server (MOSS) document library using the SharePoint adapter, initiating a MOSS workflow that will create tasks for the HR department. This is a common pattern in which BAM alerts activate a new business process either through an orchestration or by sending a message to some other system.

You can use this technique to allow the user to modify the business rules for a business process. At AWO, the factory manager can use the BAM Portal to change the order size that triggers the HR business process. We wouldn't advise implementing complex business logic using BAM alerts, however. Instead, consider using BizTalk's business rules engine, which is another tool that allows end users to modify the behavior of a business process. To modify human-to-human workflows, you should also consider Microsoft Office SharePoint Designer, which can be used to modify workflows in Microsoft Office SharePoint Server.

EXERCISE 7-1. BUILDING THE MARKETING CUBE

In Chapter 5, you created three views of the Orders activity. The Manufacturing view has no aggregations. The OrderStatus view uses real-time aggregations, so you don't need to take any actions to see the data. The Marketing view, however, uses a scheduled aggregation. In order to see data in this view, you will need to build the cube before trying to examine the data.

■Note If you didn't run any data through the system in Chapter 6, the exercises in this chapter won't display any data. If you didn't do the exercises in Chapter 6, run the batch file C:\pro bam samples\ chapter six\finished.bat.

■Note In a production system, the package that builds the cube would normally be scheduled to run on a regular basis. Details of scheduling BAM jobs will be covered in Chapter 13.

■Note If you don't build the cube, as described in this exercise, any scheduled (non-real-time) aggregations will not be populated, and you'll be left wondering why there is no data in the portal.

1. Open SQL Server Management Studio, click the Connect button in the Object Explorer, and connect to SQL Server Integration Services on your database server.

2. Open Stored Packages, and then open MSDB. If you did the exercises in Chapter 5, you should see a package called BAM_AN_Marketing.

3. Right-click the BAM_AN_Marketing package, and select Execute Package if you are using SQL Server 2005 or Run Package if you are using SQL Server 2008.

4. In the Execute Package Utility dialog box, click the Execute button (see Figure 7-4).

5. A Package Execution Progress window will be displayed. Wait until the package has completed execution, and then click the Close button to close the Package Execution Progress window.

6. Click the Close button to close the Execute Package utility.

7. In SQL Server Management Studio, click the Connect button in the Object Explorer, and connect to SQL Server Analysis Services on your database server.

8. Open the Databases icon to show a list of Analysis Services databases. You should see a database called BAMAnalysis that contains BAM's aggregation cubes.

9. Open the BAMAnalysis database to open the database objects.

10. Open the Cubes icon to show a list of cubes.

11. Right-click the Marketing cube icon and select Browse. A browse window will appear that contains a list of measures and dimensions. Drag the AgentNumber field to the Row Fields zone. Drag CustomerCountry to the Column Fields zone. Drag Price to the Detail Fields zone. You should see a matrix of total sales by agent number and country, as shown in Figure 7-5.

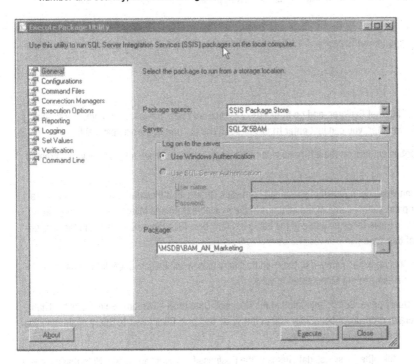

Figure 7-4. *The Execute Package Utility dialog box*

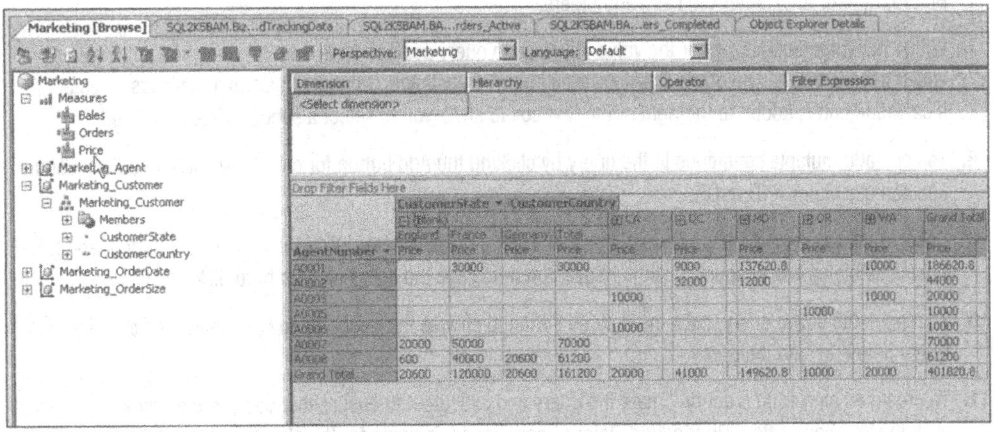

Figure 7-5. *The matrix as it appears in SQL Server Management Studio*

EXERCISE 7-2. EXAMINING DATA USING THE ACTIVITY SEARCH PAGE

This exercise will demonstrate how to query the views you defined in Chapter 5. In Chapter 5, you created three views onto the order data: Manufacturing, Marketing, and OrderProgress.

Note This exercise depends on Exercise 7-1. Please complete Exercise 7-1 before attempting to use the BAM Portal.

1. Open a new copy of Internet Explorer, and go to `http://<your server name>/bam`. If you are running everything on one computer, you can just enter `http://localhost/bam` in the address field.

2. Examine the navigation column on the left-hand side of the page. You should see a list of the views created in Chapter 5.

3. In the Manufacturing view, open Activity Search and then click Orders. In the center of the page, you'll see a Column Chooser pane. Select some of the columns in the Available Data and Milestones box, and then click the >> button to move these columns to the Items to Show box. (See Figure 7-1 earlier in the chapter for an illustration of this page.)

4. When the Items to Show box has items in it, the Execute Query button will be active. Click Execute Query to display a list of all the items in the Manufacturing view.

5. Take a look at the Query pane. Select BaleCount in the Business Data drop-down box. Select Greater Than or Equal in the Operator drop-down box. Enter **400** in the Value text box. Click Execute Query again, and you will see a list of orders for more than 400 bales.

6. Try selecting some of the other business data items in the Business Data drop-down box. Note that after you select the item, the Operator drop-down list will change to reflect the type you selected. For instance, if the data type is a Business Milestone, the Operator drop-down will change to include operators such as At, On or Before, Before, After, After the Last, and others.

7. Within the Value text box, enter the value you wish to query against. Note that the value you enter varies based upon the data type of the Business data item. For instance, if the data type is a Business Milestone, a calendar icon is added to the right of the text box to allow you to select a specific date and time.

8. You can add multiple conditions to the query by clicking the Add button for each new condition. Each condition can use either AND or OR.

9. Once you have created a useful query, you can save it for reuse later. Click the Save Query button, and a File Download dialog box appears. Click the Save button to save the query on your hard disk.

10. To reopen the saved query, click the Browse button to choose the query file to open, and then click the Open Query button to load the query.

11. To create an alert from a query, create the query and execute it to ensure that you see the correct data. Then click the Set Alert button. On the Alert Details page, provide a name for the alert and a text message to be included in files or e-mails generated by the alert (see Figure 7-6). Then click Save Alert.

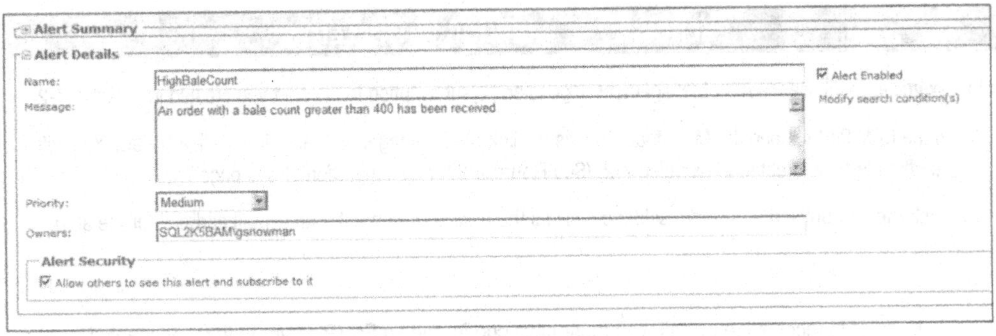

Figure 7-6. *The Alert Management page during the creation of an alert*

EXERCISE 7-3. EXAMINING DATA USING THE AGGREGATIONS PAGE

In this exercise, you'll use the Marketing view as an example of a view with aggregations.

1. In the BAM Portal, open the Marketing view, click Aggregations, and finally click AgentCountry. You will see an Excel pivot table and an Excel chart; both of these are implemented using Office Web Components. (See Figure 7-2 earlier in this chapter for an illustration of this page.)

2. Both the pivot table and the chart provide the power of Excel in the browser. Click the Field List button in the pivot table (see Figure 7-7) to bring up a list of available measures and dimensions.

3. Once the Field List is displayed, you can drag dimensions to the rows or columns, and drag measures to the data area. Try dragging CustomerCountry back to the field list, and then drag OrderSize to the Columns area. The button to the right of the Field List button is the Help button; click the Help button to learn more about working with pivot tables in Excel.

4. The Field List button is also available in the Chart View. Again, try changing the measures and dimensions that are used in the chart.

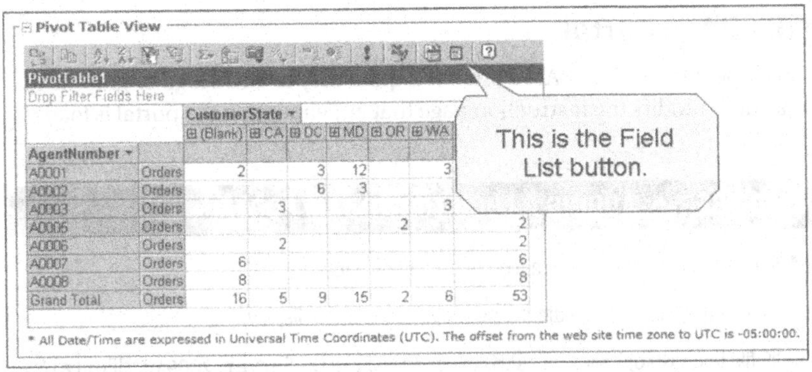

Figure 7-7. *The Aggregation page showing the location of the Field List button*

EXERCISE 7-4. WORKING WITH ALERTS

In this exercise, you'll use the Alert Management page to add a subscription to the alert you created in Exercise 7-2.

1. In the BAM Portal, open the Manufacturing view, click Alert Management, and finally click Orders. You will see the alert you created in Exercise 7-2. (See Figure 7-3 for an illustration of this page.)

2. Click the Add Subscriber button, select e-mail as the transport, and enter an e-mail address for the alert.

■**Note** In order to receive the e-mail, you must have configured an SMTP server with relay enabled as part of the BAM configuration.

Managing Permissions

Like other resources in Windows, a user needs appropriate permissions to see a BAM view. As the administrator of a BizTalk implementation, you will be able to see all views, but your users will need to be added to each view before they get access. To give a user permissions to see a view, use the bm add-account command. As an example, the command bm add-account -AccountName:SERVER1\Tony -View:Marketing will give user Tony permissions to see the Marketing view. The bm remove-account command can be used to remove permissions, and the bm get-accounts command returns a list of accounts that have permission to access a view.

Indexing a View

If your users often search on a specific field in an activity, you can improve performance by indexing that field. Use the bm create-index command to create an index. The index will be implemented as a SQL Server database index. The get-index and remove-index commands are also available to manage indexes.

Customizing the BAM Portal

You can customize the appearance of the BAM Portal. It is quite easy to add a logo or graphic to each page of the portal, or to modify the instruction page that appears when the portal is loaded.

EXERCISE 7-5. ADDING A LOGO TO THE BAM PORTAL

In this exercise, you modify the BAM Portal by adding a logo to each of its pages.

1. Using Paint or your favorite graphics tool, create the new logo you want to display.

2. Save the logo as a GIF file in C:\Program Files\Microsoft BizTalk Server 2009\BAMPortal\ Images.

3. Using Notepad, open the file C:\Program Files\Microsoft BizTalk Server 2009\BAMPortal\ Styles\StyleSheet.css.

4. Search until you find the headerLogo div class. (This is not the same as the headerlogo class.)

5. Change the background-image element to refer to your new logo.

In this exercise, you modify the BAM Portal by changing the instructions that are displayed on the home page of the portal. The home page is a great place to display information that is specific to your organization. As an example, you could explain the use of each of the views in your observation model.

1. Create an HTML page that provides instructions to your users on how to use the BAM Portal. You can use the file at C:\Program Files\Microsoft BizTalk Server 2009\BAMPortal\MainPageContent.HTM as a starting point.

2. Save your HTML page in C:\Program Files\Microsoft BizTalk Server 2009\BAMPortal\.

3. Using Notepad, open the file C:\Program Files\Microsoft BizTalk Server 2009\BAMPortal\ web.config.

4. Find the line <add key="MainPageContentUrl" value="~/MainPageContent.htm"/> and modify it to point to your instruction page.

Aggregating Data from Multiple BAM Implementations

If you have multiple instances of BAM in your organization, you can provide a single instance of the BAM Portal that allows your users to navigate to all of the available activities and views across all instances of BAM. Use the bm enable-reference command to add links to another set of BAM databases. As an example, if you have two servers, AWO1 and AWO2, and each is a single server implementation of BAM, you would run the command bm enable-reference -TargetServer:AWO2 -TargetDatabase:BAMPrimaryImport on server AWO1 to enable a user viewing the portal on AWO1, http://AWO1/bam, to navigate to the views on AWO2. Similarly, the command bm enable-reference -TargetServer:AWO1 -TargetDatabase:BAMPrimaryImport on server AWO2 will allow navigation in the opposite direction, providing the appearance of a completely seamless integration between the two BAM implementations.

Using Excel to View BAM Aggregations

When you initially created your BAM views in Excel, the BAM Add-In for Excel automatically created pivot tables within the Excel workbook for any view that contained measure and dimensions. Because the pivot table operates on aggregated data, it will only be created for aggregated views.

When you deploy the Excel file, the bm.exe command-line utility will notify you that activity, view, and security have completed successfully, and that it has saved a copy of your workbook file with the extension _LiveData to the same location from which you referenced the definition file.

■**Note** If you export the BAM definition as XML, and then deploy the XML file, the live data workbook won't be created. In order to create the live data workbook, you must deploy the Excel workbook that contains the view.

This _LiveData workbook is the same structure as the original workbook except that connection strings and database connections have been added to it. Just as the name implies, the workbook is now feeding off of raw data from your BAM infrastructure.

EXERCISE 7-7. VIEWING BAM DATA USING EXCEL

In this exercise, you'll use the live version of the Excel workbook to view aggregated data.

■**Note** Once again, this exercise assumes that you deployed the activities created in Chapter 5 and populated them in Chapter 6.

1. Examine the Excel workbook you created during the Chapter 5 exercises, and confirm that you have an XLS file. If you have an XLSX file (i.e., your file is saved in Excel 2007 format), open the file using Excel and then save it in the C:\BAM folder using Excel 97-2003 format.

2. From the Start menu, right-click Command Prompt, and then select Run As Administrator. This will start a command shell with administrator privilege.

3. Change directory to the folder containing the workbook with the activity and view definitions.

■**Note** You must be a local administrator to run the bm.exe command. These instructions assume that you have a single server installation and you used the default database names. If that is not the way your system is set up, you may need to add the -Server and -Database parameters to the bm.exe command.

4. Enter the following commands:

    ```
    path %path%;C:\Program Files\Microsoft BizTalk Server 2009\Tracking
    bm regenerate-livedataworkbook –workbookname:awo.xls
    ```

5. Using Excel, open the awo_livedata.xls file that was just created. This will open the newly created live data version of the Excel workbook.

6. Click the Marketing and OrderProgress tabs to view live data in Excel, as shown in Figure 7-8.

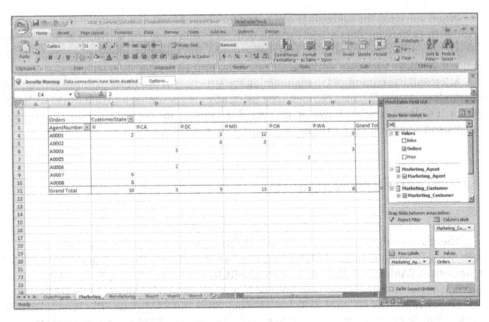

Figure 7-8. *The Excel workbook showing live data*

The BAM Databases

BAM uses five primary databases, as listed in Table 7-1. Four of the databases are relational; the BAM Analysis database is stored in SQL Server Analysis Services.

Table 7-1. *Databases in BAM*

Database	Type	Default Database Name	Contents
BizTalk Message Box	SQL	BizTalkMsgBoxDb	Messages that are being processed by BizTalk
BAM Primary Import	SQL	BAMPrimaryImport	Data that has been captured by BAM
BAM Star Schema	SQL	BAMStarSchema	Staging data used by the DTS package that populates the BAM Analysis database
BAM Analysis	OLAP	BAMAnalysis	OLAP cubes for BAM views
BAM Archive	SQL	BAMArchive	Business activity data that is older than the archive window

If you need to access the data from a custom application, the recommended approach is to do so through the SQL Server views that are created by the bm.exe tool.

When you issue the deploy-all command for your observation model, BAM automatically creates the underlying data model for your activities and views. The activities in BAM Primary Import are partitioned for archival and performance purposes into multiple tables, so it's best to use the SQL Server views, which aggregate data from all the partition tables.

Microsoft has committed to maintaining the structure of the views in future versions of the product, so you can read the view data using any programming tool that works with SQL Server. It's recommended, however, that you don't update the database directly; use the BAM API instead when you need to write new activity data.

Note The BAM API is covered in Chapter 10.

There's a vocabulary problem that makes this topic confusing. The term *view* is used with two different meanings. A SQL Server view is a virtual table that is defined using a SELECT statement. A BAM view is derived from an activity by subsetting, aggregation, or aliasing. SQL Server views are used to implement both BAM activities and BAM views. Table 7-2 lists the SQL Server views that are used to define BAM activities and BAM views. The Type column in Table 7-2 indicates whether each SQL Server view is part of a BAM activity or a BAM view.

Table 7-2. *SQL Server Views in the BAM Primary Import Database*

SQL View Name	Type	Purpose
bam_<Activity>_ActiveInstances	Activity	All instances of the activity that are currently in the active state
bam_<Activity>_AllInstances	Activity	All instances of the activity regardless of state
bam_<Activity>_AllRelationships	Activity	List of all relationships for activity instances
bam_<Activity>_CompletedInstances	Activity	All completed instances of the activity
bam_<Activity>_InstancesForArchive	Activity	All instances of the activity that will be archived on next execution of the DTS package
bam_<Activity>_RelationshipsForArchive	Activity	All relationships for the activity instances that will be archived on next execution of the DTS package
bam_<Activity>_<View>_ActiveAliasView	View	Items currently in the active state by alias
bam_<Activity>_<View>_ActiveView	View	Items currently in the active state
bam_<Activity>_<View>_CompletedAliasView	View	Items currently in the completed state by alias
bam_<Activity>_<View>_CompletedView	View	Items currently in the completed state
bam_<Activity>_<View>_View	View	All items in the view

Reading Data from SQL Server

Reading data from the SQL Server views is quite simple. Listing 7-1 shows some C# code that reads data from the BAM Primary Import database.

Listing 7-1. *ADO.NET Code Sample to Read from a SQL Server View*

```
//This code assumes the view name has been generated
//in a secure manner. Do not let the user enter the
//view name because of the risk of SQL injection
//attacks.
public SqlDataReader GetView(string viewName)
    {
        //Create connection
        string connectionString = @"Server=BIZTALK2009;Database=BAMPrimaryImport;"+
@"User ID=BIZTALK2009\Administrator;Password=password;"+
@"Trusted_Connection=False;";
        SqlConnection myConnection = new
            SqlConnection(connectionString);

        //Create command
        SqlCommand myCommand =
            myConnection.CreateCommand();
        myCommand.CommandText =
            "SELECT * FROM " + viewName;
        myCommand.CommandTimeout = 120;

        //Mark the Command as text
        myCommand.CommandType = CommandType.Text;

        //Execute the command and return
        //the SqlDataReader result
        myConnection.Open();
        return myCommand.ExecuteReader
            (CommandBehavior.CloseConnection);
    }
```

BAM and OLAP

Scheduled aggregation data is stored in the BAM Analysis database so that it may be aggregated over time and analyzed. Because the data is stored in a cube as opposed to a traditional SQL table, you would query the data using multidimensional technologies such as MDX and ADOMD.NET.

ADOMD.NET is a set of .NET objects used to read from OLAP-based cubes in the Microsoft. AnalysisServices.AdomdClient namespace. To use these objects, you'll need to reference the Microsoft.AnalysisServices.ADOMDclient.dll file. MDX, or Multidimensional Expressions, is a query language. It's analogous to SQL but allows you to query multidimensional databases. The query shown in Listing 7-2 will get a list of average order prices tabulated by agent and quarter from the Marketing view cube.

Listing 7-2. *An MDX Query for the MOLAP Cube Created in Chapter 5*

```
WITH MEMBER [Measures].[Average Price]
AS 'AVG({[Marketing_Agent].[Marketing_Agent].Members}, [Measures].[Price])'
SELECT
NON EMPTY
{
CROSSJOIN
(
{[Measures].[Orders],
[Measures].[Price],
[Measures].[Average Price]},
[Marketing_OrderDate].[Marketing_OrderDate].&[2009].Children
)
} ON COLUMNS,
{
ORDER({[Marketing_Agent].[Marketing_Agent].Members}, [Measures].[Orders], DESC)
} ON ROWS
FROM
[Marketing]
```

EXERCISE 7-8. VIEWING BAM DATA IN SQL SERVER MANAGEMENT STUDIO

In this exercise, you'll take another look at the data you've already viewed in the portal, but this time you'll drill into the structure of the data by using SQL Server Management Studio.

■**Note** Once again, this exercise assumes that you deployed the activities created in Chapter 5 and populated them in Chapter 6.

1. From the Start menu, click either Microsoft SQL Server 2005 *or* Microsoft SQL Server 2008, and then select SQL Server Management Studio.

2. Connect to the relational database engine on whatever server holds the BAM Primary Import databases (see Figure 7-9).

3. You should see several BAM-related databases. The data you captured in Chapter 6 will be in the BAMPrimaryImport database. Click the plus sign next to the database name, and then click the plus sign next to the Tables icon. You should see several tables that have names beginning with bam_. Some of these tables contain activities, and some contain metadata. The Orders activity you created in Chapter 5 is contained in tables that have names that begin with bam_Orders.

4. Right-click the bam_Orders_Active table, and then select Open Table. This table should contain the activity items that are still in flight. These are the items indicating where either the orchestration has not completed or the manufacturing instructions have not been sent.

5. Right-click the bam_Orders_Completed table, and then select Open Table. You should observe the completed activities, as shown in Figure 7-10.

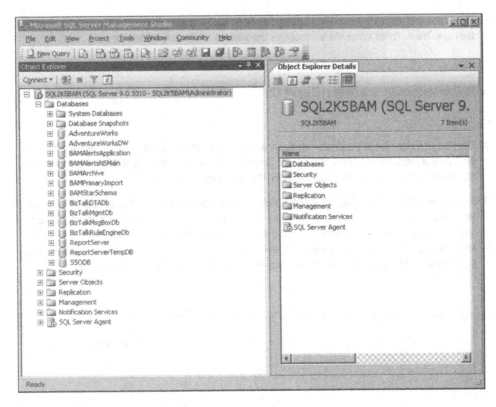

Figure 7-9. *Viewing the BAM databases*

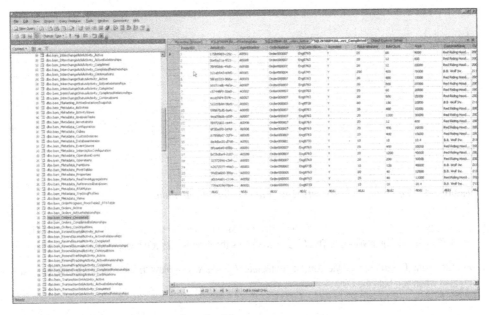

Figure 7-10. *The bam_Orders_Completed table*

6. Right-click bam_Orders_ActiveRelationships and bam_Orders_CompletedRelationships, and then open them. These tables will be empty, as there are no relationships in this data.

■**Note** Relationships are described in Chapter 12.

---

7. Click the plus sign next to the Views icon, to show the list of views defined in the database. Note that one BAM view corresponds to a set of several SQL Server views. The manufacturing BAM view is contained in SQL views that have names that start with bam_Manufacturing_ViewOrders.

8. Right-click bam_Manufacturing_ViewOrders_View and then select Open View. You will see all the activities in the view, including the aliases (see Figure 7-11). Because this is a view, the data is only stored once, although it can be selected from the view using either its original name or the alias name.

9. Right-click bam_Manufacturing_ViewOrders_View and select Script View As ➤ CREATE TO ➤ New Query Editor Window. This view is defined as the union of the active items and the completed items.

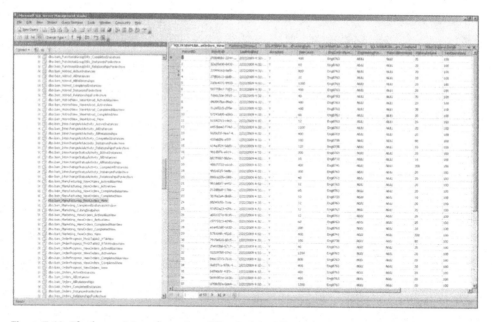

Figure 7-11. *The bam_Manufacturing_ViewOrders_View view*

10. Right-click bam_Manufacturing_ViewOrders_CompletedAliasView and select Script View As ➤ CREATE TO ➤ New Query Editor Window. This SQL view defines the aliases that you designed back in Chapter 5.

11. Examine bam_OrderProgress_ViewOrders_CompletedAliasView. This view defines the durations that you created when you built the COO view.

12. The OrderProgress view uses real-time aggregation, so let's examine the way this is implemented. Right-click bam_OrderProgress_ViewOrders_view and select Open View. You will see the individual data items in the view.

13. Right-click bam_OrderProgress_ProgressTable_RTAWindowView and select Open View. You will see the aggregate data for the view.

14. Return to the Tables list, and find the BAM_Orders_Active table. Open the Triggers list for this table, and then double-click the bam_ OrderProgress_ProgressTable_RTAActiveTrigger. You will see that each time a row is inserted, updated, or deleted, the trigger fires to keep the aggregations up to date.

15. Find the BAM_Orders_Completed table. Open the Triggers list for this table, and then double-click the bam_ OrderProgress_ProgressTable_RTACompletedTrigger. This trigger fires when a new item is inserted into the BAM_Orders_Completed table.

■**Note** See Exercise 7-1 for an example of viewing data from the BAM Analysis database in SQL Server Management Studio.

Enhancing BAM Data with Lookups

When you're designing your observation models, you'll need to decide how much information to include. At AWO, the BAM activity just includes the agent number, but a less normalized observation model might also have included the agent name, state, and country. Another example is customers; the activity could have included just the customer number, or it could also include the customer name, state, country, industry code, and so forth. The smaller activity will use less database space and perform better. An activity that includes additional information will allow users to see information in a format that is easier for them with no additional effort from the development team.

Usually, we prefer to optimize for performance by capturing just the key data. As an example, we would capture just agent number and customer number, because agent number is the key for the agent table in our database, and customer number is the primary key for customers. Then we'll use the data presentation tier to expand the captured data so that users can query and display the fields they want to see.

We have used two main techniques for showing additional data to the users. For scheduled aggregations, you can modify the cube and aggregation package to add additional lookup data. For real-time aggregations, we often use SQL Server Reporting Services Report Builder to query the data and create a report model that links the BAM data to the appropriate lookup tables.

Often, after the BAM solution has been in production for a while, it is realized that showing additional data to the users would have been helpful. Using lookup techniques allows additional fields to be added without compromising the BAM data that has already been captured.

As an example, at AWO, the agent's name, the order creation date, and the name of the engineer responsible for accepting or rejecting the order were not captured in the BAM activity. SQL Server Reporting Services are used to create reports that include additional details on both agents and customers.

Summary

This chapter has focused on consuming BAM data. There are two built-in presentation tools for BAM data: an ASP.NET application called the BAM Portal and live data Excel workbooks. The chapter described both these tools and provided exercises. An additional exercise described the process for building a scheduled view.

BAM data is stored in SQL Server and may be queried by using SQL Server views that are created when the observation model is loaded using bm.exe. The chapter described the BAM databases and the SQL Server views they contain. Finally, the chapter also covered the concept of lookups.

Chapter 11 will show more examples of reading data directly from the SQL Server views, including an exercise that uses SQL Server Reporting Services.

Part 2 of the book has covered the complete process for implementing BAM to capture data from BizTalk. Part 3, which starts with the next chapter, focuses on other data sources: Windows Communication Foundation, Windows Workflow Foundation, and the BAM API.

PART 3

Capturing Application Data for BAM

By this point, you should have a firm understanding of BAM, its tools, and how to use those tools to consume BAM data captured as a result of flowing through BizTalk orchestrations. Orchestrations, however, aren't the only means by which data may be propagated into BAM.

In Part 3, we'll examine the interceptor architecture for WCF, WF, and BizTalk interceptors.

Then, you'll learn the basics of capturing data using Windows Communication Foundation (WCF) and Windows Workflow Foundation (WF), and using the BAM application programming interfaces (APIs).

Each chapter will include an introduction to the technology, the means by which BAM interfaces with the technology, and context around how to best take advantage of that interaction.

■ ■ ■

CHAPTER 8

Capturing Data from WCF

In Part 2, you learned how to consume BAM data from orchestration events that were popu-lated by BizTalk. BAM is incredibly powerful when coupled with BizTalk as a message broker and a tool for business choreography. However, one of BAM's most underutilized and perhaps most useful features is its ability to monitor Windows Communication Foundation services.

One of the chief criticisms of WCF and WF, especially within the .NET Framework 3.5, is the lack of out-of-the-box tools to effectively manage workflow status and the performance of WCF service. Microsoft is expected to address that criticism in its next version of .NET, 4.0, with a set of technologies collectively named "Dublin."

Rather than waiting for its release and having to perhaps restructure and rewrite your application, BAM and BizTalk 2009 offer the ability to intercept data travelling through ser-vices and workflows today.

This chapter will cover

- Architecture of the interceptors

- How WCF and BizTalk integrate

- The syntax of a WCF interceptor file

- A walkthrough with common IC file examples

- Configuring the BAM WCF interception

- Fault handling in the WCF interceptor

- Loading the WCF interceptor using the BAM API

- BAM WCF performance counters

- Hosting and security considerations

This chapter assumes you have basic working knowledge of Windows Communication Foundation, XML, Visual Studio 2008, and BizTalk Server administration.

Architecture of the Interceptors

Before we describe the WCF interceptor, it's worth stepping back and providing an overview of the way interceptors work.

Interceptor Architecture Overview

One of the advantages that an enterprise server product has over a small desktop application is an architecture with many components and many integration points. Having so many "moving pieces" allows other applications to access the various functionalities offered in the server stack.

However, if you wanted to monitor method invocation and overall health and activity data throughout that stack, adding monitoring mechanisms at multiple points would cause additional latency throughout invocation. In order to provide robust monitoring capabilities, the technology would need to implement a type of "wiretapping" mechanism that would provide the ability to intercept method invocations without interfering with their performance in any way.

As of BizTalk Server 2004, Microsoft introduced the ability to intercept data as it flows through the solution, record date and time information, and look at the actual data as processes are executed. As of BizTalk Server 2006, Microsoft further enhanced that capability to include interception of data as it flows through WCF services and WF workflows.

The interceptors do so by implementing a notification callback mechanism, providing the means to gather the data at various checkpoints, recognize that an interception has occurred, and then record that data within a BAM data store. This intentional design provides high degrees of scalability such that locking is not likely to occur as a result of the interceptor "firing."

Within a typical BizTalk solution, there exist four major mechanisms through which data flows: adapters, pipelines, maps, and orchestrations (see Figure 8-1). Of these, Microsoft has prebuilt interceptors for each, with the exception of maps. In order to intercept map information, code must be written to send data directly through the interceptor framework APIs. In general, this is not a recommended practice as it tends to "bloat" maps and make them unmanageable. If you must absolutely intercept data as it flows through a map, we recommend using a well-thought-out utility class that encapsulates writing to the BAM API through a BufferedEventStream.

The mechanism through which data flows is referred to as an *Event Bus* or *Event Stream*. Data flowing through a pipeline flows through pipeline interceptors in the Messaging Event Bus (MessagingEventStream). Data flowing through orchestrations flows through orchestration interceptors in the Orchestration Event Bus (OrchestrationEventStream). When you utilize the Tracking Profile Editor, you are creating and configuring an interceptor for the MessagingEventStream and the OrchestrationEventStream.

Adapters, however, differ in that there are only interceptors for WCF and WF, instead of for all adapters. Data flowing through these adapters flows through the Direct Event Bus (DirectEventStream). There are two approaches to intercepting data for a custom adapter. Because the adapter will likely interface with an orchestration, you can use the Tracking Profile Editor and set a port mapping. If you're rolling your own adapter using a tool like the LOB Adapter Pack, and would like to highly customize your BAM interception, you may do so as well. Deciding where to intercept largely depends upon the design of your application.

Utilizing an interceptor includes two steps: creation and configuration. For messaging and orchestration interception, the Tracking Profile Editor is used to create the interceptors, and set forth a configuration for the pipeline and orchestration interceptors. WCF and WF differ, however, in that the interceptors have already been created. It is the role of the developer to enable and configure that interception, and map it to corresponding activities within the BAM database. Before jumping that far ahead, let's take a step back to the basics of a WCF service.

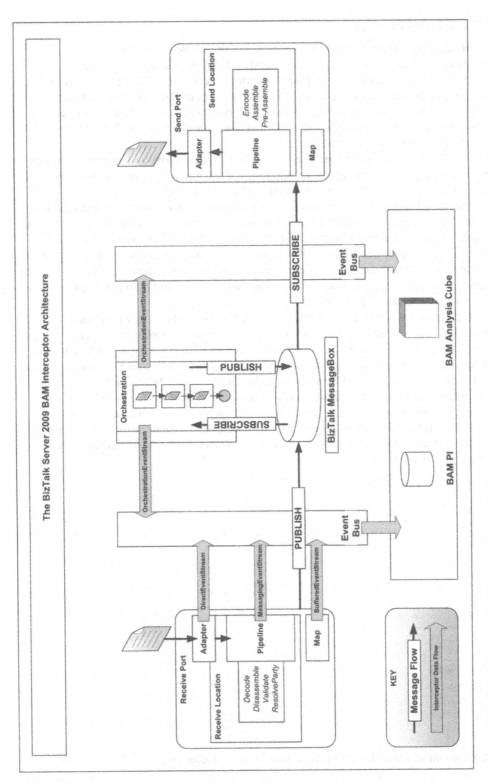

Figure 8-1. The BizTalk Server 2009 BAM interceptor architecture

The WCF Interceptor

As you'll recall, a WCF service is typically composed of three layers. All WCF services must implement a ServiceContract and a DataContract. The ServiceContract defines the OperationContracts, or operations, that the service may perform. The Service layer, or ServiceModel, includes the address, binding, contract, and behaviors. The DataContract defines the DataMembers, or data structures, that the service will support. At a lower level, WCF also provides the ability to access the Channel layer, surfacing protocols, transport, and encoding features (see Figure 8-2).

When WCF services are generated, they include both a client proxy and a server dispatcher. The client proxy and server dispatchers are duplicates of one another, and within the individual components include aspects that may be customized (see Figure 8-3).

Because they may be customized and ultimately extended, they also provide the means to gather data for BAM and send it to the BAM data store. Areas for extensibility include services, operations, endpoints, custom bindings, custom encoders, and custom transports.

The WCF interceptor was architected in this way. BizTalk has a custom endpoint behavior implemented using the Parameter Inspector and Message Inspector classes of the WCF service to gather BAM checkpoint data, listen for events as they are fired, and then create the resultant DirectEventStream to send data to the BAM Primary Import tables.

The BAM infrastructure allows WCF services (service dispatchers) or WCF clients (client proxies) to record data against a BAM activity. By attaching itself to a WCF endpoint, the WCF endpoint behavior provides the same level of functionality a traditional MessagingEventStream-based or OrchestrationEventStream-based interceptor does: continuations, document references, and recordation of BAM activity data. When the WCF channel is first opened, the WCF endpoint loads the WCF behavior, and interception begins.

For the WCF Receive adapter, the WCF channel is opened through a class derived from the ServiceHost base class if an in-process BizTalk host is used. When the receive location is started, the channel is opened. If the BizTalk Host is isolated, a ServiceHost factory-derived class opens the WCF channel.

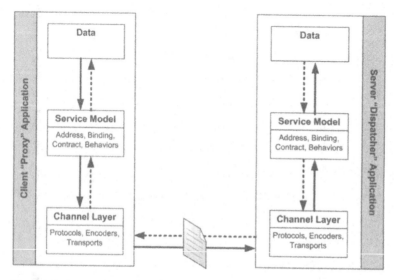

Figure 8-2. *Communications between a WCF proxy and WCF dispatcher*

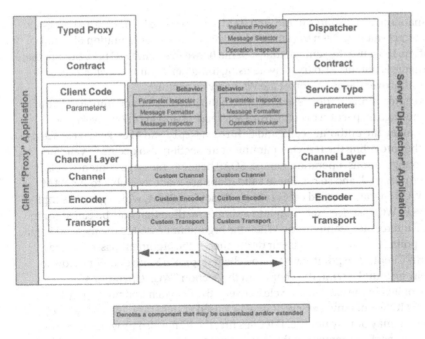

Figure 8-3. *Customization points between a WCF proxy and WCF dispatcher*

For the WCF Send adapter (the proxies), when a subscription criteria is met for the adapter, the WCF channel is opened. A dynamic ChannelFactory is created and the message(s) are sent out.

The specific WCF endpoint behavior that is attached to the WCF channel may be found within the Microsoft.BizTalk.Interceptors.dll. The DLL includes namespaces for both WCF and WF, and may be found in the Tracking directory of the BizTalk Server 2009 installation. BAMEndPointBehaviorExtension is a class in the DLL that reads from the WCF configuration information in order to create the BAM WCF interceptor, and set the connection string to the BAM Primary Import database as well as the polling interval value to query for new interceptor configurations. The behavior is applied, the interceptor is initialized, and interception continues until the WCF channel is disposed. The WCF interceptor is loaded and configured within either the ApplyClientBehavior or ApplyDispatchBehavior of the WCF framework.

Aside from its data to activity mapping, the IC file must be deployed to the BAM database for a number of other reasons. One of the most important is that the deployment process executed using bm.exe verifies that the manifest set forth in the IC file maps to a valid DLL. Upon initialization of the WCF service, an internal utility, named InterceptorConfiguration-Management, queries the BAM database to retrieve a rowset of interceptor configurations. The results are filtered by technology type: WCF or WF. Because the rowset may contain multiple interceptor configurations, the tracking profile may span multiple WCF services or multiple WF workflows, and multiple BAM activities that use the same .NET assembly containing the ServiceContracts or workflows.

What does this mean to the developer? If you have a service that exposes a ServiceContract, you may have multiple interceptor configurations. Setting the source and the manifest to use is performed using the interceptor configuration EventSource element, as described later in this chapter. It's important, if not crucial, however, that between multiple deployed IC files the combination of a manifest, event source name, and BAM activity name be unique. Otherwise, you risk having incorrect values written to your BAM activity by other configuration files and their definitions. If you must use the same manifest name between separate IC files, be sure that your event source name is unique. Also try to avoid using the generic contracts whenever possible, if you have control over the definition of the WCF service contract.

Once the interceptor configuration is loaded within the interceptor and initialized, four events within the message inspection occur: BeforeSendRequest and AfterReceiveReply (within the proxy making the outbound call), and BeforeSendReply and AfterReceiveRequest (within the dispatcher providing the reply). A parameter inspection also occurs to validate endpoint names, configurations, operation names, SOAP headers, message contents, SOAP faults that may have occurred, and so on. These validations are made available to the BAM developer using a WCF operation called GetServiceContractCallPoint, which greatly simplifies the many stages of WCF service execution into a simple method that may be called (or in the case of the WCF interceptor, configured). When the argument passed to the method begins with "Service," the point is within the service or dispatcher. If the argument passed to the method begins with "Client," the point is within the client or proxy. More details on how to use this method may be found later in the chapter in the section "WCF Operations."

These tracking points in the execution cycle between the dispatch and proxy may be filtered against in the IC file, meaning an event may be raised at this stage. By setting forth criteria for this event, it may or may not fire. If it does fire, the IC file also provides an action to perform, such as an Update statement to the BAM activity (more on updates later within the chapter in the section "The OnEvent Element").

Now with an understanding of how the interceptor technology works, let's dive into how to set it up.

WCF and BizTalk: So Happy Together

It's important to remember that WCF integrates with BizTalk in three ways: via the adapter, the publication of an orchestration as a WCF service endpoint, and the interceptor.

The WCF adapters provide the capability for BizTalk to communicate with WCF-based applications through the many WCF bindings. BizTalk includes five WCF adapters preconfigured to work with specific bindings: BasicHttpBinding, WsHttpBinding, NetTcpBinding, NetNamedPipeBinding, and NetMsmqBinding. The adapters that correspond to these bindings are the WCF-BasicHttp adapter, WCF-WSHttp adapter, WCF-NetTcp adapter, WCF-NetNamedPipe adapter, and WCF-NetMsmq adapter. BizTalk also includes the WCF-Custom adapter and WCF-CustomIsolated adapter to allow for custom or nondefault binding scenarios. The WCF adapters are used in a scenario when you have created an application that surfaces specific capabilities through a service façade into the application's data store. When BizTalk must call into that façade layer, the adapter is used. Of these adapters, the WCF-Custom adapter and WCF-CustomIsolated adapter may be used for BAM interception. The remaining adapters, however, do not support adding custom behavior extensions.

The publication of an orchestration as a WCF service is used when the opposite scenario occurs: your application wishes to call into BizTalk and instantiate an orchestration using WCF. The BAM interceptor may be used in this scenario as well: the publication of an orchestration as a WCF service is essentially building a custom adapter. By default, the ability to intercept BAM data travelling through the custom adapter, however, is not enabled. The interception of BAM data is performed using a WCF behavior attached to the WCF service endpoint.

The WCF interceptor provides the capability to support the tracking of data within WCF services, regardless of whether the BizTalk engine is interfacing with them.

In order for the interceptor to work properly, the behavior must be made available to WCF-based adapters. This can be done in multiple files, including app.config and machine.config. Because BAM solutions include executables for the BizTalk engine, tracking and interception, and ServiceHosts for WCF, it is recommended that the BAM interceptor behavior be added at the machine.config level.

EXERCISE 8-1. ADDING THE BAM INTERCEPTOR BEHAVIOR TO THE MACHINE.CONFIG FILE

If you're using the BizTalk WCF adapter and you wish to enable it to work with the BAM WCF interceptor, you must first add a behavior to the machine.config file on which the BizTalk host instance of the adapter is running. There are two ways to do this: either edit the machine.config file to include the behavior or use the Service Configuration Editor to include the behavior. As it's a great deal faster, we'll cover the manual method.

1. To edit the machine.config file manually, first open the file, which is located in the Microsoft .NET configuration folder: select Start ➤ Run, type **notepad c:\WINDOWS\Microsoft.NET\Framework\ v2.0.50727CONFIG\machine.config**, and then click OK.

■**Note** The .NET Framework 3.0 and 3.5 "wrap" the machine.config file used within the .NET Framework 2.0. Therefore, the folder you select should be v2.0.50727.

---

2. Update the machine.config file to include the following behavior extensions:

```
<system.serviceModel>
<extensions>
<behaviorExtensions>
<add name="BAMEndPointBehaviorExtension"
type="Microsoft.BizTalk.Bam.Interceptors.Wcf.BamEndpointBehavior,
Microsoft.BizTalk.Bam.Interceptors, Version=3.0.1.0, Culture=neutral,
PublicKeyToken=31bf3856ad364e35" />
</behaviorExtensions>
</extensions>
</system.serviceModel>
```

3. Close and save the machine.config file.

Adding BAMEndPointBehaviorExtension to the machine.config file will make the extension available for any WCF service on the machine. If you want to expose your orchestration as a WCF service and wish to track either the message data or service calls into the service using BAM, you must follow these three steps:

1. Create a WCF service using the BizTalk WCF Service Publishing Wizard.

2. Configure the BizTalk Server receive and send locations and ports using the BizTalk Administration Console.

3. If hosted within IIS, configure the web service application pool and directory security to provide the proper level of access.

By this point of the book, you should have a basic working knowledge of using BizTalk's wizards and know how to create a WCF service to expose the orchestration using a binding and corresponding adapter of your choosing. Therefore, this content is not covered here.

EXERCISE 8-2. CONFIGURING RECEIVE AND SEND LOCATIONS AND PORTS FOR BAM WCF INTERCEPTION

Once BAMEndPointBehaviorExtension is made available to all WCF services on the machine, it must also be linked to the specific location and port you wish to associate it with.

1. Open the BizTalk Administration Console.

2. Expand the console tree and navigate to the Receive Locations node for your BizTalk application. Click BizTalk Server 2006 Administration, click Applications, click the application you selected in the WCF Service Type dialog box, and then click Receive Locations. If you have created your WCF service properly, there will be a new receive location corresponding to the one you created. It will be in disabled status.

3. Double-click the receive location. This will open the Receive Location Properties dialog box. Choose WCF-Custom as the transport type.

4. Click the Configure button to open the Transport Properties dialog box.

5. Click the Binding tab and select the binding you want to use.

6. Click the Behavior tab, right-click the EndpointBehavior node, and then select Add Extension.

7. Select the BAMEndPointExtension (the extension you added to the machine.config file), and then click OK.

8. Select the extension you just created, set the PollingIntervalSec to 10, and set the ConnectionString to

   ConnectionString: Integrated Security=SSPI;Persist Security Info=False;
   Initial Catalog=BAMPrimaryImport;Data Source=<your server name>

9. Click OK.

10. In the Receive Location Properties dialog box, select PassThruReceive from the Receive Pipeline drop-down list, and then click OK.

11. Enable the receive location and refresh the Administration Console. If the status is started, the setup was successful.

The Syntax of a WCF Interceptor File

So now you've enabled calls to your orchestration via the WCF Service Publishing Wizard to be intercepted by BAM, or you've begun to consider intercepting calls to WCF services that don't interface with BizTalk. It's time to define how that message data or calls to services will map to your observation model. That mapping, within WCF and WF, is done by creating an interceptor file.

The interceptor file is based upon XML Schemas stored in the <Installation Path>\Microsoft BizTalk Server 2006\SDK\Samples\BAM\InterceptorXSDs directory. These files, CommonInterceptorConfiguration.xsd, WcfInterceptorConfiguration.xsd, and WorkflowInterceptorConfiguration.xsd, are used by the bm.exe utility to validate the configuration file before deployment.

The CommonInterceptorConfiguration schema, shown in Figure 8-4, is shared between both the WCF and WF interceptors, with additional validation specified by the additional schemas. Specific portions of the schema are of great interest when building your IC file.

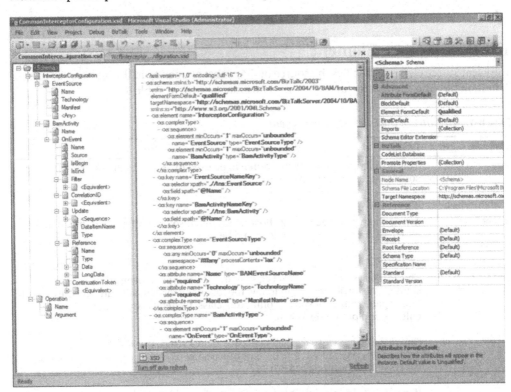

Figure 8-4. *The CommonInterceptorConfiguration schema file when opened in Visual Studio 2008*

When creating the IC file for your BAM WCF interceptor, it's important to understand the key portions of the schema. The IC file is not only a means to map data items the service processes to your observation model, but also a definition of how the specific methods within the interceptor should process that data. Five methods of specific interest exist within the code of the WCF interceptor. Rather than having to write code against them, the IC file is a means to map the data input to parameters fed into those methods. The interceptor uses the file to call these methods within the BAM API:

- BeginActivity(activityName, activityInstance)

- UpdateActivity(activityName, activityInstance, params object[] data)

- EndActivity(activityName, activityInstance)

- EnableContinuation(activityName, activityInstance, continuationToken)

- AddReference(activityName, activityID, referenceType, referenceName, referenceData, longReferenceData)

■**Note** More information on these methods as well as the BAM API may be found in Chapter 10.

The EventSource Element

The EventSource element specifies the source of the events appearing in the interceptor configuration file. The element includes the three attributes shown in Table 8-1.

Table 8-1. *Attributes of the EventSource Element*

Attribute	Details
Name	This is the name of the event source to be used by OnEvent entries to refer to the source. An example would be Name="ProcessingService"
Technology	This is the type of technology hosting the event source indicated in the manifest, either WCF or WF. An example would be Technology="WCF"
Manifest	This is the assembly-qualified class name of the type to be used as an event source. The attribute should follow the following format, substituting the correct namespace, subnamespace, containing class, nested class, assembly, version, culture, and public key token. Manifest = TopNamespace.SubNameSpace.ContainingClass+NestedClass, MyAssembly, Version=1.0.0.0, Culture=neutral, PublicKeyToken=d92g5g029353n25 If you do not have a public key token, specify PublicKeyToken=null.

An example of an EventSource element containing the preceding example would be

```
<ic:EventSource Name="ProcessingService" Technology="WCF" Manifest="
TopNamespace.SubNameSpace.ContainingClass+NestedClass, MyAssembly, Version=1.0.0.0,
Culture=neutral, PublicKeyToken=d92g5g029353n25"/>
```

The BAMActivity Element

The BAMActivity element simply defines the name of the BAM activity and is a container for other elements. The element includes only one attribute, listed in Table 8-2.

Table 8-2. *Attributes of the BAMActivity Element*

Attribute	Details
Name	This is the name, as defined by the user, of the BAM activity. An example would be Name="Order"

Following is an example of a BAMActivity element containing the preceding example:

```
<ic:BamActivity Name="Order">
   ...
</ic:BamActivity>
```

The OnEvent Element

The OnEvent element is the heart of the config file definition. It defines a logical event that is mapped to the BAMActivity element that encloses it. The OnEvent element contains four attributes, and these are presented in Table 8-3.

Table 8-3. *Attributes of the OnEvent Element*

Attribute	Details
Name	This is the name of the event as defined by the user. An example would be Name="OrderValidation"
Source	This is the name of the event source as you defined it in the EventSource element. An example would be Source="ProcessingService"
IsBegin	This is a Boolean flag indicating whether the event is the beginning of a new BAM activity (true) or not (false). An example would be IsBegin="true"
IsEnd	This is a Boolean flag indicating whether the event is the end of a BAM activity (true) or not (false). An example would be IsEnd="false"

Following is an example of an OnEvent element containing the preceding example:

```
<ic:OnEvent Name="OrderValidation"  Source="ProcessingService"
IsBegin="true" IsEnd="false">
   ...
</ic:OnEvent>
```

The OnEvent element will also include child elements, shown in Table 8-4.

Table 8-4. *Child Elements of the OnEvent Element*

Element	Details
Filter	This is a means to limit the event to specific criteria. Filter elements are top-level elements with no attributes. They contain Expression elements. If the expression evaluates to true, the event is processed. If the expression evaluates to false, the event is skipped. For example

```
<ic:Filter>
  <ic:Expression>
    <wcf:Operation Name="GetServiceContractCallPoint"/>
      <ic:Operation Name ="Constant">
        <ic:Argument>ServiceRequest</ic:Argument>
      </ic:Operation>
      <ic:Operation Name ="Equals"/>   </ic:Expression>
</ic:Filter>
```

This expression will be processed when the current contract call point for the WCF service is equal to ServiceRequest.

Element	Details
CorrelationID	This element specifies the activity instance ID for correlation purposes. CorrelationID elements are top-level elements with no attributes. They contain Expression elements. The expression can retrieve data from a message for correlation purposes, such as the Social Security number. Such retrieval is done via XPath, for example:

```
<ic:CorrelationID>
  <ic:Expression>
    <wcf:Operation Name ="XPath">       <wcf:Argument>//s:Body/social:SSN</
wcf:Argument>
    </wcf:Operation>
  </ic:Expression>

</ic:CorrelationID>
```

Operations excluded within a CorrelationID element include And and Equals.

Element	Details
Continuation-Token	This element specifies the continuation token ID, which is used for correlation as well. The ContinuationToken element correlates the event with future events that will contribute to the same activity instance. For instance, for a specific activity or process, it may be that different identifiers would better correlate the activity throughout the course of its life cycle within BAM. One such example would be BillingAddressID, ShippingAddressID, and FulfillmentCenterAddressID, each a unique address-related data item provided during different parts of the order process. However, in order to correlate these addresses, a common token must be identified. In this instance, an OrderID would be common between them all. The ContinuationToken element token is a top-level element with no attributes. It contains Expression elements. For example

```
<ic:ContinuationToken>
  <ic:Expression>
    <wcf:Operation Name="XPath">
    <wcf:Argument>//Order/OrderID</wcf:Argument>
    </wcf:Operation>
  </ic:Expression>
</ic:ContinuationToken>
```

Operations not allowed within a ContinuationToken element are And and Equals. Continuations were covered in Chapter 6.

Element	Details
Update	This element specifies the data to extract from the event and import into the BAM activity. It is a top-level element with two attributes, DataItemName (the BAM activity checkpoint name, or column, that will be updated with the extracted data) and Type (given as NVARCHAR, DATETIME, INT, or FLOAT). For example

```
<ic:Update DataItemName="Name" Type="NVARCHAR">
   <ic:Expression>
     <wcf:Operation Name="XPath">
       <wcf:Argument>//s:Body/ccservice:*/ccservice:creditCard/
creditcard:FirstName</wcf:Argument>
     </wcf:Operation>
     <wcf:Operation Name="XPath">
       <wcf:Argument>//s:Body/ccservice:*/ccservice:creditCard/
creditcard:LastName</wcf:Argument>
     </wcf:Operation>
     <ic:Operation Name ="Concatenate"/>
   </ic:Expression>
  </ic:Update>
```

This configuration will update the Name column within the BAM activity data item with the concatenation of the FirstName and LastName data within the message that is passed through the a credit card processing service. Operations not allowed within an Update element are And and Equals.

Element	Details
Reference	This element adds a reference to a BAM activity. It is a top-level element that contains either Data or LongData elements (Data is used for strings up to 128 characters, and LongData is for anything longer). References and relationships are covered in Chapter 12.

The Reference element has two attributes, Name (which is an arbitrary string that names the relationship that will be attached to the activity) and Type (another arbitrary string or BAM Reference type string that defines the type of relationship to be attached to the BAM activity). For example

```
<ic:Reference Name="Student Progress" Type="Student">
  <ic:Data>
    <ic:Expression>
      <ic:Operation Name="Constant">
        <ic:Argument>Student ID: </ic:Argument>
      </ic:Operation>
      <wcf:Operation Name="XPath">
        <wcf:Argument>//s:Body//session:StudentID</wcf:Argument>
      </wcf:Operation>
      <ic:Operation Name="Concatenate" />
    </ic:Expression>
  </ic:Data>
  <ic:Data>

    <ic:Expression>
      <ic:Operation Name="Constant">
        <ic:Argument>Total Session Hours: </ic:Argument>
      </ic:Operation>
      <wcf:Operation Name="XPath">
```

(continued)

Table 8-4. *Child Elements of the OnEvent Element*

Element	Details

Reference	`<wcf:Argument>//s:Body//session:Note</wcf:Argument>`
	`</wcf:Operation>`
	`<ic:Operation Name="Concatenate" />`
	`</ic:Expression>`
	`</ic:LongData>`
	`</ic:Reference>`
	
	When a parent calls to inquire about his or her child's e-learning bill, it's helpful for each correlated e-learning session to be correlated to the bill. The preceding Reference element references the StudentID, total number of sessions to date, and notes from the instructor so that the parent may track the student's progress against number of hours to determine whether the e-learning sessions are working. You guessed it, operations not allowed within a Reference element are And and Equals.

Expression Elements

You may have noticed that the appearance and syntax for Expression elements and their enclosing elements seem a bit strange. That's because the IC config file uses postfix notation, otherwise referred to as reverse Polish notation (no, we didn't make that up), or RPN.

The basic principle of RPN is that the operator appears after the operands. As an example, consider adding three to four. In this expression, the operators are the numbers 3 and 4. The operand is plus (+). The traditional arithmetic notation is *infix* notation, where the operator occurs between the operands. In infix notation, three added to four is represented as 3 + 4. RPN is a postfix notation, where that expression would be represented as 3 4 +. (And before you ask, there's another notation called prefix or forward Polish notation, where the same expression would be represented as + 3 4.) RPN was widely used with early programmable calculators. Many engineers will be familiar with the classic HP-41C calculator that used RPN.

RPN has two advantages. It makes the syntax for nested expressions very simple, and it's very easy to implement an RPN expression evaluator. Let's consider another expression: (3 + 4) * (5 + 6). This expression is equal to 7 * 11 = 77. In traditional infix notation, there's no way to write this expression without brackets. In RPN, you would write it as 3 4 + 5 6 + *. The way to understand this is to think about how RPN expressions are evaluated. When a number is seen, it is pushed onto the stack. When an operator is seen, it operates on the top two elements of the stack. Table 8-5 breaks the expression 3 4 + 5 6 + * down in terms of the stack contents.

Table 8-5. *Stack Contents of Expression 3 4 + 5 6 + **

Item	Stack Contents	Comments
3	3	Add 3 to stack.
4	4 3	Add 4 to stack.
+	7	Add top two items on stack, leave result on stack.
5	5 7	Add 5 to stack.
6	6 5 7	Add 6 to stack.
+	11 7	Add top two items on stack, leave result on stack.
*	77	Multiply top two items on stack, leave result on stack.

Stack-based evaluation makes it very easy to work with complex expressions. In IC files, the RPN expressions are expressed in XML. One operation that's defined in IC files is the Concatenate operation, which does a string concatenation. Here's an example of an RPN expression written in XML:

```
<ic:Expression>
    <ic:Operation Name="Constant">
        <is:Argument>Jeff</ic:Argument>
    </ic:Operation>
    <ic:Operation Name="Constant">
        <is:Argument>Geoff</ic:Argument>
    </ic:Operation>
    <ic:Operation Name="Concatenate" />
</ic:Expression>
```

This generates the string JeffGeoff. When it is evaluated, the constant "Jeff" is pushed on the stack, the constant "Geoff" is pushed on the stack, and then the two top elements on the stack are evaluated. You'll see many more examples of RPN later in the chapter.

Data items within the BAM interceptor file come in two flavors: filter expressions and data expressions. Filter expressions expect the result of the RPN expression to be a Boolean value of true or false, while data expressions expect a single value on the stack.

Filter Expressions

Filter expressions evaluate to true or false and are used in WCF or WF interception to detect when a specific event has occurred. In the case of WCF, it's common to want to get the name of the WCF service endpoint being accessed as well as the operation. Using the WCF operations (covered in the next section), a call to GetEndpointName and GetOperationName would return those values. If the endpoint name returned was CreditCardProcessorService and the operation was ValidateNumber, you could filter the data as

```
(GetEndpointName = "CreditCardProcessorService") &&
(GetOperationName = "ValidateNumber")
```

Converting this to RPN yields

```
GetEndpointName "CreditCardProcessorService" == GetOperationName
"ValidateNumber" == &&
```

Converting this expression to the equivalent expression for the interceptor configuration file results in the following XML:

```
<ic:Filter>
  <ic:Expression>
    <wf:Operation Name="GetEndpointName"/>
    <ic:Operation Name="Constant">
      <ic:Argument>CreditCardProcessorService</ic:Argument>
    </ic:Operation>
    <ic:Operation Name="Equals"/>
    <wf:Operation Name="GetOperationName"/>
    <ic:Operation Name="Constant">
      <ic:Argument>ValidateNumber</ic:Argument>
    </ic:Operation>
    <ic:Operation Name="Equals"/>
    <ic:Operation Name="And"/>
  </ic:Expression>
</ic:Filter>
```

Data Expressions

Data expressions are simply used to define a single string value. A data expression may be defined as any expression that is not enclosed by a `Filter` element. Data expressions are used by the `OnEvent` elements `CorrelationID`, `ContinuationToken`, `Reference`, and `Update`.

Following is an example of a data expression:

```
<ic:Operation Name="Constant">
    <ic:Argument>Blue</ic:Argument>
</ic:Operation>
```

Interceptor Operations

Three operation types are utilized when defining an interceptor configuration file: WCF operations, WF operations, and common or shared operations, which are used with both technologies.

Shared Operations

Table 8-6 lists the four operations that are exposed to both the WCF and WF interceptors to be used within your filter expressions:

```
<ic:Filter>
  <ic:Expression>
...
  </ic:Expression>
</ic:Filter>
```

Table 8-6. *Shared Operations*

Operation	Details
And	The And operation is typically used if you need to evaluate multiple statements as true or false. For example, if (A = "Value1") AND (B = "Value2") The syntax is given as <ic:Operation Name="And"/>. Note the IC prefix.
Concatenate	The Concatenate operation is typically used if you want to concatenate multiple string values, either as constants or as the result of calls to operations. You can use these in a filter expression or an update expression. An example would be wanting to update based upon the start time of the call to the WCF service: ```<ic:Expression>\n <ic:Operation Name="Constant">\n <ic:Argument>StartTime: </ic:Argument>\n </ic:Operation>\n <wcf:Operation Name="GetContextProperty">\n <wcf:Argument>EventTime</wf:Argument>\n </wcf:Operation>\n <ic:Operation Name="Concatenate" />\n</ic:Expression>``` The syntax is given as <ic:Operation Name="Concatenate" />
Constant	The Constant operation simply treats the value as a string. An example would be ```<ic:Operation Name="Constant">\n <ic:Argument>Blue</ic:Argument>\n</ic:Operation>``` The syntax is given as <ic:Operation Name="Constant"> and requires an argument as well.
Equals	The Equals operation simply compares the two expressions. An example would be ```<ic:Filter>\n <ic:Expression>\n <ic:Operation Name="Constant">\n <ic:Argument>Apples</ic:Argument>\n </ic:Operation>\n <ic:Operation Name="Constant">\n <ic:Argument>Apples</ic:Argument>\n </ic:Operation>\n <ic:Operation Name="Equals"/>\n </ic:Expression>\n</ic:Filter>``` which would allow you to compare apples to apples. The syntax is given as <ic:Operation Name="Equals"/>.

WCF Operations

The WCF Interceptor provides six operations, listed in Table 8-7, to extend filter and updating capabilities within an interceptor configuration file.

Table 8-7. *WCF Operations*

Operation	Details

AutoGenerateCorrelationToken	The AutoGenerateCorrelationToken operation is typically used when there is no correlation token present in the message, but you still want to correlate the information from a request and a reply. Using the operation will allow you to correlate a particular request/reply on either the client or the service side. This operation is typically used with continuations.
	An example, which shows the syntax of the operation, would be
	
	`<ic:CorrelationID>`
	`  <ic:Expression>`
	`    <wcf:Operation Name="AutoGenerateCorrelationToken"/>`
	`  </ic:Expression>`
	`</ic:CorrelationID>`

GetContextProperty	The GetContextProperty operation will return either the current date and time or the workflow session ID. This operation is used perhaps the most frequently to determine milestones. An example used in an update element would be
	
	`<ic:Update DataItemName ="Card Processing Time" Type ="DATETIME">`
	`  <ic:Expression>`
	`    <wcf:Operation Name ="GetContextProperty">`
	`    <wcf:Argument>EventTime</wcf:Argument>`
	`    </wcf:Operation>`
	`  </ic:Expression>`
	`</ic:Update>`
	
	This expression would retrieve the current date and time and map them to the credit card processing time.

GetEndpointName	The GetEndpointName operation will return the name of the current service endpoint (the name value) or `<binding>_<contract>` if the name value is not set. The syntax of the operation is `<wcf:Operation` `Name="GetEndpointName" />`.

GetOperationName	The GetOperationName operation will return a string representing the name of the current operation. An example would be
	
	`<ic:Filter>`
	`  <ic:Expression>`
	`    <wcf:Operation Name="GetOperationName" />`
	`    <ic:Operation Name="Constant">`
	`<ic:Argument>ValidateCreditCard</ic:Argument>`
	`    </ic:Operation>`
	`  </ic:Expression>`
	`</ic:Filter>`

Operation	Details
GetServiceContractCallPoint	The GetServiceContractCallPoint operation is used to intercept the contract at during different stages in the lifetime of interacting with a WCF service. Specifically, the contract may be intercepted at ClientReply, ClientRequest, ClientFault, ServiceReply, ServiceRequest, ServiceFault, CallbackRequest, CallbackReply, and CallbackFault. This operation, when used in conjunction with the GetOperationName and GetEndpointName operations, can be very powerful.
XPath	The XPath operation will extract the string value from a valid XPath expression that's provided.

A Walkthrough with Common IC File Examples

There are a number of common scenarios found in IC files. You may have noticed that certain methods tend to be called more often than others. In general, writing an IC file can be broken down into four repeatable steps:

1. Define the event source; that is, what general name you are going to refer to the event source as, which technology it uses (WCF or WF), and what manifest is to be used as the event source.

2. Define the BAM activity, that is, what activity you are defining to view in the BAM Portal or what your consuming application is. Remember to make this unique and specific to your scenario.

3. Define the event or events, that is, on which event or events in the client/proxy processing cycle you want to want to perform some action.

4. Define your actions to perform, that is, whether you want to update data in the BAM activity or utilize continuations, correlations, or references.

Let's walk through a couple common examples of building IC files.

Example 1: Sales and Fulfillment by Region

Because WCF services are oftentimes exposed using SOAP and XML, the XPath capabilities of the WCF interceptor may be considered invaluable.

The AWO Corporation allows its sales force in the field to create orders on their laptops for customers while disconnected, and then, when near an access point, submit the XML-based orders to a WCF service. Orders are fulfilled in several regional manufacturing centers in the following geographic regions: Northeast, Middle Atlantic, Southeast, Central, South, Northwest, and Southwest. A customer submitting an order in the Northeast may or may not have his or her order fulfilled there. The selection of the region to fulfill the orders is based upon a number of factors, including local labor costs (regional unions, average wage per employee, etc.), regional transportation costs (diesel fuel, highway taxes, etc.), and availability of raw materials in the region.

The AWO Logistics group has devised numerous calculations that will derive the most cost-effective region in which to fulfill the order, and has been tasked with identifying order patterns and developing techniques to reduce long-term costs for AWO. Long-term costs may be reduced by having the correct number of trucks at a facility rather than having to drive them from a nearby facility, thus increasing costs; or by examining regional fuel costs and attempting to maximize the amount of goods to be shipped in a truck.

The Logistics group approaches IT and asks that from each order the following data be captured and made available to its members via a Logistics BAM Portal: CustomerName, CustomerRegion, ItemName, ItemQuantity, ItemWeight, OrderDate, and DeliveryDate.

Fortunately, the sales catalog made available on each salesperson's laptop includes those data points. An excerpt of the XML order message is as follows:

```xml
<?xml version="1.0" encoding="utf-8"?>
 <order id="A6242966-BB0E-48f6-B654-1D3321AC2C77">
  <history>
   <creation>
    <dateTime>20090801 14:02:30 EST</dateTime>
    <user>Babe</user>
   </creation>
   <lastNodified>
    <dateTime>20090815 01:08:35 EST </dateTime>
    <user>Porky</user>
   </lastModified>
   <estimatedDelivery>
    <dateTime>20090817 12:00:00 EST</dateTime>
    <promissor>Piggy, Ms.</promissor>
   </estimatedDelivery>
   ...
  </history>
  <customer id="B38CE334-8527-4b06-B81A-60397C1C696F">
   <name>Petunia Pig</name>
   <salesRegionId>4</salesRegionId>
   ...
  </customer>
  <manifest>
   <item id="C18028DB-D7B7-4a35-A3E2-CF2FA7E14A1E">
   <name>Porcus Home Wrap - 20 ft. roll</name>
   <quantity>5</quantity>
   <description>Protects your structure from the elements.</description>
   <dimensions>
    <weightQuantity>50</weightQuantity>
    <weightUoM>kg</weightUoM>
   </dimensions>
   ...
   </item>
  </manifest>
 </order>
</xml>
```

Now that we have what we need, let's build the IC file.

First, let's start out with the basics of the file, and then create the event source. We start with the document declaration and namespace reference for WCF interception.

```xml
<?xml version="1.0" encoding="utf-8"?>
<ic:InterceptorConfiguration xmlns:ic="http://schemas.microsoft.com/BizTalkServer/
2004/10/BAM/InterceptorConfiguration" xmlns:wcf="http://schemas.microsoft.com/
BizTalkServer/2004/10/BAM/WcfInterceptorConfiguration" >
```

Next, we define the event source. In this case, it's the order processing service exposed by AWO.

```xml
<ic:EventSource Name="AWOOrderProcessingServiceSource" Technology="WCF"
Manifest="AWOServices.IProcessOrders, AWOServices, Version=1.0.0.0, Culture=neutral,
PublicKeyToken=null">
    <wcf:NamespaceMappings>
      <wcf:Namespace Prefix ="order" Uri="http://tempuri.org/"/>
      <wcf:Namespace Prefix="s" Uri="http://www.w3.org/2003/05/soap-envelope" />
    </wcf:NamespaceMappings>
  </ic:EventSource>
```

Then we create the activity we wish to define in BAM and our observation model.

```xml
<ic:BamActivity Name="OrdersProcessingByRegion">
```

We next define an event to be raised (condition to be met). Because our activity is self-contained, IsBegin and IsEnd can be set to true. We set Source to our event source defined previously.

```xml
<ic:OnEvent IsBegin="true" IsEnd ="true" Name ="Create"
Source="AWOOrderProcessingServiceSource">
```

Now that we have our container for the event, we have to actually provide the condition to be met using a Filter element. Each order makes a request to a WCF service, specifically, to the ProcessOrder method. Knowing that, we can decide to use the GetServiceContractCall-Point operation to make sure we're examining each request to the service, but also limit it to only requests made to the ProcessOrder method by using GetOperationName. We have two criteria: GetServiceContractCallPoint = "ServiceRequest", and GetOperationName = "ProcessOrder". Using RPN, the logic would look something like this:

```
GetServiceContractCallPoint
ServiceRequest
Equals
GetOperationName
ProcessOrder
Equals
And
```

Formatting this as XML, we get the following:

```
<ic:Filter>
   <ic:Expression>
     <wcf:Operation Name="GetServiceContractCallPoint" />
     <ic:Operation Name="Constant">
       <ic:Argument>ServiceRequest</ic:Argument>
     </ic:Operation>
     <ic:Operation Name="Equals" />
     <wcf:Operation Name="GetOperationName" />
     <ic:Operation Name="Constant">
       <ic:Argument>ProcessOrder</ic:Argument>
     </ic:Operation>
     <ic:Operation Name="Equals" />
     <ic:Operation Name="And" />
   </ic:Expression>
</ic:Filter>
```

Let's consider any correlation or continuation needs. We need to identify a correlation token. In our case, the Logistics department will drive its business needs off of the SalesRegionId. The business activity will be driven based upon this value, so it makes sense for us to set it up as a correlation token.

```
<ic:CorrelationID>
   <ic:Expression>
     <wcf:Operation Name ="XPath">
       <wcf:Argument>//salesRegionId</wcf:Argument>
     </wcf:Operation>
   </ic:Expression>
</ic:CorrelationID>
```

Lastly, we need to update BAM with the information that the Logistics department requested. The exact names the department requested were not found in the XML, so we'll have to do some simple mapping using Update statements to retrieve and map. For each data item, we need to create a separate update node, as follows:

```
<ic:Update DataItemName="CustomerName" Type="NVARCHAR">
       <ic:Expression>
         <wcf:Operation Name ="XPath">
           <wcf:Argument>//customer/name</wcf:Argument>
         </wcf:Operation>
       </ic:Expression>
     </ic:Update>
     <ic:Update DataItemName="CustomerRegion" Type="NVARCHAR">
       <ic:Expression>
         <wcf:Operation Name ="XPath">
           <wcf:Argument>//customer/salesRegionId</wcf:Argument>
         </wcf:Operation>
       </ic:Expression>
     </ic:Update>
```

```
    <ic:Update DataItemName="ItemName" Type="NVARCHAR">
      <ic:Expression>
        <wcf:Operation Name ="XPath">
          <wcf:Argument>//item/name</wcf:Argument>
        </wcf:Operation>
      </ic:Expression>
    </ic:Update>
    <ic:Update DataItemName="ItemQuantity" Type="NVARCHAR">
      <ic:Expression>
        <wcf:Operation Name ="XPath">
          <wcf:Argument>//item/quantity</wcf:Argument>
        </wcf:Operation>
      </ic:Expression>
    </ic:Update>
    <ic:Update DataItemName="ItemWeight" Type="NVARCHAR">
      <ic:Expression>
        <wcf:Operation Name ="XPath">
          <wcf:Argument>//item/dimensions/weightQuantity</wcf:Argument>
        </wcf:Operation>
        <wcf:Operation Name ="XPath">
          <wcf:Argument>//item/dimensions/weightUoM</wcf:Argument>
        </wcf:Operation>
        <ic:Operation Name="Concatenate" />
      </ic:Expression>
    </ic:Update>
    <ic:Update DataItemName="OrderDate" Type="NVARCHAR">
      <ic:Expression>
        <wcf:Operation Name ="XPath">
          <wcf:Argument>//order/history/creation/dateTime</wcf:Argument>
        </wcf:Operation>
      </ic:Expression>
    </ic:Update>
    <ic:Update DataItemName="DeliveryDate" Type="NVARCHAR">
      <ic:Expression>
        <wcf:Operation Name ="XPath">
          <wcf:Argument>//order/history/estimatedDelivery/dateTime</wcf:Argument>
        </wcf:Operation>
      </ic:Expression>
    </ic:Update>
```

Note that we aggregated the two weight values together to provide Logistics with an easy-to-read value with context. Lastly, we have to close all of the tags:

```
    </ic:OnEvent>
  </ic:BamActivity>
</ic:InterceptorConfiguration>
```

The final IC file is as follows:

```xml
<?xml version="1.0" encoding="utf-8"?>
<ic:InterceptorConfiguration xmlns:ic="http://schemas.microsoft.com/
BizTalkServer/2004/10/BAM/InterceptorConfiguration"
xmlns:wcf="http://schemas.microsoft.com/BizTalkServer/2004/10/
BAM/WcfInterceptorConfiguration" >
  <ic:EventSource Name="AWOOrderProcessingServiceSource" Technology="WCF"
Manifest="AWOServices.IProcessOrders, AWOServices, Version=1.0.0.0, Culture=neutral,
PublicKeyToken=null">
    <wcf:NamespaceMappings>
      <wcf:Namespace Prefix ="order" Uri="http://tempuri.org/"/>
      <wcf:Namespace Prefix="s" Uri="http://www.w3.org/2003/05/soap-envelope" />
    </wcf:NamespaceMappings>
  </ic:EventSource>
  <ic:BamActivity Name="OrdersProcessingByRegion">
    <ic:OnEvent IsBegin="true" IsEnd ="true" Name ="Create"
      Source="AWOOrderProcessingServiceSource">
    <ic:Filter>
      <ic:Expression>
        <wcf:Operation Name="GetServiceContractCallPoint" />
        <ic:Operation Name="Constant">
          <ic:Argument>ServiceRequest</ic:Argument>
        </ic:Operation>
        <ic:Operation Name="Equals" />
        <wcf:Operation Name="GetOperationName" />
        <ic:Operation Name="Constant">
          <ic:Argument>ProcessOrder</ic:Argument>
        </ic:Operation>
        <ic:Operation Name="Equals" />
        <ic:Operation Name="And" />
      </ic:Expression>
    </ic:Filter>
    <ic:CorrelationID>
      <ic:Expression>
        <wcf:Operation Name ="XPath">
          <wcf:Argument>//salesRegionId</wcf:Argument>
        </wcf:Operation>
      </ic:Expression>
    </ic:CorrelationID>
    <ic:Update DataItemName="CustomerName" Type="NVARCHAR">
      <ic:Expression>
        <wcf:Operation Name ="XPath">
          <wcf:Argument>//customer/name</wcf:Argument>
        </wcf:Operation>
      </ic:Expression>
    </ic:Update>
    <ic:Update DataItemName="CustomerRegion" Type="NVARCHAR">
```

```
      <ic:Expression>
        <wcf:Operation Name ="XPath">
          <wcf:Argument>//customer/salesRegionId</wcf:Argument>
        </wcf:Operation>
      </ic:Expression>
    </ic:Update>
    <ic:Update DataItemName="ItemName" Type="NVARCHAR">
      <ic:Expression>
        <wcf:Operation Name ="XPath">
          <wcf:Argument>//item/name</wcf:Argument>
        </wcf:Operation>
      </ic:Expression>
    </ic:Update>
    <ic:Update DataItemName="ItemQuantity" Type="NVARCHAR">
      <ic:Expression>
        <wcf:Operation Name ="XPath">
          <wcf:Argument>//item/quantity</wcf:Argument>
        </wcf:Operation>
      </ic:Expression>
    </ic:Update>
    <ic:Update DataItemName="ItemWeight" Type="NVARCHAR">
      <ic:Expression>
        <wcf:Operation Name ="XPath">
          <wcf:Argument>//item/dimensions/weightQuantity</wcf:Argument>
        </wcf:Operation>
        <wcf:Operation Name ="XPath">
          <wcf:Argument>//item/dimensions/weightUoM</wcf:Argument>
        </wcf:Operation>
        <ic:Operation Name="Concatenate" />
      </ic:Expression>
    </ic:Update>
    <ic:Update DataItemName="OrderDate" Type="NVARCHAR">
      <ic:Expression>
        <wcf:Operation Name ="XPath">
          <wcf:Argument>//order/history/creation/dateTime</wcf:Argument>
        </wcf:Operation>
      </ic:Expression>
    </ic:Update>
    <ic:Update DataItemName="DeliveryDate" Type="NVARCHAR">
      <ic:Expression>
        <wcf:Operation Name ="XPath">
          <wcf:Argument>//order/history/estimatedDelivery/dateTime</wcf:Argument>
        </wcf:Operation>
      </ic:Expression>
    </ic:Update>
  </ic:OnEvent>
 </ic:BamActivity>
</ic:InterceptorConfiguration>
```

Example 2: WCF Service Usage

As simple as it sounds, a common and prevalent usage of BAM with WCF is to determine use of the service or methods the service offers. Versioning of publicly exposed WCF services can be a challenge: you create a service to perform some processing, and after some time, realize that additional features or capabilities need inclusion. Because service contracts are explicit, by changing the contract, you risk compatibility issues. Many times during the service life cycle, a developer must decide whether the new service or operation should deprecate the older functionality.

As a sample scenario, consider a credit card processing service. At one time, transactions online simply involved providing the name and number of the cardholder. Over time, as numbers were recorded in databases that were later compromised by malicious code, credit cards numbers found their way into the hands of hackers. As such, financial institutions began inclusion of a three- or four-digit security code on the back of each card, as well as the billing postal code of the cardholder.

In this scenario, a WCF service previously existed with a C# method signature as follows:

```
[OperationContract]
public bool Validate(string cardNumber, string cardholderName,
DateTime expirationDateTime);
```

After the financial institutions introduced the requirement to also include the security code and billing postal code, a new method was introduced, with the following signature:

```
[OperationContract]
public bool ValidateSecure(string cardNumber, string cardholderName, DateTime
expirationDateTime, int securityCode, string billingPostalCode);
```

Members of IT Operations want to know whether there are any callers to the Validate method so that they may set a date by which the older method will be no longer be supported based upon usage, and create additional revenue via an "extended support" model.

To create an IC file for this scenario, we begin with the document and namespace declarations:

```
<?xml version="1.0" encoding="utf-8"?>
<ic:InterceptorConfiguration xmlns:ic="http://schemas.microsoft.com/
BizTalkServer/2004/10/BAM/InterceptorConfiguration"
xmlns:wcf="http://schemas.microsoft.com/BizTalkServer/2004/
10/BAM/WcfInterceptorConfiguration" >
```

Next, we define the event source. In this case, it's the credit card validation service.

```
<ic:EventSource Name="CardValidationServiceSource" Technology="WCF"
Manifest="AWOServices.IValidateCards, AWOServices, Version=1.0.0.0,
Culture=neutral, PublicKeyToken=null">
    <wcf:NamespaceMappings>
      <wcf:Namespace Prefix ="card" Uri="http://tempuri.org/"/>
      <wcf:Namespace Prefix="s" Uri="http://www.w3.org/2003/05/soap-envelope" />
    </wcf:NamespaceMappings>
  </ic:EventSource>
```

Then we create the activity we wish to define in BAM and our observation model.

```
<ic:BamActivity Name="CallsToDeprecatedService">
```

We next define the event to be raised. The activity is self-contained, so IsBegin and IsEnd can be set to true. We set Source to our event source defined previously.

```
<ic:OnEvent IsBegin="true" IsEnd ="true" Name ="ValidateCall" Source="
CardValidationServiceSource ">
```

Next, we provide the condition to be met using a Filter element. We need to use two methods, Validate and ValidateSecure. Simply enough, we're looking for any requests to the service (ServiceRequest) where the method being called is the deprecated method, Validate. Again, we use the GetServiceContractCallPoint operation to make sure we're examining each request to the service, and limit it to only requests made to the Validate method by using GetOperationName. We have two criteria: GetServiceContractCallPoint = "ServiceRequest" and GetOperationName = "Validate". Using RPN, the logic would look something like this:

```
GetServiceContractCallPoint
ServiceRequest
Equals
GetOperationName
Validate
Equals
And
```

Formatting this as XML, we get the following:

```
<ic:Filter>
  <ic:Expression>
    <wcf:Operation Name="GetServiceContractCallPoint" />
    <ic:Operation Name="Constant">
      <ic:Argument>ServiceRequest</ic:Argument>
    </ic:Operation>
    <ic:Operation Name="Equals" />
    <wcf:Operation Name="GetOperationName" />
    <ic:Operation Name="Constant">
      <ic:Argument>Validate</ic:Argument>
    </ic:Operation>
    <ic:Operation Name="Equals" />
    <ic:Operation Name="And" />
  </ic:Expression>
</ic:Filter>
```

There's no real need here to correlate information between requests or activities. Once a single call is made, IT Operations has no intent of keeping a record of which card numbers or postal codes were sent, just that the service was called. As such, we can autogenerate a correlation token like this:

```
<ic:CorrelationID>
  <ic:Expression>
```

```
    <wcf:Operation Name="AutoGenerateCorrelationToken"/>
  </ic:Expression>
</ic:CorrelationID>
```

Next, we create the action to perform, an `Update` block, to track the call and record the date and time of the call:

```
<ic:Update DataItemName ="ValidateMethodRequestInstance" Type ="DATETIME">
  <ic:Expression>
    <wcf:Operation Name ="GetContextProperty">
     <wcf:Argument>EventTime</wcf:Argument>
    </wcf:Operation>
  </ic:Expression>
</ic:Update>
```

Finally, we close our tags.

```
</ic:OnEvent>
  </ic:BamActivity>
</ic:InterceptorConfiguration>
```

The final IC file is as follows:

```
<?xml version="1.0" encoding="utf-8"?>
<ic:InterceptorConfiguration xmlns:ic="http://schemas.microsoft.com/
BizTalkServer/2004/10/BAM/InterceptorConfiguration"
xmlns:wcf="http://schemas.microsoft.com/BizTalkServer/2004/
10/BAM/WcfInterceptorConfiguration" >
<ic:EventSource Name="CardValidationServiceSource" Technology="WCF"
Manifest="AWOServices.IValidateCards, AWOServices, Version=1.0.0.0,
Culture=neutral, PublicKeyToken=null">
    <wcf:NamespaceMappings>
      <wcf:Namespace Prefix ="card" Uri="http://tempuri.org/"/>
      <wcf:Namespace Prefix="s" Uri="http://www.w3.org/2003/05/soap-envelope" />
    </wcf:NamespaceMappings>
  </ic:EventSource>
<ic:BamActivity Name="CallsToDeprecatedService">
<ic:OnEvent IsBegin="true" IsEnd ="true" Name ="ValidateCall" Source="
CardValidationServiceSource ">
    <ic:Filter>
      <ic:Expression>
        <wcf:Operation Name="GetServiceContractCallPoint" />
        <ic:Operation Name="Constant">
          <ic:Argument>ServiceRequest</ic:Argument>
        </ic:Operation>
        <ic:Operation Name="Equals" />
        <wcf:Operation Name="GetOperationName" />
        <ic:Operation Name="Constant">
          <ic:Argument>Validate</ic:Argument>
        </ic:Operation>
```

```
            <ic:Operation Name="Equals" />
            <ic:Operation Name="And" />
         </ic:Expression>
      </ic:Filter>
<ic:CorrelationID>
  <ic:Expression>
    <wcf:Operation Name="AutoGenerateCorrelationToken"/>
  </ic:Expression>
</ic:CorrelationID>
<ic:Update DataItemName ="ValidateMethodRequestInstance" Type ="DATETIME">
  <ic:Expression>
    <wcf:Operation Name ="GetContextProperty">
    <wcf:Argument>EventTime</wcf:Argument>
    </wcf:Operation>
  </ic:Expression>
</ic:Update>
</ic:OnEvent>
   </ic:BamActivity>
</ic:InterceptorConfiguration>
```

Configuring the BAM WCF Interception

Chapter 3 provides end-to-end coverage of how to configure WCF for interception and how to capture data from a WCF service external to BizTalk. By this point, you should have enabled the machine.config file, set the necessary send and receive ports and locations, and written an IC file that will provide the observation model you desire.

Fault Handling WCF Interception

In the event an exception occurs during the processing of a WCF request or response, the default behavior for WCF is not to return that exception to the client unless it is thrown as a FaultException (or inherited subtype) or if a FaultContract is implemented. It's important to consider fault handling in the context of the interceptor insomuch that as the number of activities grows and your BAM infrastructure monitors multiple systems, you'll have less time to track down individual errors as they occur. It is of paramount importance to develop a fault-handling strategy from the beginning.

Fortunately, BAM and the interceptor configuration file provide a means for doing so. The GetServiceContractCallPoint method includes the ability to pass a Constant argument as an argument representing the fault track point (e.g., ServiceFault, ClientFault, CallbackFault) and map to the point of a specific update action within the message to execute.

Unfortunately, there are limitations to this implementation due to the way in which WCF returns faults, specifically during the ServiceFault and ClientFault track points. In fact, the fault-handling strategy for the IC file is largely dependent upon how the WCF service handles faults itself. Provided you have captured the fault as part of your WCF response, you may use XPath to retrieve the fault and update it in your BAM activity.

The IC file with comments for such an approach follows:

```xml
<!-- Define an event that will populate your BAM Activity //-->
<ic:OnEvent IsBegin ="true" IsEnd="false" Name="AuthorizationServiceReply"
Source="ESCreditCardService">

<!-- This block filters on the fault track point ServiceReply, and on the
ValidateCreditCard method being invoked. //-->
<!-- When a ServiceReply occurs for method invocation, the filter will fire. //-->
  <ic:Filter>
    <ic:Expression>
      <wcf:Operation Name="GetServiceContractCallPoint"/>
      <ic:Operation Name ="Constant">
        <ic:Argument>ServiceReply</ic:Argument>
      </ic:Operation>
      <ic:Operation Name ="Equals"/>
      <wcf:Operation Name="GetOperationName" />
      <ic:Operation Name="Constant">
        <ic:Argument>ValidateCreditCard</ic:Argument>
      </ic:Operation>
      <ic:Operation Name ="Equals" />
      <ic:Operation Name ="And" />
    </ic:Expression>
  </ic:Filter>

<!-- This block is added to create a correlation token between the request and
the reply //-->
  <ic:CorrelationID>
    <ic:Expression>
      <wcf:Operation Name="AutoGenerateCorrelationToken"/>
    </ic:Expression>
  </ic:CorrelationID>

<!-- If a reply has occurred to the ValidateCreditCard operation at the
ServiceReply fault track point, mark the "Status" of the BAM Activity as
"Success" //-->
  <ic:Update DataItemName="Status" Type="NVARCHAR">
    <ic:Expression>
      <ic:Operation Name="Constant">
        <ic:Argument>Success</ic:Argument>
      </ic:Operation>
    </ic:Expression>
  </ic:Update>

<!-- If a reply has occurred to the ValidateCreditCard operation at the
ServiceReply fault track point, set the "Result" of the BAM Activity to
the value returned by the XPath expression provided below within the WCF
response message //-->
```

```xml
      <ic:Update DataItemName="Result" Type="NVARCHAR">
        <ic:Expression>
          <wcf:Operation Name ="XPath">
            <wcf:Argument>//s:Body/CreditCardService:*/CreditCardService:
ValidateCreditCardResult</wcf:Argument>
          </wcf:Operation>
        </ic:Expression>
      </ic:Update>

<!-- If a reply has occurred to the ValidateCreditCard operation at the
ServiceReply fault track point, set the "Service Call Date" of the
BAM Activity to the current date and time //-->
      <ic:Update DataItemName ="Service Call Date" Type ="DATETIME">
        <ic:Expression>
          <wcf:Operation Name ="GetContextProperty">
            <wcf:Argument>EventTime</wcf:Argument>
          </wcf:Operation>
        </ic:Expression>
      </ic:Update>

</ic:OnEvent>


<!-- If you wish, define another event that will populate your BAM Activity //>
<ic:OnEvent IsBegin ="true" IsEnd="false" Name="AuthorizationServiceFault"
Source="ESCreditCardService">

<!-- This block filters on the fault track point ServiceFault, and on
the ValidateCreditCard method being invocated. //-->
<!-- When a Service Fault occurs for method invocation, the filter will fire. //-->
  <ic:Filter>
    <ic:Expression>
      <wcf:Operation Name="GetServiceContractCallPoint"/>
      <ic:Operation Name ="Constant">
        <ic:Argument>ServiceFault</ic:Argument>
      </ic:Operation>
      <ic:Operation Name ="Equals"/>
      <wcf:Operation Name="GetOperationName" />
      <ic:Operation Name="Constant">
        <ic:Argument>ValidateCreditCard</ic:Argument>
      </ic:Operation>
      <ic:Operation Name ="Equals" />
      <ic:Operation Name ="And" />
    </ic:Expression>
  </ic:Filter>
```

```
<!-- This block is added to create a correlation token between the request
and the reply //-->
  <ic:CorrelationID>
    <ic:Expression>
      <wcf:Operation Name="AutoGenerateCorrelationToken"/>
    </ic:Expression>
  </ic:CorrelationID>

<!-- If a fault has occurred to the ValidateCreditCard operation at
the ServiceFault fault track point, mark the "Status" of the BAM Activity as
"Fault" //-->
  <ic:Update DataItemName="Status" Type="NVARCHAR">
    <ic:Expression>
      <ic:Operation Name="Constant">
        <ic:Argument>Fault</ic:Argument>
      </ic:Operation>
    </ic:Expression>
  </ic:Update>

<!-- If a fault has occurred to the ValidateCreditCard operation at the
ServiceFault fault track point, mark the "Source" of the BAM Activity as
the value returned by the XPath expression provided below within the WCF
response message within Reason/Text //-->
      <ic:Update DataItemName="Source" Type="NVARCHAR">
        <ic:Expression>
          <wcf:Operation Name ="XPath">
            <wcf:Argument>//s:Body/Fault/Reason/Text</wcf:Argument>
          </wcf:Operation>
        </ic:Expression>
      </ic:Update>

<!-- If a fault has occurred to the ValidateCreditCard operation at
the ServiceFault fault track point, mark the "Service Call Date" of the
BAM Activity to the current date/time //-->
  <ic:Update DataItemName ="Service Call Date" Type ="DATETIME">
    <ic:Expression>
      <wcf:Operation Name ="GetContextProperty">
        <wcf:Argument>EventTime</wcf:Argument>
      </wcf:Operation>
    </ic:Expression>
  </ic:Update>

</ic:OnEvent>
```

Loading the WCF Interceptor Using the BAM API

While Chapter 10 more comprehensively covers the BAM API, we felt it important to cover manual loading of the BAM interceptors in this chapter.

While it's not common, in some scenarios you would want to load the WCF interceptor using the BAM API rather than using a configuration file. Values within the config file, especially those in Filter elements or within Update elements, are static. Therefore, if you would like to change the values of the tracking profile on-the-fly, or if you would prefer to call your own methods against which to compare constants, you'll need to load the WCF interceptor manually using the BAM API.

The SDK utilizes the following (corrected) code to load the BAM interceptors using the BAM API. However, there are many ways in which this may be done. The BAM API, while largely undocumented, does include a great deal of functionality for interfacing with BAM via the API. More information on the BAM API may be found in Chapter 10.

In the code that actually opens the service, add a reference to the Microsoft.BizTalk. Interceptors.dll and add a using statement to Microsoft.BizTalk.Interceptors.Wcf. Add the following code:

```
internal class MyBamBehaviorExtension : BamBehaviorExtension
{
    internal MyBamBehaviorExtension(string connectionString,
        int pollingInterval)
        : base()
    {
        this.PrimaryImportConnectionString = connectionString;
        this.PollingIntervalSec = pollingInterval.ToString();
    }

    internal IEndpointBehavior Create()
    {
        return (IEndpointBehavior) this.CreateBehavior();
    }
}
```

Within the code that executes just before the service is actually opened, include the following code to add the endpoint behavior to the service:

```
MyBamBehaviorExtension bamBehaviorExtension =
new MyBamBehaviorExtension(ConfigurationManager.AppSettings["ConnectionString"],
int.Parse(ConfigurationManager.AppSettings["PollingIntervalSec"]));
    IEndpointBehavior bamBehavior = bamBehaviorExtension.Create();
    foreach (ServiceEndpoint endpoint in myServiceHost.Description.Endpoints)
    {
        if (endpoint.Behaviors.Find<MyBamBehaviorExtension>() == null)
            endpoint.Behaviors.Add(bamBehavior);
    }
```

This code also assumes that you are reading the ConnectionString value from the config file.

BAM Interceptor Performance Counters

There are six performance counters that are of interest to BAM WCF developers. These performance counters enable you to not only monitor performance, but also identify bottlenecks for your BAM WCF implementation. While a wiretapping pattern incurs negligible degradation, it is still helpful to have the counters to identify where activities may need to be restructured, or when calls to a WCF service are taking too long as a result of the binding endpoint behavior.

All of these performance counters, listed in Table 8-8, may be accessed by examining the performance counter category "BAM Interceptor."

Table 8-8. *Performance Counters*

Counter Name	Description
Avg. Failed BAM Events/ Flush Avg	The average number of failed BAM events that occurred during a flush of data to the Primary Import database. This number should be low or 0. If you are noticing increases, your BAM solution is likely encountering high amounts of traffic, or there are problems communicating with the Primary Import database. Consider archiving your BAM data, examining network latency, determining whether other processes are running on your BAM Primary Import database, examining transaction failures, or determining whether your BAM Activities are "too heavy" (meaning that entirely too much data is being collected within an activity definition).
Successful BAM Events/ Flush	The average number of successful BAM events that occurred during a data flush to the Primary Import database. The events may not be persisted to the database if the transaction is rolled back. Ideally this number should be as high as possible.
Avg. Extraction sec/ BAM Event	The average amount of time spent extracting BAM events. Remember, the design pattern used is a wiretapping one with the goal of the least amount of intrusion possible. Very detailed XPath queries, concatenations with a high number of data items, or very, very detailed filter expressions tend to cause a larger time period for extractions.
Avg. Flush sec/ BAM Event	The average amount of time spent flushing BAM events. This counter is something to monitor over several weeks and months as your BAM solution grows. At some point, you may want to scale up and scale out, and this is a great justification for doing so.
Total Failed BAM Events During Flush	The total number of failed BAM events that occurred during the data flush. If, when adding a WCF service to be monitored, you notice a spike in this number, your IC for that service definitely has some issues. However, most of the time, it's not that easy to determine. Use basic math between this and the Total Successful BAM Events During Flush to determine where your pain points lie.
Total Successful BAM Events During Flush	The total number of successful BAM events flushed to the Primary Import database. The events may not be persisted to the database if the transaction is rolled back.

Hosting and Security Considerations

When considering the many "moving pieces" in a solution that involves SQL Server, IIS, WCF, BAM, and the file system, it's clear that security and hosting options play a key role in the health of the overall solution.

The security roles you use when intercepting the WCF adapter are the same as those used for other BAM solutions. The additional considerations for intercepting the WCF adapter involve selecting the correct user and event writer role to use.

When using WCF services and the WCF adapter, all BAM-related data is written to the BAM Primary Import database by the selected role.

You can select the proper user role configuration by assessing your solution scenario. If your solution requires many new services that are tracked by many different activities and are all run under the same user account, it is advantageous to use the BAM event writer super role to write the intercepted events.

Note Users must be added to the BAM event writer super role. When adding a user to the super role, it is important to remember that the user will then be able to write to all the activities in the system.

If your solution requires greater control of the events written, you should use activity-specific roles.

Note Users must be added to the activity-specific event writer role for each activity.

Summary

In this chapter, we covered the architecture of the interceptors, diving into the implementation details, and then specifying the implementation for WCF. This chapter also covered the three ways that BizTalk and WCF integrate and went through an extensive (and hopefully exhaustive) coverage of the interceptor configuration file syntax. The chapter included fault-handling techniques within the WCF interceptor, as well as a code sample and a scenario on when and how to load the WCF interceptor programmatically. The chapter finished with tips on when to use each BAM performance counter and hosting and security considerations.

The next chapter will build upon the information provided in this chapter, covering how the BAM WF interceptor may be used to intercept data within WF workflows.

CHAPTER 9

■ ■ ■

Capturing Data from WF

Windows Workflow Foundation, or WF, is oftentimes compared to BizTalk's orchestration-underlying XLANG language. WF's underlying XAML language, like the XLANG language, provides an extensible and declarative means to describe the execution of a business process. Within BizTalk, this business process is implemented in the form of an orchestration. Within WF, the business process is executed as either a sequential or a state machine workflow.

Since WF's introduction and given the striking similarities to BizTalk orchestrations, BizTalk architects have wondered how WF is aligned with BizTalk, and whether that alignment takes advantage of the umbrella of ancillary technologies, such as BAM, that BizTalk has to offer. The answer is that WF may be positioned alongside BizTalk and BAM quite nicely, complementing BizTalk, BAM, and other technologies that are a part of BizTalk.

This chapter will cover the following:

- WF overview and concepts

- BizTalk orchestrations vs. WF workflows

- The WF interceptor architecture

- Understanding a WF tracking profile

- How to monitor a WF workflow with the WF interceptor

- The syntax of a WF interceptor file

- Editing the app.config file

- Exercises on monitoring WF with BAM

This chapter assumes you have basic knowledge of workflow within applications, XML, Visual Studio 2008, and BizTalk Server Administration.

While Microsoft has announced significant changes will be coming within .NET Framework 4.0 with regard to WF and WCF (effectively dubbed *WCF+WF 4.0*), you may assume that the next version of BizTalk, built upon the .NET Framework 4.0, will be updated to include these changes.

WF Overview and Concepts

Although it was known that Microsoft had an SOA product (Indigo) in the works at the time of Microsoft's Professional Developer's Conference 2005, little was known about its companion product, Windows Workflow Foundation, which was announced at the conference.

As the portfolio of Microsoft's server offerings has grown, so too has the number of proprietary implementations of workflow-like technology. While BizTalk implemented its own business process workflow first as orchestrations and then later added Human Workflow Services, products such as Content Management Server hosted long-running workflows some time ago. Microsoft also had no application-level workflow offering by which developers could build .NET applications without resorting to third-party offerings, such as K2 or Skelta.

With each server implementing its own flavor of workflow, it made sense for Microsoft to provide some "foundational" workflow APIs by which application-level workflows could be constructed and upon which additional capability could be built (e.g., Microsoft Office Share-Point Server builds its workflows using WF).

As WF emerged, many questioned whether it would replace XLANG as the execution engine of BizTalk. While the same team worked on both technologies, it was ultimately decided that the two technologies would coexist as they target different environments. In fact, Microsoft, as part of its pledge toward future BizTalk versions, has made it clear that existing investments within XLANG will never be sacrificed at the expense of the "latest and greatest."

Application Workflows

Within WF, a *workflow* represents the implementation of a specific process. Application code, in general, is the implementation of a specific process. What differentiates application code from a workflow is the means in which it executes and the way in which that execution is represented.

Workflows within WF execute in one of two ways: either sequentially or as a result of an event firing or a condition being met (referred to as *state machine workflows*). BizTalk orchestrations may be thought of as sequential as well. Figures 9-1 and 9-2 depict a sequential BizTalk orchestration and a sequential WF workflow. Note the similarities.

In building an orchestration, it's oftentimes known what the proposed outcome will be or what the set of steps to take place are. Sequential workflows lend themselves to the same design pattern: a fixed set of steps that largely follows a path from A to B and may take some tangents.

State machine workflows are more geared toward human interaction or interaction from an outside force. They are less fixed, less rigid, and more adept at handling events as they occur (see Figure 9-3). Over time, message and orchestration design patterns have emerged within BizTalk as a result of a desire to handle events in a nonlinear fashion. Publish-subscribe responds to the event of a message publication. The convoy pattern fully accepts message events will occur out of order and expects to build some mechanism to deal with them. The same may be said of the aggregator pattern.

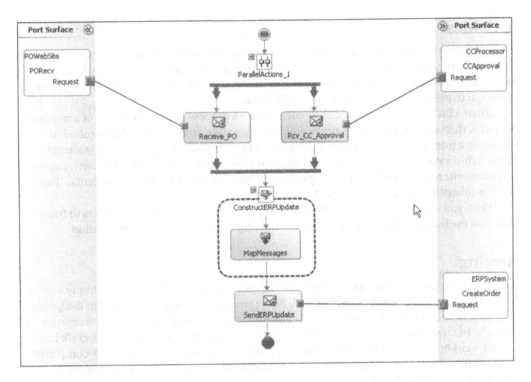

Figure 9-1. *BizTalk orchestration (sequential)*

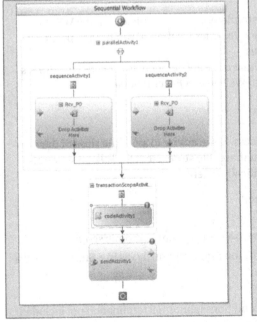

Figure 9-2. *WF sequential workflow*

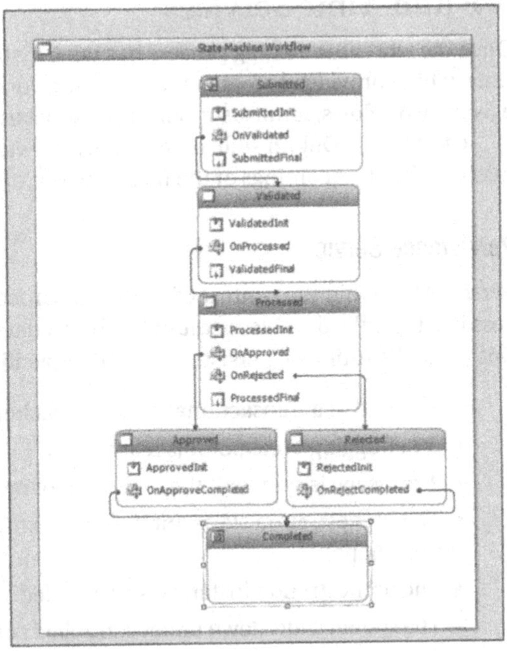

Figure 9-3. *A state machine workflow*

Activities

If a workflow represents the implementation of a specific process, activities represent the individual tasks or units of work of that process. Out of the box, BizTalk provides activities in the form of shapes within the toolbox. WF provides similar capabilities, but also the ability to build custom activities by inheriting from the activity class.

When a BizTalk developer wishes to encapsulate a process or promote reuse of a sequence of events, this is accomplished by either building a separate orchestration that is called or started by a primary orchestration or calling into a custom code component within a code shape. Within WF, a developer may encapsulate multiple activities in a single activity, known as a *composite activity*, instead of calling across activities (or their BizTalk equivalents). This is done by inheriting from the CompositeActivity class.

When you use the activities and the WF designer within Visual Studio, it begins to become clear that the toolset is largely geared toward building workflow within an application.

Hosting

From a purely physical standpoint, after creation, an orchestration file (ODX) is simply a code file. Likewise, a WF workflow is code as well. Both provide a rich visual interface for designing the code. BizTalk, however, has the distinct advantage of providing for not only the creation of the code, but also the execution environment, known as the BizTalk run time or BizTalk host.

WF workflows, in the form of WF libraries, must be executed using a .NET 2.0–compliant hosting process, such as a Windows Forms application, WPF application, Windows service, web application, console application, etc.

WF Run-Time Services

Once the workflow hosting process has been instantiated, it communicates to the WF run time, which provides access to the WF framework. In order for the WF run time to properly execute workflows, it must support three services.

Of note, the Dublin suite of technologies, while not fully detailed, is expected to address many of the shortcomings of the management of WCF and WF technologies.

Persistence Service

Persistence, within the context of a business process, is the ability to store the state of the process in a typically durable medium (such as a database, file store, etc.). BizTalk implements this capability utilizing persistence points, specifically when

- The end of a transactional scope is reached.
- A debugging breakpoint is reached.
- A message is sent with the exception of message being sent in atomic scope.
- The orchestration starts another orchestration asynchronously (as in a Start Orchestration shape).
- The orchestration instance is suspended.
- The system shuts down under controlled conditions (abnormal termination not included).
- The engine determines that the instance should be dehydrated.
- The orchestration instance is finished.

Some argue that the fact that BizTalk automatically provides management of its persistence points is beneficial to the developer; others argue that this persistence mechanism should be surfaced via an API and that calls to it should be made more explicit.

Because it is unknown where the WF run time will be hosted, WF implements a PersistenceService, which provides the ability to persist, dehydrate, or rehydrate the state of a workflow. A Windows Forms application, WPF application, or Windows service that runs continually manages the state of the workflow within the execution space of the application or service. But for an ASP.NET application, the state of the workflow must be maintained in some external store. In instances where the request made to the ASP.NET application is load balanced across multiple servers, there is no guarantee that the same server will receive the successive request. As such, some medium must be in place between changes to the business process to maintain the state of the workflow.

As with BizTalk, there are times when it is necessary to "sleep" a process, awaiting either external input or for a specific period of time to elapse. From a memory management standpoint, especially when considering scalability, keeping each workflow in memory soon becomes unrealistic.

WF provides one out-of-the-box persistence mechanism, SQL Server, using SqlWorkflowPersistenceService. Fortunately, unlike BizTalk, WF provides you the ability to "roll your own" persistence service by creating a class that inherits from the WorkflowPersistenceService class. As with SqlWorkflowPersistenceService, your persistence service then serializes the state of the workflow in the following instances:

- When a workflow becomes idle.
- When a workflow completes or terminates.
- When a TransactionScopeActivity completes.
- When a CompensatableSequenceActivity completes.
- When a custom activity that is decorated with the PersistOnCloseAttribute completes.
- When one of the methods on a WorkflowInstance is invoked that causes a persistence operation, such as Unload and TryUnload. The Load method results in a previously unloaded and persisted workflow being retrieved and loaded back into memory.

The mechanism utilized to persist to the store, binary representation and GZIP compression, is identical between BizTalk and WF.

Tracking Service

The WF Tracking Service is to HAT what WF workflows are to BizTalk orchestrations. The WF Tracking Service provides visibility into the execution process of a workflow, such as duration, decision points made and route taken, and completion state of activities executed therein. While many comparisons have been made between the WF Tracking Service and BAM, it's important to remember that BAM is business and activity focused, whereas the WF Tracking Service and HAT are message based.

As may be surmised, WF ships with one tracking service out of the box, the SqlTrackingService, which provides the ability to write tracking data to a SQL Server–based data store. Additional tracking services may be created to persist data and aggregated during the execution process (with some performance penalty, of course).

As with BAM, there are two primary phases to the design of a tracking profile for WF. However, BAM provides you at least one tool for the creation of an observational model, whereas

WF leaves implementation and configuration to the developer. Again, expect this shortcoming to be introduced with the Dublin suite of technologies, currently slated to be released at the time of Visual Studio 2010.

Scheduling Service

The WF Scheduling Service manages how workflow instances are scheduled by the workflow run-time engine. While not directly analogous, the WF Scheduling Service is akin to the service window capabilities found within a BizTalk receive or send location, providing for a specific date/time during which an orchestration may be executed.

The WF Scheduling Service provides two out of the box classes: `DefaultWorkflowScheduler-Service` and `ManualWorkflowSchedulerService`. The difference between the two largely has to do with the threading model; while the former is more positioned toward Windows Forms and WPF apps, the latter is geared toward ASP.NET applications.

Rules Engine

The purpose of a rules engine tool is the centralization of an application's or enterprise's business rules. From a central repository, rules are made accessible for reuse by multiple business processes and may be efficiently and consistently maintained while avoiding the need to change code in multiple places. Additionally, redeployments of rule sets are often unnecessary for small changes to variables. The underlying principles serve to promote reuse of code and abstraction of logic.

While BizTalk provides a rules engine in the form of the BRE, WF also provides its own rules engine in the form of the WFRE. Although they were engineered by the same team, the BRE and the WFRE differ greatly in their design and implementation.

BAM in the BizTalk vs. WF Debate

While similar in concept and designed by the same team, BizTalk and WF are strikingly different in their implementation. Table 9-1 summarizes those differences.

What emerges clearly from this comparison chart involving BAM are the following assertions:

- BizTalk orchestrations are better suited for business processes that execute across multiple systems.

- WF workflows execute best within a domain-specific application space.

- The tools and workflow technologies differ in their offerings.

- It is important to utilize the proper technology.

- BAM is the only technology that may take advantage of BizTalk, WCF, and WF by abstracting messages, activities, message data, or service calls into a higher level.

Think of BizTalk as executing business processes between systems. Think of WF as executing business processes within a system. Think of WCF as the entry points to and exit points from a system. Also, remember that as of .NET 3.5, WCF can be used to instantiate a WF workflow.

So how may the contents of a WF workflow or activity provide data to BAM? We'll explore that next.

Table 9-1. *A Feature-Based Comparison of BizTalk and WF As They Relate to BAM*

	BizTalk Orchestrations	WF Workflows	What This Means
Hosting model	Server-hosted. The BizTalk server run time executes the orchestration within a Windows service.	Application-hosted. The WF run time executes the workflow within a host, which may reside within an application executable (such as a console app, Winform app, or WPF app), or a Windows service (such as a Windows system service or ASP.NET).	BizTalk is more targeted toward SOA, B2B, EAI, and BAM—think "workflow for systems." WF is more targeted toward applications that humans use—think "workflow for people." Ultimately, workflow (that is, business process) is involved with both technologies. BAM may be used to monitor BizTalk workflow and WF workflow.
Activation	Orchestrations may be initiated when a message is received or when called by another orchestration.	WF workflows may be initiated when an activity is initiated or when a specific state is met.	Because BizTalk defines its idea of an event as a message being received or published, it is message-based. WF workflows may executed in the same means as code, but may also be initiated when a non-message-based event occurs. Within BizTalk, message execution, states, or data may be abstracted into BAM activities. Within WF, activities themselves may be considered BAM activities—there is less need for abstraction. BAM may monitor both regardless of activation model.

Continued

Table 9-1. *Continued*

	BizTalk Orchestrations	WF Workflows	What This Means
Processing models	Sequential. State machine workflows may be approximated by using messaging design patterns and/or implementing polling mechanisms to determine the state of an activity or message.	Sequential and state machine	A sequential workflow executes in a definite beginning-to-end flow (think "start to end"). Sequential workflows work best when the expected behavior is known at design time. A state-machine workflow executes when a specific event fires (think OnEventOccurs). State-machine workflows don't always execute in a predefined sequence and are usually centered around human interaction. Regardless of how the business process executes, BAM may monitor it from start to finish or at a single point on an event being raised—the processing model has no effect on the capabilities of BAM.
Persistence	BizTalk persists its message and orchestration instance state to a SQL Server–based persistence store at predefined persistence points automatically.	WF persists its workflow instance state to a durable relational database automatically, as well as binary files or XML via customization. Persistence occurs automatically or when manually specified using specific activity types (search MSDN for the WF "PersistOnCloseAttribute").	The persistence model for WF is a great deal more robust and is especially necessary given the robustness of human workflow scenarios. Because persistence is abstracted from a BizTalk orchestration and a WF workflow, BAM data may be sent at any point in the life cycle of execution. A BizTalk orchestration or a WF workflow may be rehydrated after several weeks or even months and suddenly begin reporting additional BAM data.

	BizTalk Orchestrations	WF Workflows	What This Means
Integration	BizTalk provides the ability to connect business processes between different systems or applications via adapters.	All WF integration must be created manually or by using tools such as the BizTalk LOB Adapter pack.	As long as the scope of the workflow is constrained to one application or one domain of processing, WF is a good choice. Beyond that, BizTalk is a better tool.
			Because BAM may be used to monitor BizTalk orchestrations, which cross systems, and WF workflows within a system, BAM provides an additional level of abstraction above the processing layer.
Business rules engine	Implemented through the BizTalk BRE.	Implemented through the WF Rules Engine.	Both technologies provide the means to assert whether specific conditions have been met, and to perform resultant steps accordingly. BAM is not tied to either rules engine. An advantage is that BAM is not tightly coupled, but a disadvantage is that the status or a rule being met or the value set within the rule must explicitly be reported to BAM. It's important to remember that if you wish for rules values to be reported to BAM, you must build the mechanism within your orchestration or WF activity.

Continued

Table 9-1. *Continued*

	BizTalk Orchestrations	WF Workflows	What This Means
Tracking	Tracking of both orchestrations (service instances) and messages comes out of the box with the BizTalk Management Console.	Instrumentation comes out of the box using the System.Workflow.Runtime. Tracking DLL and namespace and the WF Tracking Service. Developers may also implement their own tracking mechanisms.	BizTalk's ability to track execution of orchestrations is a powerful and compelling reason for its usage. Remember that tracking is limited to the scope of the message being processed within BizTalk. WF's tracking involves some enhancement and modification. Remember though that the tracking is limited to the application space with WF. With BizTalk, tracking is targeted toward the message level. With WF, tracking is targeted toward the (code) activity. While the WF model is more like BAM in the tracking of activities, WF does not differentiate between a business-based activity and a code activity. Additionally, when monitoring between BizTalk, WF, and WCF, BAM is the only way to provide a single view into activities that occur between the three technologies and provide some correlation or means to connect the transactions as they occur.
Transactions	BizTalk provides the ability to create both long-running and atomic transactions through the usage of Scope shapes and persistence points.	Implemented using a Transaction-ScopeActivity.	BizTalk transactions can span multiple systems, as long as those systems support enlistment in a distributed transaction. WF transactions are limited to the application execution space. The performance of a call into BAM depends upon the EventStream type being utilized. However, both Direct-EventStream and BufferedEventStream are transaction consistent.

	BizTalk Orchestrations	WF Workflows	What This Means
Administration and management tools	Orchestrations may be administered through the BizTalk Server Administration Console.	WF workflows must be administered through a custom application. The WF SDK provides some samples that help with basic management.	Expect to see more functionality surrounding WF administration with the Dublin release of tools. BAM does not figure into administration and management of either technology, unless the BAM activities being defined within the observation model are the messages or WF activities themselves. BAM, however, may be used to monitor BizTalk and WF solutions.

The WF Interceptor Architecture

As the overall interceptor architecture was covered in detail in Chapter 8, we won't revisit it again. However, it is important to understand how the WF interceptor works.

The WF interceptor is implemented as a WF Tracking Service named BamTrackingService, which inherits from the base TrackingService class and implements the IProfileNotification interface. The WF run time sends three types of events to a tracking service: workflow events, activity events, and user events. These events are implemented as track points.

Workflow events, as you may imagine, provide visibility into the life cycle of the workflow instance with events such as Created, Completed, Idle, Suspended, Resumed, Persisted, Unloaded, Loaded, Exception, Terminated, Aborted, Changed, and Started.

Activity events describe and provide visibility into the life cycle of an activity instance. Status events for an activity include Executing, Closed, Compensating, Faulting, and Canceling.

User events are defined by the developer of the workflow and the activity. Each activity offers a TrackData() method with two overloads. The objectData or key and objectData passed to this method is passed to the tracking service as a User event.

The tracking run time, which executes within the host application, uses a tracking profile similar to BAM's to filter which events will be reported to the tracking service. Because BamTrackingService determines the items to be tracked based upon what the BAM developer determines should be tracked via the IC file, the implementation of BamTrackingService is unique.

When BamTrackingService is first initialized, it first creates a new instance of a BamProfileManager, the primary class used to manage BAM tracking profiles as they relate to WF tracking profiles, validating and managing track points, and validating activities, users, and workflows. The configuration file is read to set the ConnectionString to the PI tables as well as the polling interval, and then WF event source names are read into a collection.

The first functional event that occurs is a TryGetProfile() call from the tracking run time to the tracking service, requesting a specific workflow type and tracking profile. The first attempt is to retrieve a local WF tracking profile. An attempt is then made to retrieve an interceptor configuration from the PI tables for the specific workflow event source. Providing everything is successful, BamProfileManager then takes over and begins parsing the interceptor configuration via the SetupMetadata and HelpSetupMetadata methods. A TrackingProfile object is returned. This object is the mechanism that communicates which events, by way of its call to the PI tables, are to be observed rather than monitoring *all* events that occur within the WF workflow.

The tracking run time then calls the GetTrackingChannel() method from BamTrackingService. A BamTrackingChannel is a mechanism to handle the tracking events and data that occur within the workflow instance. It's important to note that in its construction, the BamTrackingChannel instantiates a DirectEventStream object and a WorkflowInspector object. The WorkflowInspector object actually transforms tracking data and produces events that are recorded to the BAM Primary Import database.

At execution time, events and data that the service requested through the tracking profile are sent to the tracking channel for the instance via the Send method of the tracking channel. A new tracking channel is used for each WF workflow instance, preventing synchronization and locking issues from occurring as each workflow instance runs on a single thread.

Understanding a WF Tracking Profile

WF tracking profiles are much like BAM tracking profiles. WF tracking profiles include workflow track points, activity track points, and user track points. So what is a track point? Simply a construct that defines information on the type of data to collect and when to collect it.

A WF tracking profile is simply a collection of track points. The BAM WF interceptor, by way of the SetupMetadata method, actually performs mapping between the WF interceptor configuration (which in essence is a BAM tracking profile) and the WF tracking profile.

Without going into too much detail here (you can find detailed info on MSDN by searching for "Windows Workflow Foundation: Tracking Services Deep Dive"), the WF tracking profile is structured as follows:

- WorkflowTrackPoints
  - MatchingLocations
    - Events
  - Annotations
- Activity TrackPoint
  - Matching/Excluded Locations
    - ActivityType
    - MatchDerivedTypes
    - ExecutionStatusEvents (for example, Executing or Closed)
    - Conditions
      - Member
      - Operator (Equals/Not Equals)
      - Value
  - Annotations
  - Extracts
    - Workflow Extract
    - Activity Extract
- User TrackPoint
  - Matching/Excluded Locations
    - ActivityType
    - MatchDerivedActivityTypes
    - ArgumentType
    - MatchDerivedArgumentTypes
    - KeyName
    - Conditions
      - Member
      - Operator (Equals/Not Equals)
      - Value

- Annotations
- Extracts
  - Workflow Extract
  - Activity Extract

From a cursory glance, a BAM tracking profile/interceptor configuration and a WF tracking profile appear rather similar.

How to Monitor a WF Workflow with the WF Interceptor

The basic process for enabling BAM to monitor WF workflows is as follows:

1. Create the WF workflow(s) within a WF class library.

2. Decide upon a hosting model for the workflow.

3. Install the BAM Eventing software if it is not already installed.

4. Create and deploy an observation model.

5. Create and deploy the interceptor configuration file.

6. Ensure that the user under which the WF host application executes is set with the correct (bam_<activity>_EventWriter) SQL Server roles to enable the application to read the interceptor configuration information and write to the BAM activities.

7. Modify the WF application app.config file to load the BAM Tracking Service or manually load the BAM Tracking Service within your code, and then restart the application.

With a little experience with WF, you should be familiar with each of these steps with the exception of creating the interceptor configuration file targeted toward WF applications and modifying the app.config file. Let's cover the WF IC file first.

The Syntax of a WF Interceptor File

The WF interceptor file is based upon XML Schemas stored in the <Installation Path>\Microsoft BizTalk Server 2009\SDK\Samples\BAM\InterceptorXSDs directory. These files, CommonInterceptorConfiguration.xsd, WcfInterceptorConfiguration.xsd, and WorkflowInterceptorConfiguration.xsd, are used by the bm.exe utility to validate the configuration file before deployment.

Chapter 8 covered the WCF interceptor schema as well as the CommonInterceptor-Configuration schema. The WorkflowInterceptorConfiguration schema includes the following:

```
<xs:element name="Operation">
  <xs:complexType>
    <xs:sequence>
      <xs:element name="Argument" type="xs:string" minOccurs="0"
          maxOccurs="unbounded" />
    </xs:sequence>
    <xs:attribute name="Name" type="WorkflowOperationType" use="required" />
  </xs:complexType>
</xs:element>

<xs:simpleType name="WorkflowOperationType">
  <xs:restriction base="xs:string">
    <xs:enumeration value="GetActivityName" />
    <xs:enumeration value="GetActivityEvent" />
    <xs:enumeration value="GetWorkflowEvent" />
    <xs:enumeration value="GetActivityType" />
    <xs:enumeration value="GetUserDataType" />
    <xs:enumeration value="GetUserKey" />
    <xs:enumeration value="GetUserData" />
    <xs:enumeration value="GetWorkflowProperty" />
    <xs:enumeration value="GetActivityProperty" />
    <xs:enumeration value="GetContextProperty" />
  </xs:restriction>
</xs:simpleType>
```

As stated in Chapter 8, the config file for your BAM WF interceptor is really just a means for BAM to call specific methods without requiring you to write code, namely

- `BeginActivity(activityName, activityInstance)`

- `UpdateActivity(activityName, activityInstance, params object[] data)`

- `EndActivity(activityName, activityInstance)`

- `EnableContinuation(activityName, activityInstance, continuationToken)`

- `AddReference(activityName, activityID, referenceType, referenceName, referenceData, longReferenceData)`

The EventSource Element

The EventSource element specifies the source of the events appearing in the interceptor configuration file. The element includes the three attributes listed in Table 9-2.

Table 9-2. *Attributes for the EventSource Element*

Attribute	Details
Name	This is the name of the event source to be used by OnEvent entries to refer to the source. An example would be Name="ProcessingWorkflow".
Technology	This is the type of technology hosting the event source indicated in the manifest, either WCF or WF. For WF, the setting is Technology="WF".
Manifest	This is the assembly-qualified class name of the type to be used as an event source. An example would be Manifest = TopNamespace.SubNameSpace.ContainingClass+ NestedClass, MyAssembly, Version=1.0.0.0, Culture=neutral, PublicKeyToken= d92g5g029353n25. If you do not have a public key token, specify PublicKeyToken=null.

Following is a complete example of an EventSource element for WF:

```
<ic:EventSource Name="ProcessingWorkflow" Technology="WF"
Manifest="SimpleWorkflow.OrderWorkflow, SimpleWorkflow, Version=0.0.0.0,
Culture=neutral, PublicKeyToken=null"/>
```

The BAMActivity Element

The BAMActivity element simply defines the name of the BAM activity and is a container for other elements. The element includes only one attribute, which is listed in Table 9-3.

Table 9-3. *Attributes for the BAMActivity Element*

Attribute	Details
Name	This is the name, as defined by the user, of the BAM activity. An example would be Name="Order".

Following is an example of a BAMActivity element containing the preceding example:

```
<ic:BamActivity Name="Order">
    ...
</ic:BamActivity>
```

The OnEvent Element

The OnEvent element is the heart and soul of the config file definition. It defines a logical event that is mapped to the BAMActivity element that encloses it. The OnEvent element contains the four attributes listed in Table 9-4.

Table 9-4. *Attributes for the* OnEvent *Element*

Attribute	Details
Name	This is the name of the event as defined by the user. An example would be Name="OrderValidation".
Source	This is the name of the EventSource as defined in the EventSource element. An example would be Source="ProcessingWorkflow".
IsBegin	This is a Boolean flag indicating whether the event is the beginning of a new BAM activity (true) or not (false). An example would be IsBegin="true".
IsEnd	This is a Boolean flag indicating whether the event is the end of a BAM activity (true) or not (false). An example would be IsEnd="false".

The OnEvent element will also include child elements, as listed in Table 9-5.

Table 9-5. *Child Elements of the* OnEvent *Element*

Element	Details
Filter	This is a means to limit the event to specific criteria. A Filter element is a top-level element with no attributes. It contains Expression elements. If the expression evaluates to true, the event is processed. If the expression evaluates to false, the event is skipped. For example ``` <ic:Filter> <ic:Expression> <wf:Operation Name="GetActivityName"/> <ic:Operation Name="Constant"> <ic:Argument>CompareBuildingMaterials</ic:Argument> </ic:Operation> <ic:Operation Name="Equals"/> <wf:Operation Name="GetActivityEvent"/> <ic:Operation Name="Constant"> <ic:Argument>Closed</ic:Argument> </ic:Operation> <ic:Operation Name="Equals"/> <ic:Operation Name="And"/> </ic:Expression> </ic:Filter> ``` This filter will limit the event processing to when the call to GetActivityName returns the value CompareBuildingMaterials and when the call to GetActivityEvent equals Closed.
CorrelationID	This element specifies the activity instance ID for correlation purposes. CorrelationID elements are top-level elements with no attributes. They contain Expression elements. The expression can retrieve data from a message for correlation purposes, such as the BuilderID, a common value stored between all workflows as a property. For example ``` <ic:CorrelationID> <ic:Expression> <wf:Operation Name="GetWorkflowProperty"> <wf:Argument>BuilderID</wf:Argument> </wf:Operation> </ic:Expression> </ic:CorrelationID> ```

Continued

Table 9-5. *Continued*

Element	Details

ContinuationToken	This element specifies the continuation token ID, which is used for correlation as well. The ContinuationToken element correlates the event with future events that will contribute to the same activity instance. For instance, for a specific activity or process, it may be that different identifiers would better correlate the activity throughout the course of its life cycle within BAM. One such example would be BillingAddressID, ShippingAddressID, and FulfillmentCenterAddressID, each a unique address-related data item provided during different parts of the Order process. However, in order to correlate these addresses, a common token must be identified. In this instance, an OrderID would be common between them all. Within each workflow, a workflow property named ContinuationToken is defined and stores the OrderID. For example
	`<ic:ContinuationToken>`
	`  <ic:Expression>`
	`    <wf:Operation Name="GetWorkflowProperty">`
	`      <wf:Argument>ContinuationToken</wf:Argument>`
	`    </wf:Operation>`
	`  </ic:Expression>`
	`</ic:ContinuationToken>`
	Use ContinuationToken if you have a singular BAM activity for which you wish to record data from multiple events.
	Use CorrelationID if you have multiple BAM activities that you wish to correlate.

Update	This element specifies the data to extract from the event and import into the BAM activity. It is a top-level element with two attributes, DataItemName (the BAM activity checkpoint name, or column, that will be updated with the extracted data) and Type (given as NVARCHAR, DATETIME, INT, or FLOAT). For example
	`<ic:Update DataItemName="StartHistoryLookup" Type="DATETIME">`
	`  <ic:Expression>`
	`    <wf:Operation Name="GetContextProperty">`
	`      <wf:Argument>EventTime</wf:Argument>`
	`    </wf:Operation>`
	`  </ic:Expression>`
	`</ic:Update>`
	In the preceding example, the call to GetContextProperty will retrieve the current date and time and store it as the value StartHistoryLookup within the BAM activity.

Reference	This element adds a reference to a BAM activity. It is a top-level element that contains either Data or LongData elements (Data is used for strings up to 128 characters, and LongData is for anything longer).
	The Reference element has two attributes, Name (which is an arbitrary string that names the relationship that will be attached to the activity) and Type (another arbitrary string or BAM Reference type string that defines the type of relationship to be attached to the BAM activity). For example
	`<ic:Reference Name="Generated Document" Type="DocumentUrl">`
	`  <ic:Data>`
	`    <ic:Expression>`
	`      <wf:Operation Name="GetUserData" />`
	`    </ic:Expression>`
	`  </ic:Data>`
	`</ic:Reference>`
	A good example of when to use a Reference value is when data in the activity would be useful to be included in an output alert or BAM activity. In this example, the call to GetUserData returns the UserData stored within the WF activity and stores it in the BAM activity.

WF Interceptor Operations

You may have noticed within the WF interceptor schema an enumeration of WFOperationTypes. The WF interceptor provides the ten operations listed in Table 9-6 to extend filter and updating capabilities within an interceptor configuration file.

Table 9-6. *Operations Specific to the WF Interceptor*

Operation	Description

GetActivityEvent	There are several states through which a WF activity is assigned during the lifetime of a workflow instance. GetActivityEvent will filter for a specific execution status of the WF activity.
	 Execution statuses included are Canceling, Closed, Compensating, Executing, and Faulting.
	 It's important to remember in your filter expression to filter on both the name of the WF activity as well as the WF activity event.
	 For example, the following will filter for when the PerformCreditCheck WF activity reaches a Closed state:
	 `<ic:Filter>`
	 `  <ic:Expression>`
	 `    <wf:Operation Name="GetActivityName"/>`
	 `    <ic:Operation Name="Constant">`
	 `      <ic:Argument>PerformCreditCheck</ic:Argument>`
	 `    </ic:Operation>`
	 `    <ic:Operation Name="Equals"/>`
	 `    <wf:Operation Name="GetActivityEvent"/>`
	 `    <ic:Operation Name="Constant">`
	 `      <ic:Argument>Closed</ic:Argument>`
	 `    </ic:Operation>`
	 `    <ic:Operation Name="Equals"/>`
	 `    <ic:Operation Name="And"/>`
	 `  </ic:Expression>`
	 `</ic:Filter>`

GetActivityName	As you may surmise from the previous example, the GetActivityName operation returns the name of an activity and can be used with a constant to look for a specific activity.

GetActivityProperty	One of the *major* advantages BamTrackingService has over the default tracking service is the ability to expose data items within classes. Remember that WF workflows have code behind them, which may include classes exposed as property members.
	 The GetActivityProperty operation retrieves the value of the members of the class exposed as a property within your WF activity.
	 For example, if you have a CreditCard class with a Number string property, you could filter that value as follows:
	 `<ic:Filter>`
	 `  <ic:Expression>`
	 `    <wf:Operation Name="GetActivityProperty">`
	 `<wf:Argument>CreditCard.Number</wf:Argument>`
	 `    </wf:Operation>`
	 `    <ic:Operation Name="Constant">`
	 `      <ic:Argument>1234-5678-9012-3456</ic:Argument>`
	 `    </ic:Operation>`
	 `    <ic:Operation Name="Equals"/>`
	 `  </ic:Expression>`
	 `</ic:Filter>`
	 It's important to note that property names are case sensitive first, and then case insensitive. When in doubt, use the case-sensitive version, and try to keep your class property names unique.

Continued

Table 9-6. *Continued*

Operation	Description

GetActivityType	The GetActivityType operation will return the assembly-qualified name of the WF activity as it is named within the DLL that contains it. The format is as follows:
	`TopNamespace.SubNameSpace.ContainingClass+NestedClass, MyAssembly, Version=1.5.0.0, Culture=neutral, PublicKeyToken=31bf3856ad364e35, processorArchitecture=MSIL`
	While it is technically feasible to filter off of this value, it's not practical, and ultimately is better for providing type information via an Update element, as follows:
	`<ic:Update DataItemName="TextData" Type="NVARCHAR">`
	`  <ic:Expression>`
	`    <wf:Operation Name="GetActivityType" />`
	`  </ic:Expression>`
	`</ic:Update>`

GetContextProperty	The GetContextProperty operation is analogous to the GetContextProperty operation for the WCF interceptor. However, rather than EventTime and SessionId, the arguments available are EventTime and InstanceId, where InstanceId will return the workflow instance ID.
	The GetContextProperty operation and EventTime argument are frequently used with Update elements, while InstanceId is often used with Correlation, as follows:
	`<ic:CorrelationID>`
	`  <ic:Expression>`
	`    <wf:Operation Name="GetContextProperty">`
	`      <wf:Argument>InstanceId</wf:Argument>`
	`    </wf:Operation>`
	`  </ic:Expression>`
	`</ic:CorrelationID>`

GetUserData	The GetUserData operation returns data that the WF workflow developer sent to the tracking service via the Activity.TrackData() method or one of its overloads. It's important to note that this operation cannot be used within a filter.
	An example of its usage, which effectively extracts data from a WF activity, maps it, and flushes it to a BAM activity, is as follows:
	`<ic:Update DataItemName="UserData" Type="NVARCHAR">`
	`  <ic:Expression>`
	`    <wf:Operation Name="GetUserData" />`
	`  </ic:Expression>`
	`</ic:Update>`

GetUserDataType	The GetUserDataType operation is similar to the GetActivityDataType operation with the exception that only the class and member are returned, not the assembly-qualified name.
	Because one of the overloads of the Activity.TrackData() method accepts any object, this method may be used to filter on its type. An example of its usage would be as follows:
	`<ic:Filter>`
	`  <ic:Expression>`
	`    <wf:Operation Name="GetUserDataType" />`
	`    <ic:Operation Name="Constant">`
	`      <ic:Argument>CreditCard.Number</ic:Argument>`
	`    </ic:Operation>`
	`    <ic:Operation Name="Equals" />`
	`  </ic:Expression>`
	`</ic:Filter>`

Operation	Description

GetUserKey	There are two overloads to the WF TrackData method: void `Activity.TrackData(object userData)` and void `Activity.TrackData(string userDataKey, objectUserData)`.
	
	Much like the `GetUserData` operation, `GetUserKey` will return the string value that is passed in this method.
	
	An example of its usage would be to filter when the string value passed describes `objectUserData` in some way, such as
	
	`<ic:Filter>`
	`  <ic:Expression>`
	`    <wf:Operation Name="GetUserKey" />`
	`    <ic:Operation Name="Constant">`
	`      <ic:Argument>Credit Card number for processing</ic:Argument>`
	`    </ic:Operation>`
	`    <ic:Operation Name="Equals" />`
	`  </ic:Expression>`
	`</ic:Filter>`

GetWorkflowEvent	Where activities may be assigned a series of states according to their execution, so too may workflows. For workflows, the following states may occur: Changed, Completed, Created, Exception, Idle, Loaded, Persisted, Resumed, Started, Suspended, Terminated, and Unloaded.
	
	The `GetWorkflowEvent` operation accepts one of the states as an argument and allows for filtering on that event. An example that fires when the WF workflow has been loaded is as follows:
	
	`<ic:Filter>`
	`  <ic:Expression>`
	`    <wf:Operation Name="GetWorkflowEvent" />`
	`    <ic:Operation Name="Constant">`
	`      <ic:Argument>Created</ic:Argument>`
	`    </ic:Operation>`
	`    <ic:Operation Name="Equals" />`
	`  </ic:Expression>`
	`</ic:Filter>`

GetWorkflowProperty	The `GetWorkflowProperty` operation is used within Update elements only and is similar to the `GetActivityProperty` operation. It is a powerful operation that allows members exposed within the workflow to be extracted to BAM, mapped, and updated to a BAM activity.
	
	An example that maps the number of times a credit card applicant has been delinquent on paying his bills from the applicant's credit history is as follows:
	
	`<ic:Update DataItemName="DelinquencyTotal" Type="NVARCHAR">`
	`  <ic:Expression>`
	`    <wf:Operation Name="GetWorkflowProperty">`
	`      <wf:Argument>CreditHistory.LineOfCredit.NumberOfTimesDelinquent</wf:Argument>`
	`    </wf:Operation>`
	`  </ic:Expression>`
	`</ic:Update>`

While incredibly useful when extracting data from WF activities, mapping to WF activities, and flushing that data to BAM, these operations also have their limitations due to the implementation of the WF interceptor, as you may have noticed.

Each of these operations (as well as Equals, And, Concatenate, and Constant) may only be used against specific track point categories. As you may recall from Chapter 8, Filter elements and data extraction or manipulation operations are defined within an IC file.

Tables 9-7 and 9-8 summarize whether the operations may be used in filter expression operations and whether they may be used within data extraction or manipulation operations.

Table 9-7. *Filter Expression Operation Usage Limitations by Track Point Type*

Filter Expression Operation	May Be Used with Activity Track Point	May Be Used with Workflow Track Point	May Be Used with User Track Point
Equals	Yes	Yes	Yes
And	Yes	Yes	Yes
Concatenate	No	No	No
Constant	Yes	Yes	Yes
GetActivityEvent	Yes	No	No
GetActivityName	Yes	No	Yes
GetActivityProperty	Yes	No	Yes
GetActivityType	Yes	No	Yes
GetContextProperty	No	No	No
GetUserData	No	No	No
GetUserDataType	No	No	Yes
GetUserKey	No	No	Yes
GetWorkflowEvent	No	Yes	No
GetWorkflowProperty	No	No	Yes

Table 9-8. *Data Extraction and Manipulation Operation Usage Limitations by Track Point Type*

Data Extraction or Manipulation Operation	May Be Used with Activity Track Point	May Be Used with Workflow Track Point	May Be Used with User Track Point
Equals	Yes	Yes	Yes
And	Yes	Yes	Yes
Concatenate	Yes	Yes	Yes
Constant	Yes	Yes	Yes
GetActivityEvent	Yes	No	No
GetActivityName	Yes	No	Yes
GetActivityProperty	Yes	No	Yes
GetActivityType	Yes	No	Yes
GetContextProperty	Yes	Yes	Yes
GetUserData	No	No	Yes
GetUserDataType	No	No	Yes
GetUserKey	No	No	Yes
GetWorkflowEvent	No	Yes	No
GetWorkflowProperty	Yes	No	Yes

Now, with a thorough understanding of the WF IC config, the last step is to edit the WF application's app.config file.

Editing the app.config File

The app.config file edit is really a simple process. Open the app.config file in Notepad or Visual Studio 2008. Locate the Configuration element, and within it paste the following:

```
<WorkflowServiceContainer>
  <Services>
    <add type="Microsoft.BizTalk.Bam.Interceptors.Workflow.BamTrackingService,
        Microsoft.BizTalk.Bam.Interceptors, Version=3.0.1.0, Culture=neutral,
        PublicKeyToken=31bf3856ad364e35"
        ConnectionString="Integrated Security=SSPI;
        Data Source=.;Initial Catalog=BAMPrimaryImport"
      PollingIntervalSec="5"/>
  </Services>
</WorkflowServiceContainer>
```

You'll need to make sure the Section element is the same name as the one used by your application code when using the WorkflowRuntime class. You'll also need to modify the ConnectionString section to point to the BAM PI database, save the file, and restart your application.

BAM and WF at AWO

Now that you have a better understanding of how BAM and WF complement one another, we'll detail how the Arnold, Wilbur, and Olivia Corporation (AWO) utilizes the two technologies to complement one another.

As you'll recall, AWO is an international leader in specialty building materials construction. AWO began in the 1840s because of combined contributions from its founders Jacobs and Lang. AWO is nearing some 170 years of accrued business knowledge and expertise in the building materials construction space.

Over time, separate and distinct applications have emerged under the guidance and supervision of the enterprise architect at AWO. Some of these systems include

- An externally-facing ASP.NET 3.5–based web application (BuilderWeb) used by builders to place orders for and check the availability of specialty building materials. BuilderWeb hosts WF activities to provide users with an updated status of their order at all times using sequential and state machine workflows.

- A Microsoft Office SharePoint Server 2007 implementation (PigPen) that includes Microsoft InfoPath server. AWO quality inspectors perform random spot checks of many of their suppliers to ensure that only quality materials are being utilized. They fill out InfoPath forms via tablet PCs in the field, which are then submitted to MOSS and a BizTalk WCF endpoint. The form data stored within MOSS is used for collaboration.

The form data sent to the WCF endpoint is published to BizTalk and sent to the AWO CRM system (HogCall). Within HogCall, the data undergoes a series of WF custom workflows that generate documents and e-mails that are sent to suppliers to notify them if the standards are not met.

- A WPF security application (SheepDetector) used to detect fraudulent orders, enforce perimeter security, and prevent trade materials from falling into the hands of AWO's largest competitor, BBWolf LLC. AWO and BBWolf have a history of legal entanglements stemming from the death of BBWolf's founder and former CEO on AWO property in a ghastly but contained fire. SheepDetector hosts a number of WF workflows that periodically execute against the WF rules store.

- A BizTalk Server 2009 implementation that integrates all enterprise applications.

Figure 9-4 presents the diagram for this enterprise architecture.

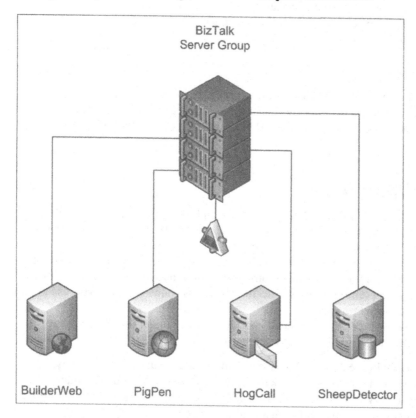

Figure 9-4. *The BizTalk and WF architecture at AWO*

The BizTalk Server 2009 implementation utilizes the WF interceptor to monitor WF workflows within each of the applications and provide an end-to-end systems integration business process for builders.

One of the big "value-adds" for AWO over its competitors is that BuilderWeb is fed with real-time data from the enterprise in BAM. When a builder visits the application and browses the catalog, he is able to determine not only whether the building material is in stock and the current price, but also whether there have been any problems in the past with the material and whether the supplier has had a track record of problems. This is important because builders provide a warranty to their houses from defects in materials. Comprehending this risk provides the builder a better understanding of whether the material will withstand a huff and a puff.

BAM is able to monitor outstanding workflow complaints from customers and correspondence that has gone out to suppliers from HogCall, monitor attempts to order materials by BBWolf as part of SheepDetector, and monitor whether BuilderWeb is selling enough materials to meet expected sales.

AWO's enterprise architect has also contacted AWO's Microsoft Partner account manager and asked that the next version of SharePoint Server include the ability for BAM to monitor SharePoint Server–based workflows. Currently, BAM may not be used to monitor MOSS workflows as MOSS is a "closed" workflow system.

EXERCISE 9-1. CREATING A WF SEQUENTIAL WORKFLOW TO MONITOR

While this chapter provides an overview of WF workflows and activities, there are still many items outside of the scope of this book related to creating WF sequential workflows including custom activities, binding, integration of custom entities, and so forth.

Great resources are available on the Internet for learning WF, as well as training available from independent sources. We recommend *Pro WF: Windows Workflow in .NET 3.5* by Bruce Bukovics (Apress, 2008).

This example will simulate the validation and preapproval of a credit card charge. Many times when you go to a restaurant and use a credit card as payment, the card will be validated first to ensure it meets certain criteria. A preapproval amount will be established, and a final approved amount will be calculated based upon current balance, credit limit, and a number of other factors (such as protecting you from a waitstaff member providing herself a 500% tip).

In the exercises in this chapter, you will create the sequential workflow to monitor and use BAM to monitor the workflows as they take place. This scenario is common in the real world, as BAM is used by fraud detection systems to alert a cardholder to the card being used too frequently at a single merchant or within a timespan, to detect patterns where a card may be used multiple times at a single merchant without the cardholder's knowledge, to alert the cardholder that he may be nearing his credit limit, and other scenarios. Because the workflow merely performs the work, BizTalk and BAM may raise alerts to perform other actions, temporarily suspend the card should fraudulent activity be detected, or even e-mail the cardholder of the activities that are taking place.

1. Open Visual Studio 2008. Click Create and from the New Project dialog, select the Visual C# > Workflow tab, and then select the Sequential Workflow Console Application. Name the project and solution appropriately (in this case, ProBAM2009.WFConsoleApp), and click OK. We have you select a sequential workflow here because it is a closer model to the validation process than a state machine workflow.

2. Double-click `Program.cs` and, at the end of the `Main` method, within the end of the `using` block after `waitHandle.WaitOne();`, add the following code and save the file:

```
Console.WriteLine("Press any key to exit");
Console.ReadKey();
```

3. Double-click Workflow1.cs. Using the Toolbox, between the green and red indicators drop two Code Activity shapes and an IfElse Activity shape, and within the left branch of the IfElse shape, drop a third Code Activity shape.

4. Click the topmost Code Activity shape, named codeActivity1, click the Properties tab, and then rename codeActivity1 to GenerateRequestActivity.

5. Click the Code Activity shape beneath GenerateRequestActivity, named codeActivity2, click the Properties tab, and then rename codeActivity2 to ValidateRequestActivity.

6. Click the IfElse activity, click the Properties tab, and rename the activity from ifElseActivity1 to ifIsValidActivity.

7. Click the left branch of ifIsValidActivity, click the Properties tab, and rename ifElseBranchActivity1, the left branch of the activity, to isValidBranchActivity.

8. Click the right branch of the activity and change its name from ifElseBranchActivity2 to isInvalidBranchActivity.

9. Click the Code Activity shape within the left branch, named codeActivity3, and change its name to SetFinalAmountActivity. Your workflow should now look as shown in Figure 9-5.

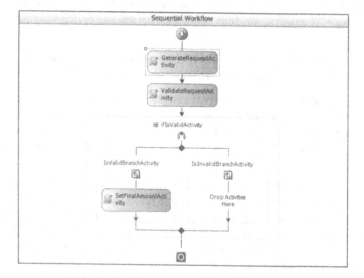

Figure 9-5. *The sequential workflow after the basic setup*

10. Right-click Workflow1.cs within Solution Explorer and select View Code. Beneath the following code segment:

```
public Workflow1()
 {
InitializeComponent();
}
```

enter the following code and save the file:

```
public partial class CreditCard
    {
        public CreditCard()
        {
        }

        public int CardId;
        public string AccountNumber;
        public DateTime ExpirationDate;
        public string CardHolderName;
        public string BillingPostalCode;
        public int SecurityCode;

        public Double CreditLimit;
        public Double CurrentBalance;
    }

    public partial class Purchase
    {
        public Purchase()
        {
        }

        public Guid PurchaseId;
        public Guid MerchantId;
        public Double PreapprovalAmount;
        public Double FinalApprovedAmount;
    }

    public partial class ValidationRequest
    {
        public ValidationRequest(CreditCard cardInstance, Purchase
            purchaseInstance)
        {
            CardInstance = cardInstance;
            PurchaseInstance = purchaseInstance;
        }

        public CreditCard CardInstance;
        public Purchase PurchaseInstance;
        public bool IsValid = true;
    }

    public CreditCard myCreditCard;
    public Purchase myPurchase;
    public ValidationRequest myValidationRequest;
```

```csharp
private int GenerateRandomIntegerInRange(int min, int max)
{
    Random random = new Random();
    return random.Next(min, max);
}

private DateTime GenerateRandomDateTimeInRange(DateTime fromDateTime,
    DateTime toDateTime)
{
    System.Random random = new Random();
    TimeSpan range = new TimeSpan(toDateTime.Ticks -
        fromDateTime.Ticks);
    return fromDateTime + new TimeSpan((long)(range.Ticks *
        random.NextDouble()));
}

private void WriteConsoleData(CreditCard creditCard)
{
    Console.WriteLine("Credit Card instance data generated");
    Console.WriteLine("  Card Account Number: " +
        creditCard.AccountNumber);
    Console.WriteLine("  Card Billing Postal Code: " +
        creditCard.BillingPostalCode);
    Console.WriteLine("  Card Holder Name: " +
        creditCard.CardHolderName);
    Console.WriteLine("  Card Id: " + creditCard.CardId.ToString());
    Console.WriteLine("  Card Credit Limit: " +
        creditCard.CreditLimit.ToString());
    Console.WriteLine("  Card Current Balance: " +
        creditCard.CurrentBalance.ToString());
    Console.WriteLine("  Card Expiration Date: " +
        creditCard.ExpirationDate.ToShortDateString());
    Console.WriteLine("  Card Security Code: " +
        creditCard.SecurityCode.ToString());
}

private void WriteConsoleData(Purchase purchase)
{
    Console.WriteLine("Purchase instance data generated");
    Console.WriteLine("  Purchase Merchant Id: " +
        purchase.MerchantId.ToString());
    Console.WriteLine("  Purchase Id: " +
        purchase.PurchaseId.ToString());
    Console.WriteLine("  Purchase Pre-Approval Amount: " +
        purchase.PreapprovalAmount.ToString());
}
```

11. Double-click `Workflow1.cs`, and then double-click the GenerateRequestActivity shape. This should auto-matically create an event handler for the `execute` method of the activity. Enter the following code for the event handler:

```
// Generate card data
myCreditCard = new CreditCard();
myCreditCard.AccountNumber =
GenerateRandomIntegerInRange(1, 9999).ToString() + "-" +
GenerateRandomIntegerInRange(1, 9999).ToString() + "-" +
GenerateRandomIntegerInRange(1, 9999).ToString() + "-" +
GenerateRandomIntegerInRange(1, 9999).ToString();
myCreditCard.BillingPostalCode =
GenerateRandomIntegerInRange(10000, 99999).ToString() + "-" +
GenerateRandomIntegerInRange(0, 9999).ToString();
myCreditCard.CardHolderName = "Jeff Sanders";
myCreditCard.CardId = GenerateRandomIntegerInRange(1, 641000000);
myCreditCard.CreditLimit = 3500;
myCreditCard.CurrentBalance = GenerateRandomIntegerInRange(0, 4150);
myCreditCard.ExpirationDate =
GenerateRandomDateTimeInRange(DateTime.Today.AddYears(-1),
DateTime.Today.AddYears(3));
myCreditCard.SecurityCode = GenerateRandomIntegerInRange(0, 999);

WriteConsoleData(myCreditCard);

// Generate purchase data
myPurchase = new Purchase();
myPurchase.MerchantId = System.Guid.NewGuid();
myPurchase.PurchaseId = System.Guid.NewGuid();
myPurchase.PreapprovalAmount = 100;

WriteConsoleData(myPurchase);

// Generate validation request
myValidationRequest = new ValidationRequest(myCreditCard, myPurchase);
// Generate card data
myCreditCard = new CreditCard();
myCreditCard.AccountNumber =
GenerateRandomIntegerInRange(1, 9999).ToString() + "-" +
GenerateRandomIntegerInRange(1, 9999).ToString() + "-" +
GenerateRandomIntegerInRange(1, 9999).ToString() + "-" +
GenerateRandomIntegerInRange(1, 9999).ToString();
myCreditCard.BillingPostalCode =
GenerateRandomIntegerInRange(10000, 99999).ToString() + "-" +
GenerateRandomIntegerInRange(0, 9999).ToString();
myCreditCard.CardHolderName = "Jeff Sanders";
myCreditCard.CardId = GenerateRandomIntegerInRange(1, 641000000);
myCreditCard.CreditLimit = 3500;
```

```
myCreditCard.CurrentBalance = GenerateRandomIntegerInRange(0, 4150);
myCreditCard.ExpirationDate =
GenerateRandomDateTimeInRange(DateTime.Today.AddYears(-1),
DateTime.Today.AddYears(3));
myCreditCard.SecurityCode = GenerateRandomIntegerInRange(0, 999);

WriteConsoleData(myCreditCard);

// Generate purchase data
myPurchase = new Purchase();
myPurchase.MerchantId = System.Guid.NewGuid();
myPurchase.PurchaseId = System.Guid.NewGuid();
myPurchase.PreapprovalAmount = 100;

WriteConsoleData(myPurchase);

// Generate validation request
myValidationRequest = new ValidationRequest(myCreditCard, myPurchase);
}
```

12. Double-click `Workflow1.cs` again, and double-click the ValidateRequestActivity shape. Within the event-handler code, enter the following:

```
private void ValidateRequestActivity_ExecuteCode(object sender, EventArgs e)
{
// Is it an expired card
if (myValidationRequest.CardInstance.ExpirationDate < DateTime.Today)
        {
            myValidationRequest.IsValid = false;
        }

        // Does the amount to debit exceed the credit limit
        // e.g., a $10,000 charge on a card with a $1,000 limit
        if (myValidationRequest.PurchaseInstance.PreapprovalAmount >
            myValidationRequest.CardInstance.CreditLimit)
        {
            myValidationRequest.IsValid = false;
        }

        // Other logic
        // ...

        Console.WriteLine("Is Valid: " +
            myValidationRequest.IsValid.ToString());
    }
```

13. Finally, double-click `Workflow1.cs` again, and double-click the SetFinalAmountActivity shape. Within the event-handler code that is generated, enter the following:

```
private void SetFinalAmountActivity_ExecuteCode(object sender, EventArgs e)
{
    myValidationRequest.PurchaseInstance.FinalApprovedAmount =
        myValidationRequest.PurchaseInstance.PreapprovalAmount * 1.3;

    Console.WriteLine();
    Console.WriteLine("Final Approved Amount for request: " +
        myValidationRequest.PurchaseInstance.FinalApprovedAmount
        .ToString());
}
```

14. Once again, double-click Workflow1.cs. You'll notice an exclamation icon within the IfElse activity. Click it, and then click the window option Property "Condition" is not set.

15. In the Properties window, under the Condition property, set the drop-down value to Declarative Rule Condition. A + sign will appear to the left of the word "Condition." Double-click the ellipses in the ConditionName value property, which will open the Select Condition dialog.

16. Click the New button, which will open the Rule Condition Editor. In the dialog, type the following and click OK:

```
this.myValidationRequest.IsValid == True
```

17. Rename the condition (Condition1) to IsValidRequest, and click OK to close all dialogs. Your workflow should now build. If it does not build, remedy any problems that occur.

Your WF should now generate a sample credit card validation for a purchase and through random number generation provide sample data that is within statistical norms (e.g., there are 641 million credit card numbers currently in circulation, the average credit limit per card is $3,500, the average current balance per card is $8,300, cards are usually replaced after every 2–3 years, etc.). The validation should appear similar to what you see in Figure 9-6.

Figure 9-6. *An example of the WF console application output*

18. Run the workflow several times just to examine the different scenarios. You should see a couple instances in which the purchase is not valid because either the card is expired or the amount to charge exceeds the credit limit.

EXERCISE 9-2. CREATING A WF OBSERVATION MODEL

The purpose of this exercise is to create a simple, but effective observation model for the sequential workflow created in Exercise 9-1.

1. Open Microsoft Excel 2007, and ensure that the BAM Add-In for Excel is still functioning. If it is not, follow the instructions in Chapter 3 to enable it.

2. Click the Add-Ins tab, click the BAM button drop-down, and select BAM Activity.

3. Click New Activity and set the activity name to CardValidationActivity.

4. Click New Item and create the new activity items listed in Table 9-9.

Table 9-9. *Items for CardValidationActivity*

Name	Item Type	Data Type	Max Length
AccountNumber	Business Data – Text	Text	19
BillingPostalCode	Business Data – Text	Text	10
CreditLimit	Business Data – Decimal	Decimal	
CurrentBalance	Business Data – Decimal	Decimal	
ExpirationDate	Business Milestones	DateTime	
MerchantId	Business Data – Text	Text	100
PreApprovalAmount	Business Data – Decimal	Decimal	
SecurityCode	Business Data – Integer	Integer	

5. Click OK to close dialogs until the Business Activity Monitoring View Creation dialog appears, and then click Next.

■**Note** At this point, it's important to mention that this gathered data could be used in numerous scenarios. For instance, a check could be done simply with AccountNumber and SecurityCode to determine how frequently a SecurityCode was not being provided. If frequent, it's likely that someone had a copy of the card number, but not the actual card itself, and was trying to use it for fraudulent activities.

BillingPostalCode and CurrentBalance could be used together to determine the average current balance per postal code. In tough economic times, many people charge excess amounts on their credit cards to cover other expenses. This data could be used to detect likelihood of default by geographic region when correlated with median income values.

6. Select Create a new view and click Next. Specify a view name of ViewPurchase and select the CardValidationActivity. Click Next.

7. In this scenario, you'd simply like to provide all data for analysts to consume within the BAM Portal. In the New BAM View: View Items screen, select Select all items and click Next.

8. In the New BAM View: Aggregation Dimensions and Measures screen, add a new dimension. Set the dimension name to PostalCodeDimension, set the dimension type to Data Dimension, and add BillingPostalCode to the DimensionLevels.

9. In the same screen, add a new measure. Set the measure name to AvgCurrentBalance, set the base data item to CurrentBalance (CardValidationActivity), and set the aggregation type to Average. Click OK, and then click Next.

10. Review the items to be created, and click Next.

11. Click Finish.

12. Save your workbook, and use the BAM Add-In for Excel to export the XML file for the observation model definition. Name it `WFCreditValidationActivity.xml`.

13. Populate the PivotTable with some basic data elements.

14. Deploy `WFCreditValidationActivity.xml` to BAM using the `bm.exe` utility.

You now should have an observation model in place, as well as the necessary tables and views against which BAM will aggregate data.

Your XML file should contain the following values (note that it's OK for the `CubeRefs` and `ID` values to be unique):

```xml
<?xml version="1.0" encoding="UTF-16"?>
<BAMDefinition xmlns="http://schemas.microsoft.com/BizTalkServer/2004/10/BAM">
    <Activity Name="CardValidationActivity"
        ID="ID927C20DBBC5B4360AC2991AD02ED502D">
        <Checkpoint Name="BillingPostalCode" ID="
            IDF3883587FB8243D58F5EDACB409C8C53" DataType="NVARCHAR"
            DataLength="10"/>
        <Checkpoint Name="CreditLimit" ID="ID79EC19C7C8C04D979468C2791BEFC2AD"
            DataType="FLOAT"/>
        <Checkpoint Name="CurrentBalance" ID="ID8033A8365BC74AB8AF2293FA8D85AE30"
            DataType="FLOAT"/>
        <Checkpoint Name="ExpirationDate" ID="ID5EE406D8D8D7486CAA8BB1A74868651B"
            DataType="DATETIME"/>
        <Checkpoint Name="MerchantId" ID="IDFB18611CF38A4F1CA867F6930781C015"
            DataType="NVARCHAR" DataLength="100"/>
        <Checkpoint Name="AccountNumber" ID="IDF03617B6A25249B890279DAEE5A4F06C"
            DataType="NVARCHAR" DataLength="19"/>
        <Checkpoint Name="SecurityCode" ID="IDEE671F746E664BE694BF30DE240C7386"
            DataType="INT"/>
        <Checkpoint Name="PreApprovalAmount" ID=
            "ID9B3F0A326FF445DD8A53352725441B2C" DataType="FLOAT"/>
    </Activity>
    <View Name="ViewPurchase" ID="ID097F3E17C4E84609BE7DECC429B7A73D">
        <ActivityView Name="ViewCardValidationActivity" ID=
            "ID8F0EE5D172964234830CBF4D9F71A7FB"
            ActivityRef="ID927C20DBBC5B4360AC2991AD02ED502D">
            <Alias Name="AccountNumber" ID="ID6773829E971349AA851C989C9D352A73">
                <CheckpointRef>IDF03617B6A25249B890279DAEE5A4F06C</CheckpointRef>
            </Alias>
```

```
        <Alias Name="BillingPostalCode" ID=
           "ID4F345643B9304B02A45293476F996E69">
          <CheckpointRef>IDF3883587FB8243D58F5EDACB409C8C53</CheckpointRef>
        </Alias>
        <Alias Name="CreditLimit" ID="IDBEF71A3909D04C998CCB7D4F2F5F26D8">
          <CheckpointRef>ID79EC19C7C8C04D979468C2791BEFC2AD</CheckpointRef>
        </Alias>
        <Alias Name="CurrentBalance" ID="IDAEE685FF52584DB5B6601AD3788F3F61">
          <CheckpointRef>ID8033A8365BC74AB8AF2293FA8D85AE30</CheckpointRef>
        </Alias>
        <Alias Name="ExpirationDate" ID="IDBE1DD6F03F374A749864137ABDDF9A83">
          <CheckpointRef>ID5EE406D8D8D7486CAA8BB1A74868651B</CheckpointRef>
        </Alias>
        <Alias Name="MerchantId" ID="ID197A3A90897740EFB728B7E2E6BE551B">
          <CheckpointRef>IDFB18611CF38A4F1CA867F6930781C015</CheckpointRef>
        </Alias>
        <Alias Name="PreApprovalAmount" ID=
           "IDAE119D3964DB4379BCD34465BA3BDC38">
          <CheckpointRef>ID9B3F0A326FF445DD8A53352725441B2C</CheckpointRef>
        </Alias>
        <Alias Name="SecurityCode" ID="ID577A4D74D3CB4457B4D259E291CA4A10">
          <CheckpointRef>IDEE671F746E664BE694BF30DE240C7386</CheckpointRef>
        </Alias>
      </ActivityView>
  </View>
  <Cube Name="ViewPurchase" ID="IDF4EB46891D044808AA3F2965EAECBAFF"
     CreateOlapCube="true" ActivityViewRef=
     "ID8F0EE5D172964234830CBF4D9F71A7FB">
     <Measure Name="AvgCurrentBalance" ID="ID1E123759207842D3A6D4B9A47A905665"
        AliasRef="IDAEE685FF52584DB5B6601AD3788F3F61" AggregationFunction=
        "Avg"/>
     <DataDimension Name="PostalCodeDimension" ID=
        "IDF06F6EA6D4B24802A7B2ED30AAEBE626">
        <LevelAliasRef>ID4F345643B9304B02A45293476F996E69</LevelAliasRef>
     </DataDimension>
  </Cube>
  <Extension>
     <OWC xmlns:x="urn:schemas-microsoft-com:office:excel">
        <PivotTableView CubeRef="IDF4EB46891D044808AA3F2965EAECBAFF">
           <x:PivotTable>
              <x:ConnectionString/>
              <x:DataMember>Sample</x:DataMember>
              <x:PivotField>
                 <x:Name>AvgCurrentBalance</x:Name>
                 <x:SourceName>[Measures].[AvgCurrentBalance]</x:SourceName>
                 <x:SourceHierarchy>[Measures].[AvgCurrentBalance]
                    </x:SourceHierarchy>
              </x:PivotField>
```

```
        <x:PivotField>
            <x:Name>BillingPostalCode</x:Name>
            <x:SourceName>[PostalCodeDimension].[BillingPostalCode]
                </x:SourceName>
            <x:Orientation>Row</x:Orientation>
            <x:Position>1</x:Position>
            <x:SourceHierarchy>[PostalCodeDimension]</x:SourceHierarchy>
        </x:PivotField>
        <x:PivotField>
            <x:Name>Data</x:Name>
            <x:Orientation>Row</x:Orientation>
            <x:Position>-1</x:Position>
            <x:DataField/>
        </x:PivotField>
        <x:PivotField>
            <x:Name>AvgCurrentBalance</x:Name>
            <x:Orientation>Data</x:Orientation>
            <x:Position>1</x:Position>
            <x:ParentField>[Measures].[AvgCurrentBalance]</x:ParentField>
        </x:PivotField>
        <x:PivotView>
            <x:IsNotFiltered/>
            <x:Label>
                <x:Caption>PivotTable1</x:Caption>
            </x:Label>
        </x:PivotView>
      </x:PivotTable>
    </PivotTableView>
  </OWC>
 </Extension>
</BAMDefinition>
```

EXERCISE 9-3. CREATING THE WF INTERCEPTOR CONFIGURATION

The purpose of this exercise is to create an interceptor configuration by which simple collection of WF activity data will occur. Now that you have a thorough understanding of interceptor configuration files from both Chapters 8 and 9, this exercise should come fairly easy.

1. In Visual Studio 2008, create a new XML file. Name it `WFCCValidationIC.xml`.

2. The following configuration is simply a pass-through of data from the WF workflow. Because you allow the analyst to better refine the data, the data items selected are captured and persisted to BAM. Enter the configuration as follows:

```
<?xml version="1.0" encoding="utf-8" ?>
<ic:InterceptorConfiguration xmlns:ic="http://schemas.microsoft.com/
    BizTalkServer/2004/10/BAM/InterceptorConfiguration" xmlns:wf=
```

```
   "http://schemas.microsoft.com/BizTalkServer/2004/10/BAM/
   WorkflowInterceptorConfiguration">
<ic:EventSource Name="Workflow1" Technology="WF" Manifest=
   "ProBAM2009.WFConsoleApp.Workflow1, ProBAM2009.WFConsoleApp,
   Version=1.0.0.0, Culture=neutral, PublicKeyToken=null"/>
<ic:BamActivity Name="CardValidationActivity">
  <!--Purchase Validated Received...-->
  <ic:OnEvent Name="SetFinalApprovalAmount"  Source="Workflow1" IsBegin=
     "true" IsEnd="true">
    <ic:Filter>
      <ic:Expression>
        <wf:Operation Name="GetActivityName" />
        <ic:Operation Name="Constant">
          <ic:Argument>ValidateRequestActivity</ic:Argument>
        </ic:Operation>
        <ic:Operation Name="Equals" />
      </ic:Expression>
    </ic:Filter>
    <ic:CorrelationID>
      <ic:Expression>
        <wf:Operation Name="GetContextProperty">
          <wf:Argument>InstanceId</wf:Argument>
        </wf:Operation>
      </ic:Expression>
    </ic:CorrelationID>
    <ic:Update DataItemName="AccountNumber" Type="NVARCHAR">
      <ic:Expression>
        <wf:Operation Name="GetWorkflowProperty">
          <wf:Argument>myValidationRequest.CardInstance.AccountNumber
          </wf:Argument>
        </wf:Operation>
      </ic:Expression>
    </ic:Update>
    <ic:Update DataItemName="BillingPostalCode" Type="NVARCHAR">
      <ic:Expression>
        <wf:Operation Name="GetWorkflowProperty">
          <wf:Argument>myValidationRequest.CardInstance.BillingPostalCode
          </wf:Argument>
        </wf:Operation>
      </ic:Expression>
    </ic:Update>
    <ic:Update DataItemName="CreditLimit" Type="FLOAT">
      <ic:Expression>
        <wf:Operation Name="GetWorkflowProperty">
          <wf:Argument>myValidationRequest.CardInstance.CreditLimit
          </wf:Argument>
        </wf:Operation>
```

```
      </ic:Expression>
    </ic:Update>
    <ic:Update DataItemName="CurrentBalance" Type="FLOAT">
      <ic:Expression>
        <wf:Operation Name="GetWorkflowProperty">
          <wf:Argument>myValidationRequest.CardInstance.CurrentBalance
          </wf:Argument>
        </wf:Operation>
      </ic:Expression>
    </ic:Update>
    <ic:Update DataItemName="ExpirationDate" Type="DATETIME">
      <ic:Expression>
        <wf:Operation Name="GetWorkflowProperty">
          <wf:Argument>myValidationRequest.CardInstance.ExpirationDate
          </wf:Argument>
        </wf:Operation>
      </ic:Expression>
    </ic:Update>
    <ic:Update DataItemName="SecurityCode" Type="INT">
      <ic:Expression>
        <wf:Operation Name="GetWorkflowProperty">
          <wf:Argument>myValidationRequest.CardInstance.SecurityCode
          </wf:Argument>
        </wf:Operation>
      </ic:Expression>
    </ic:Update>
    <ic:Update DataItemName="MerchantId" Type="NVARCHAR">
      <ic:Expression>
        <wf:Operation Name="GetWorkflowProperty">
          <wf:Argument>myValidationRequest.PurchaseInstance.MerchantId
          </wf:Argument>
        </wf:Operation>
      </ic:Expression>
    </ic:Update>
    <ic:Update DataItemName="PreApprovalAmount" Type="FLOAT">
      <ic:Expression>
        <wf:Operation Name="GetWorkflowProperty">
          <wf:Argument>myValidationRequest.PurchaseInstance.PreapprovalAmount
          </wf:Argument>
        </wf:Operation>
      </ic:Expression>
    </ic:Update>
  </ic:OnEvent>
 </ic:BamActivity>
</ic:InterceptorConfiguration>
```

3. Save the file, and use bm.exe with the deploy-interceptor command to deploy it.

EXERCISE 9-4. LOADING THE WF INTERCEPTOR RUNTIME

Finally, you must either modify the app.config file included with the console application to enable it for BAM tracking or add to the Program.cs file the code to manually load the BAM Tracking Service. By default, console applications don't include app.config files, so you'll elect to manually load the BAM Tracking Service using code.

1. Open the Visual Studio 2008 console application. Open the Program.cs file.

2. Right-click the References folder and select Add References.

3. Click the Browse tab, navigate to <BizTalk Installation Drive>\Program Files\Microsoft BizTalk Server 2009\Tracking, click the Microsoft.BizTalk.Bam.Interceptors.dll file, and click OK.

4. Within the Program.cs file, add a using directive at the top of the file:

    ```
    using Microsoft.BizTalk.Bam.Interceptors.Workflow;
    ```

5. After the following line within the auto-generated code:

    ```
    AutoResetEvent waitHandle = new AutoResetEvent(false);
    ```

    insert the following code:

    ```
    string connectionString = "Integrated Security=SSPI;Data Source=.;
    Initial Catalog=BAMPrimaryImport";
    int interceptorConfigurationPollingInterval = 5;
    workflowRuntime.AddService(new BamTrackingService(connectionString,
    interceptorConfigurationPollingInterval));
    ```

6. Save your solution and rebuild the application. Open the BAM Portal within a web browser, and access CardValidationActivity within the Activity Search menu item.

7. Run the WF console application five to ten times. Execute a query to include all available data and milestones. You should see the BAM data that was captured in BAM from WF, as shown in Figure 9-7.

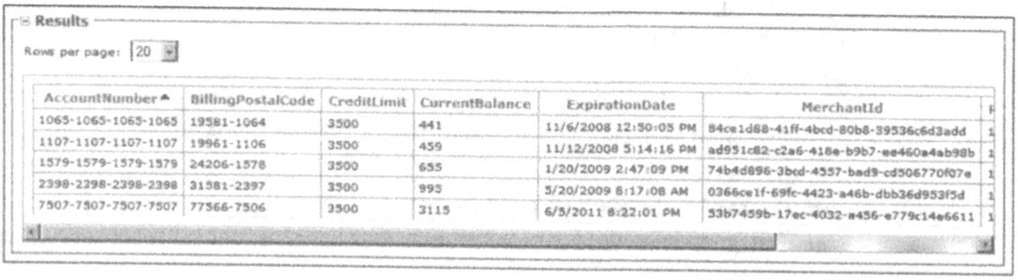

Results

Rows per page: 20

AccountNumber▲	BillingPostalCode	CreditLimit	CurrentBalance	ExpirationDate	MerchantId	
1065-1065-1065-1065	19581-1064	3500	441	11/6/2008 12:50:05 PM	84ce1d68-41ff-4bcd-80b8-39536c6d3add	1
1107-1107-1107-1107	19961-1106	3500	459	11/12/2008 5:14:16 PM	ad951c82-c2a6-418e-b9b7-ee460a4ab98b	1
1579-1579-1579-1579	24206-1578	3500	655	1/20/2009 2:47:09 PM	74b4d896-3bcd-4557-bad9-cd506770f07e	1
2398-2398-2398-2398	31581-2397	3500	995	5/20/2009 8:17:08 AM	0366ce1f-69fc-4423-a46b-dbb36d953f5d	1
7507-7507-7507-7507	77566-7506	3500	3115	6/5/2011 8:22:01 PM	53b7459b-17ec-4032-a456-e779c14e6611	1

Figure 9-7. *WF activity data intercepted, mapped to BAM, and displayed within the BAM Portal*

Summary

Windows Workflow Foundation is a strong complementary technology to BAM.

In this chapter, you learned about WF and the context of BAM within BizTalk and WF. The chapter included coverage of the WF interceptor architecture, how a WF tracking profile is structured, and how to monitor a WF workflow using the WF interceptor. The chapter also covered the syntax of a WF interceptor configuration file and how to edit the app.config file to enable monitoring of WF workflows within BAM.

Sometimes it is useful to get at an even more granular level when writing data to BAM or when you want to monitor an application that doesn't utilize BizTalk, WCF, or WF. The next chapter will cover the BAM API and how it may be used to capture and process BAM data.

CHAPTER 10

■■■

The BAM API

The BAM API is used to write data into BAM programmatically. There are two main reasons you would use the BAM API:

- The BAM API is used to store BAM data from a .NET application that's not part of BizTalk, such as an ASP.NET page or a SharePoint event handler. It's more common to use BAM from code running on a server, but it can even be used on the client in a Windows Forms application.

- Some BAM needs within BizTalk can't be addressed using the TPE. Sometimes you might find it convenient to write to BAM by using code from within an orchestration or a pipeline component, and special classes exist to support these requirements. One case where this is useful is dealing with repeating data. The TPE can't intercept data from repeated elements, such as line items within an order. The TPE also can't intercept data that doesn't have a schema, such as binary data or any message in an orchestration of type string or type System.Xml.XmlDocument. If you want to capture these types of data, you need to use the API.

This chapter starts by describing the major objects of the BAM API, followed by three exercises:

- Capturing data from a console application using the BAM API

- Adding a second BAM API application and implementing a continuation between the two applications

- Capturing data within an orchestration using the BAM API

The chapter concludes with discussions of working with the MessagingEventStream object and the BAM Management API.

The BAM API Objects

The BAM API defines four main classes: `DirectEventStream`, `BufferedEventStream`, `OrchestrationEventStream`, and `MessagingEventStream`. All of these classes, which are described in Table 10-1, are derived from the base class `EventStream`, and most of the BAM API consists of methods inherited from `EventStream`.

Table 10-1. *Classes That Inherit from EventStream*

Class	Inherits From	Purpose
BufferedEventStream	EventStream	Used in a .NET application to do a buffered write of data to BAM
DirectEventStream	EventStream	Used in a .NET application to do an unbuffered write of data to BAM
OrchestrationEventStream	EventStream	Used when writing to BAM programmatically within an orchestration; provides transactional consistency with the orchestration
MessagingEventStream	EventStream	Used when writing to BAM programmatically within a pipeline; provides transactional consistency with the messaging engine

You're probably wondering when you should use each of these classes. `DirectEventStream` and `BufferedEventStream` can be used in any application that supports .NET, no matter whether the application is running in BizTalk. `DirectEventStream` is a synchronous call; when you execute an update on a `DirectEventStream`, the call won't return until after the database write is committed. `BufferedEventStream` is asynchronous. When you update a `BufferedEventStream`, the update is cached and written later. If your goal is to maximize throughput, use `BufferedEventStream` and take advantage of the cache. If your application can't ever afford to lose data, even if the server crashes immediately after an update completes, use `DirectEventStream`.

`OrchestrationEventStream` is available only when executing in the context of the orchestration engine. It has two advantages:

- *Performance*: It can piggyback its database writes on the orchestration persistence points for maximum performance.

- *Consistency*: Because it writes during orchestration persistence points, even in the event of a server crash, the state of the orchestration recorded by BAM is guaranteed to be consistent with the last orchestration persistence point.

`MessagingEventStream` is available only when executing in a BizTalk pipeline. It has similar performance and consistency advantages as `OrchestrationEventStream`.

Table 10-2 lists the members of the `EventStream` class. `DirectEventStream`, `BufferedEventStream`, `OrchestrationEventStream`, and `MessagingEventStream` all implement each of these methods.

Table 10-2. *Members of the EventStream Class*

Member	Comments
AddRelatedActivity	Relationships are covered in Chapter 12, which has an example of working with this method.
BeginActivity	Opens an activity for updates.
Clear	Clears the buffered data. If called before Flush, any UpdateActivity() calls are discarded.
EnableContinuation	Keeps the activity open so additional data can be added later. See Exercise 10-2 for an example.
EndActivity	Closes the activity so that no more updates are possible.
Equals	Inherited from System.Object.
Flush	Flushes data to the database.
GetHashCode	Inherited from System.Object.
GetType	Inherited from System.Object.
StoreCustomEvent	Stores an object that has the IPersistQueryable interface. This member is intended for internal use by HAT, Human Workflow Services, and the business rules engine, which used it to store DelayedSpCall objects that are executed as stored procedure calls by the Event Bus Service.
ToString	Inherited from System.Object.
UpdateActivity	Takes a list of field names and values to store.

EXERCISE 10-1. USING THE BAM API

In this exercise, you will implement a simple "Hello World" application to write some BAM events.

1. Use Microsoft Excel and the BAM Add-In for Excel to create an activity called APIDemo with the fields listed in Table 10-3.

Table 10-3. *Activity Items for the BAM API Sample*

Field	Type
Key	Business Data – Text
Data1	Business Data – Integer
Data2	Business Data – Integer
Data3	Business Data – Integer

2. Use the View Creation Wizard to create a simple view that contains all the fields from the activity.

3. Use bm deploy-all to deploy the activity and view.

■Note Detailed instructions for creating and deploying activities and views are in Chapter 5.

4. Open Visual Studio 2008, and from the File menu select New ➤ Project. In the Project Types tree view, select Visual C# Windows projects, and then click Console Application. Create a new console application called APIDemo1.

5. In Solution Explorer, right-click References, and then select Add Reference. Click the Browse tab, browse to the `C:\Program Files\Microsoft Biztalk Server 2009\Tracking` folder, and click `Microsoft.BizTalk.Bam.EventObservation.dll`. Click the OK button to add a reference.

6. Replace the code in `program.cs` with the following:

```
using System;
using System.Text;
using Microsoft.BizTalk.Bam.EventObservation;

namespace APIDemo
{
    class Program
    {
        static void Main(string[] args)
        {
            /*Check for enough arguments*/
            if (args.Length < 3)
            {
                Console.WriteLine("Insufficient arguments supplied.");
                return;
            }

            try
            {
                /*Create an instance of BufferedEventStream*/
                string connString = "Integrated Security=SSPI;Data"
                    +" Source=.;Initial Catalog=BizTalkMsgBoxDb";
                BufferedEventStream eventStream = new
                    BufferedEventStream(connString, 0);

                /*activityGuid will be used to uniquely*/
                /*identify this row in the table*/
                string activityGuid = Guid.NewGuid().ToString();
                Console.WriteLine("Writing Activity : {0}", activityGuid);
```

```
            //Write data to the activity
            eventStream.BeginActivity("APIDemo", activityGuid);
            int data1 = int.Parse(args[1]);
            eventStream.UpdateActivity("APIDemo",
                activityGuid, "Key", args[0], "Data1", data1);
            int data2 = int.Parse(args[2]);
            eventStream.UpdateActivity("APIDemo",
                activityGuid, "Data2", data2);
            eventStream.EndActivity("APIDemo", activityGuid);

            /*Flush the data to the database*/
            eventStream.Flush();
        }
        catch (Exception excep)
        {
            Console.WriteLine("Exception Caught : {0}", excep.ToString());
        }

    }
  }
}
```

This console application writes its arguments to the activity called APIDemo. Once it has checked that the user gave it some arguments, it creates a new instance of the BufferedEventStream class in a variable called eventStream. The constructor takes two parameters: the connection string to the message box database and an integer that indicates how many writes to accept before the event stream is automatically flushed. In this code, we pass a zero, which means don't autoflush the event stream.

The next step is to generate a globally unique identifier (GUID). This GUID will be stored in the BAM Primary Import database as the activity ID.

A GUID is a 128-bit number that is guaranteed to be unique. The activity table needs a unique value to act as the primary key. When you're using the TPE, if you don't assign the activity ID, the TPE will automatically generate a GUID for you. If we had a natural key, such as a Social Security number or order number, we could use the natural key instead of creating a GUID. However, the best practice is to use a GUID, as sometimes natural keys can be repeated unexpectedly, messing with the structure of the database. The exception is when two BAM activities are connected by a relationship. In that case, it may be necessary to use a field from the data as the activity ID.

■Note Related activities are covered in Chapter 12, which provides an example of using an order number as the activity ID.

The next step is to call the BeginActivity() method, which makes the activity available for write. Each of the two UpdateActivity() calls adds data to the activity. You can add data to as many fields as you wish during a call to UpdateActivity(). Finally, EndActivity() marks the activity as completed, and Flush() forces the writing of events accumulated in memory to the store-and-forward database so that they can be processed by the Event Bus Service.

7. Check that the tracking host is running on your BizTalk server.

Note Chapter 13 explains the concept of a tracking host. The bottom line is that if the BizTalk service isn't running, you won't be able to capture BAM data.

---

8. In Solution Explorer, right-click the project name, and select Properties. In the Debug tab of the Project Properties dialog box, enter the command-line arguments test1 123 456.

9. Press F11 to step into the sample, and step through it in the debugger. Note the GUID generated by the program.

10. Once the sample completes, you can go and take a look at the data. Open SQL Server Management Studio from the Start menu.

11. Press F8 to display the Object Explorer.

12. Click Connect, select Database Engine, and connect to the database server where your BizTalk databases are stored.

13. Open the Databases folder, and then open the BAM Primary Import database. Right-click the BAM_APIDemo_Completed table, and select Open Table.

You should see the data you entered in the command-line arguments stored in the BAM database, as shown in Figure 10-1.

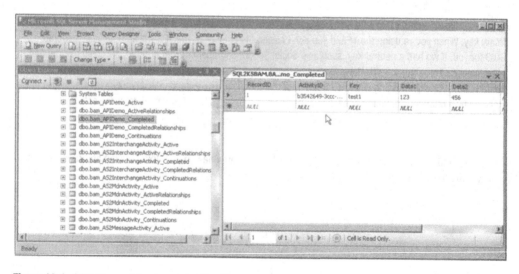

Figure 10-1. *SQL Server Management Studio*

14. Run the application a couple more times, and then refresh the data in SQL Server Management Studio. You should see additional lines being written to the table.

In this exercise, you created a simple .NET application that used the BAM API. Next, you'll extend this application by adding support for continuation.

EXERCISE 10-2. ADDING A CONTINUATION

Continuation allows you to write part of an activity in one application, and then write the rest of it in a separate application. You use a continuation value that is known to both applications to correlate the two writes.

■**Note** You'll find a lot more detail on how continuation works in Chapter 5.

1. In Visual Studio, edit the `program.cs` file from the previous exercise by adding this line before the call to `EndActivity()`:

```
eventStream.EnableContinuation("APIDemo", activityGuid, args[0]);
```

This line tells BAM that another application will write additional data into this activity later. With the surrounding lines, it should read as follows:

```
int data2 = int.Parse(args[2]);
eventStream.UpdateActivity("APIDemo", activityGuid, "Data2", data2);
eventStream.EnableContinuation("APIDemo", activityGuid, args[0]);
eventStream.EndActivity("APIDemo", activityGuid);
```

2. Press F5 to run the sample application again, and then refresh the BAM_APIDemo_Completed table in SQL Server Management Studio. You'll notice that this time, the application didn't add any lines to the table. That's because this table shows completed activities.

3. In SQL Server Management Studio, right-click the table BAM_APIDemo_Active, and select Open Table. You should see one row in this table; it's the activity waiting for additional data.

4. In Visual Studio 2008 Solution Explorer, right-click the solution name and select Add ➤ Select New Project.

5. In the Project Types tree view, select Visual C# Windows projects, and then click Console Application. Create a second console application called APIDemo2.

6. In Solution Explorer, under APIDemo2, right-click References, and then select Add Reference. Click the Browse tab, browse to the C:\Program Files\Microsoft Biztalk Server 2009\Tracking folder, and click Microsoft.BizTalk.Bam.EventObservation.dll. Click the OK button to add the reference.

7. Replace the code in `program.cs` with the following:

```
using System;
using System.Text;
using Microsoft.BizTalk.Bam.EventObservation;

namespace APIDemo
{
    class Program
    {
        static void Main(string[] args)
        {
            if (args.Length < 2)
            {
                Console.WriteLine("Insufficient arguments supplied.");
                return;
            }

            try
            {
                /*Create an instance of BufferedEventStream*/
                string connString = "Integrated Security=SSPI;Data"
                    +" Source=.;Initial Catalog=BizTalkMsgBoxDb";
                BufferedEventStream eventstream = new
                    BufferedEventStream(connString, 0);

                Console.WriteLine("Continuing : {0}", args[0]);

                /*Write data to the activity*/
                int data3 = int.Parse(args[1]);
                eventstream.UpdateActivity("APIDemo", args[0], "Data3", data3);
                eventstream.EndActivity("APIDemo", args[0]);

                /*Flush the data to the database*/
                eventstream.Flush();
            }
            catch (Exception excep)
            {
                Console.WriteLine("Exception Caught : {0}", excep.ToString());
            }

        }
    }
}
```

You'll notice that in this program, there's no call to the BeginActivity() method. That's because the activity has already been created by the previous application. All this application has to do is update the activity, and then end the update. You'll also notice that instead of using a GUID as the activity ID, the program uses the first parameter from the command-line arguments. The first parameter on the command line should be the same when you run the second program as it was when you ran the first program. That way, BAM can use the first parameter to establish a continuation between the two different applications.

8. In Solution Explorer, right-click the APIDemo2 project, and select Properties. In the Debug tab of the Project Properties dialog box, enter the command-line arguments test1 789.

9. Press F11 to step into the sample, and step through it in the debugger.

10. In SQL Server Management Studio, refresh the BAM_APIDemo_Completed table. An extra row should have appeared in this table.

11. Refresh the BAM_APIDemo_Active table. It should be empty again.

12. Open a command window and set the path to include both sample applications. Investigate the behavior of the applications by running them with different values for the key, which is the first argument for each application. Remember that APIDemo1 creates a new activity, stored in BAM_APIDemo_Active. The activity will wait until APIDemo2 is run with the same value for the key, when Data3 is filled in and the activity moves to the BAM_APIDemo_Completed table.

In this series of two exercises, you have built two separate applications that both use the BAM API. When they are run in sequence, a complete activity will be captured by BAM. The continuation allows two different applications to contribute to the same activity.

EXERCISE 10-3. USING ORCHESTRATIONEVENTSTREAM

In this exercise, you'll learn how to use OrchestrationEventStream within an orchestration.

For simplicity, you can use the same activity you created for the previous exercises. If you didn't do Exercise 10-1, go back and create an activity and view as described in Step 1.

1. Open Visual Studio 2008, and from the File menu select New ➤ Project. In the Project Types tree view, select BizTalk Server projects, and then click Empty BizTalk Server Project. Create a new project called OrchAPIDemo.

2. In Windows Explorer, create a new folder called C:\pro bam samples\chapter eleven\filedrops\OrchAPIin. Set permissions on the folder so all users have access.

3. In Solution Explorer, right-click the project name and select Add ➤ New Item. Click BizTalk Orchestration, and then click OK.

4. If the Orchestration View isn't visible, from the View menu select Other Windows ➤ Orchestration View.

5. In Orchestration View, right-click the Messages folder, and then select New Message.

6. In Orchestration View, click the message you just created, and then press F4 to bring up its properties. Set the message type to System.Xml.XmlDocument.

7. Drag a receive shape from the Toolbox to the orchestration.

8. Drag an expression shape from the Toolbox to the orchestration, so that it occurs after the receive shape, as shown in Figure 10-2.

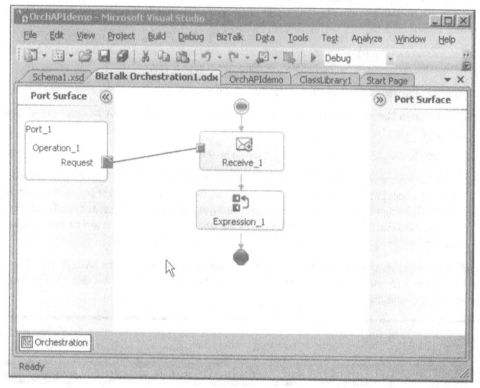

Figure 10-2. *The completed sample orchestration*

9. Right-click Port Surface at the left of the Orchestration Designer and select New Configured Port.

10. When the Port Configuration Wizard opens, click the Next button.

11. Accept the default port name, Port_1, and click the Next button.

12. On the Select a Port Type screen, shown in Figure 10-3, accept the defaults and click the Next button.

13. On the Port Binding screen, shown in Figure 10-4, select I'll always be receiving messages on this port as the port direction, and select Specify now as the port binding.

■**Note** We don't recommend specifying a port binding in an orchestration for production code; however, it's a great way to put together quick prototypes.

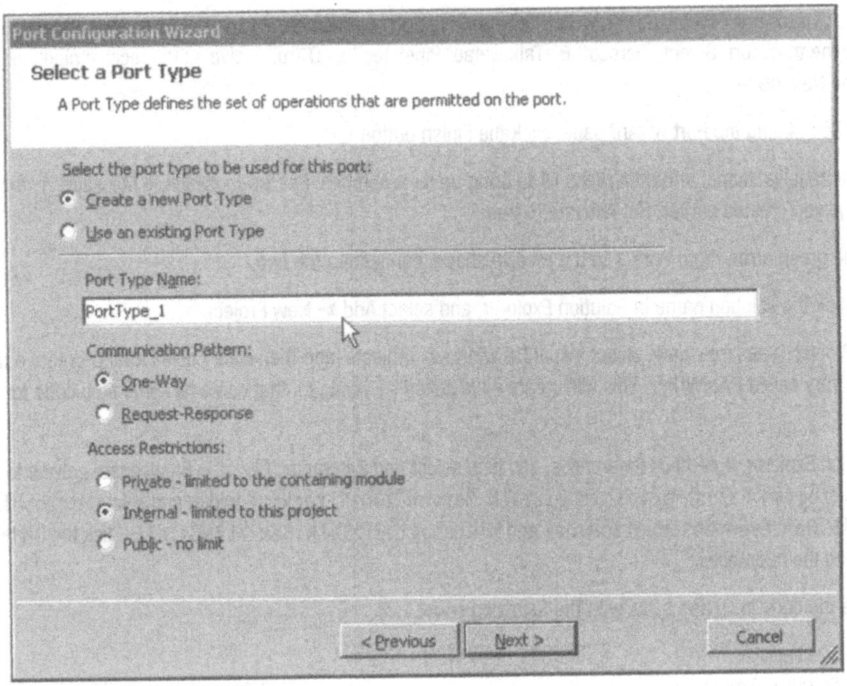

Figure 10-3. *The Select a Port Type wizard page*

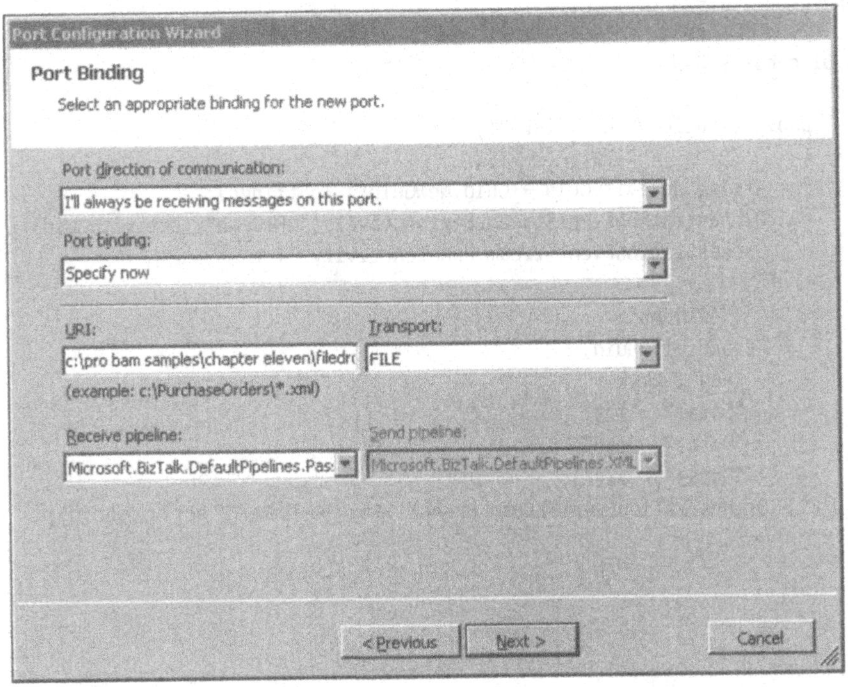

Figure 10-4. *The Port Binding wizard page*

14. Select C:\pro bam samples\chapter eleven\filedrops\OrchAPIin*.xml as the URL. Select FILE as the transport. Select Microsoft.BizTalk.DefaultPipelines.PassThruReceive as the receive pipeline. Click the Next button.

15. On the Completing the Port wizard page, click the Finish button.

16. Click the receive shape, and then press F4 to bring up its properties. Set the message to Message_1, the message you created earlier. Set Activate to true.

17. Drag the green arrow from Port_1 to the receive shape, connecting the two.

18. Right-click the solution name in Solution Explorer, and select Add ➤ New Project.

19. In the Project Types tree view, select Visual C# Windows projects, and then click Class Library. Create a new class library called BAMWriter. This will create a file called Class1.cs that contains some stub code for a class.

20. In Solution Explorer, right-click References, and then select Add Reference. Click the Browse tab, browse to the C:\Program Files\Microsoft Biztalk Server 2009\Tracking folder, and select Microsoft. BizTalk.Bam.EventObservation.dll and Microsoft.BizTalk.Bam.XLANGs.dll. Click the OK button to add the references.

21. Replace the code in Class1.cs with the following code:

```
using System;
using System.Text;
using Microsoft.BizTalk.Bam.EventObservation;

namespace BAMWriter
{
    public class BAM
    {
        public static void WriteBAM()
        {
            string activityGuid = Guid.NewGuid().ToString();
            OrchestrationEventStream.BeginActivity("APIDemo", activityGuid);
            OrchestrationEventStream.UpdateActivity
            (
                "APIDemo",
                activityGuid,
                "Key", "mykey",
                "Data1", "123",
                "Data2", "456",
                "Data3", "789");
            OrchestrationEventStream.EndActivity("APIDemo", activityGuid);
        }
    }
}
```

22. Right-click the BAMWriter project and select Rebuild. Confirm the code builds without errors.

23. Right-click the BAMWriter project and select Properties. Click the Signing tab, and check the Sign the Assembly check box (see Figure 10-5). In the Choose a strong name key file drop-down box, select New, and create a new key file. Don't protect the key file with a password.

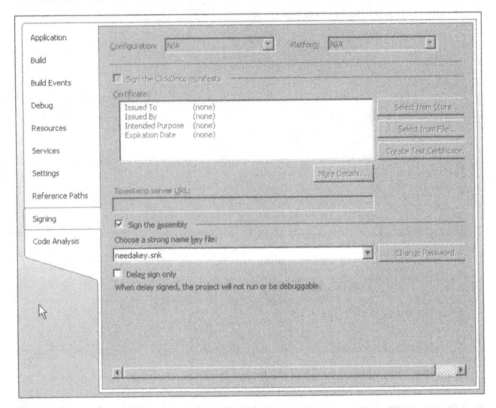

Figure 10-5. *The Signing tab in the Project Properties designer*

24. From the Start menu, select Microsoft Visual Studio 2008 ➤ Visual Studio Tools ➤ Visual Studio 2008 Command Prompt. This opens a new command line.

25. Change directory to the folder that contains BAMWriter.DLL.

26. Run the following command:

```
gacutil /i bamwriter.dll
```

27. Right-click the OrchAPIDemo project, and select Properties. Click the Signing tab, and check the Sign the Assembly check box. In the Choose a strong name key file drop-down box, select Browse, and browse to the key file you created in the previous step.

28. In the OrchAPIDemo Project Properties designer, click the Deployment tab. Enter **OrchAPIDemo** as the application name, as shown in Figure 10-6.

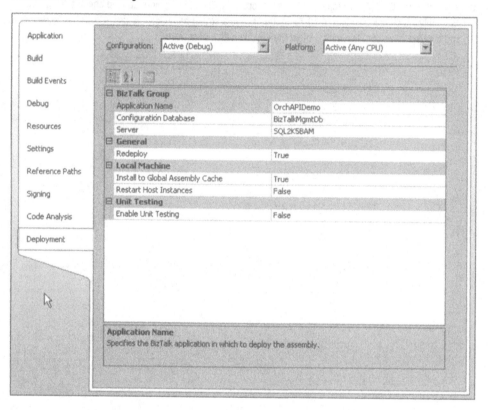

Figure 10-6. *The Deployment tab in the Project Properties designer*

29. In Solution Explorer, right-click References, and then select Add Reference. Click the Projects tab, and then select BAMWriter. Click the OK button to add a reference.

30. Double-click the orchestration to open it in the Orchestration Designer. Double-click the expression shape to bring up the BizTalk Expression Editor. Enter an expression that calls the method in your class library. The correct code is shown in Figure 10-7.

31. Click OK to close the Expression Editor.

32. In Solution Explorer, right-click the solution name and select Deploy. Check the Output pane to confirm that the solution was deployed correctly.

33. From the Start menu, open BizTalk Server Administration Console.

34. Open the BizTalk Group folder, and then open the Applications folder. You should see a new application called OrchAPIDemo. Open the OrchAPIDemo application, and then click Orchestrations. Double-click the orchestration to bring up its properties. Click the Bindings tab, and then set the host to BizTalkServerApplication, as shown in Figure 10-8. (If you have modified the hosts running on your BizTalk Server, you can use any host that you wish.)

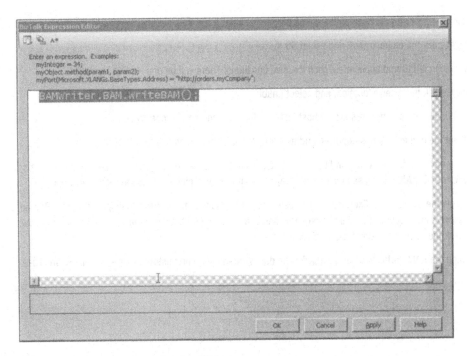

Figure 10-7. *The BizTalk Expression Editor*

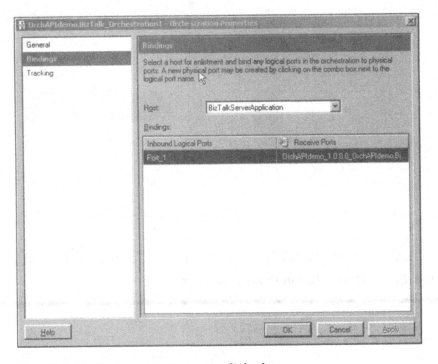

Figure 10-8. *The Orchestration Properties dialog box*

35. Click the OK button to dismiss the dialog box.

36. Right-click the orchestration and select Start.

37. In the OrchAPIDemo application, click Receive Locations. There will be one receive location.

38. Right-click the receive location, and select Enable.

39. In the platform settings, restart the host instance that is running the orchestration.

At this point the orchestration is deployed and available to run. The next step is to test it.

40. Copy any XML file you wish, and paste it into `C:\pro bam samples\chapter eleven\filedrops\ OrchAPIin`. After a few seconds it will disappear—it has been picked up by the receive location.

41. Follow the directions in Exercise 10-1 to use SQL Server Management Studio to inspect the BAM Primary Import database. You should see a new row has been written into the database. If you don't see the row, check the Application event log for error messages.

42. Using the BAM Portal, you can search for the data written by the orchestration, as shown in Figure 10-9.

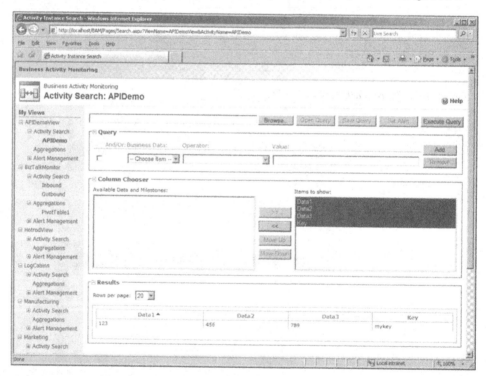

Figure 10-9. *The BAM Portal showing orchestration data*

Working with MessagingEventStream

MessagingEventStream is used inside a pipeline component to write to BAM as part of the messaging transactions. It shares the EventStream base class with the other classes you've already learned, so the code will look quite familiar.

If you examine a BizTalk pipeline component, it usually does its work in the Execute method of the IComponent interface. Execute has two parameters: an IPipelineContext that contains the pipeline context and an IBaseMessage that contains the message being processed. The pipeline context has a GetEventStream method that returns a MessagingEventStream. So you might see the following code inside a pipeline component:

```
public IBaseMessage Execute(IPipelineContext context, IBaseMessage baseMessage)
{
    //Other pipeline behavior omitted for clarity

    //Get the Messaging Event Stream
    MessagingEventStream eventStream = context.GetEventStream();

    //This code uses the event stream to write to BAM
    string activityGuid = Guid.NewGuid().ToString();
    eventStream.BeginActivity("PipelineTracking",activityGuid);
    eventStream.UpdateActivity("PipelineTracking ",activityGuid,
        "MessageTime", System.DateTime.Now().ToString(),
        "MessageID", baseMessage.MessageID);
    eventStream.EndActivity("PipelineTracking",activityGuid);
    eventStream.Flush();
}
```

As you can see, once you've used the context to get a MessagingEventStream object, the code is the same as in the previous exercises.

The BAM Management API

BAM provides a management web service available at http://<your server>/BAM/ BamManagementService/BamManagementService.asmx. It supplies the methods listed in Table 10-4.

These methods would be useful to a developer building a clone of the BAM Portal. Also, if your application needed to create alerts or subscriptions on behalf of the user, this API would be useful. As an example, consider a Sales department where each state is associated with a different sales representative. Sales representative allocations change frequently and are managed in an ERP application. Whenever an order is received for a state, the salesperson for that state could be notified. A BizTalk application that monitors the ERP system could use the BAM Management Web Service to ensure the sales order alerts were set correctly whenever the salesperson allocations were changed in the ERP system.

BAM provides another web service available at `http://<your server>/BAM/BamQueryService/BamQueryService.asmx`. It supplies only one method: `GetInstanceData()`. Unlike the BAM Management Web Service, the BAM Query Service is undocumented, and Microsoft recommends that application developers don't use it. We agree with this recommendation. The syntax for this web service is bizarre; it's hard to use and unsupported. Instead, we recommend querying the SQL Server views directly. Although it's counterintuitive, going directly to the database is more supportable and flexible, and we recommend connecting directly to SQL Server in your applications. If you must have a web service for interoperability, don't use the Query Service. Instead, create your own web service, or use ADO.NET Data Services to provide a Representational State Transfer (REST) interface to BAM.

Table 10-4. *Methods in the BAM Management API*

Method	Comments
AddSubscription	Adds a subscription to an existing alert.
CreateAlert	Creates a new BAM alert.
DeleteAlert	Deletes a BAM alert.
GenerateEventForArtifact	Generates an entry in the event log asking for help with the activity.*
GetAlert	Gets information about an alert.
GetAlertsSummary	Retrieves a list of alerts associated with a view.
GetCapabilities	Provides information on the database version and whether OLAP and alerts are available.
GetPivotViewXml	Returns XML that allows Office Web Components to be used to display a pivot view.
GetReferences	Returns a list of related artifacts for an activity instance. The artifacts can be a BizTalk service, message ID, activity ID, document URL, instance ID or arbitrary user type.
GetRelatedActivityInstances	Returns a list of directly related activity instances.
GetViewDetailsAsXml	Returns the BAM definition XML for a view.
GetViewSummaryForCurrentUser	Returns data on all views the current user can access.
RemoveSubscription	Removes a subscription for an alert.
UpdateAlert	Adds and removes alert owners and subscriptions.
UpdateSubscription	Updates existing subscriptions for an alert.

* See Chapter 7 for more information on generating help requests in the BAM Portal.

Summary

In this chapter, you learned about four classes: `DirectEventStream`, `BufferedEventStream`, `OrchestrationEventStream`, and `MessagingEventStream`. Each of these classes allows you to write to BAM programmatically. `DirectEventStream` and `BufferedEventStream` allow you to write to BAM from a .NET application that is not written in WCF, WF, or BizTalk. `OrchestrationEventStream` and `MessagingEventStream` allow you to write code in BizTalk to provide capabilities that are not available in the TPE. You also learned how to implement continuations using the API and about the BAM Management Web Service.

PART 4

■ ■ ■

Advanced Topics in BAM

Finishing out the book, Part 4 covers some advanced topics in BAM.

Chapter 11 discusses BAM and business intelligence (BI), including using applications and servers within Microsoft's BI offerings to display data from the BAM databases.

Chapter 12 covers relationships between BAM activities. Relationships between activities are analogous to foreign key relationships in a relational database. In the chapter example, a relationship exists between one BAM activity that captures order header information and another activity that captures line items that you'll discover has many applications.

Chapter 13 covers managing BizTalk servers, including database administration. To keep your BAM databases healthy, you'll want to schedule certain database jobs. Chapter 13 explains these jobs and provides some tips and tricks for the BAM Management utility.

Chapter 14 covers monitoring BizTalk servers using BAM instead of out-of-the-box tools. BAM can provide a more efficient alternative to using tracking data in large BizTalk installations.

The final chapter of the book, Chapter 15, wraps up and talks about some developments we expect to see in BAM and enterprise performance monitoring over the next few years.

CHAPTER 11

BAM and Business Intelligence

Enterprise Performance Management is a practice that usually involves multiple tools (BI, BAM, CEP, etc.), methodologies (Six Sigma, Total Quality Management, Activity-Based Costing, etc.), and practices that blend both tools and methodologies (Balanced Scorecard, Integrated Strategic Management, etc.).

As Sun Tzu said in *The Art of War*: "Measurement owes its existence to Earth; Estimation of quantity to Measurement; Calculation to Estimation of quantity; Balancing of chances to Calculation; and Victory to Balancing of chances." The more comprehensive, more integrated, and more "balanced" your Enterprise Performance Management practice, the more likely your chance of victory.

This chapter describes the relationship between BAM and business intelligence (BI) tools. It includes

- An overview of BI concepts, including key performance indicators and dashboards

- An overview of integrating BAM and Microsoft's BI tools

- Alternative integration notes for including other Microsoft tools in your BI strategy

This chapter should be considered just one stone of a foundation for building an Enterprise Performance Management practice. Careful attention must be paid to the development and implementation of methodologies and practices within that foundation as well.

Business Intelligence Concepts

Business intelligence is a collection of technologies that transform raw data into useful information to enable more effective decision making. The aim of BI technologies is to provide a view into the health of business processes; BI is a high priority for CIOs because it has a high potential to deliver business value.

■**Note** Chapter 1 includes an overview of the relationship between BI and BAM.

Traditionally, BI tools have been fed from transactional databases by extract-transform-load (ETL) tools. Typically, these implementations upload data to a data warehouse on a periodic basis, often daily or hourly. BAM can be used with a BI strategy as an additional source of data, providing a view of the business that is closer to real time. A comprehensive BI strategy is likely to involve combining BAM data with traditional BI data to provide a holistic view of the organization.

Before we drill into the technical details of combining BAM with BI, it's useful for you to know some of the more well-known and common BI concepts: key performance indicators (KPIs), measurable objectives, scorecards, strategy maps, and dashboards.

KPIs

The first step in a BI project is for the organization to define a set of *key performance indicators*. KPIs are the specific measurable data points a business tracks in order to identify its progress. When businesses define their KPIs, they set forth the metrics by which their efforts will be measured against their objectives. Examples of KPIs are *average cost of recruiting an employee, median number of days required to process an order*, or *average cost of handling an insurance claim*.

A KPI is the most granular aspect of a BI solution. When defining KPIs, you should seek to assess complex business strategies through measurable numbers. In a BAM project, KPIs are likely to be based on measures in an aggregated BAM view.

Measurable Objectives

KPIs are rolled up into objectives. In order to be useful, objectives need to be measurable. Measurable objectives include five elements: an action, a KPI, a benchmark, a target, and a timeframe. An example of a measurable objective is *reduce average cost of recruitment per employee from $15,000 to $9,000 by end of fiscal year 2010*. It's quite simple to take this objective and parse out the five key elements, as shown in Table 11-1.

Table 11-1. *An Example Measurable Objective*

Element	Example
Action	Reduce . . .
KPI	. . . average cost of recruitment per employee . . .
Benchmark	. . . from $15,000 . . .
Target	. . . to $9,000 . . .
Timeframe	. . . by end of fiscal year 2010.

The action is the effect that is desired, the KPI is the value that's being measured, the benchmark is the current value of the KPI, the target is the desired value of the KPI, and the timeframe is the date when the desired value of the KPI should be achieved. Another example of an objective is to control travel costs. In order to make this objective measurable, the current benchmark value should be measured, and then a target and timeframe must be set.

A measurable objective would be *reduce travel expenses from 5% to 2% of overall revenue by December*. While the BAM Portal does provide real-time observation capabilities, when dealing with BAM data, an objective is likely to be implemented with a tool like PerformancePoint Server or PerformancePoint Services using data from a BAM scheduled aggregation.

Scorecards

A *scorecard*, then, is the set of measurable objectives that are used to judge a team or organization. Often, these objectives are grouped as strategic, operational, or tactical. Scorecards also seek to grow accountability by assigning ownership of the objectives.

The biggest challenge in designing a scorecard is ensuring the correct balance of incentives. As an example, consider designing a scorecard for a group of telephone support representatives who answer technical questions from computer owners. Long support calls cost more than short support calls, so you might assume that the scorecard should measure reps based on the number of calls they handle during an eight-hour shift. It's easy to use the call center infrastructure to measure the number of calls taken by a rep, so imagine that the company pays each rep a $50 bonus if he takes more than 50 calls during a shift.

How will the reps respond? Some reps, when they realize that their shift is almost over and they haven't answered 50 calls, will start hanging up two minutes into each call, whether the technical question has been resolved or not. Hanging up abruptly will have three main effects. It will ensure the rep gets $50, which is good for the rep. It will have a serious negative effect on customer satisfaction, which is bad for both the computer company and its customers. It will also increase technical support costs, because the customers will call back and start work on their problem again from the beginning. In this case, the scorecard has caused behavior that is the exact opposite of the company's business goals; the reps having succeeded in "gaming" the system.

Historically, scorecards in practice went wrong because they contain only financial measures, which often encourage the wrong behaviors. A balanced scorecard is a scorecard that contains both financial and nonfinancial measurements. Often the measurements are grouped under four perspectives: financial perspective, customer perspective, internal process perspective, and learning and organizational growth perspective.

In the call center example, you could improve the quality of service the reps provide by calling customers back to survey their satisfaction with customer service and give a bonus only to reps who achieve an appropriate customer satisfaction rating in addition to a fast average call time. Even with a balanced scorecard, there's a danger that people will attempt to beat the system. Imagine that the call center modifies its bonus scheme to pay a bonus to reps who have a 90% customer satisfaction rating in addition to 50 calls per month. This bonus scheme tells reps that they can get the bonus as long as they don't do more than five fast hangups per shift.

A real example of a scorecard system that created perverse incentives was the British government's attempt to improve access to medical appointments under the National Health Service. One of the goals of the policy was to ensure that patients could be seen quickly when requesting an appointment. A scorecard was created that judged doctors' offices on the length of time between making the appointment and seeing the patient; the government's goal was that patients should be seen within 48 hours. Many doctors responded by declining to book appointments more than 48 hours in advance. If no appointment was available within 48 hours, their offices would refuse to book a later appointment. Instead, they told their patients to call back a couple of days later, when an appointment might be available. One patient described the effects of the scorecard as follows:

You have to sit on the phone for three hours in the morning trying to get an appointment because you are not allowed to ask for the appointment before that, because by making it 48 hours beforehand they are missing the government target.

Diana Church of Essex on BBC One's *Question Time*

Strategy Maps

Strategy maps (see Figure 11-1) were introduced in response to the challenges associated with scorecards. If KPIs and scorecards are based on the idea that *you can't manage what you can't measure*, strategy maps are based on the idea that *you can't measure what you can't describe*. In this approach, measures are selected by plotting strategic objectives on a strategy map.

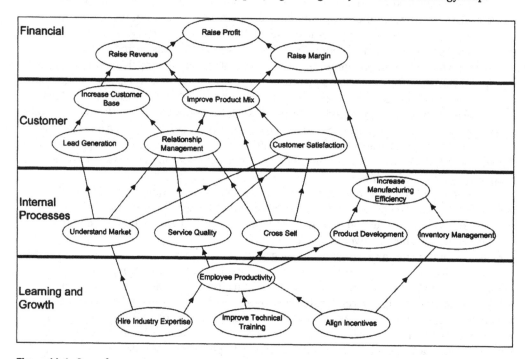

Figure 11-1. *Sample strategy map*

In the sample strategy map shown in Figure 11-1, the organization's most important objective is *raise profit*. This objective, however, cannot be implemented in a vacuum. Instead, *raise profit* has been decomposed into a set of strategies for achieving the objective. An arrow between two strategies indicates a cause-and-effect relationship. In our sample, *raise profit* is caused by *raise revenue* and *raise margin*. *Raise margin*, in turn, is caused by *improve product mix* and *increase manufacturing efficiency*.

In a real example of a strategy map, a military command within the U.S Department of Defense created a goal of *equipping the warfighter to win.* Strategies that supported that goal included *quality systems equipment, expert life-cycle management, operational efficiency,* and *high-performance organization.*

Dashboards

Dashboards are a visual representation of performance data, which may include a composite of scorecards, strategy maps, charts, graphs, and other information. A dashboard may best be thought of as a view of the BI data relevant to the person or department. A dashboard may include a single scorecard or many scorecards. As an example, a salesperson's dashboard might include just the scorecard for the salesperson's territory. A sales manager would see a dashboard that included each territory's scorecard, allowing the manager to assess the relative performance of each salesperson.

When shown on a dashboard, scorecards usually include indicators that visually depict performance against the plan, such as arrows, stoplights, or thumbs up/thumbs down images. Drill-through to additional detail is often provided so that the user can analyze why targets are being met or missed.

Through the use of scorecards and dashboards, the user will see relevant data and can develop initiatives that support the organization's objectives. Dashboards may also include trend data that supports forecasting future performance. As with objectives, scorecards and dashboards based on BAM data are often implemented with a tool like PerformancePoint using data from a BAM scheduled aggregation.

Integrating BAM and BI

BI architectures may be broken down into three logical tiers:

- Data presentation
- Data processing
- Data input

BizTalk's BAM stack provides all three tiers. The BAM Portal is a presentation application, the BAM infrastructure provides the processing logic, and the BAM interceptors provide the data inputs. In a more traditional BI architecture, data presentation is provided by a dashboard tool such as PerformancePoint or a reporting tool such as Crystal Reports or SQL Server Reporting Services (SSRS), data processing is provided by an online analytical processing (OLAP) server such as SQL Server Analysis Services (SSAS), and data input is provided by an extract-transform-load tool such as Informatica PowerCenter or SQL Server Integration Services (SSIS).

Several architectures that combine BI with BAM are possible; the most common is an architecture in which BAM is used as an input to a broader BI strategy. In this approach, BAM would be one of several sources of information that are accepted by a data warehouse, and reports or dashboards would be created that use data from both BAM and more traditional sources.

In BizTalk Server 2009, BAM provides the ability to view complex data on current business events, whereas more traditional BI solutions represent a snapshot of data at a specific period in time or over a period of time.

Strategies for Process Monitoring

In the Gartner research paper "Intelligent Process Monitoring: BPM, BAM, and BI Combined," Gartner introduced a four-level process-monitoring framework. Gartner's four levels of process monitoring are as follows:

- *Monitoring a single process instance*: This allows you to answer questions like *What is the state of Mr. Smith's insurance claim?* and *How long have we been working on Mr. Smith's claim?* BizTalk provides this with BAM activities.

- *Monitoring all active process instances*: This allows you to answer questions like *How long on average does it takes to process an insurance claim?* and *Which part of the process takes the longest?* BizTalk provides this with BAM aggregated views.

- *Monitoring all active and completed process instances*: This allows you to answer questions like *Has the time taken to handle claims changed over the last month?* and *Is the underwriting department doing better or worse than this time last month?* Implementing this on the Microsoft platform is likely to require creating a custom solution that combines data from BAM with information from either an archive of historical BAM data or information from a traditional data warehouse. In some cases, trending information from the BAM archive or the data warehouse may be enough, and integration with real-time data may not be needed.

- *Monitoring related external events*: This allows you to answer questions like *What effect do hurricanes have on the time taken to process a claim?* This will be complex to implement, requiring some kind of ESB feeding events to BAM and a solution that combines external events from the ESB, BAM data, and information from a data warehouse. If you plan to reach this level of monitoring, you may want to consider acquiring a complex event processing (CEP) system that had broader capabilities than BizTalk's BAM offering.

Note For more information on CEP and on context on building better BAM, see Chapter 15. Microsoft has announced it will introduce a CEP offering before the end of 2009.

It's important to understand that these aren't either/or choices. A comprehensive strategy will include all levels of process monitoring. Most likely, you will want to start by monitoring individual processes, and then move up the stack to provide aggregated data later. Over time, you can add the third and fourth levels of the framework to your BAM solution.

Monitoring should not require a human being to watch the data. Use BAM alerting and other alerting capabilities to notify business users when a process requires human intervention.

Integrating BAM with Microsoft's BI Tools

Microsoft provides a rich set of technologies for implementing BI solutions. The next sections provide overviews of the BI capabilities in Microsoft's database, middleware, and presentational BI software, and a roadmap for these technologies as Microsoft rolls out the next generation of Microsoft Office.

SQL Server Integration Services Overview

SQL Server Integration Services is an extract-transform-load tool. SSIS is capable of moving data between a large variety of data sources and destinations, and transforming the data format as the data is processed. The most common uses for SSIS are moving data between instances of relational databases and moving data from an operational database to a data warehouse. In many cases, SSIS packages perform a series of steps as they move data. SSIS provides conditional workflow capabilities; the next step in a package may depend on whether the previous step succeeded or failed. If a step fails, SSIS can revert to a checkpoint earlier in the package and retry.

SSIS was released with SQL Server 2005. SQL Server 2000 included Data Transformation Services (DTS), a much simpler ETL tool with fewer data sources and more limited data transformation, management, and workflow capabilities. DTS is incompatible with SSIS, so DTS was also provided with SQL Server 2005 for backward compatibility.

Integrating BAM with SSIS or DTS

BAM uses DTS packages to move data from the BAM Primary Import database to the BAM Archive and BAM Analysis databases. The correct packages are automatically created by the BAM Management utility, bm.exe.

There are a myriad of means by which BAM and SSIS may be integrated other than the ones by which it already does. Because SSIS offers tasks to perform full CRUD operations, send mail, interface with WMI, perform schema management, prepare and scrub data, and others, SSIS oftentimes is used as "glue" to accommodate and enhance functionality in a BAM implementation once it has been deployed. For example, lookups are great for adding additional context to BAM activities and views. However, if the data within the lookups is external to the instance of SQL Server on which BAM is hosted, or even external to the organization, SSIS provides "scheduled job"–like capabilities to regularly update the lookup data from external sources, thus keeping your lookup data relevant.

The most frequently used means for SSIS when integrating with BAM is to move data from BAM to your organization's data warehouse. We recommend creating all new packages in SSIS only, as DTS may not be supported in future SQL Server versions.

SQL Server Analysis Services Overview

SQL Server Analysis Services provides OLAP databases. The most common format for SSAS databases is a *cube*. Cubes are databases that are organized using the concepts of *measures* and *dimensions*. A measure is simply an aggregated data item, such as *total price, item count*, or *total revenue*. A dimension is an attribute that is used to organize data, such as *order date*, *customer location*, or *product category*. The advantage of the cube format is that measures can be aggregated for any combination of dimensions very quickly.

OLAP databases can actually come in several varieties. Multidimensional OLAP (MOLAP) stores data as a cube, relational OLAP (ROLAP) stores data in relational tables, and hybrid OLAP (HOLAP) stores detail data in relational tables but aggregate data in cubes. In addition to OLAP databases, SSAS allows KPIs to be defined and calculated in the database.

Integrating BAM and SSAS

BAM stores aggregated views as cubes in SSAS. The cube structure is automatically created by the BAM Management utility based on the view definition created in Excel.

One of the scenarios in integrating BAM and SSAS we've witnessed is to create cubes that combine data from BAM with data from other sources. As an example, consider the Arnold, Wilbur, and Olivia Corporation (AWO) sample described in Chapter 5. The BAM data captured in Chapter 6 was used to populate a marketing view that contains information on agents, customer state and country, and order size. If AWO has a customer database that includes additional data about corporate customers, such as industry classification (North American Industry Classification System, or NAICS) code, annual revenue, and number of office locations, it would be useful to add this data to the marketing view as additional dimensions. Because this data is not captured directly by BAM, it would be necessary to create a new set of databases for the additional data. The implementation would probably include a custom *star schema* database. Star schema is a relational database format that is used as a staging area for measures and dimensions that will be used to build a cube. A custom SSIS package would be used to move data from the BAM Primary Import database to the star schema database.

■**Note** NAICS is a system for classifying economic data, where each industry is given a standard code. As an example, the code 33994 is used for the manufacturing of office supplies other than paper.

SQL Server Reporting Services Overview

SQL Server Reporting Services allows developers and end users to create printed or interactive reports based on data in relational databases, SSAS cubes, or other data formats. SSRS is extensible, so it's relatively easy for a .NET developer to write code that connects SSRS to a custom data source. Because BAM data is stored in SQL Server, it doesn't require any custom coding to create reports based on data stored in BAM views.

Developers can design reports in the Visual Studio Report Designer and publish them to a report server so they are available to users. Developers can also create *report models* that define the relationships between tables in a database, making it easy for nontechnical users to define their own reports. Users can also create reports by working in Query Builder directly with cubes or relational data, but that requires the users to understand the data model they are working with.

One of the major benefits that SSRS has over a tool like the BAM Portal is its ability to create report subscriptions. That is, if there is specific data you feel users of the BAM Portal should receive on a regular basis that a BAM alert may not necessarily provide, SSRS may be used to distribute that data via e-mail or even for rendering to a mobile device.

Integrating BAM and SSRS

Integrating BAM and SSRS is a fairly straightforward process. BAM may be used as the data source for SSRS reports, or to provide additional, real-time contextual data to preexisting reports.

EXERCISE 11-1. REPORTING ON BAM DATA

In this exercise, you will use SQL Server Reporting Services to report on data in a BAM view.

Note Perform this exercise on a machine that has SQL Server Reporting Services installed. If that's not the machine that has BizTalk installed, you will need network connectivity to your BAM Primary Import database.

---

1. If you didn't complete the exercises in Chapter 6, run the batch file C:\pro bam samples\chapter six\finished.bat.

2. If you have SQL Server 2005, from the Start menu, select Microsoft SQL Server 2005 ➤ SQL Server Business Intelligence Development Studio.

3. If you have SQL Server 2008, from the Start menu, select Microsoft SQL Server 2008 ➤ SQL Server Business Intelligence Development Studio.

4. From the File menu, select New ➤ Project.

5. Select Report Server Project, set the project name to BAM Reports, and then click OK.

6. In Solution Explorer, right-click Reports, and then select Add New Report, displaying the first page of the Report Wizard. Click Next to display the Select the Data Source page.

7. Click the Edit button to edit the database connection string.

8. Using the Server name drop-down box, select the name of the server that contains your BAM Primary Import database.

9. Using the Select or Enter a Database Name drop-down box, select the BAM Primary Import database, as shown in Figure 11-2.

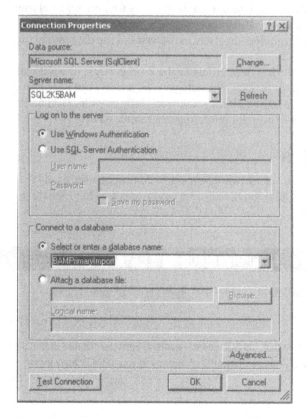

Figure 11-2. *The Connection Properties dialog box*

10. Click OK to close the Connection Properties dialog box and return to the Select the Data Source page, which should now look as shown in Figure 11-3.

11. Click Next to display the Design the Query page.

12. Click the Query Builder button to display the Query Builder.

13. Click the Generic Query button, shown in Figure 11-4, to bring up the Visual Designer.

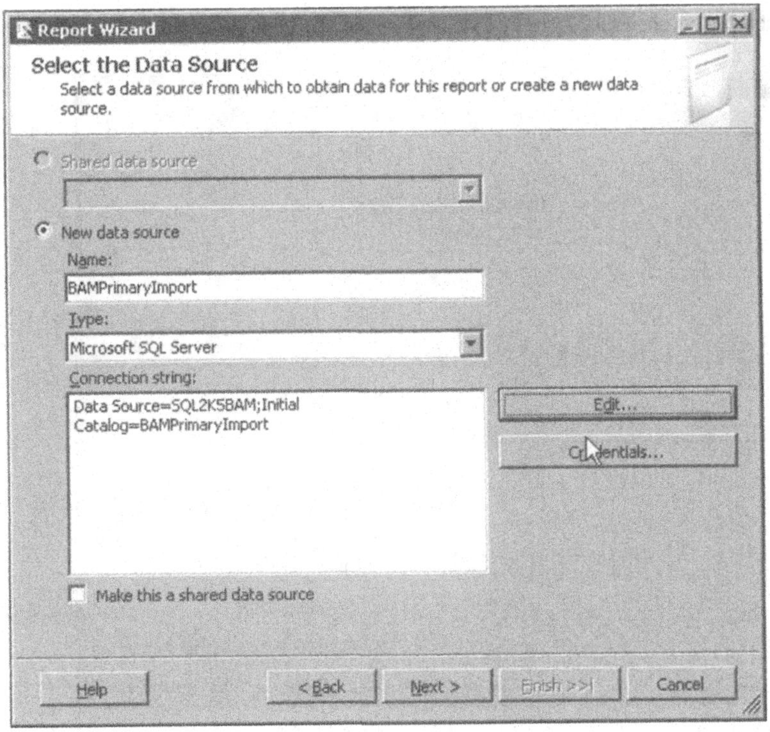

Figure 11-3. *The Select the Data Source page in the Report Wizard*

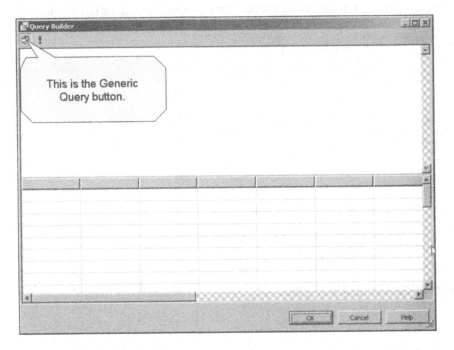

Figure 11-4. *The Generic Query button*

14. Press the Add Table button, shown in Figure 11-5, to bring up the Add Table dialog box.

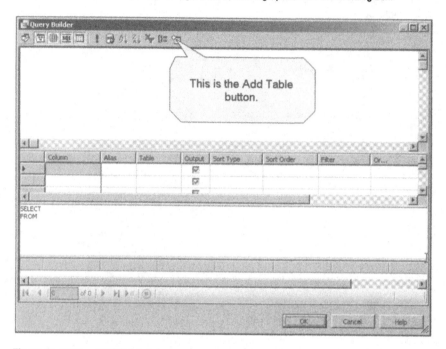

Figure 11-5. *The Add Table button*

15. Select the Views tab, and then select the bam_Orders_AllInstances view, as shown in Figure 11-6.

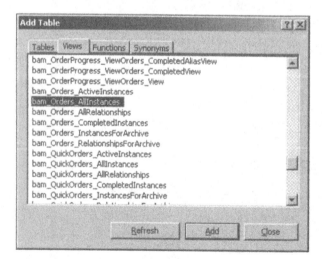

Figure 11-6. *The Add Table dialog box*

16. Click the Add button, and then click the Close button to close the Add Table dialog box.

17. Select the fields shown in the following list. Your Query Builder should now resemble what you see in Figure 11-7.

- AgentNumber
- OrderNumber
- Price
- BaleCount
- CustomerName
- CustomerState
- CustomerCountry

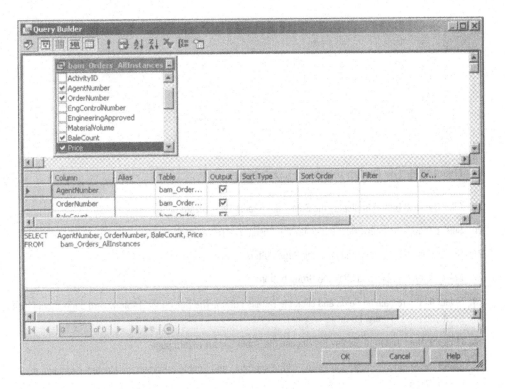

Figure 11-7. *The Query Builder*

18. Click the OK button to close the Query Builder and return to the Design the Query page, shown in Figure 11-8.

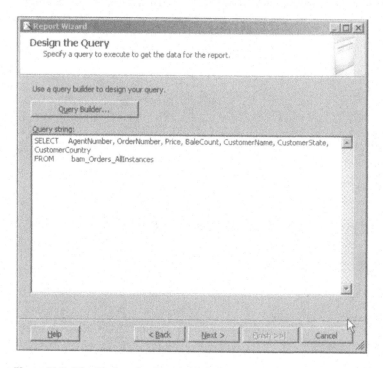

Figure 11-8. *The Design the Query wizard page*

19. Click the Next button to display the Select the Report Type wizard page.

20. Select Tabular and click Next to display the Design the Table wizard page.

21. Select CustomerCountry and click the Page button.

22. Select AgentNumber and click the Group button.

23. Select all the remaining fields and click the Details button. The Design the Table wizard page should look like what you see in Figure 11-9.

24. Click the Next button to display the Choose the Table Layout wizard page.

25. Select the Stepped format, and leave Include subtotals and Enable drilldown unselected, as shown in Figure 11-10.

26. Click the Next button to display the Choose the Table Style wizard page.

27. Click each of the available styles to view the choice of color scheme. Select one that appeals to your artistic side. (If you don't have an artistic side, choose the Generic style.)

28. Click the Next button to display the Completing the Wizard page.

29. Name the report Orders.

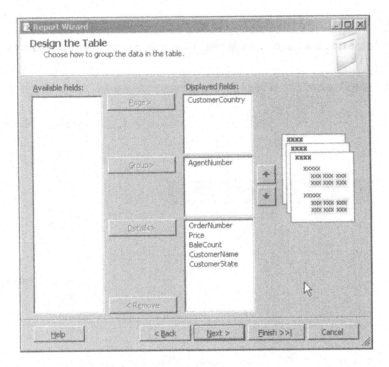

Figure 11-9. *The Design the Table wizard page*

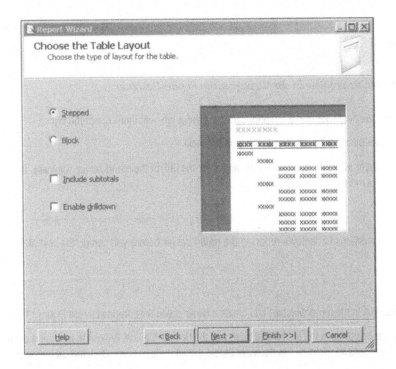

Figure 11-10. *The Choose the Table Layout wizard page*

30. Click the Finish button.

31. The report will now be open in Visual Studio Report Designer. Click the Preview tab to see a preview of the report (see Figure 11-11).

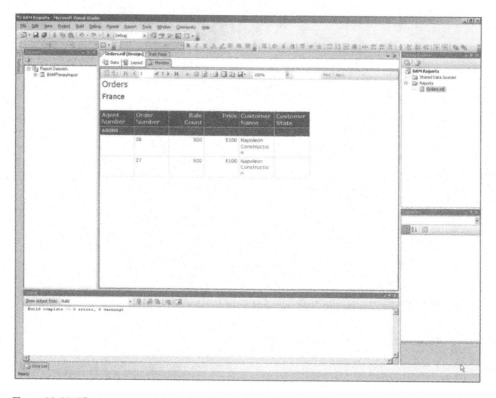

Figure 11-11. *The report preview in the Visual Studio Report Designer*

32. If you wish to change the field widths in the report, click the Layout tab, and then correct the layout.

33. Save all files, and close Business Intelligence Development Studio.

34. if you have a report server available, open a browser and enter the URL of the report server. Typically, the URL will be `http://<server name>/reports`.

■Note You will need permissions to deploy a report to the report server before you can do the rest of the exercise.

---

35. Click the New Folder link in the navigation bar, and create a folder called BAM Reports (see Figure 11-12).

36. Click the BAM Reports link to open the folder, and then click the Upload File line. Browse to the report definition you created in Business Intelligence Development Studio, called `orders.rdl`. Click the OK button to load the file.

37. A new Orders link should be visible in the folder. Click the link to see your report, which should look like the one in Figure 11-13.

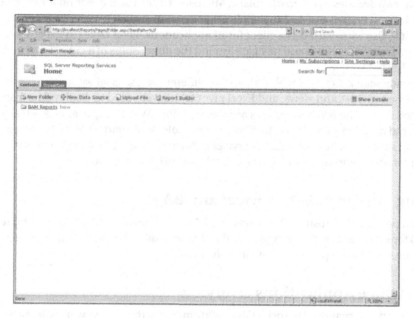

Figure 11-12. *The Report Manager showing the new folder*

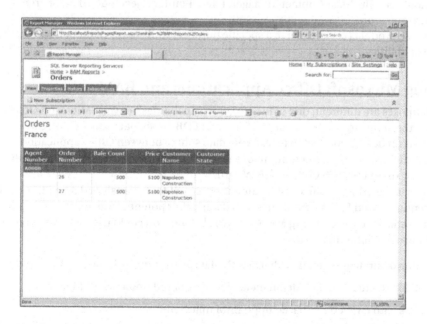

Figure 11-13. *The report displayed in the Report Manager*

Microsoft Office Excel Overview

After more than two decades in the marketplace, Microsoft Office Excel needs no introduction. Although Excel is best known as a desktop application for simple calculations and records management, it is also widely used as a client for BI applications. Pivot tables in Excel allow users to see data from SSAS cubes and navigate around the dimensions of a cube. Excel also supports SSAS KPIs.

You've already seen Excel used with BAM in two different ways. Excel was used in several chapters to define activities and views, and Excel pivot tables were used to display data from BAM aggregated views. The BAM Portal uses Microsoft's Office Web Components, a server component based on Excel's code base, to display pivot tables and charts. (Office Web Components are still supported; however, Excel Services in Microsoft Office SharePoint Server, or MOSS, is the preferred approach for displaying Excel spreadsheets in a browser.)

Integrating Microsoft Office Excel and BAM

The integration points of Microsoft Office Excel and BAM have been covered in prior chapters. See Chapter 5 for exercises that define aggregated BAM views using Excel. See Chapter 7 for exercises that use Excel to display BAM data in a pivot table.

Microsoft Office Applications Overview

In its latest released incarnation, Microsoft Office 2007 includes the following desktop products in various SKUs: Access, Accounting, Communicator, Excel, Groove, InfoPath, OneNote, Outlook, Outlook with Business Contact Manager, PowerPoint, Project, Publisher, SharePoint Designer, Visio, and Word.

Each of these products seeks to serve a specific purpose, while many of them have slightly overlapping capabilities.

Integrating Microsoft Office Applications and BAM

While their purposes are different, one of the common capabilities between Microsoft Office applications is the ability to connect to an ODBC- or OLEDB-based data source. You can find instructions on how to connect to an external data source between Office applications by searching the Office help documentation for the topic "Import data into Office Publisher, Visio, or Word by using the Data Connection Wizard."

While Excel is the primary Office application used as a BI tool to analyze data within BAM (Access is oftentimes used for its wizards to scrub data), other potential integration and data consumption scenarios emerge. Using Microsoft Word alone, you could use BAM data and the data connection capabilities to create

- A meeting or strategic agenda with live BAM data as supporting information

- Budget documents that include financial numbers based upon live BAM data

- Calendars with target dates based upon BAM milestones

- Contracts and operating agreements (e.g., Service-Level Agreements) utilizing BAM uptime data as supporting evidence

- Mail merge envelopes and letters to recipients who have met a specific BAM threshold

- Invoices, packing slips, or work orders to be sent out based upon purchase orders from BAM data

- Letters with BAM data as supporting information (e.g., a letter to the head of a real estate broker office notifying her of the top sellers for the month)

- Memos, business plans, or project plans that use BAM data to support a strategic or tactical position

- A customer service report utilizing BAM data to substantiate customer service ratings

- Timesheets for a professional services organization that submits its time via a WCF web service monitored by BAM

If you've ever created a network diagram in Visio, the idea of a network diagram fed with live BAM data that indicates the number of service requests for a WCF service or the health of a BAM solution is a very powerful concept.

While these solutions are not provided out of the box, they are feasible and greatly enhanced by a well-defined BAM observation model.

Microsoft Office PerformancePoint Server Overview

Microsoft Office PerformancePoint Server is Microsoft's entry in the Corporate Performance Management (CPM) market. PerformancePoint provides three main capabilities: monitoring, analytics, and planning. These three capabilities were developed separately and are not especially well integrated. Each module's heritage is clearly visible, and the tools used to manage each module are different.

In BizTalk Server 2009, Microsoft modified the BAM database structures to ensure that they are compatible with PerformancePoint. BAM data from BizTalk Server 2006 or BizTalk Server 2006 R2 may have issues working with BAM databases.

The monitoring module manages and displays KPIs, dashboards, and reports. It is based on Business Scorecard Manager 2005, which was an earlier Microsoft product for building dashboards. KPIs, scorecards, and dashboards are designed in the Dashboard Designer tool and published to WSS sites. The Strategy Map Designer is a Visio add-in that supports strategy maps. Monitoring is the part of PerformancePoint that is most likely to be useful to a BAM project. If you are using PerformancePoint dashboards in your organization, you should consider extending the dashboards to include BAM data.

The analytics module is used primarily for analyzing data stored in SSAS. The analytics module contains additional tools, such as ProClarity Dashboard, that overlap with the monitoring module. The tools in the analytics module were originally developed by ProClarity Corporation, which was acquired by Microsoft in 2006.

ProClarity's decomposition trees and heat maps are not available in the monitoring module. The heat map provides a color-coded, two-dimensional graphic that groups data of like values; it allows the user to visually spot KPIs that are out of range. This tool would be very useful with BAM, but the authors recommend caution in adopting tools from the analytics module until the SharePoint 14 roadmap becomes clearer.

The planning module was developed by Microsoft for release with PerformancePoint under the code name Biz#; the first version of the planning module shipped with PerformancePoint in 2007. It supports budgeting and forecasting, and is not typically used with BAM data.

Integrating PerformancePoint Server and BAM

The most common (and recommended) integration point for BAM and PerformancePoint Server is the monitoring server module, specifically because PerformancePoint focuses upon using SSAS to access data in the BAM Analysis database.

While an exercise on integrating BAM and PerformancePoint would be useful, we must note that the setup of PerformancePoint Server should not be included on your BizTalk Server virtual machine. In fact, PerformancePoint Server requires SQL Server 2005 and has specific conflicts with.NET Framework 3.5 Service Pack 1 (along the lines of ASP.NET AJAX server extensions), and it caused a number of Windows Workflow Foundation problems in our tests when we tried to host within WSS. Rather than include an exercise here, we will endeavor to provide one on the Apress web site and in the code downloads for this book.

If you have a PerformancePoint Server implementation already up, the general process you'll want to follow to integrate BAM and PerformancePoint Server Monitoring Server is as follows:

1. Import the Activity View cube into PerformancePoint Server Dashboard Designer by using the Create a Scorecard Wizard against the BAM cube. This will generate the BAM KPIs in which you are interested.

2. Alter the KPIs to the criteria relevant to the business process.

3. Combine the KPIs into a scorecard.

4. Add the scorecard to PerformancePoint Server dashboard and publish to a monitoring server.

SharePoint Server is actually involved at this point, as the dashboard is rendered using the PerformancePoint Server Dashboard Viewer web part. Bear in mind, this is purely for observation purposes and doesn't really provide for collaboration. That's where a tool like SharePoint Server comes in.

Microsoft SharePoint Server Overview

Microsoft Office SharePoint Server is a collaboration, web content management, search, and portal product that is widely used as an intranet framework. SharePoint Server 2007 shipped in November 2006. SharePoint Server 2010 will probably ship with version 14 of Microsoft Office in 2010. MOSS provides several BI tools, including the Business Data Catalog (BDC), KPI support, web-based reporting, and server-based spreadsheet management. SharePoint's user interface can be customized using a technology called *web parts*. Each web part provides part of the page; users can edit the appearance of the portal by dragging web parts from place to place.

MOSS builds on Windows SharePoint Services (WSS) 3.0. WSS is a feature of Windows Server that provides some basic support for collaboration. MOSS adds many additional features to WSS, but is fully compatible with WSS web parts.

The Business Data Catalog is a SharePoint service that extracts data from other data sources, including databases and business applications. BDC data can be searched by SharePoint and can be included in SharePoint pages and lists. As an example, customer data stored in Siebel could be displayed in a list or searched using MOSS Enterprise Search.

MOSS supports creating and displaying KPIs. KPIs can be displayed in a SharePoint list, which can be included in a portal or dashboard as a web part. These KPI lists provide a simple approach to implementing business scorecards. KPIs can be manually entered, based on cells in Excel spreadsheets, based on KPIs in SSAS, or based on data in SharePoint lists.

MOSS provides tools for publishing and displaying reports. Dashboard reports present information from multiple sources, including scorecards as KPI lists, and tables from databases, spreadsheets, or other applications that are available through the Business Data Catalog. Report libraries support Excel reports, SSRS reports, and SharePoint dashboards.

Excel Services is a MOSS component that runs Excel spreadsheets and performs calculations. Calculations are performed on the application server, allowing shared access to spreadsheet data through the browser and a web services API.

SSRS supplies WSS web parts for displaying reports in SharePoint. SSRS reports can easily be included in a SharePoint page.

Integrating Microsoft SharePoint Server and BAM

There are many ways by which SharePoint Server may be integrated with BAM including the following:

- By serving as a portal mechanism to display BAM data (typically done using web parts)

- By using the MOSS dashboard and portal to display KPIs from the BAM API (views)

- By integrating the MOSS BDC with BAM using custom code

- By serving as a content repository for SSRS reports that utilize BAM data

- By providing Excel Services online workbooks that users may manipulate

- By providing as part of its BI offerings reports, dashboards, Excel workbooks, analytic views, scorecards, and plans

One of the means by which SharePoint 2007 and BAM should not be integrated, however, is by simply uploading a BAM Live Workbook to SharePoint Server's Excel Services. Because the BAM Live Workbook contains pivot tables as well as VBA code, it is unsupported within Excel Services (see http://blogs.msdn.com/excel/archive/2005/12/01/499206.aspx). We also highly recommend you don't attempt this; while most times we have received "The following unsupported feature(s) were detected" message when we've tried this, we have also seen it bring down entire server farms. It is likely the ability to upload "enhanced" workbooks is something the SharePoint Server Excel Services product team is focused upon for the next version of SharePoint Server.

BI Roadmap

At this point, you may be puzzled by the relationship between MOSS and PerformancePoint. MOSS provides tools for defining KPIs and designing dashboards. PerformancePoint also provides tools for defining KPIs and designing dashboards. There is clearly some overlap between the two products and even between different modules in PerformancePoint.

By 2010, we expect the confusion to be resolved. In January 2009, Microsoft announced that PerformancePoint would not be continued as a separate product. The Microsoft Business Intelligence Blog stated the following:

Based on customer feedback, we're announcing today that Microsoft is consolidating the scorecard, dashboard, and analytical capabilities from PerformancePoint Server into SharePoint Server as PerformancePoint Services, making these capabilities available to millions of SharePoint users around the world. This move helps us extend our vision to deliver BI more broadly to everyone in the organization at a lower total cost of ownership.

Post by Nic Smith on the Microsoft Business Intelligence Blog

SharePoint Server 14 should provide a unified set of dashboard tools that implement the BI functions of both MOSS 2007 and the monitoring and analytics modules of PerformancePoint. Microsoft plans to stop investing in the planning module, so we don't recommend building new applications on that technology.

In the short term, prior to the release of SharePoint Server 14, you will face some challenges deciding what technology to use for your dashboards. The migration story is much clearer for MOSS than PerformancePoint. On the other hand, PerformancePoint has much richer monitoring and analytics capabilities than MOSS 2007. We would not recommend starting a new CPM project on PerformancePoint without very specific guidance from Microsoft on the upgrade path to SharePoint 14.

Alternate Integration Scenarios

Because BAM data is exposed via SQL Server views and an Analysis Services database, the utilization of BAM beyond traditional BI tools is possible, but not one that immediately comes to mind when conceptualizing whether BAM fits within your BI implementation. BAM data stores may either serve as the destination for data from other Microsoft applications or expose data those applications make available.

We've included this section as we feel that learning how to use BAM is just as important as how to apply it. If your business is e-mail, the role Microsoft Exchange plays in your BI strategy is likely of great importance. Likewise, if you are an online merchant utilizing Microsoft Commerce Server, details down to the transaction level are likely a big part of your BI strategy.

With tools such as Microsoft Exchange, however, as with most server-level enterprise applications, it's important to identify the most appropriate tool for monitoring. If availability, scalability, and volume are to be monitored, BAM is probably not the best choice given the architecture of Microsoft Exchange. However, if the business-level interchange of data is to be monitored, for example, and if that data flows through a custom .NET application that could be enhanced to write data to BAM using the BAM API, then BAM is an appropriate choice.

Of course, there are limitations to integrations to specific products. For instance, the integration of BizTalk Server 2009 with Commerce Server is not supported as of the publication of this book. However, BizTalk Server 2006 with SP1 is supported. It is equally important to ask these questions as you integrate applications into your BI strategy.

As the number of applications for which you desire business activity monitoring grows, you can expect challenges. However, using the integration capabilities of BizTalk to connect via adapter, or using the WCF and WF interceptors, it's possible to bring business activity monitoring to applications such as the Managed Services Engine, Microsoft Exchange, Commerce Server 2009, Team Foundation Server, the Microsoft Dynamics Suite of products, and others.

Summary

In this chapter, you learned about the intersection between BI and BAM. A complete BI strategy is likely to include traditional data sources such as operational databases fed through ETL tools as well as BAM data from business processes. The chapter described some important BI concepts: KPIs, measurable objectives, balanced scorecards, strategy maps, and dashboards. The chapter also described Microsoft's BI platform and roadmap. An exercise showed how to integrate BAM with SQL Server Reporting Services.

In large enterprises, you will inevitably find an incumbent BI strategy, and a BAM project will only be successful if it integrates with the strategy. Creating dashboards in the preferred BI tool, and using ETL to move BAM data into a data warehouse, will be essential if you want your organization's management to use the data generated by your BAM project.

In the next chapter, we'll show you how to create BAM relationships.

■ ■ ■

CHAPTER 12

Relationship Advice

In this chapter, you'll learn how to create BAM relationships using either the TPE or the BAM API. BAM relationships are used whenever two activities need to be connected by shared data. Usually, the relationship is a one-to-many relationship, such as order header and order detail, or customers and orders.

As an example, consider the manufacturing process at a small specialty manufacturer of custom engine parts that supplies several NASCAR and Formula One teams. Each request for a part is converted by the engineering team into a part itinerary, which describes the steps required to manufacture that part. Each part itinerary contains header information and a series of manufacturing steps. Each manufacturing step contains information on the machine tool to use, the tool settings, and the detailed process for manufacturing the part.

BAM is used to capture information on manufacturing performance. There are two related activities: part and step. The part activity contains the part start time, completion time, and request number for the part. The step activity contains the request number, tool number, manufacturing time, and the status returned by the tool. The request number is shared across the two activities, allowing a BAM relationship to be set up. When a manufacturing step is viewed in the BAM Portal, a link is displayed that allows the user to navigate from manufacturing step to the request header information.

This chapter contains several exercises that cover the following:

- Creating related activities
- Examining the sample BizTalk application
- Creating a tracking profile for related activities
- Testing the application and capturing data
- Viewing relation data in SQL Server Management Studio
- Creating related activities using the BAM API

The Relationship Sample

Arnold, Wilbur, and Olivia (AWO), the specialized construction products company, has diversified into the manufacture of kits for building log cabins. Each kit consists of special hardware that is used to connect lumber together to form a cabin. (It's assumed the contractor constructing the cabin will provide the sticks.) Because there are a limited number of orders, and lumber size varies, each hardware kit is manufactured to order.

Each order contains a list of the hardware components needed as line items. When the order is received, BizTalk's XML receive pipeline breaks the interchange into separate messages for each line item; the subscribed send port stores each line item as a separate file.

Because of AWO's success with BAM in the Straw Bale division, the company has decided to implement BAM in the Log Cabin Hardware division. However, a single activity won't work to track the set of line items associated with a single order. Instead, two activities will be created: one that stores information from order headers and another that captures information from line items. An obvious relationship exists between these two activities, which is analogous to the foreign key relationship between order headers and order details in a relational database. In this case, instead of a relational database foreign key, the BAM activities are connected by using the BAM concept of a relationship. In this chapter, you will work through several exercises that implement this relationship.

EXERCISE 12-1. CREATING RELATED ACTIVITIES

In this exercise, you'll create the activities that will be used to capture order information for the Log Cabin Hardware division.

■Note Detailed instructions on creating activities and views are in Chapters 3 and 5.

---

1. Open Excel, and select BAM Activity from the BAM menu. Click the New Activity button, and create a new activity called Header that contains the items listed in Table 12-1.

Table 12-1. *Header Activity Items*

Name	Item Type
CustomerName	Business Data – Text
LumberType	Business Data – Text
OrderNumber	Business Data – Integer

2. Click the New Activity button again, and create a second new activity called LineItem that contains the items shown in Table 12-2.

Table 12-2. *LineItem Activity Items*

Name	Item Type
ConnectorType	Business Data – Text
Diameter	Business Data – Decimal
OrderNumber	Business Data – Integer
Quantity	Business Data – Integer

3. Click OK to close the Activity Definition dialog box.

4. In the Business Activity Monitoring View Creation Wizard, create a simple view called LogCabins that contains all the items from both activities, but no measures, dimensions, aliases, or durations.

5. If you completed Exercise 5-1, save the spreadsheet in your Excel Workbooks folder. If you didn't complete that exercise, save the spreadsheet in any convenient folder. If you're using Excel 2003, name the workbook Chap_12.xls. If you're using Excel 2007, name the workbook Chap_12.xlsx.

6. Open a new command-line window as an administrator.

7. Change directory to your Excel Workbooks folder.

8. If you are using Excel 2003, run the following commands:

```
path %path%;C:\Program Files\Microsoft BizTalk Server 2009\Tracking
bm deploy-all –DefinitionFile:Chap_12.xls
bm add-account -AccountName:<your account name> -View:LogCabins
```

9. If you are using Excel 2007, run the following commands:

```
path %path%;C:\Program Files\Microsoft BizTalk Server 2009\Tracking
bm deploy-all –DefinitionFile:Chap_12.xlsx
bm add-account -AccountName:<your account name> -View:LogCabins
```

EXERCISE 12-2. EXAMINING THE SAMPLE BIZTALK APPLICATION

The sample BizTalk application used in this chapter is very simple; it has one receive port, one send port, and no orchestrations. In this exercise, you'll examine the sample application that you'll use as the source for your data.

■Note This exercise assumes you have downloaded the sample code.

1. Run the installation batch file for the sample code at C:\pro bam samples\chapter twelve\ prepare.bat.

2. Using Visual Studio 2008, open the solution Relate.sln in C:\pro bam samples\chapter twelve\ code.

3. The solution contains two schemas and a receive pipeline. One schema is the envelope that contains the order header information, and the other schema represents an individual line item. Examine the properties of the Envelope schema by clicking the schema node and pressing F4. You will notice that the Envelope property is set to Yes.

4. In Solution Explorer, double-click the pipeline to open it in the Pipeline Designer (see Figure 12-1). It contains only one component, the XML disassembler. The envelope schema for the disassembler is Envelope.XSD. The document schema for the disassembler is LineItem.XSD.

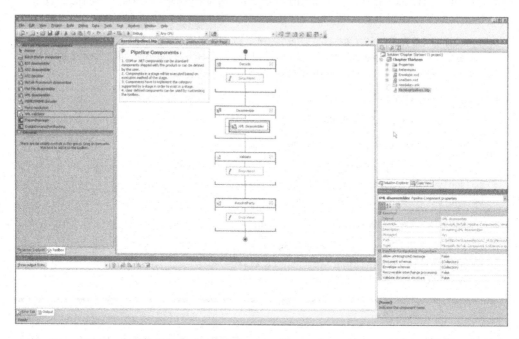

Figure 12-1. *The Pipeline Designer with a receive pipeline*

5. Open the BizTalk Administration Console, and examine the bindings that have been set up for the Relate application.

6. The folder C:\pro bam samples\chapter twelve\filedrops\data contains three sample input files. Double-click one of the files to view it in Internet Explorer.

7. Copy one of the sample files to C:\pro bam samples\chapter twelve\filedrops\in, and then examine the folder C:\pro bam samples\chapter twelve\filedrops\out. You should notice that one output file exists for each line item in your input file.

■Note If the application does not appear to be working, check the Application event log for any messages that identify the problem.

EXERCISE 12-3. CREATING TRACKING PROFILES FOR RELATED ACTIVITIES

Now you have created an activity and tested the BizTalk application. The next step is to create tracking profiles that capture information from the sample application.

1. From the Start menu, select BizTalk Server 2009 ➤ Tracking Profile Editor.

■**Note** For detailed instructions on the using the Tracking Profile Editor, see Chapter 6.

2. Click the link in the left-hand pane and select the Header activity. Click OK to display the Header activity in the TPE.

3. You will notice a new node type in the TPE. Because you defined two activities in the same workbook, the TPE assumes they are related and displays a relationship node called LineItem. Click the Select Event Source button near the top-right corner of the TPE, and then click Select Messaging Payload. The Select Event Source Parent Assembly dialog box will be displayed.

4. In the Select Event Source Parent Assembly dialog box, choose the Chapter Twelve assembly. Click the Next button to display the Select Schema dialog box.

5. In the Select Schema dialog box, choose the Envelope schema. Click the OK button to return to the TPE.

6. Drag the OrderNumber, CustomerName, and LumberType fields from the schema to the corresponding items in the activity.

7. Right-click the OrderNumber field, select Set Port Mappings, and then set the port to Ch12In. Repeat the process to set the ports for CustomerName and LumberType to Ch12In.

The relationship between Header and LineItem requires a shared piece of data that can be used to relate the activities. In Chapter 6, you left the Activity ID node blank, and BAM generated a globally unique identifier (GUID) for the activity ID. In order to support related activities, you need a shared number that is available in both the line item and the header. The order number is shared between the header and the line item, so it's ideal for the purpose of this exercise. In the header, you will use the order number as the activity ID.

8. Drag the OrderNumber field from the schema to the Activity ID node. This ensures that the order number will be stored in the activity's ID field, instead of a random GUID.

9. Right-click the OrderNumber field under the Activity ID node, select Set Port Mappings, and then set the port to Ch12In.

■**Note** In the Header activity, leave the LineItem relationship node blank.

10. Select Apply Tracking Profile from the Tools menu to apply the tracking profile.

11. If you completed Exercise 5-1, select Save from the File menu to save the tracking profile into your Tracking Profiles folder. If you didn't complete Exercise 5-1, save the tracking profile into any convenient folder.

Figure 12-2 shows how the Header activity should now look in the TPE.

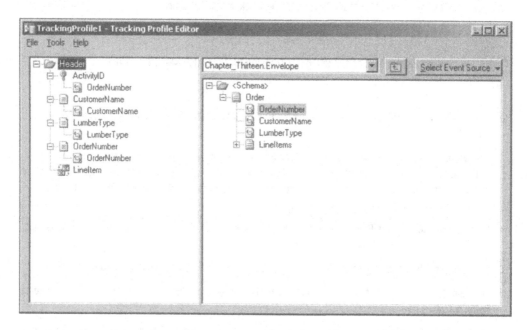

Figure 12-2. *The TPE showing the completed Header activity*

12. From the File menu, select Import BAM Activity Definition. The Import BAM Activity Definition dialog box will be displayed.

13. Choose the LineItem activity, and then click the OK button.

14. Click the Select Event Source button near the top-right corner of the TPE, and then click Select Messaging Payload. The Select Event Source Parent Assembly dialog box will be displayed.

15. In the Select Event Source Parent Assembly dialog box, choose the Chapter Twelve assembly. Click the Next button to display the Select Schema dialog box.

16. In the Select Schema dialog box, choose the LineItem schema. Click the OK button to return to the TPE.

17. Drag the ConnectorType, Diameter, OrderNumber, and Quantity fields from the schema to the corresponding items in the activity.

18. Right-click the OrderNumber field, select Set Port Mappings, and then set the port to Ch12Out. Repeat the process to set the ports for ConnectorType, Diameter, and Quantity to Ch12Out.

19. The Header activity uses the order number as the activity ID. In the LineItem activity, you will store the order number in the Header relationship node. This will create a relationship between the two activities.

20. Drag the OrderNumber field from the schema to the Header relationship node. This creates a link between the two activities.

21. Right-click the OrderNumber field under the Activity ID node, select Set Port Mappings, and then set the port to Ch12Out.

Note Don't associate any data with the Activity ID node in the LineItem activity. If you were to use order number as the activity ID, only one line item could be written for each order number, and data would be lost.

Figure 12-3 shows how the LineItem activity should now look in the TPE.

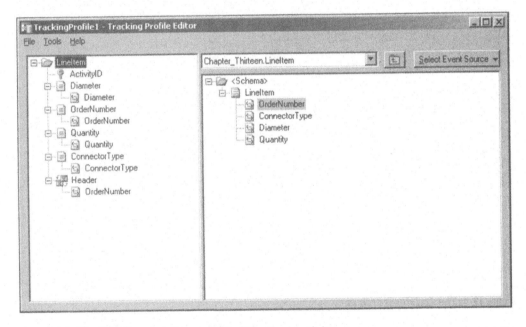

Figure 12-3. *The TPE showing the completed LineItem activity*

22. Select Apply Tracking Profile from the Tools menu to apply the tracking profile.

23. If you completed Exercise 5-1, select Save from the File menu to save the tracking profile into your Tracking Profiles folder. If you didn't complete Exercise 5-1, save the tracking profile into any convenient folder.

EXERCISE 12-4. TESTING THE APPLICATION AND CAPTURING DATA

In this exercise, you will run the sample application and capture data, and then use the portal to look at the data.

1. Copy all three of the sample files from C:\pro bam samples\chapter twelve\filedrops\data to C:\pro bam samples\chapter twelve\filedrops\in, and then examine the folder C:\pro bam samples\chapter twelve\filedrops\out. You should notice that several line items were created, one for each line item in your input files.

2. Using Internet Explorer, browse to http://localhost/bam.

3. In the left-hand navigation bar, you will see a list of views. One of the views should be the LogCabins view that you created in Exercise 12-1. Open the LogCabins view, and then click the Header activity under Activity Search (see Figure 12-4).

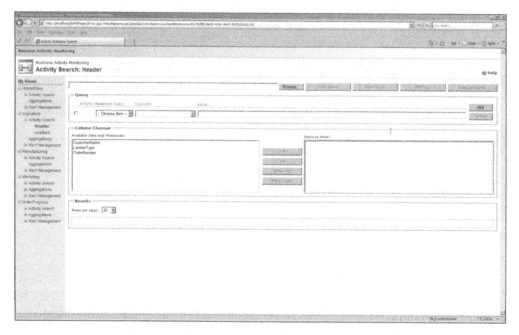

Figure 12-4. *The Activity Search view*

4. In the Available Data and Milestones box of the Column Chooser, click CustomerName to select it.

5. Hold down the Shift key, and then click OrderNumber to select the other two column names.

6. Click the >> button to move all three column names to the Items to Show box.

7. Click the Execute Query button to display a list of orders that have been captured by BAM, as shown in Figure 12-5.

8. Double-click the header with order number 2, bringing up the detailed data for order number 2, as shown in Figure 12-6.

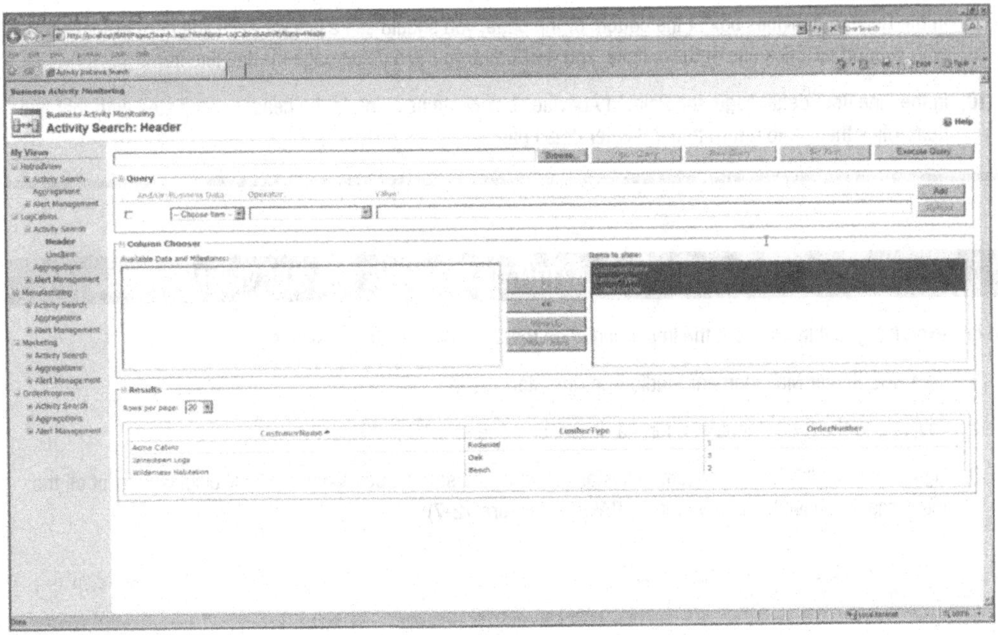

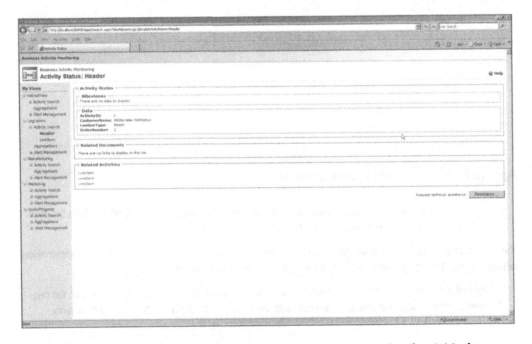

Figure 12-5. *The list of captured orders*

Figure 12-6. *Detailed data about an order. There are three links in the Related Activities box near the bottom of the page.*

9. In the Related Activities box at the bottom of the page, you should see a link for each line item associated with your order. Click one of these links, and it will take you to a detail page for that line item.

10. In the Line Item detail page, the Related Activities box contains a link to the header associated with that line item. Click the link to return to the Header detail page.

EXERCISE 12-5. VIEWING RELATION DATA IN THE SQL SERVER MANAGER

In this exercise, you'll learn about the implementation that underlies related activities.

1. Start SQL Server Management Studio from the Start menu.

2. Navigate to the BAM Primary Import database, and open the Views folder.

3. Right-click the dbo.bam_LineItem_AllInstances view and select Open View. This will display a list of all the line items that have been captured by BAM (see Figure 12-7).

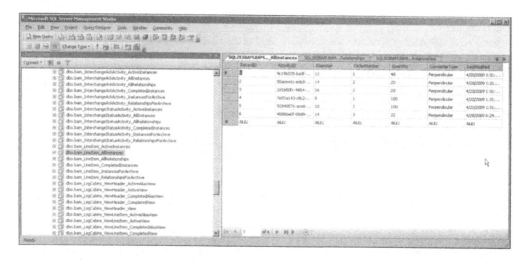

Figure 12-7. *The bam_LineItem_AllInstances view*

4. Right-click the dbo.bam_LineItem_AllRelationships view and select Open View. This will display a list of all the line items that have been captured by BAM (see Figure 12-8).

The relationships of interest to you will have the string "Header" in the reference name. Each of these relationships will contain a GUID for the activity ID and the order number in the reference data.

5. Right-click the dbo.bam_Header_AllRelationships view and select Open View. This view is empty; the relationship implementation stores reference data with the referencing activity, not the referenced activity.

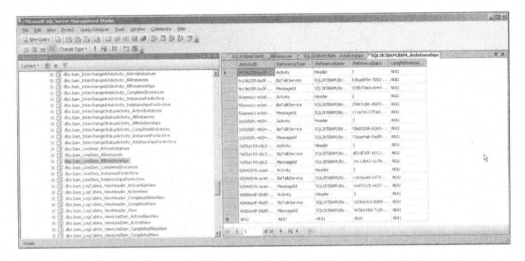

Figure 12-8. *The bam_LineItem_AllRelationships view*

EXERCISE 12-6. CREATING RELATED ACTIVITIES USING THE BAM API

In this exercise, you will populate the related activity using the BAM API. You'll use the same activity as in the previous exercises so as to avoid taking the time to create another activity. You'll also use console applications for simplicity.

1. If you didn't complete the previous exercises in this chapter, run the batch file `C:\pro bam samples\ chapter twelve\finished.bat`. This will create the activities and view you need for the exercise.

2. Open Visual Studio 2008, and from the File menu select New ➤ Project. In the Project Types tree view, select Visual C# Windows projects, and then click Console Application. Create a new console application called RelateAPIDemo.

3. In Solution Explorer, right-click References, and then select Add Reference. Click the Browse tab, browse to the `C:\Program Files\Microsoft Biztalk Server 2009\Tracking` folder, and click `Microsoft. BizTalk.Bam.EventObservation.dll`. Click the OK button to add a reference.

4. Replace the code in `program.cs` with the following:

```
using System;
using System.Text;
using Microsoft.BizTalk.Bam.EventObservation;

namespace APIDemo
{
    class Program
    {
        static private string connString = "Integrated " +
            "Security=SSPI;Data Source=.;" +
            "Initial Catalog=BizTalkMsgBoxDb";
```

```csharp
static void Main(string[] args)
{
    try
    {
        for (int orderNumber = 10;
            orderNumber < 18;
            orderNumber++)
        {
            WriteHeader(orderNumber);
            for (int itemNumber = 0;
                itemNumber < (orderNumber - 8);
                itemNumber++)
            {
                WriteLineItem(orderNumber, itemNumber);
            }
        }
        return;
    }
    catch (Exception excep)
    {
        Console.WriteLine(
            "Exception Caught : {0}",
            excep.ToString());
    }
}

static void WriteHeader(int orderNumber)
{
    //Create an instance of BufferedEventStream
    BufferedEventStream eventstream =
        new BufferedEventStream(connString, 0);

    //activityGuid will be used to uniquely
    //identify this row in the table
    string activityID = orderNumber.ToString();
    Console.WriteLine("Writing Order Number : {0}",
        activityID);

    //Write data to the activity
    eventstream.BeginActivity("Header", activityID);
    eventstream.UpdateActivity("Header", activityID,
        "OrderNumber", orderNumber.ToString(),
        "CustomerName", "Piggy Palaces",
        "LumberType", "Oak");
    eventstream.EndActivity("Header", activityID);

    //Flush the data to the database
```

```
        eventstream.Flush();

    }

    static void WriteLineItem(int orderNumber, int itemNumber)
    {

        //Create an instance of BufferedEventStream
        BufferedEventStream eventstream =
            new BufferedEventStream(connString, 0);

        //activityGuid will be used to uniquely
        //identify this row in the table
        string activityGuid = Guid.NewGuid().ToString();
        Console.WriteLine("Writing Line Item : {0}",
            activityGuid);

        //Write data to the activity
        eventstream.BeginActivity("LineItem", activityGuid);
        eventstream.UpdateActivity("LineItem", activityGuid,
            "OrderNumber", orderNumber.ToString(),
            "Diameter", (itemNumber + 3.2).ToString(),
            "Quantity", (5 * itemNumber + 4).ToString(),
            "ConnectorType", "Straight");
        //Set up the relationship
        eventstream.AddRelatedActivity("LineItem",
            activityGuid, "Header", orderNumber.ToString());
        eventstream.EndActivity("LineItem", activityGuid);

        //Flush the data to the database
        eventstream.Flush();
    }
  }
}
```

The vast majority of the code in this sample should be familiar to you, as it closely resembles code in Chapter 10.

■**Note** More information on the BAM API is in Chapter 10.

The new API method is AddRelatedActivity in the WriteLineItem method.

```
        //Set up the relationship
        eventstream.AddRelatedActivity(
            "LineItem", activityGuid,
            "Header", orderNumber.ToString());
```

This method tells BAM that Header is a related activity, and that the relationship uses `orderNumber` as the foreign key.

5. Press F5 to run the application. (It's best to only run the application once to avoid generating duplicate order numbers.)

6. Browse to `http://localhost/bam` and investigate the new rows that were added. You should see several new rows in the Header and LinkItem activities.

7. If you wish, continue examining the data by using SQL Server Management Studio.

Summary

In this chapter, you learned two different ways to implement a relationship in BAM: the TPE and the BAM API. Related activities are an important feature of BAM as they allow data to be captured even when it doesn't fit conveniently into a single table.

Relationships, as you recall, differ from continuations in that relationships span activities, whereas continuations span business processes.

As your BAM solutions grow in breadth, depth, and scope, you'll find managing BAM from a data flow and solution perspective is key to the success of your implementation. The next chapter will cover an overview of the tools and processes of what you need to know to effectively manage BAM.

■ ■ ■

CHAPTER 13

Managing BAM

In this chapter, you'll learn about managing BAM. BAM is all about data flows, and the chapter starts by reviewing the databases and data flows in BAM. This section also contains exercises that teach two important administrative functions: setting up a tracking host and scheduling data archiving. The health of a BizTalk server is dependent on the underlying databases. If BizTalk's databases are healthy, BizTalk itself is usually healthy. To keep the databases healthy, certain database jobs should be scheduled, and you'll learn about these here.

The next section provides a reference for the commands available in the BAM Management utility, bm.exe. The final section provides tips and tricks for managing BAM, including step-by-step instructions for some advanced administration techniques.

Data Flow in BAM

The heart of the BAM architecture is several SQL Server databases, shown in Table 13-1.

Table 13-1. *Databases Used by BAM*

Database	Type	Default Database Name	Description
BizTalk Message Box	SQL	BizTalkMsgBoxDb	This database stores all messages being processed by BizTalk and the state of all BizTalk orchestrations.
BizTalk Management	SQL	BizTalkMgmtDb	This database contains BizTalk configuration, including TDDS configuration and orchestration to activity mappings.
BAM Primary Import	SQL	BAMPrimaryImport	This is the most important BAM database. Data collected by BAM is moved into this database first. Real-time views are calculated in this database.
BAM Star Schema	SQL	BAMStarSchema	This database contains staging data for building the cubes in the BAM Analysis database.
BAM Analysis	OLAP	BAMAnalysis	This database contains the cubes used by scheduled views.

Continued

Table 13-1. *Continued*

Database	Type	Default Database Name	Description
BAM Archive	SQL	BAMArchive	Old business activity data is moved here to minimize the amount of accumulated data in the BAM Primary Import database.
BAM Alerts Main	SQL	BAMAlertsNSMain	This database contains instance information specifying how a system connects to SQL Server Notification Services. Supports BAM alerts.
BAM Alerts Application	SQL	BAMAlertsApplication	This database contains alert information in SQL Server Notification Services. Supports BAM alerts.

Figure 13-1 shows the way data flows between the BAM databases.

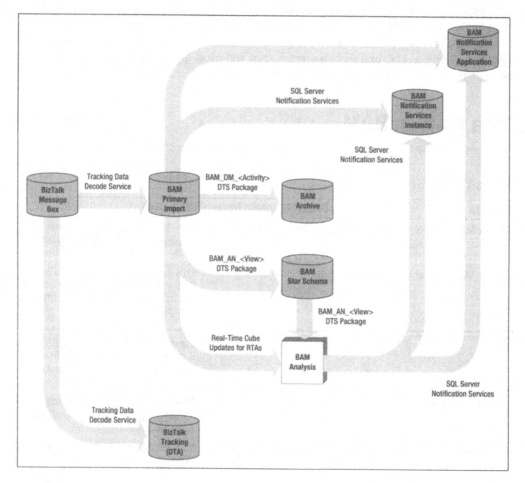

Figure 13-1. *Data flows in BAM*

The data flows fall into three categories:

- *TDDS*: The Tracking Data Decode Service (TDDS) runs in a BizTalk host instance and despools data from the Message Box database to the BAM Primary Import database and the BizTalk Tracking database.

- *DTS packages*: Each scheduled view has an associated job that builds the view's cube in the BAM Analysis OLAP database. In addition, each activity has a job that moves old data out of BAM Primary Import into the BAM Archive database.

- *SQL Server Notification Services*: The BAM Notification Services Instance (Alerts Main) and Application (Alerts Application) databases are used to support BAM alerts, and are populated by SQL Server Notification Services.

BizTalk Hosts, Host Instances, and Groups

TDDS runs in a BizTalk host called the *tracking host*. In order to understand the concept of a tracking host, you'll need to know a little about BizTalk *hosts*, *host instances*, and *groups*. Readers who are BizTalk experts may want to skip ahead to the next section. In BizTalk, receive ports, send ports, and orchestrations are run by host instances. Each host instance is a Windows service running on a particular machine.

Figure 13-2 shows the Windows services on a server with four running BizTalk host instances. BizTalkServerApplication is the default name of a host that is created when BizTalk is installed. This host instance is currently stopped. OneSampleHost, AnotherSampleHost, and ThirdSampleHosts were created later. All three are currently running.

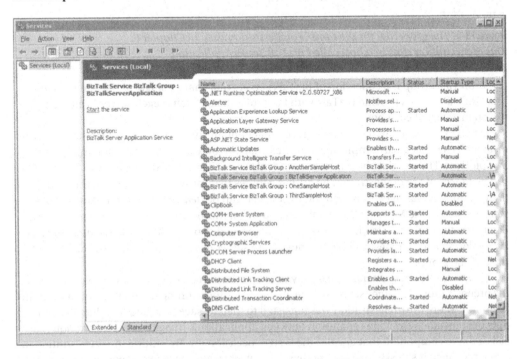

Figure 13-2. *Services Administration Console showing four BizTalk host instances*

So how does BizTalk decide what to run in a specific host instance? It uses the concept of a host. Each BizTalk port or orchestration is associated with a host. Each host may have one or more instances, and each instance runs the ports and orchestrations associated with that host, as shown in Figure 13-3.

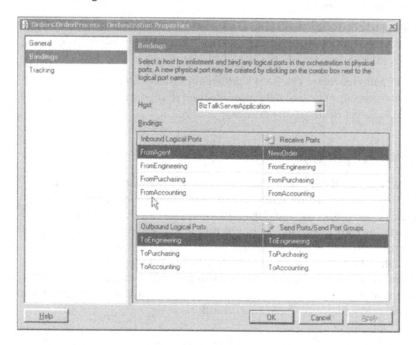

Figure 13-3. *The properties for the sample orchestration used in Chapter 6. This orchestration runs in a host called BizTalkServerApplication.*

A BizTalk group is a collection of BizTalk servers that share a single management database. BizTalk groups provide BizTalk with fault tolerance, because each server in a group may run an instance of each host.

As an example, imagine a BizTalk group that contains two servers, and each server has an instance of a host called SampleHost. Further imagine there is an orchestration that runs in SampleHost. The multiple host instances provide scalability to the orchestration; BizTalk will run instances of the orchestration on both machines to improve performance. When a BizTalk orchestration is waiting for an inbound message, it can be *dehydrated*. This means that its state is saved to the Message Box database, and the orchestration is removed from memory. Each time the orchestration is rehydrated, it will be loaded on the first host instance that has available capacity. Orchestrations can move from server to server to maximize scalability of the BizTalk group.

The multiple host instances also provide fault tolerance. If one server fails while running the orchestration, the other server will be able to continue running the orchestration from the last point where the orchestration was persisted to the Message Box database. Finally, multiple host instances provide separation between applications. Imagine an orchestration that calls a rogue component that crashes the system occasionally. By putting the orchestration in a separate host, it's possible to ensure that the orchestration can't take down anything else.

Now that the review is over, you're ready to learn about tracking hosts.

The Tracking Data Decode Service

The Tracking Data Decode Service, which is also known as the BAM Event Bus Service, is responsible for the following:

- Moving BAM data from the Message Box database to the BAMPrimaryImport database.

- Moving Health and Activity Tracking (HAT) data from the Message Box database to the BizTalkDTAdb database. This book doesn't cover HAT, as we don't recommend using it in high-performance environments.

TDDS runs in a BizTalk host instance. We recommend that you create a separate host that does only tracking, and turn off tracking in any host that contains ports or orchestrations, to ensure that tracking is insulated from ports and orchestrations. This provides better scalability and fault tolerance.

EXERCISE 13-1. SETTING UP A TRACKING HOST

In this exercise, you'll set up a new host and host instance, and configure them for tracking. This ensures that your server has a dedicated tracking host, following the recommended practice for scalability and fault tolerance.

1. From the Start menu, open the BizTalk Server Administration Console.

2. Open the BizTalk group.

3. In Platform Settings, right-click hosts and select New ➤ Host.

4. In the Host Properties dialog box, shown in Figure 13-4, enter **Tracking** as the name of the host, ensure the host type is InProcess, and select the Allow Host Tracking check box. Enter **BizTalk Application Users** as the Windows group. You can ignore the Advanced and Certificate tabs.

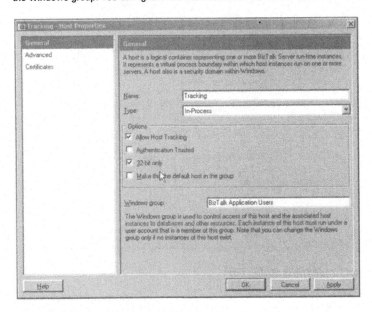

Figure 13-4. *The Host Properties dialog box*

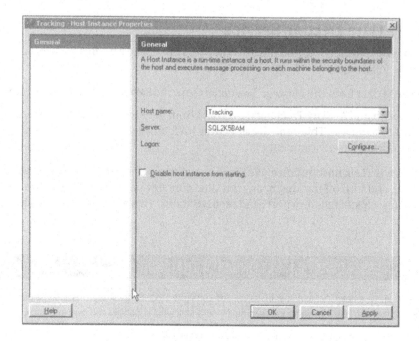

Figure 13-5. *The Host Instance Properties dialog box*

8. Click the Configure button, and enter logon details, as shown in Figure 13-6.

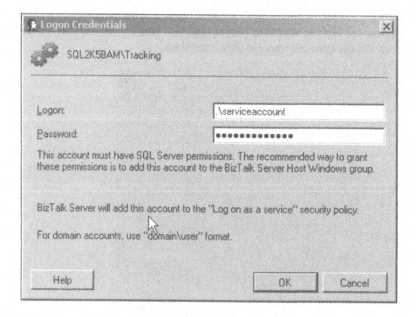

Figure 13-6. *The Logon Credentials dialog box*

If you have more than one server in your BizTalk group, you should add an instance of the Tracking host on each server in the group.

9. In BizTalk Server Administration Console, click the Host Instances icon. Right-click the Tracking host instance, and select Start.

10. In BizTalk Server Administration Console, click the Hosts icon. If you accepted the default installation, you will see a host called BizTalkServerApplication. Double-click the BizTalkServerApplication host, and disable the Allow Host Tracking check box. Click OK to close the dialog box. If you get a warning telling you to restart the host instance, click the OK button to close it.

11. In BizTalk Server Administration Console, click the Host Instances icon. Right-click the BizTalkServer-Application host instance, and select Restart. If you have multiple servers, you will need to restart the host instance on each server.

12. Repeat the last two steps to disable tracking on any other hosts that exist on your server.

In this exercise, you created a new host to run TDDS and disabled TDDS on your other hosts. If you have multiple tracking hosts, whether they are on the same server or within different servers, BizTalk will automatically load balance the tracking duties across the tracking hosts; different ports and orchestrations may be tracked by different hosts, but BizTalk will ensure that each message is tracked exactly once. Each running instance of TDDS sends heartbeat messages to the TDDS_Heartbeats table in the BizTalk Management database to ensure coordination of tracking hosts. If a host fails, perhaps because the server running it shuts down, another tracking host will pick up the sessions it was running to prevent loss of data.

We recommend that you have only one host that is enabled for tracking, but have instances of that host on each machine in your BizTalk group.

A stored procedure called TDDS_UpdateSetting allows you to change the refresh interval, SQL command time-out, session timeout, event logging interval, and retry count for TDDS. We strongly recommend that you don't change these parameters unless specifically instructed by Microsoft Product Support Services, as this is likely to lead to unexpected changes in behavior.

Archiving BAM Data

BAM is intended to provide information about the status of active business processes; it's not recommended that you keep historical data in the BAM Primary Import database. Instead, you should move old data out of BAM Primary Import and into the BAM Archive database.

Each time you use bm.exe to load a new BAM activity, a SQL Server Integration Services (SSIS) package called BAM_DM_<Activity> is created. As an example, when you created the Orders activity in Chapter 5, you created a package called BAM_DM_Orders, shown in Figure 13-7, that is stored in MSDB. This package is used to move old BAM data into the BAM Archive database.

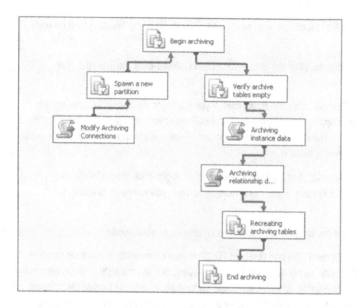

Figure 13-7. *The* BAM_DM_Orders *package in Visual Studio 2005*

If you want to inspect the package, you can use the dtutil utility to export it to a file. The following code line exports the package called BAM_DM_Orders stored in MSDB to a file called C:\ssis\bam_dm_orders.dtsx:

```
dtutil /SQL BAM_DM_Orders /COPY "FILE;c:\pro bam samples\chapter
  fourteen\bam_dm_orders.dtsx"
```

After you have exported the package to a file, you can open SQL Server Business Intelligence Development Studio from the SQL Server folder in the Start menu and open the file.

The package has two functions:

- It partitions the data in BAM Primary Import.

- It removes old data from BAM Primary Import. By default, it moves it into the BAM Archive database.

Data is partitioned by creating new tables in BAM Primary Import to contain activity data. An example is shown in Figure 13-8. The archive package has just run and partitioned the bam_Orders_Completed table by creating an additional partition table called bam_Orders_4BD3B6B1_763A_4698_BF74_9986E9155576. The bam_Orders_CompletedRelationships table has been partitioned by the creation of the bam_Orders_4BD3B6B1_763A_4698_BF74_9986E9155576_Relationships table.

Partitioning data into separate tables is a performance improvement, especially for real-time aggregations. It also simplifies the archival process. When the package runs, it looks for partitions that are available to archive, and processes the entire partition.

```
    dbo.bam_metadata_views
⊞   dbo.bam_OrderProgress_PivotTable2_RTATable
⊞   dbo.bam_Orders_4BD3B6B1_763A_4698_BF74_9986E9155576
⊞   dbo.bam_Orders_4BD3B6B1_763A_4698_BF74_9986E9155576_Relationships
⊞   dbo.bam_Orders_Active
⊞   dbo.bam_Orders_ActiveRelationships
⊞   dbo.bam_Orders_Completed
⊞   dbo.bam_Orders_CompletedRelationships
⊞   dbo.bam_Orders_Continuations
⊞   dbo.bam_QuickOrders_Active
```

Figure 13-8. *Detail from SQL Server Management Studio after running* BAM_DM_Orders. *Additional partition tables have been created on the order view.*

Caution If you write code against the BAM Primary Import database, it's essential to use the views, not the underlying tables. If you write code directly against the underlying tables, BAM data may disappear when the job runs and partitions the table.

A partition is available to archive if all scheduled views that depend on the partition have been processed, and the partition is older than the online window for the activity. By default, the online window for an activity is six months. You can change the online window using BM. As an example, the following command changes the online window for the orders activity to 14 days:

```
bm set-activitywindow -activity:orders -timelength:14 -timeunit:day
```

Note bm.exe is in the folder C:\Program Files\Microsoft BizTalk Server 2009\Tracking, so set the path appropriately before running the command.

It's important to bear in mind that the package only archives partitions older than the online window. As an example, imagine an activity where the archive package has never been run. There is a year's worth of data in the BAM Primary Import database, but there are no partitions. The online window is the default: six months. Now consider what happens if you schedule the archive package to run each day. The first day the package runs and creates a partition table in BAM Primary Import. This partition table contains a year's worth of data. However, there are no partitions older than six months, so no data is removed from BAM Primary Import. The next day, the package runs again, and a second partition table is created. This partition will contain one day's worth of data. The partition table created the previous day is only 24 hours old, and so it will be left in BAM Primary Import. If the online window remains six months, it will be a full six months after the job is scheduled before any data is removed from BAM Primary Import, but then a full year of data will be removed in one day.

You can configure whether or not data is moved to the BizTalk Archive database using BM. This command causes old data to be purged from the Orders activity, instead of moving it to the BizTalk Archive:

```
bm set-archive -activity:orders -shouldarchive:false
```

This command causes old data to be archived to the BizTalk Archive database:

```
bm set-archive -activity:orders -shouldarchive:true
```

The purge flag and the online window can be confirmed by examining the BAM_Metadata_ Activities table in the BAM Primary Import database.

You have two design decisions to make when setting up archiving: the length of the online window and how often the archive job runs. The length of the archive window is driven by business needs for historical data. Longer online windows will require more disk space, and will also have an impact on the time taken to back up the BizTalk databases. In very large installations of BizTalk, the total time taken to back up the BizTalk databases can become a significant issue.

The archive job should be run on a regular basis. For many organizations, running this job daily or weekly will be a good choice. Running the job more often will create more partitioning in the database, which may provide a slight improvement in write performance at the cost of complicating the database structure by creating many more partitions.

EXERCISE 13-2. SCHEDULING DATA ARCHIVING

In this exercise, you'll learn how to schedule the activity archive package that you created in Chapter 5 when you deployed the BAM activity for the orders process. If you don't have the Orders activity from Chapter 5, you can use any other BAM activity that you have loaded by changing the name of the DTS package. The goal of the exercise is to manage the size of the BAM Primary Import database by archiving old data to the BAM Archive database.

1. From the Start menu, select Open SQL Server Management Studio.

2. Press F8 to display the Object Explorer.

3. Click Connect, select Database Engine, and connect to the database server where your BizTalk databases are stored.

4. Scroll to the bottom of the Object Explorer, open SQL Server Agent, and then open the Jobs folder.

5. Right-click Jobs and select New Job to bring up the dialog box shown in Figure 13-9.

6. Enter **Archive Orders** as the name of the job, and enter a description if you wish.

7. Click Steps in the Select a page pane, and click the New button to create a new job step.

8. Enter **Run Package** as the step name and specify SQL Server Integration Services package as the package type. This will display a set of tabs that allow you to enter information on the package.

9. In the General tab, select SQL Server as the package source, and choose the correct database server in the Server drop-down list (see Figure 13-10). Click the Browse button next to the Package text box, and select BAM_DM_Orders.

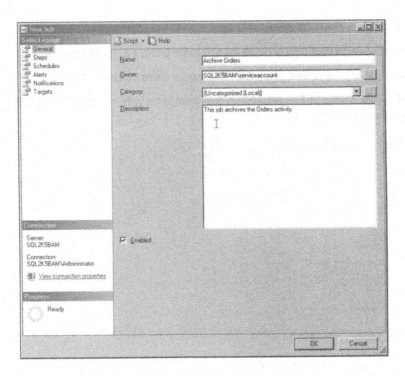

Figure 13-9. *The New Job dialog box*

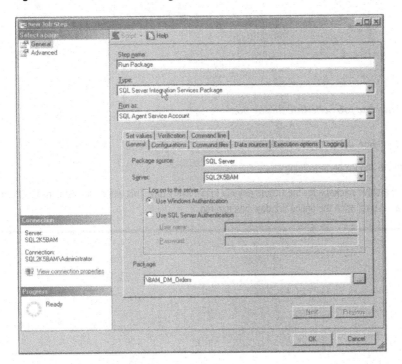

Figure 13-10. *The New Job Step dialog box*

10. Click OK to close the New Job Step dialog box.

11. Click Schedules in the Select a Page pane, and click the New button to create a new job schedule.

12. If you get a prompt to change the success action of the step you just created, click the OK button.

13. Name the schedule Daily, change the Frequency Occurs drop-down box to Daily, and check that the Daily Frequency is to occur once at midnight (see Figure 13-11).

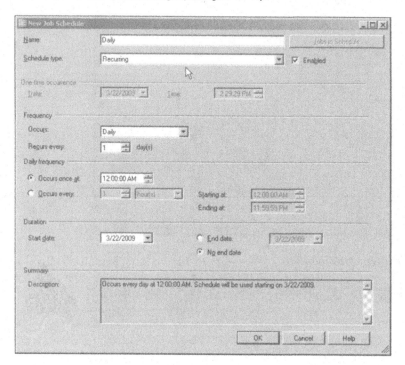

Figure 13-11. *The New Job Schedule dialog box*

14. Click OK to close the New Job Schedule dialog box.

15. Click OK to close the Job Properties dialog box.

You have scheduled the archive package for the Orders activity to run every day. This will partition the data for efficiency and will remove old data once the online window has expired.

Scheduling a Cube Build

Scheduled aggregated views require the aggregations to be built before they are available to users. In Chapter 7, you learned how to run the BAM_AN_Marketing DTS package from SQL Server Management Studio to build the Marketing view on the Orders activity. In production, it won't work to build views by hand; they should be built using scheduled SQL Server jobs.

Whenever you create a new view that requires a cube to be built, follow the steps in Exercise 13-2, but use the package name BAM_AN_<View> to schedule the cube build.

Note Chapter 7 contains instructions on building the cube for an aggregated view using SQL Server Management Studio.

Backing Up the BizTalk Databases

Your organization may have a standard approach to backing up SQL Server databases, and the DBA team may tell you they have backups under control. If they haven't dealt with BizTalk before, don't believe them.

Several BizTalk databases participate in cross-database transactions. These include BizTalk Message Box, BizTalk Management, BizTalk Tracking (DTA), and BizTalk Primary Import. If you back up each of these databases separately, the backups will be useless to you. That's because additional transactions that complete after the first backup but before the second backup will make the databases transactionally inconsistent.

The only way to back up BizTalk is to use the Backup BizTalk Server job that is installed in SQL Server by the BizTalk installation. This job will put a mark in the transaction log for each of the BizTalk databases at a specific point in time. When you restore the databases, you will restore to the transaction log mark, ensuring that all databases are transactionally consistent.

To check the list of databases that will be backed up for you by the Backup BizTalk Server job, take a look at the admv_BackupDatabases view in the BizTalk Management database. (It's fine to look at this view, just don't edit it.)

Cleaning Up the Alerts Chronicle Table

If you are using BAM alerts, there's a table called BAM_Metadata_AlertChronicles in the BAM Alerts Application database that audits all alerts fired by the notification services infrastructure. Each time an alert is fired, a new row is added to this table. For each view you create, you will also see a job called bam_<View Name>_<Activity View>_DelAlertHistJob. This job cleans up the auditing data.

You should run each of these jobs occasionally, perhaps monthly or quarterly, to clean up old audit information.

Enjoy Your BM

Many aspects of a BAM solution are managed using bm.exe. You've already seen some examples of bm.exe. It was used in Chapter 5 to deploy activities and views, and in Chapter 3 to deploy interceptor configuration files. It was used earlier in this chapter to adjust archiving behavior.

This section documents the complete set of commands implemented by bm.exe in BizTalk Server 2009. Some of these commands are not available in earlier versions of BizTalk Server.

Help Commands

The BM utility provides help for its many commands. help gets a description for each of the BM commands.

Database and Infrastructure Commands

The BM utility provides commands to manage databases and infrastructure, as listed in Table 13-2.

Table 13-2. *Database and Infrastructure Commands Available Through* bm.*exe*

Command	Description
setup-databases	Creates a fresh copy of the BAM databases: Primary Import, Star Schema, Archiving, Analysis, and Alerts. The command takes a configuration file as a parameter. An example of the configuration file format is provided in the section "Changing BAM Runtime Settings" later in this chapter.
migrate-sql	Moves the BAM databases between different versions of SQL Server. Use this command immediately after upgrading from one version of SQL Server to another.
migrate-rta	Creates new OLAP cubes for real-time aggregations compatible with BizTalk Server 2009.
get-config	Gets the current BAM database configuration and saves it in a file. You can later use setup-databases with the file to reinstall the BAM databases. For an example, see Exercise 13-6.
update-config	Updates the BAM database configuration based on a configuration file. For an example, see Exercise 13-6.
enable-reference	Sets up a reference to another BAM Primary Import database. When you do this, the BAM Portal will show all views the user has access to on either the local database or the remote database. When the user clicks a remote view, the portal will automatically link to the instance of the BAM Portal that contains that view. See Chapter 7 for an example.
disable-reference	Deletes an external database reference.
get-references	Lists all external database references.
get-changes	Gets a list of all changes that have been made to the BAM configuration (see Figure 13-12).

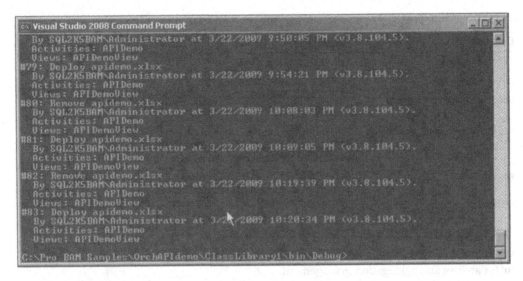

Figure 13-12. *The BM get-changes command*

Observation Model Commands

The commands listed in Table 13-3 focus on administration of objects contained within an observation model.

Table 13-3. *Observation Model Commands Available with bm.exe*

Command	Description
deploy-all	Deploys activities and views defined in an Excel workbook or an XML file. See Chapters 3 and 5 for examples.
update-all	Updates activities and views defined in an Excel workbook or an XML file.
remove-all	Removes activities and views defined in an Excel workbook or an XML file.
get-activities	Lists the activities defined on the system.
remove-activity	Removes a single activity.
get-views	Lists views for a specific activity or all views in the database.
remove-view	Removes a view. Causes an error if the view has alerts.
add-account	Gives an account permissions to see a view. Adding an account will make the view visible to the user in the BAM Portal, as well as allowing the user to run code that queries the view directly. See Chapters 3 and 7 for examples.
remove-account	Denies an account permissions to see a view.
get-accounts	Lists accounts that have permissions to see a view.
create-index	Creates a database index on an activity for more efficient searching. See Chapter 7 for an example.

Continued

Table 13-3. *Continued*

Command	Description
delete-index	Deletes an index.
get-index	Lists the indexes on an activity.
update-livedataworkbook	Updates the database connection string in an Excel live data workbook.
regenerate-livedataworkbook	Generates the live data workbook from a workbook that contains activities and views, without deploying the activities and views. For an example, see Exercise 13-5.
get-defxml	Gets a file that contains all activities and views defined in the system. For an example, see Exercise 13-5.

Archive and Aggregation Management

When it comes to management of BAM databases, the commands listed in Table 13-4 are useful for archive and aggregation management.

Table 13-4. *Archive and Aggregation Management Commands Made Available in* bm.exe

Command	Description
set-archive	Sets the archive flag. The flag is true if older data is archived to BAM Archive, false if older data is purged.
get-archive	Gets the archive flag.
set-activitywindow	Sets the online window for an activity. Data outside the online window will be either purged or archived when the BAM_DM_<Activity> package is run.
get-activitywindow	Gets the online window.
set-rtawindow	Sets the real-time aggregation window for a view. This is the length of time that data is included in a real-time aggregation.
get-rtawindow	Gets the real-time aggregation window for a view.

Alert Commands

Administration of BAM alerts visible in the BAM Portal is greatly enhanced by the commands listed in Table 13-5.

Table 13-5. *Alert Commands Available in* bm.exe

Command	Description
get-alerts	Lists alerts for a specific view or all alerts in the database
remove-alerts	Removes all alerts associated with a view
add-subscription	Adds a subscription for an alert
remove-subscription	Removes a subscription for an alert
get-subscriptions	Lists all subscribers for an alert
enable-alerts	Enables alerts for a view
disable-alerts	Disables alerts for a view

Interceptor Configuration Commands

With the BAM interceptors available, bm.exe also includes commands to manage artifacts related to the interceptors, as shown in Table 13-6.

Table 13-6. *Interceptor Configuration Commands Available in bm.exe*

Command	Description
deploy-interceptor	Deploys an IC file.
get-interceptorlist	Gets a list of all interceptors in the database.
get-interceptor	Gets a copy of an IC file from the database. Use this if you have lost your IC file after you deployed it.
remove-interceptor	Removes an interceptor.

Tracing BAM Management

You can trace the behavior of the BAM Management utility to investigate its behavior. This will provide a log of the internal operations of the utility.

EXERCISE 13-3. TRACING BAM MANAGEMENT

The BM utility performs a series of actions "behind the scenes" with little transparency as to what exactly is happening. If you want to know more, work through this exercise, and you'll be able to investigate the individual steps.

1. In Windows Explorer, browse to C:\Program Files\Microsoft BizTalk Server 2009\Tracking.

2. Make a copy of bm.exe.config so you can revert back to it at the end of the exercise.

3. Right-click the file bm.exe.config, and then select Open With ➤ Visual Studio 2008.

4. Uncomment the following text:

```
<switches>
<add name="bm" value="1" />
<add name="Microsoft.BizTalk.Bam.Management" value="1" />
</switches>
```

5. Run the bm.exe commands of interest.

6. Using Notepad, open the file C:\Program Files\Microsoft BizTalk Server 2009\Tracking\ BamManagerTrace.log and review the contents.

7. In Windows Explorer, replace BM.exe.config with the copy of the original file you made earlier.

Advanced Topics

This section includes information on some advanced topics in BAM management.

Removing Orphaned Tracking Profiles

Imagine the following scenario: you create and deploy a BAM activity, and then you use the TPE to create a tracking profile that captures data from your BizTalk application. Later, you undeploy the activity. What's going to happen? The tracking profile is still active and will attempt to capture data and store it in the activity. All the tables that support the activity, however, will be missing from the database.

In this scenario, you will start seeing errors showing up in the Application event log. The text will be similar to this:

```
Event Type: Error
Event Source: BAM EventBus Service
Event Category: None
Event ID: 6
Date:  03/22/2009
Time:  11:33:17
User:  N/A
Computer: SQL2K5BAM
Description:
Execute event error. Error(s) occurred while executing events, see
TDDS_FailedTrackingData table for more details.  SQLServer: SQL2K5BAM,
Database: BAMPrimaryImport.
```

The TDDS_FailedTrackingData table will contain entries similar to this:

```
Could not find stored procedure 'dbo.bam_Orders_PrimaryImport'.
TDDS failed to execute event. Could not find stored procedure
'dbo.bam_Orders_AddRelationship'.
TDDS failed to execute event. Could not find stored procedure
'dbo.bam_Orders_EnableContinuation'.
TDDS failed to execute event. Could not find stored procedure
'dbo.bam_Orders_PrimaryImport'.
TDDS failed to execute event. Parameter is not valid.
```

This is known as the orphaned tracking profile problem. In order to fix it, you need to use TPE to remove the orphaned tracking profile, so you'll need to run through the following steps:

1. Find the file that defines the activity.

2. Deploy the activity using BM.

3. Start TPE, select the activity you just loaded, and then retrieve the tracking profile that corresponds to that activity.

4. Undeploy the tracking profile.

5. Remove the activity using BM.

This sounds easy enough, but sometimes during development you will be deploying and removing activities for testing, editing the definitions as you go. A few hours later, you notice the signs of an orphaned profile, realize you deleted the activity definition file, and have no choice but to say "Oh, Fiddlesticks!"

At that point, the urge to start editing BAM Primary Import by hand will become overwhelming. If you're on a production box, don't even think about it. If you mess with the database, your server is immediately unsupported by Microsoft support, and your best choice is to go back to a recent backup before the problem started. However, if you're willing to attempt an unsupported fix, here's the process.

Caution This process is unsupported. Back up your databases before using this process. Do not use this process on production systems.

---

1. Compare BAM_Metadata_TrackingProfiles with the list of activities returned by bm get-activities. If you have orphaned profiles, there will be activity names in BAM_Metadata_TrackingProfiles that aren't currently deployed.

2. Take a backup of all BizTalk databases.

3. Run TRUNCATE TABLE against the following tables in BizTalkMgmtDB:

   - BAM_TrackingProfiles
   - BAM_TrackPoints
   - StaticTrackingInfo

4. Run TRUNCATE TABLE against the following tables in BAMPrimaryImport:

   - BAM_Metadata_TrackingProfiles
   - BAM_Metadata_Annotations

Tracing TDDS

You can trace the behavior of TDDS. If you have issues with the performance of tracking, it might be worth tracing TDDS to examine the details of its behavior.

EXERCISE 13-4. TRACING TDDS

In this exercise, you set up a trace on TDDS to investigate its behavior.

1. In Windows Explorer, browse to C:\Program Files\Microsoft BizTalk Server 2009\.

2. Make a copy of BTSNTSvc.exe.config so you can revert back to it at the end of the exercise.

3. Right-click the file BTSNTSvc.exe.config, and then select Open With ➤ Visual Studio 2008.

4. Add the following text immediately before the `</configuration>` tag that closes the file:

```
<system.diagnostics>
<switches>
<add name="Microsoft.BizTalk.Bam.EventBus" value="1" />
</switches>
<trace autoflush="true" indentsize="4">
<listeners>
<add name="Text" type="System.Diagnostics.TextWriterTraceListener"
    initializeData="c:\tdds.log"/>
</listeners>
</trace>
</system.diagnostics>
```

5. Save the file and close Visual Studio.

6. Restart all running host instances.

7. Execute any of the sample code in this book that uses TDDS. The samples in Chapter 6 or Chapter 10 would both work.

8. Open the file C:\tdds.log in Notepad, and you'll see a trace of the behavior of TDDS, as shown in Figure 13-13.

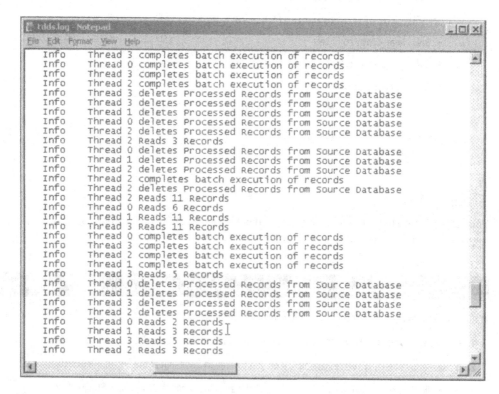

Figure 13-13. *Trace of TDDS*

9. In Windows Explorer, replace BTSNTSvc.exe.config with the copy of the original file you made earlier.

10. Restart all running host instances.

Regenerating a Live Data Workbook

If you have lost the files associated with an activity, you can still create an Excel workbook with live data by using bm.exe.

EXERCISE 13-5. REGENERATING A LIVE DATA WORKBOOK

In this exercise, you will generate a live data workbook that will allow you to view the data associated with the Orders activity created in Chapter 5. This exercise assumes that you created the activity in Chapter 5 and that it is still loaded on your system.

1. Open a new command-line window as an administrator.

2. Change directory to your BamDefinitions folder.

3. Enter the following commands:

```
path %path%;C:\Program Files\Microsoft BizTalk Server 2009\Tracking
bm get-defxml -filename:def.xml
```

4. Open Microsoft Excel.

5. Select Import XML from the BAM menu.

■Note If you don't have the BAM Add-In for Excel loaded, you won't be able to see the BAM menu. Refer to Chapter 3 for instructions on loading the add-in and navigating to the BAM menu.

6. Browse to your BamDefinitions folder and select def.xml.

7. Click the Open button to load def.xml.

8. Remove any BAM views that you don't want to see in your Live Workbook by selecting BAM View from the BAM menu and using the wizard to delete unneeded views.

9. Using the tabs at the bottom of the workbook, navigate to the aggregated view that you wish to work with in Excel.

10. Drag items from the Pivot Table field list into the pivot table to build the table you need.

11. If you're using Excel 2007, save the file by clicking the Office button and selecting Save As. Save the workbook in your ExcelWorkbooks folder as orders_new.xlsx.

12. If you're using Excel 2003, save the file by selecting Save As from the File menu. Save the workbook in your ExcelWorkbooks folder as orders_new.xls.

13. Close the workbook, but leave Excel open.

14. In the command-line window, change to the directory to your `ExcelWorkbooks` folder.

15. Enter one of the following commands, depending on the name of the file you saved:

```
bm.exe regenerate-livedataworkbook -workbookname:orders_new.xlsx
bm.exe regenerate-livedataworkbook -workbookname:orders_new.xls
```

16. In Excel, open `C:\bam\orders_new_livedata.xlsx`.

17. Examine the pivot tables, which now contain live data.

In this exercise, you learned to re-create and Excel workbook with live data when the original file is missing.

Changing BAM Runtime Settings

Several configuration settings can be changed using `bm.exe`. The `get-config` command creates a file that contains the BAM configuration. To change a setting, such as changing the name of a database, you can edit the file and then reload the configuration using the `update-config` command.

Listing 13-1 shows an example configuration file.

Listing 13-1. *Sample Generated by Using* BM `Get-Config` `-filename:config.xml`

```xml
<?xml version="1.0" encoding="UTF-8" ?>
<BAMConfiguration xmlns="http://schemas.microsoft.com/BizTalkServer/
      2004/10/BAM">
  <GlobalProperty Name="BAMVRoot">http://sql2k5bam:80/BAM</GlobalProperty>
  <GlobalProperty Name="MaxAlertableActivityViews">63</GlobalProperty>
  <DeploymentUnit Name="PrimaryImportDatabase">
    <Property Name="ServerName">SQL2K5BAM</Property>
    <Property Name="DatabaseName">BAMPrimaryImport</Property>
  </DeploymentUnit>
  <DeploymentUnit Name="StarSchemaDatabase">
    <Property Name="ServerName">SQL2K5BAM</Property>
    <Property Name="DatabaseName">BAMStarSchema</Property>
  </DeploymentUnit>
  <DeploymentUnit Name="AnalysisDatabase">
    <Property Name="ServerName">SQL2K5BAM</Property>
    <Property Name="DatabaseName">BAMAnalysis</Property>
  </DeploymentUnit>
  <DeploymentUnit Name="ArchivingDatabase">
    <Property Name="ServerName">SQL2K5BAM</Property>
    <Property Name="DatabaseName">BAMArchive</Property>
  </DeploymentUnit>
  <DeploymentUnit Name="CubeUpdateDTS">
    <Property Name="ConnectionTimeOut">120</Property>
```

```
      <Property Name="UseEncryption">0</Property>
  </DeploymentUnit>
  <DeploymentUnit Name="DataMaintenanceDTS">
    <Property Name="ConnectionTimeOut">120</Property>
    <Property Name="UseEncryption">0</Property>
  </DeploymentUnit>
  <DeploymentUnit Name="Alert">
      <Property Name="DBServer">SQL2K5BAM</Property>
      <Property Name="ApplicationDatabaseName">Application</Property>
      <Property Name="InstanceDatabaseName">BAMAlerts</Property>
      <Property Name="GeneratorServerName">SQL2K5BAM</Property>
      <Property Name="ProviderServerName">SQL2K5BAM</Property>
      <Property Name="DistributorServerName">SQL2K5BAM</Property>
      <Property Name="SmtpServerName">SQL2K5BAM</Property>
      <Property Name="AlertMailFrom">BAM@microsoft.com</Property>
      <Property Name="FileDropUNC">\\SQL2K5BAM\alerts</Property>
  </DeploymentUnit>
</BAMConfiguration>
```

EXERCISE 13-6. ENCRYPTING TRAFFIC TO ANALYSIS SERVICES

In this exercise, you change a configuration setting to encrypt traffic between the BAM Primary Import database and SQL Server Analysis Services. The main reason we include this exercise is to provide an example of changing BAM configuration data using the update-config command, but this may also be a useful technique to know if you are capturing confidential data.

1. Open a new command line as administrator.

2. Change directory to your BAMDefinitionFiles folder.

3. Enter the following commands:

   ```
   path %path%;C:\Program Files\Microsoft BizTalk Server 2009\Tracking
   bm get-config -filename:config.xml
   copy config.xml config_old.xml
   ```

4. Using Notepad, open the file config.xml.

5. Find the following element:

   ```
   <DeploymentUnit Name="CubeUpdateDTS">
   ```

6. Edit the UseEncryption element to read as follows:

   ```
       <DeploymentUnit Name="CubeUpdateDTS">
         <Property Name="ConnectionTimeOut">120</Property>
         <Property Name="UseEncryption">1</Property>
       </DeploymentUnit>
   ```

7. Save the file.

8. In the command-line window, load the new configuration by entering the following command:

    `bm update-config -filename:config.xml`

9. If you now run one of the `BAM_AN_<View>` packages, information will be sent to SQL Server Analysis Services in encrypted format.

10. In the command-line window, revert to the previous configuration by entering the following command:

    `bm update-config -filename:config_old.xml`

This has now reverted to the original configuration.

In this exercise, you learned how to change the configuration of BAM by editing configuration files.

Summary

In this chapter, you learned about data flows in BAM, and learned to schedule data archiving and cube builds. You also saw how to perform several advanced maintenance procedures. The primary tool for administering BAM is bm.exe, and you've now seen examples of almost all the functions provided by this tool. While you may encounter other scenarios while managing BAM, these tend to be the most common you'll run across. As always, the Internet provides discussion forums on some of the more esoteric scenarios, as well as prescriptive guidance on how to remedy them.

You probably noticed while reading this chapter that BAM has relatively few utilities for its management and administration. In fact, out of the box, BizTalk provides applications and utilities that address the more common scenarios of using BAM and managing BizTalk. The BizTalk Server 2009 Administration Console is a very useful tool for managing BizTalk, but a custom BAM solution provides additional capabilities the Administration Console does not.

The next chapter will introduce how to monitor BizTalk using BAM as a hands-on exercise.

■■■

CHAPTER 14

Monitoring BizTalk Status Using BAM

The standard feature for tracking messages in a BizTalk server is the BizTalk Server 2009 Administration Console (which now includes the query capabilities of the tool formerly known as Health and Activity Tracking, or HAT). However, in large, multiserver BizTalk systems, Administration Console queries can cause performance issues under some circumstances; the large volume of data generated can have an impact on the TDDS service and backup jobs. Because of that, many BizTalk users have chosen to move away from Administration Console queries and implement a BAM solution for monitoring their BizTalk environment. You can use BAM to create an overview of the performance and behavior of a BizTalk server.

In this chapter, we describe one possible approach to tracking messages flowing through BizTalk Server. This approach works with both messaging-only applications and orchestrations, and can be implemented by using custom pipeline components or by using the Tracking Profile Editor (TPE).

■**Note** This is a solution for tracking messages; it's not a full health-monitoring solution for a BizTalk server farm. To monitor the health of your BizTalk servers, consider acquiring a server management product. The BizTalk Management Pack for System Center Operations Manager (SCOM) provides very detailed health monitoring for BizTalk; in our opinion, it's the best tool out there. Other server management tools, such as HP's OpenView, also provide management packs for BizTalk, but in our experience the SCOM tools provide much more detail on what's happening now in your BizTalk group.

■**Note** To disable HAT-style tracking exposed within the BizTalk Server Administration Console, use SQL Server Management Studio to open the adm_group table in BizTalkMgmtDB. This table contains only one row. Set the value of the GlobalTrackingOption field in that row to 0 to disable tracking, 1 to reenable tracking.

Observation Model

Data will be captured using two related activities; one activity is used for inbound messages, and the other is used for outbound messages.

The inbound activity contains the items shown in Table 14-1 and is shown in Figure 14-1.

Table 14-1. *Inbound Activity for BizTalk System Monitoring*

Field	Type
InterchangeID	Business Data – Text
MessageID	Business Data – Text
ReceivePort	Business Data – Text
MessageType	Business Data – Text (150 characters)
Size	Business Data – Integer
PortStartTime	Business Milestone
PortEndTime	Business Milestone

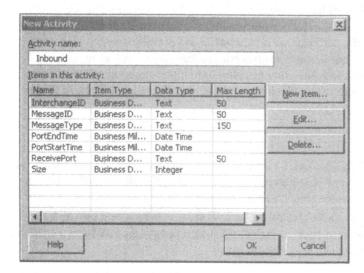

Figure 14-1. *The inbound activity*

The outbound activity contains the items shown in Table 14-2.

Two activities are used because each inbound message can potentially generate multiple outbound messages through BizTalk's publish-subscribe model. A one-to-many relationship exists between the inbound and outbound activities, implemented using BAM relationships. In your environment, if you are certain that each inbound message will never generate more than one outbound message, you can simplify the implementation by using a single activity that contains both inbound and outbound data. In this case, you would replace the one-to-many relationship with a continuation.

Table 14-2. *Outbound Activity for BizTalk System Monitoring*

Field	Type
InterchangeID	Business Data – Text
MessageID	Business Data – Text
SendPort	Business Data – Text
MessageType	Business Data – Text (150 characters)
Size	Business Data – Integer
PortStartTime	Business Milestone
PortEndTime	Business Milestone

■**Note** Instructions for creating activities and views are in Chapter 5. Instructions for implementing relationships are in Chapter 12.

Obviously, several aggregate views can be created with this data. Message size and message count are useful measures, and time, message type, and port are useful dimensions. We usually start by creating a simple aggregate view that describes the inbound data, as shown in Figure 14-2. The measures and dimensions we use are shown in Tables 14-3 and 14-4.

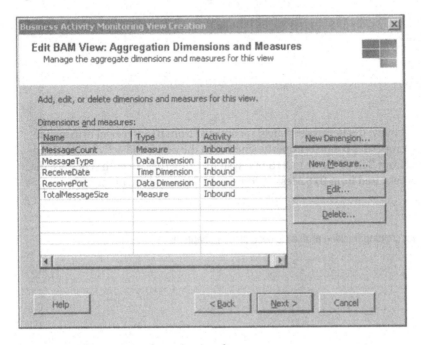

Figure 14-2. *The aggregated monitoring data*

Table 14-3. *Measures for Monitoring Biztalk Server*

Measure	Base Data	Aggregation
MessageCount	Inbound	Count
TotalMessageSize	Size (Inbound)	Sum

Table 14-4. *Dimensions for Monitoring BizTalk Server*

Dimension	Type	Derived From
Received	Time	PortStartTime (Inbound)
MessageType	Data	MessageType (Inbound)
ReceivePort	Data	ReceivePort

Tracking Profile Implementation

In the simplest implementation, two tracking profiles are used. One tracking profile captures inbound information, and the other tracking profile captures outbound information.

In each tracking profile, five of the six items in the activity come from the messaging property schema, as shown in Figure 14-3. This schema can be selected by pressing the Select Event Source button in the TPE and contains the following items:

- InterchangeID
- MessageID
- PortStartTime
- PortEndTime
- Size

In the inbound activity, the ReceivePort field is captured from BTS.ReceivePortName in the BTS.bts_system_properties context property schema. In the outbound activity, the Send-Port field is captured from BTS.SPName in BTS.bts_system_properties. In both schemas, the message type field is captured from BTS.MessageType in BTS.bts_system_properties.

Note The process for creating tracking profiles is described in Chapter 6.

In addition to capturing the six fields in each activity, a relationship between the two activities is needed. This is implemented by using the interchange ID, which is available through the InterchangeID field in the messaging property schema. The interchange ID is used as the activity ID in the inbound activity. The interchange ID is also used in the inbound relationship node in the outbound activity, as shown in Figure 14-4. In the outbound activity, leave the activity ID node empty, and BAM will generate a GUID as the activity ID for each item in the activity.

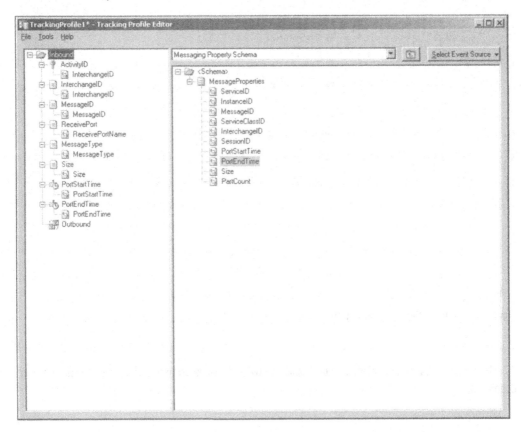

Figure 14-3. *The inbound activity tracking profile in TPE*

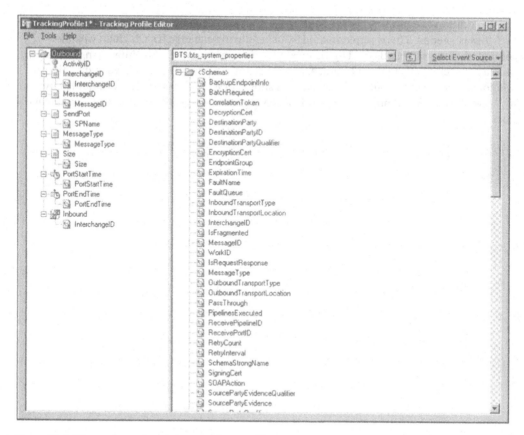

Figure 14-4. *The outbound activity tracking profile*

■**Note** The process for implementing relationships between activities using tracking profiles is described in Chapter 12.

InterchangeID works for creating this relationship because the interchange ID is preserved as the message is published to the message box and then picked up by its subscribers. If the application is a messaging-only solution, the interchange ID at the send port will be the same as the interchange ID at the receive port. If the application contains an orchestration, the interchange ID of a message sent by an orchestration will be the same as the interchange ID of the message that activated the orchestration.

A port mapping is needed for each of the seven items in the activity. If you want to monitor every port in the system, that's easy to set up. In the inbound tracking profile, right-click an item in the TPE, and select Set Port Mapping. In the Select Ports dialog box, select the Show Receive Ports check box and clear the Show Send Ports check box to display a list of receive ports (see Figure 14-5). Click the >> button, and all the receive ports on your server will be monitored using the tracking profile. For the outbound tracking profile, simply select all the send ports but not the receive ports.

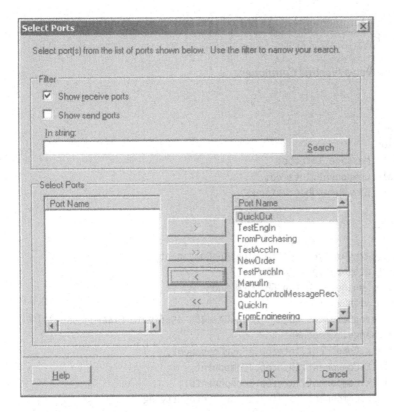

Figure 14-5. *Setting the port mappings*

Pipeline Component Implementation

As an alternative implementation, it would be possible to create custom pipeline components that used the BAM API to capture data. This would perform slightly less well than using the TPE to gather the data, as the TPE is very efficient. In most situations, the TPE is the preferred solution. Some organizations, however, may prefer to avoid administering and applying tracking profiles. In this case, it is possible to implement a similar solution using two pipeline components. One component is used in the receive pipeline, and the other component is used in the send pipeline.

Note Detailed discussion of pipeline component implementation is beyond the scope of this book. For a simple example of a custom pipeline component, refer to the book *BizTalk 2006 Recipes: A Problem-Solution Approach* by Mark Beckner et al. (Apress, 2006). (Most of the boilerplate code in this chapter was taken from this title.) For a more detailed discussion of the pipeline object model, see the book *Pro BizTalk 2006* by George Dunphy and Ahmed Metwally (Apress, 2006).

The code in Listing 14-1 implements a pipeline component that captures the inbound activity using the BAM API.

Listing 14-1. *Code for the Receive Pipeline Component*

```
using System;
using System.Text;
using System.Resources;
using System.Reflection;
using Microsoft.BizTalk.Message.Interop;
using Microsoft.BizTalk.Component.Interop;
using Microsoft.BizTalk.Bam.EventObservation;

namespace InterchangeID
{
    [ComponentCategory(CategoryTypes.CATID_PipelineComponent)]
    [ComponentCategory(CategoryTypes.CATID_Any)]
    //The GUID should be unique, so run GUIDGEN and
    //replace this GUID with your own
    [System.Runtime.InteropServices.Guid("1081A6CA-44E5-45ef-9D1D-E144FD9C5869")]
    public class InterchangeIDComponent :
        Microsoft.BizTalk.Component.Interop.IBaseComponent,
        Microsoft.BizTalk.Component.Interop.IComponent,
        Microsoft.BizTalk.Component.Interop.IComponentUI,
        Microsoft.BizTalk.Component.Interop.IPersistPropertyBag
    {

        #region Constructor
        public InterchangeIDComponent()
        {
            ;
        }
        #endregion

        #region IBaseComponent Members

        string IBaseComponent.Description
        {
            get { return "Captures Status to BAM"; }
        }

        string IBaseComponent.Name
        {
            get { return "RcvBAM"; }
        }

        string IBaseComponent.Version
        {
```

```
            get { return "1.0"; }
        }

        #endregion

        #region IComponent Members
        IBaseMessage IComponent.Execute
            (IPipelineContext pContext, IBaseMessage pInMsg)
        {
            //Get the properties we need
            string sysProps =
"http://schemas.microsoft.com/BizTalk/2003/system-properties";
            string interchangeID = pInMsg.Context.Read(
                "InterchangeID",
                sysProps).ToString();
            string messageID = pInMsg.Context.Read(
                "MessageID",
                sysProps).ToString();
            string portStartTime = pInMsg.Context.Read(
                "PortStartTime",
                sysProps).ToString();
            string portEndTime = pInMsg.Context.Read(
                "PortEndTime",
                sysProps).ToString();
            string messageSize = pInMsg.Context.Read(
                "Size",
                sysProps).ToString();
            string receivePort = pInMsg.Context.Read(
                "BTS.ReceivePortName",
                sysProps).ToString();
            string messageType = pInMsg.Context.Read(
                "BTS.MessageType",
                sysProps).ToString();


            //Get an instance of MessagingEventStream
            EventStream eventstream = pContext.GetEventStream();

            //Write to the event stream
            eventstream.BeginActivity("Inbound", interchangeID);
            eventstream.UpdateActivity("Inbound", interchangeID,
                "InterchangeID", interchangeID,
                "MessageID", messageID,
                "PortStartTime", portStartTime,
                "PortEndTime", portEndTime,
                "Size", messageSize,
                "ReceivePort", receivePort,
                "MessageType", messageType);
```

```csharp
        eventstream.EndActivity("Inbound", interchangeID);

        //Return message
        return pInMsg;

    }
    #endregion

    #region IComponentUI Members
    IntPtr IComponentUI.Icon
    {
        get { return IntPtr.Zero; }
    }

    System.Collections.IEnumerator IComponentUI.Validate(object projectSystem)
    {
        return null;
    }
    #endregion

    #region IPersistPropertyBag Members
    void IPersistPropertyBag.GetClassID(out Guid classID)
    {
        //Should match the GUID in the
        //System.Runtime.InteropServices.Guid attribute above
        classID = new Guid(
        "1081A6CA-44E5-45ef-9D1D-E144FD9C5869");
    }

    void IPersistPropertyBag.InitNew()
    {
        ;
    }

    void IPersistPropertyBag.Load(IPropertyBag propertyBag, int errorLog)
    {
        ;
    }

    void IPersistPropertyBag.Save(IPropertyBag propertyBag,
        bool clearDirty, bool saveAllProperties)
    {
        ;
    }
```

```
    #endregion
  }
}
```

The vast majority of this pipeline component is completely standard boilerplate. The method that does the actual work is the IComponent.Execute method. This method gets the items we need from the message context, gets an instance of MessagingEventStream from the pipeline context, and then uses the BAM API to write the data to the activity. The interchange ID is used as the activity ID, just as in the tracking profile implementation.

A separate pipeline component is used for the send pipeline, as it needs to create the relationship. All the code is the same as in the receive pipeline, except for the IComponent.Execute method, which is implemented using the code shown in Listing 14-2.

Listing 14-2. *The Code for the IComponent.Execute Method in the Send Pipeline Component*

```
IBaseMessage IComponent.Execute(IPipelineContext pContext,
    IBaseMessage pInMsg)
{
    //Get the properties we need
    string sysProps =
"http://schemas.microsoft.com/BizTalk/2003/system-properties";
        string interchangeID = pInMsg.Context.Read(
            "InterchangeID",
            sysProps).ToString();
        string messageID = pInMsg.Context.Read(
            "MessageID",
            sysProps).ToString();
        string portStartTime = pInMsg.Context.Read(
            "PortStartTime",
            sysProps).ToString();
        string portEndTime = pInMsg.Context.Read(
            "PortEndTime",
            sysProps).ToString();
        string messageSize = pInMsg.Context.Read(
            "Size",
            sysProps).ToString();
        string sendPort = pInMsg.Context.Read(
            "BTS.SPName",
            sysProps).ToString();
        string messageType = pInMsg.Context.Read(
            "BTS.MessageType",
            sysProps).ToString();

    //Get an instance of MessagingEventStream
    EventStream eventstream = pContext.GetEventStream();
```

```
        //activityGuid will be used to uniquely identify this row in the table
        string activityGuid = Guid.NewGuid().ToString();

        //Write to the event stream
        eventstream.BeginActivity("Outbound", activityGuid);
        eventstream.UpdateActivity("Outbound", activityGuid,
            "InterchangeID", interchangeID,
            "MessageID", messageID,
            "PortStartTime", portStartTime,
            "PortEndTime", portEndTime,
            "Size", messageSize,
            "SendPort", sendPort,
            "MessageType", messageType);
        //Set up the relationship
        eventstream.AddRelatedActivity(
            "Outbound", activityGuid,
            "Inbound", interchangeID);
        eventstream.EndActivity("Outbound", activityGuid);

        //Return message
        return pInMsg;
    }
```

In the send pipeline component, the activity ID is a globally unique identifier (GUID) that is generated randomly. The call to UpdateActivity uses the SendPort field instead of the ReceivePort field. The additional method call used is the call to AddRelatedActivity, which establishes a relationship between the inbound and outbound activities.

■**Note** Instructions for creating relationships between activities using the BAM API are in Chapter 12.

BAM Portal

Because of the related activities, you can use the BAM Portal to navigate from inbound messages to outbound messages and examine the outbound messages that were created by each inbound message. The Activity Search page, shown in Figure 14-6, allows the inbound and outbound activities to be searched.

Once you have located the activity of interest, clicking the activity displays activity details plus a list of related documents (see Figure 14-7).

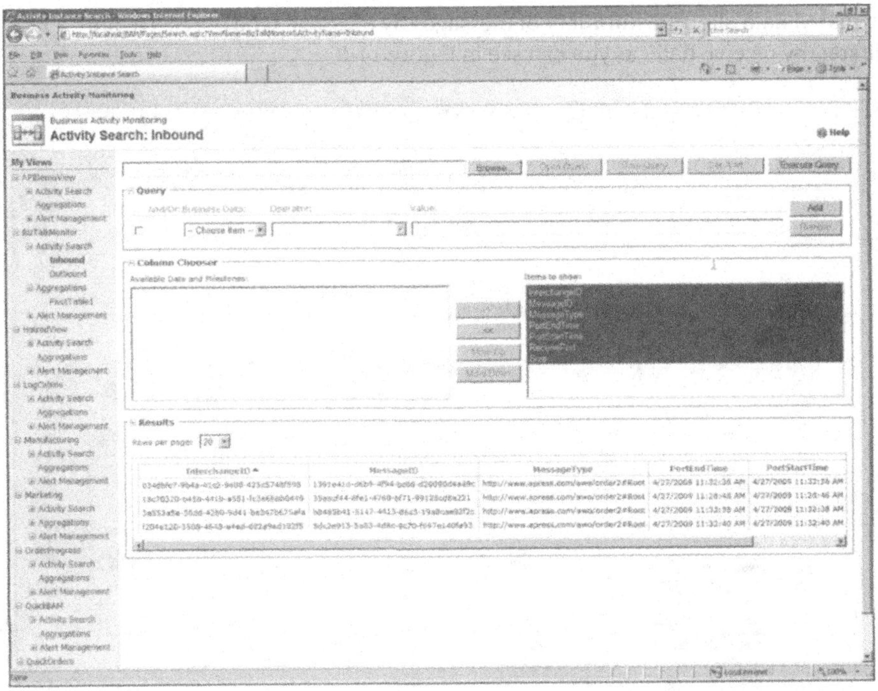

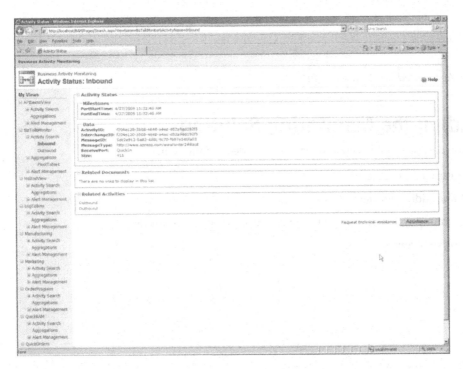

Figure 14-6. *The Activity Search page*

Figure 14-7. *The Activity Detail page showing related activities*

The aggregated data allows a summary of messages by message type or receive port, optionally filtered by receive date, as you can see in Figure 14-8.

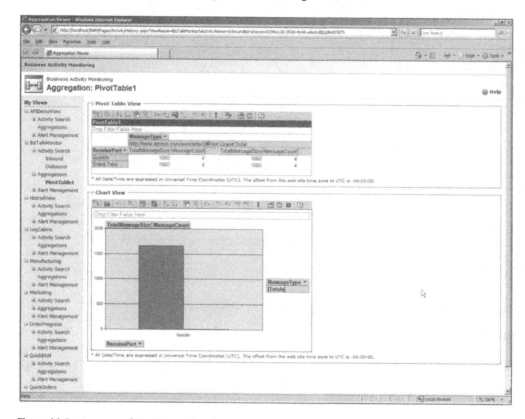

Figure 14-8. *Aggregated BAM tracking data*

Extending the Monitoring Solution

The solution described in this chapter can be extended in four main ways:

- Capturing more data
- Adding additional views
- Integrating system monitoring with business process monitoring
- Using BAM alerts

Capturing More Data

The set of data captured in the activities was very small; the data was kept small to minimize the impact on BizTalk's performance. As your experience of managing BizTalk Server grows, you will probably want to add some additional data to the inbound and outbound activities. Obviously, you should add whatever data is needed by your management process, while recognizing that capturing more fields will increase the space requirements of your BAM databases.

Some of the obvious candidates for tracking are shown in Table 14-5. If you make heavy use of a specific adapter, you may want to also add context properties for that adapter. As an example, if all your data flows through IBM's WebSphere MQ, you will probably want to add context properties provided by that adapter. If other data from the message context is useful to you, go ahead and add it.

Table 14-5. *Candidate Data Items for the Tracking Solution*

Item	Description
ServiceClassID	Values are 1—orchestration, 2—tracking, 4—messaging, 8—MSMQT, 16—other, 32—isolated adapter, 64—routing failure.
BTS.InboundTransportLocation	URL for an inbound message.
BTS.InboundTransportType	Adapter for an inbound message: File, HTTP, and so forth.
BTS.IsDynamicSend	Flag that indicates whether the message is sent through a dynamic send port.
BTS.OutboundTransportLocation	URL for an outbound message.
BTS.OutboundTransportType	Adapter for an outbound message: File, HTTP, and so forth.
BTS.ReceivePortID	ID of the receive port.
BTS.SourceParty	Party name—used with EDI Trading Party Management.
BTS.SourcePartyID	Party ID—used with EDI Trading Party Management.
BTS.SPID	ID of the send port.
BTS.WindowsUser	Name of the account that submitted the message. (This information is only available with protocols that support Windows authentication.)
FILE.ReceivedFileName	Name of a received file.
FILE.FileCreationTime	Date and time the received file was created.
SOAP.MethodName	Method name that was called on a web service.

Adding Additional Views

Once you have added additional data, additional views will also be useful to analyze the data. As an example, the aggregated view shown in Figure 14-2 displays only received data. In some cases, this may underestimate the total data processed by BizTalk Server, as one inbound message may generate many outbound messages. You may want to add a second aggregated view to show outbound message counts and sizes. Other aggregated views may also prove useful.

Integrating System Monitoring with Business Process Monitoring

In addition to the health tracking data described in this chapter, you may also be using BAM to capture data on a specific business process, with an activity that contains data that is specific to your process. You can link the business process activities with the BizTalk monitoring activities using the interchange ID. Whenever you implement a BAM activity, consider adding a relationship node that relates that activity to the inbound activity. The relationship will allow you to navigate from the business process activity to the inbound monitoring activity, and then you can navigate from the inbound activity to outbound messages associated with your business process. By creating these links, you add additional investigative capabilities to any business process view you create.

Using BAM Alerts

To create a full monitoring solution, you should supplement the BAM data with BAM alerts. Adding alerts into the solution allows administrators to be notified of unusual conditions. As an example, an administrator might want to be notified if the message load on a specific port is greater than 10,000 messages per hour.

The correct alerts for your environment will need to be determined from your specific traffic flows, but once the solution described in this chapter is in place, it's easy to create alerts as needed.

Summary

In this chapter, you learned how to track BizTalk messages using BAM. A specific observation model was recommended for capturing statistics on messages flowing through your BizTalk group, and two implementations were provided. One of the implementations used tracking profiles, and the other used pipeline components. No matter how the data is captured, the BAM Portal can be used to view tracked data.

The last section of the chapter provided some ideas for extending the solution, including adding additional data, additional views, integrating with other BAM activities, and adding BAM alerts.

Chapter 15, the final chapter in the book, describes BAM best practices and provides some perspective on future Microsoft technologies for monitoring business events.

■ ■ ■

Building Better BAM

While BAM is an incredibly powerful tool, it shouldn't be the only tool utilized in building your BPM practice. In fact, organizations with more than one operational intelligence tool are those that have much higher levels of visibility into the business and higher project success rates.

In this final chapter, we'll conclude the book by covering

- *BAM best practices*: BAM implementations built better as a result of practices within the organization

- *BAM architectural evolution*: BAM, as a technology, built better with each successive generation

- *BAM branches out*: BAM solutions built better by including multiple operational intelligence systems

- *BAM to the future*: BAM being built better by Microsoft updates to the product

While this chapter doesn't include any hands-on exercises, there are a number of exercises you may put into practice to build better BAM.

BAM Best Practices

By this point in the book, you should have a thorough understanding not only of Microsoft's implementation of BAM, but also of some technical best practices as well. Numerous recommendations for executing BAM projects, in general, emerge irrespective of vendor.

A recent Forrester Research white paper, "Best Practices: Business Activity Monitoring Adoption," captures five recommendations for BAM adoption, upon which we expand:

1. *Create a Center of Excellence (COE)*: A Center of Excellence is a learning community in which participants apply their knowledge, experience, and varied skills in leadership development, systemic change, continuous improvement, and best practices.

   In order for BAM implementations to be successful, such an environment must exist and be fostered by the executive sponsors. As IT members face common challenges involving better process and providing better metrics to decision makers, members of the COE may collaborate and deploy BAM solutions to address them. When identifying those whom you want to be part of the COE, recruit members from diverse groups within the business to provide for a wider range of opinions. Ensure that COE members have diverse skill sets; that is, avoid having a large concentration of any one role, like developer, business analyst, DBA, BI pro, and so forth.

As part of the COE creation, consider creating a BAM toolkit including templates for questions to ask when building a dashboard or an observation model.

For projects that originate from the COE, determine your project methodology up front and get buy-in from not only IT stakeholders, but also your financial stakeholders. BAM and BI projects are often assailed for taking too long and producing too little. In order to improve the operational efficiency of a process or a business over time, it is "time" that is imperative. Therefore, adopt an iterative development cycle with regular deliverables, and be sure to keep an eye on budget at all times.

The goal of the COE should be to continuously promote a stronger working relationship between IT and the business, and ensure that the relationship is reciprocal.

2. *Involve operational staff and midlevel management early:* The quality of a BAM implementation is directly related to the quality of the people involved.

If solid business planning, analysis, and design have not gone into building the observation model, your large group of data-hungry consumers expecting a heaping portion of information filet mignon will be served a small portion of last week's data leftovers. We have witnessed observation models built around describing activities for data that does not exist because a BizTalk developer or systems engineer was not involved. There have also been cases of robust observation models that provide large amounts of data, honed and processed, and further distilled into well-presented information for massive amounts of consumption. Unfortunately, the decision makers were uninformed as to the availability or the validity of the information. Get people involved and ensure that everyone understands their role in not only building the observation model, but also committing to better process management.

Remember that BAM, as a technology, is applicable to many, many different projects and models. Therefore, it's very important to choose your first BAM project very carefully and deliberately. You may select a small-scope BAM project because it provides a quick "win" to the business; or maybe you choose a large BAM project because it will bring a "win" to the most number of users possible. In general, though, we recommend starting small and "planting the seeds." There will always be processes and projects that need improvement.

If your IT environment is like most, any number of proprietary spreadsheets or custom-built web sites exist to track metrics as an evolutionary need through the years. While this approach is noble, it doesn't provide project sponsors and senior-level management with any transparency as to how metrics were defined or why they were chosen.

As with any project, IT or otherwise, expectation management is key. Have a clearly defined charter and scope for your project; be willing to expand that scope to monitor and refine other processes and complex systems; but also know when to set boundaries. Once operational staff begins to see the benefits of BAM, you'll likely be surprised how fast the enthusiasm about using it spreads. It may be that some seek to build BAM portals and track metrics for items that shouldn't necessarily fall under a BAM project. Just remember the saying, "To a hammer, everything looks like a nail." By having a COE in place, these challenges can quickly be addressed while maintaining enthusiasm.

Be very careful about the marketing of your BAM project. Using terms like "business process reengineering" implies that the processes aren't functioning as they should be and may be considered offensive to some. Tread lightly in promoting BAM projects in which BAM is utilized to monitor employee productivity or human-centric metrics. The perception may be that those who are not viewed as productive by BAM definition metrics will face some punitive action. In general, try to market your BAM effort to the broadest audience possible, but at the same time, target and distill your message.

Lastly, ensure that operational staff members know where, when, and how they may contribute. Raising an alert to a user is one thing, but if the user has no idea as to how the problem may be remedied, the alert will be ignored.

3. *Choose the right metrics*: BAM differs from operational intelligence tools like BI and reporting. Focus your BAM activities on operational metrics about how you actually perform business and how you want to perform business, as opposed to just defining KPIs.

Metrics must be defined as part of an operational intelligence project. However, the real value provided by their implementation is not the end result, but the process of defining them. Understanding how upper or midlevel management maps high-level business requirements to low-level process data and milestones is key. The activity or KPI is merely the capturing of that collaboration.

Don't consider your metrics to be set in stone—BAM activities and views and KPIs are a reflection of business milestones and data considered to be of importance at a specific point in time. At some point in the future, whether a process may be considered optimized, perfected, or meeting its target may change. Revisit your original business goals and objectives, and refine your observation model accordingly.

Remember that there are multiple viewpoints for data. Information may be interpreted differently according to many factors related to the consumer. Make it clear how the information you define in your observation model maps to specific business objectives. Also remember that mistakes happen—sometimes a milestone is defined incorrectly. Sometimes a threshold is set too high or too low. Sometimes a step in the business process is omitted. Have procedures in place to handle either misinterpretations of data or requirements, as well as "meta" information involving how data should be interpreted. Oftentimes, people see what they want to see. It's up to you to help them understand the facts and the correlating information.

Just as conclusions are presented and decisions made, commit to the betterment of that process. If a senior-level manager "wants" to make a decision, but has some hesitancy because of lack of supporting information, consider using lookups to provide greater detail, or deploying a new version of the observation model that captures additional information. The data you present is only temporary—consider using an iterative approach to expand the context of the data presented to users, and provide customization points where necessary.

The input of mapping high-level business goals to BAM activities and low-level KPIs from one person is valuable, but the input from several people is even more valuable. Different data points are of different value to different people. Be sure to include as many voices as possible, while at the same time drawing a line when necessary.

4. *Relate the COE to a business excellence team*: BAM is a means to generate, process, and consume data around business activities. Once that process is built into a repeatable, well-honed one, it's important to have an executive team that will do just that: execute.

The BAM COE functions well to help refine, define, and extend the capabilities of BAM. Having a team that utilizes the output of the COE to make measured, well-informed decisions is equally as important. We have read about and know personally of instances in which BAM or operational intelligence information was passed on to decision makers who, ultimately, decided to ignore it, at times to their downfall. Whether decision makers decide to side with BAM data or not is their choice; but at some point they must decide. A business excellence team of executives is put in place for just that purpose.

5. *Turn passive BAM dashboards into actionable dashboards*: As referred to in the chapter on consuming BAM data, providing information and alerts to consumers is just the first step. Specific, actionable, measurable tasks must be assigned as a result of BAM data, and the best place to surface and assign is in a dashboard or personalized portal. As dashboards are personalized, unlike scorecards, they may provide a more hands-on approach to viewing and acting upon BAM data.

BAM Architectural Evolution

From a technology standpoint, BAM has come a long way since its humble beginnings, especially since it was introduced in the BizTalk product line in BizTalk Server 2004. Few know that research company Gartner, Inc. actually coined the term "Business Activity Monitoring" in 2001 to describe "a style of monitoring application that provides near real-time access to business performance indicators, with the goal to improve the speed and effectiveness of business operations. A valuable characteristic of a BAM application is its ability to reveal current business conditions, correlations and causality by using events from multiple and unassociated environments."

While 2001 wasn't too long ago, in the IT world, it was another era. The architecture of BAM implementations has evolved a great deal since then to include four successive "generations."

First-generation BAM (1G BAM) may be considered, as defined by Gartner, as "a monitoring application that delivers real-time information, but its scope is limited to the context of a business application where it is embedded." As an example, think of a Windows Forms application that monitors an assembly line. The application may control the different conveyor belts or machinery on the assembly line and also provide some operational status as to how the different activities, from one end point of the assembly line to the next, progress. Figure 15-1 illustrates this generation of BAM.

The advantages of 1G BAM are that the implementation time is short and the data is readily available. The disadvantages are that it fails to extend monitoring capabilities beyond a single system, and therefore has a largely static data model contoured around the entities of the single system. There is little or no correlation to other systems or data sources, and data rules are often hard-coded.

Second-generation BAM (2G BAM), as defined by Gartner, introduces middleware and messaging, and is more "stand-alone BAM" (see Figure 15-2). Using publish-subscribe patterns, application adapters, capturing agents, log files, and other techniques, 2G BAM connects to external systems and multiple event sources, and is extensible. 2G BAM also provides the ability to transform, normalize, and standardize events so that they may be monitored. The defining mark between 1G and 2G BAM is that with 2G+, new event types, new metrics, and new custom events may be defined within the system. 2G BAM also provides the ability to monitor a process without first modeling it.

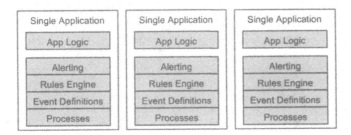

Figure 15-1. *First-generation BAM*

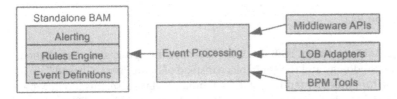

Figure 15-2. *Second-generation BAM*

The advantages of 2G BAM are that most 2G BAM products align closely with the BPM tool or suite with which they are deployed. Within the BizTalk realm, before 2006, BAM and BizTalk were very closely intertwined because of BAM's ability to only monitor BizTalk orchestrations. The disadvantages of such systems are that there tends to be a high latency involved in processing through BPM suites and applications, and that middleware tends to introduce other problems for which additional code must be written. 2G BAM is where most BAM implementations reside today, closely aligned with a product, and typically used to monitor a handful of applications or integrated systems.

Third-generation BAM (3G BAM), as defined by Gartner, "leverages the expandable data model characteristics of second-generation BAM applications, but integrates BAM within an application, a proprietary application development environment, or within a BPM Suite."

Think of 3G BAM as "embedded BAM," that is, applications monitored by a stand-alone BAM product are architected specifically to be plugged into a BAM or BPM suite instead of using adapters (see Figure 15-3). Alerts, rules, and events are exposed by 3G BAM–monitored systems in a standardized way without providing middleware (such as web services, WCF services, or on- and off-ramps) to standardize interfacing. Much like 1G BAM, 3G BAM usually involves purchasing a vendor's entire product suite as the emitters put forth by the individual applications or systems tend to work best when coupled with the BAM product offering put out by the same company.

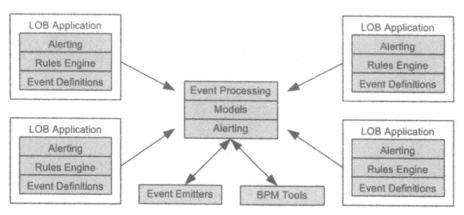

Figure 15-3. *Third-generation BAM*

The advantage of 3G BAM, much like 1G BAM, is that because the applications are aligned with a standard design methodology and toolset in place instead of being "best of breed," there tends to be less time for implementation and more familiarity. Likewise, this too may be a disadvantage as competitive tools may provide better offerings, but sometimes, IT may be forced to purchase the entire suite.

Fourth-generation BAM (4G BAM), according to Gartner, has yet to hit the marketplace. Gartner defines 4G BAM as "a vision of what could be, but is not available in 2008. Here, the BAM application is built to exploit the power of a service-oriented architecture, using external services to deliver its functions. It uses composite application development techniques, calling on data services to subscribe to events, an event processing engine to detect patterns, a rule engine to analyze changing metrics, an alerting service to handle the delivery of alerts, BI services to provide historic and predictive analysis and a portal to display the environment. The objective is to use best-of-breed services, connected together across an enterprise service bus, or Web-oriented architecture techniques such as Simple Object Access Protocol (SOAP) and representative state transfer (REST)." The diagram in Figure 15-4 depicts 4G BAM.

Portions of this vision of BAM have largely been realized with the integration of WCF and WF as means to monitor an SOA in BizTalk. BAM and BizTalk together utilize a rules engine for changing metrics (the BRE), provide alerting, and connect to composite applications using a WCF service façade. BAM in BizTalk Server 2009 may even be used to monitor SOAP and REST-based architectures (Microsoft, in January 2009, released a white paper on doing just that). Gaps between Gartner's 4G BAM vision and the Microsoft BAM of BizTalk Server 2009 exist in the areas of BI services, predictive analysis, and the tight-coupling of BAM and BizTalk.

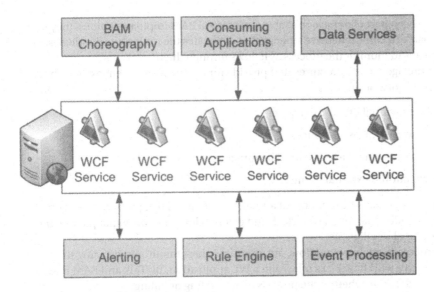

Figure 15-4. *Fourth-generation BAM*

With regard to BI services, Microsoft announced that it would discontinue its Performance-Point product, and roll the underlying business intelligence capabilities into a series of "services" to be bundled with the next version of SharePoint Server. It is not known, however, whether these BI services will offer a standardized API that provides a means to roll up into a centralized portal to display both BAM and BI information side by side.

With regard to predictive analysis, Microsoft has remained quiet on the front of predictive analysis tools, but with the industry largely moving in that direction (see "BAM to the Future" later in this chapter), this arena clearly cannot be ignored.

With regard to the tight-coupling of BizTalk and BAM, historically, BAM has "ridden the coattails" of BizTalk's BPM capabilities in order to become a more widely recognized product. While this has worked to promote knowledge of BAM, it has also hindered its adoption to some degree. The perception widely exists that in order to implement BAM, you must have BizTalk. In fact, the licensing model promoted by Microsoft requires at least one licensed BizTalk server to be in place in a network for the BAM license to be valid.

In order for Microsoft BAM to fully reach this vision, in the future, it may have to be decoupled from BizTalk altogether, perhaps as part of a larger strategy toward moving beyond the firewall (e.g., BAM reaching out to the cloud, etc.). In order to provide a more effective, more comprehensive intelligence strategy, BAM should become one pillar of many in an organization's operational intelligence strategy.

BAM Branches Out

BAM is but one component of a comprehensive operational intelligence strategy. In fact, in order to provide a truer, more accurate, complete, and transparent process monitoring and intelligence strategy, the strategies of multiple technologies, such as BAM, BPM, BI, reporting, and so forth, must be closely aligned.

When we have been part of or have read about successful BAM implementations, they have oftentimes been part of a comprehensive strategy that delineates the multiple technologies, but also provides a means to monitor the process as it flows through them.

Operational intelligence architectures that provide for the most comprehensive technique for accurate process monitoring

- Monitor an individual process instance.

- Monitor all active process instances.

- Examine processes that have occurred historically.

- Correlate monitored external events.

Those processes that have been modeled and well understood by operational users and are monitored at an individual, peer, historical, and external level are those that provide the most useful operational intelligence.

Individual processes, such as workflow, are oftentimes best monitored by using BPM tools. For instance, as a workflow kicks off within a WF application, BizTalk and BAM may use the WF adapter to determine whether the process is succeeding or failing.

Peer processes are often best monitored in the same way. Where it is useful to monitor an individual process, such as an order being submitted to a WF application, for specific metrics such as whether it was processed or rejected, it is equally useful to monitor multiple order submissions to determine patterns and alert business users as to trends that may be emerging in real time.

Over time, as the total amount of data that has been amassed in either the BAM analysis database or a BI cube has grown, tools such as the BAM pivot table or PerformancePoint Server are best used to examine historical trends and apply "smart patterns" in an offline fashion.

While BAM is great for monitoring WF applications, additional patterns may emerge as messages flow through line-of-business applications and BizTalk. Correlation of the various data into usable information should be your ultimate goal.

BAM to the Future

Microsoft BAM is a relatively mature technology, but one that has yet to witness widespread adoption. Changes to the modern software ecosystem, however, in conjunction with enhancements to BAM's underlying technologies, will serve to make BAM a great deal more commonplace.

A recent white paper examined the frustration of users in finding the information they need to do their jobs. This frustration was highlighted in a 2007 Accenture survey of 1,000 middle managers that showed managers spend up to two hours a day looking for information and that more than 50% of the information they find has no value to them.

The hypothesis of the white paper was that many users have problems finding information because the data discovery and analysis tools provided by vendors often assume, incorrectly, that the user has a detailed working knowledge of the business data involved, knows where to find it, and is able to use fairly sophisticated software tools for finding and using the business data they require.

Today we have access to more information than ever before, and while advantageous, it is also problematic: so much of that information is raw data and so little of it is useful information. Not only that, the boundaries of where data is stored and processed are quickly blurring with technologies such as cloud computing and Software as a Service (SaaS).

Additionally, disruptive technologies such as event-driven architecture (EDA) and complex event processing (CEP) are providing "smarter," more predictive intelligence at a faster rate than ever before.

BizTalk and BAM in the Software + Services World

Software + Services is Microsoft's mantra and approach to these five trends:

- Service-oriented architecture (SOA)
- Rich Internet Applications (RIAs)
- Software as a Service
- Web 2.0
- Cloud computing

The Software + Services vision was first fully detailed at the Microsoft PDC 2008 conference with the announcement of Windows Azure, the Microsoft data centers, and enhancements to a number of preexisting Microsoft technologies.

BizTalk is not part of the Software + Services cloud, but may interact with applications and operating services via service invocation. It's very likely that the next version of BizTalk will include extensive integration with .NET Services, Live Services and SQL Services on the Azure services platform via BizTalk adapters.

Although there is currently no cloud offering for Business Activity Monitoring, the question may be posed as to whether or not BAM will interface with cloud components to monitor services and workflows executing in the cloud.

The .NET Framework 4.0, which includes extensive enhancements to WCF and WF, has been structured much like a 3G BAM system, with specific tracking mechanisms built into it rather than adjoining it. As these technologies along with Windows Azure and the Microsoft cloud APIs mature, expect to see BAM and tracking capabilities within the cloud. It is also a criticism of the cloud as a hosting platform.

As one executive relayed, "I want to move some of my applications to the cloud, but I'm hesitant. While hosting costs may be lower and the premise of infinite scalability is very nice, with [operational intelligence] tools, I can tell who has dropped the ball, or discern data patterns and refine. Once that moves into the cloud, I have no visibility and no control."

BizTalk, BAM, and Complex Event Processing

Event-driven architecture is a software architecture pattern focused upon promoting the production, detection, consumption of, and reaction to events. Where the fundamental construct of BAM is the activity, in an EDA, it is the event.

An event is oftentimes thought of simply as a change in state. The scope of that change can be major or minor and may roll into a larger series of events or activities. Events have a header, which includes metadata about the event, and a body, which describes the actual event that occurred.

Event-driven systems, usually implemented within distributed architectures, typically consist of event emitters (or agents) and event consumers (or sinks).

It is the role of the emitter to generate data from various sources. Sinks then have the responsibility of acting upon that event as soon as it is presented. That action may be acted upon by the sink or routed to another mechanism to be acted upon. Sinks could potentially simply filter, transform, and forward the event to another component. Conversely, the sink may perform a series of internal actions and then route on to another component.

Sinks fall into two categories: traditional components, such as message-oriented middleware, to distribute an application across multiple heterogeneous platforms, and self-contained online actions, which require a more appropriate transactional executive framework.

Event-driven architectures, because of the nature of their design, tend to be more agile and responsive to unpredictable and asynchronous environments. Additionally, event-driven architectures fit well within or are complementary to service-oriented architectures because services within an SOA can be activated by triggers fired on incoming events. Whenever the sink is a more traditional component, the integration point within an SOA is increased because fewer dependencies exist that need to be accounted for.

Within event-driven architectures, events are processed by three means: simple, stream, and complex. The three styles are not mutually exclusive and are often used together in a mature event-driven architecture.

Simple event processing focuses upon events directly related to specific, exact, and measurable changes of condition. In the simple event-processing model, an event happens upstream that initiates downstream action(s). Simple event processing is oftentimes used to drive the real-time flow of work, reducing lag time and cost. Examples of simple events are usually in a one-to-one ratio, for example, a thermostat detects that it has become colder, and therefore turns on the heat.

In event stream processing (ESP), events that are considered both ordinary and notable happen. Ordinary events, such as an order submission, or an RFID transmission, are examined to determine whether they are considered notable and accordingly streamed to information subscribers. Event stream processing is oftentimes used to promote the real-time flow of information in and around the enterprise, which enables in-time decision making.

Complex event processing, then, is the combination of the two. CEP allows patterns of simple and ordinary events to be examined to infer that a complex event has occurred. Complex event processing, much like BAM, evaluates events and then takes action. CEP requires the employment of sophisticated event interpreters throughout the event chain, event pattern definition and matching, and correlation techniques (see Figure 15-5).

BizTalk infrastructures that generate events, by definition, are event-driven architectures. Emitters may be data feeds, network feeds, RFID feeds, ESB messages, custom applications that generate events, or packaged applications. Currently, the BizTalk Server WCF adapters provide the sink capabilities within BizTalk.

The difference between BizTalk BAM and CEP has to do with means by which queries are structured, the speed at which they are executed, and the flow of the data events through the system. In BAM, ad hoc queries or requests are created using the BAM portal to raise alerts. There may be a latency of even a couple seconds for complex activities, but at times, BAM

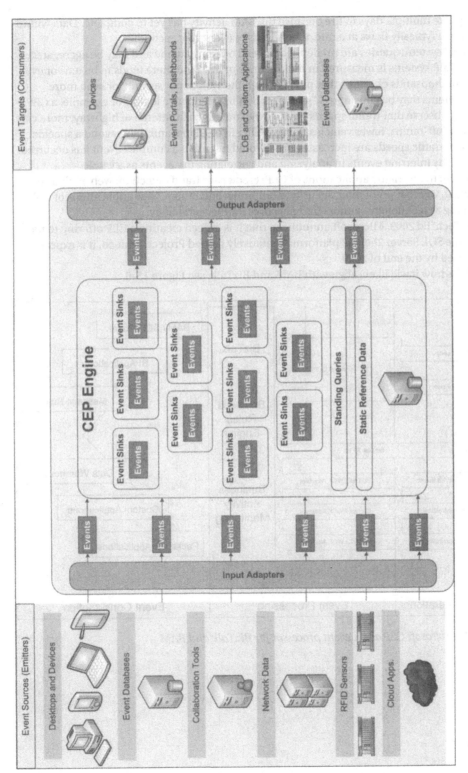

Figure 15-5. *Complex event processing within an event-driven architecture*

alerts may take multiple days to fire because the BAM activity has yet to complete. Data within a BAM system typically flows at a rate of hundreds of events per second.

In a CEP system, queries are predefined instead of being ad hoc and may be aggregated. Latency in CEP systems is measured in milliseconds or less, and there tends to be tens or even hundreds of thousands of events that pass through the system per second, or even more.

CEP systems may be considered "smart" and utilize deductive logic. For example, a CEP system may observe that traffic speeds have slowed on a specific stretch of highway, more cars are exiting at off-ramps, fewer vehicles are travelling in one lane, and that beyond a specific mile marker, traffic speeds are increasing. CEP would infer that a complex event has occurred: an accident, by inferring events in analyzing and correlating the events as a whole.

There are many, many applications of CEP: credit card fraud detection, web analytics, stock trading, weather prediction, security monitoring, and others. New applications of CEP are emerging as technology vendors find new uses for the technology.

As of Tech*Ed 2009, Microsoft announced that it is indeed creating a CEP offering to be based on the SQL Server 2008 R2 platform. Tentatively named Project Orinoco, it is expected to be released by the end of 2009.

As far as how it will likely align with BAM and BizTalk, see Figure 15-6.

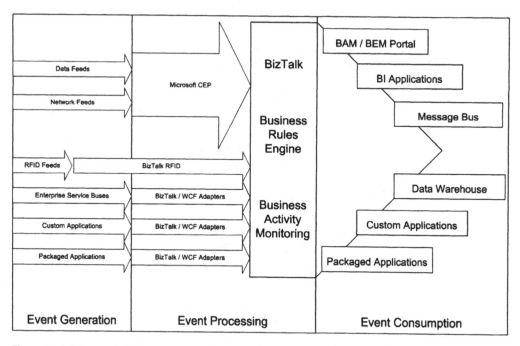

Figure 15-6. *Microsoft CEP as an event processor for BizTalk and BAM*

Summary

This final chapter focused upon best practices for BAM adoption, BAM's architectural evolution through the years and how it maps to BizTalk Server 2009 BAM, BAM as part of a comprehensive operational intelligence strategy, and where BAM may be heading in the future.

IT has become more commoditized, and the bar has been raised for developers to become architects, demonstrating technical, leadership, and business superiority in their day-to-day function. Architects are also being asked to do a great deal more with a great deal less: fewer resources, less funding, tighter deadlines, and much higher quality standards. As such, it's increasingly important to utilize the data around you to make as many informed decisions as possible using powerful technologies such as BAM. It's our hope that this book will help you to achieve that goal.

Index

You Need the Companion eBook

Your purchase of this book entitles you to buy the companion PDF-version eBook for only $10. Take the weightless companion with you anywhere.

We believe this Apress title will prove so indispensable that you'll want to carry it with you everywhere, which is why we are offering the companion eBook (in PDF format) for $10 to customers who purchase this book now. Convenient and fully searchable, the PDF version of any content-rich, page-heavy Apress book makes a valuable addition to your programming library. You can easily find and copy code—or perform examples by quickly toggling between instructions and the application. Even simultaneously tackling a donut, diet soda, and complex code becomes simplified with hands-free eBooks!

Once you purchase your book, getting the $10 companion eBook is simple:

❶ Visit **www.apress.com/promo/tendollars/**.

❷ Complete a basic registration form to receive a randomly generated question about this title.

❸ Answer the question correctly in 60 seconds, and you will receive a promotional code to redeem for the $10.00 eBook.

THE EXPERT'S VOICE™

2855 TELEGRAPH AVENUE | SUITE 600 | BERKELEY, CA 94705

Offer valid through 12/09.